DEFIANT

ALSO BY ALVIN TOWNLEY

Legacy of Honor

Spirit of Adventure

Fly Navy

DEFIANT

The POWs Who Endured Vietnam's Most Infamous Prison,
the Women Who Fought for Them, and the One Who Never Returned

ALVIN TOWNLEY

THOMAS DUNNE BOOKS ☙ ST. MARTIN'S PRESS NEW YORK

THOMAS DUNNE BOOKS.
An imprint of St. Martin's Press.

www.thomasdunnebooks.com
www.stmartins.com

Designed by Omar Chapa
Maps by J. M. McGrath

Library of Congress Cataloging-in-Publication Data

Townley, Alvin.
    Defiant : the POWs who endured Vietnam's most infamous prison, the women who fought for them, and the one who never returned / Alvin Townley.
      p. cm
    Includes bibliographical references and index.
    ISBN 978-1-250-00653-0 (hardcover)
    ISBN 978-1-250-03761-9 (e-book)
    1. Vietnam War, 1961–1975—Prisoners and prisons, North Vietnamese.
2. Prisoners of war—United States—Biography.   3. Prisoners of war—Vietnam—Biography.   4. Military spouses—United States—Biography. I. Title.
    DS559.4.T69 2014
    959.704'37—dc23

2013031164

First Edition: February 2014

10 9 8 7 6 5 4 3 2 1

To the men of the Fourth Allied POW Wing and

to the families who never forgot

CONTENTS

CONTENTS

It matters not how strait the gate,
How charged with punishments the scroll,
I am the master of my fate:
I am the captain of my soul.

—"Invictus," William Ernest Henley

HOA LO·1896   HANOI HILTON·1964·1973

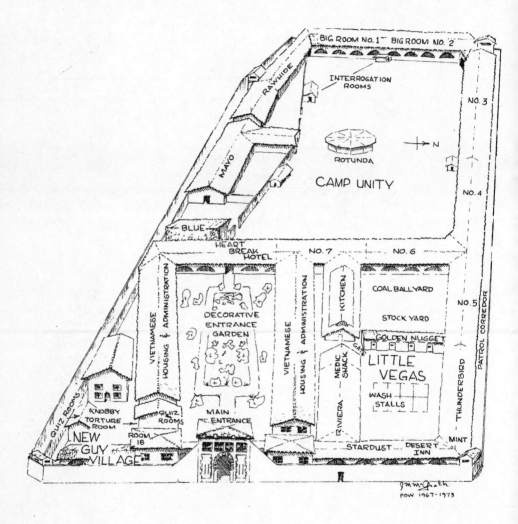

ALCATRAZ

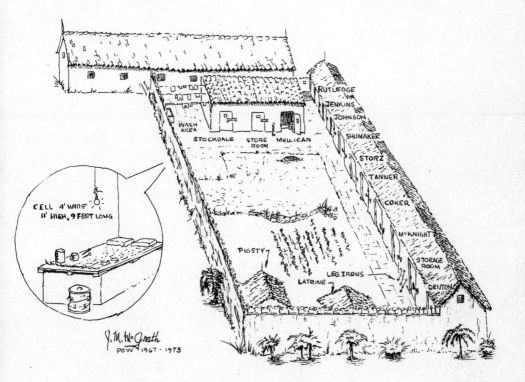

CELL 4' WIDE
11' HIGH, 9 FEET LONG

WASH AREA

STOCKDALE   STORE ROOM   MULLIGAN

RUTLEDGE
JENKINS
JOHNSON

SHUMAKER

STORZ

TANNER

COKER

McKNIGHT

STORAGE ROOM

DENTON

PIGSTY

LATRINE   LEG IRONS

J. M. McGrath
POW 1967 - 1973

Sketches by Mike McGrath,
POW, 1967 – 1973.

PROLOGUE

A DARK PLACE

He could not forget the beetle, how it stopped moving, how it rolled onto its back, dead, its stiff legs pointed to the plaster ceiling, where a single burning bulb and a meat hook hung. By now, he knew the hook wasn't intended for meat. Instead, it gave leverage to the ropes that forced him to talk, to sign confessions, to compromise the Code.

Some of the ants crawling across his own beaten and prostrate body soon began marching down to the floor and toward the dead beetle. He watched them—just inches from his face—as they bored holes through its shell, devouring it. Soon a column of the tiny scavengers formed and carried the carcass away to an unknown grave in this godforsaken prison.

After two years of interrogations, torture, and isolation, he felt just like the beetle. He lived in the same filth as the insects and vermin that inhabited the floor of Room Nineteen. He could still barely stand. The guard—Pigeye, the prisoners called him—had broken his knee again, rendering his left leg useless and leaving it twisted inward at a grotesque angle. Three weeks ago, they'd hauled him off the tile floor that he'd shared with the beetle and shoved him into a different cell. Now he spent the entire day wearing a tight blindfold across his eyes, hunched on the floor in his own waste. Mosquitoes and ants preyed freely upon him; he could fend off neither since tight iron cuffs bound his wrists behind his back. A guard removed the cuffs and blindfold once each day so he could eat the watery vegetable soup that barely sustained him. Sometimes the guards refastened the cuffs so tightly that the pain kept him from sleep, the one refuge from the horror of his imprisonment in North Vietnam. Jim Stockdale had no idea when or if this unbearable sentence would ever end, for him and for the other American pilots locked inside Hỏa Lò Prison, or, as they'd taken to calling it, the Hanoi Hilton.

The forty-three-year-old navy commander could still remember better days; they hadn't yet taken his memories from him. He recalled being a young man and wanting more than anything to attend the United States Naval Academy; he remembered the pride of joining its Brigade of Midshipmen in 1943. Recollections of Annapolis, of flight training, of long deployments with good friends helped comfort him while he lay on that prison floor. He thought often of his family, of time at home in San Diego with his wife, Sybil, and their four boys, happily playing piano together before he deployed. Back then he had felt in control of his world. He provided for his family, ensured his sons were becoming strong young men, and, with confidence, watched his career progress toward admiral. At sea aboard the USS *Oriskany*, he'd felt a similar control over the men and planes in the air wing he commanded, the powerful jets he piloted, and nearly everything he surveyed from his cockpit.

He remembered flying imperiously over the paddies and jungles of North Vietnam, this nation of peasants who still farmed with oxen, who fought in sandals, and whose weaponry, he thought, would never down a pilot like him in an airplane like an A-4 Skyhawk. Yet they'd bagged him. He'd pulled out of a perfect low-level run over the rural district of Tĩnh Gia and watched his shower of explosives dance across a row of boxcars filled with supplies for Communist guerrillas in South Vietnam. Then he'd headed straight for the clouds. Before he could reach them, a string of 57mm shells ripped into the Skyhawk's starboard side. In the cockpit, he'd felt impervious to the dangers of battlefields below; the hits shattered that sense of invincibility.

The plane pitched down, and all control slipped away. Jim was yanked forward into his shoulder harness, then slammed back into the seat as the Skyhawk plummeted toward the ground. As he struggled with the controls, he spied the blue sea just 3 miles away. If he could hold the plane together for a few more seconds, he could reach the Gulf of Tonkin, where he'd eject and rescuers could fish him from the waves.

Instead, the Skyhawk continued its dive, which would inevitably end in a fiery crash. Jim had only seconds to escape. He tried in vain to lift his arms against the g-forces to reach the overhead ejection ring. With the ground growing larger in his windshield, he grasped the alternate ejection handle between his legs and pulled. The jet's canopy shot off and the seat rocketed Jim out of the aircraft. He registered pain as he tumbled through the sky. By the time his parachute deployed, he knew he'd been injured, but he couldn't process it. Only seconds separated him from the ground, and he spent them hoping that the bullets slicing away at his parachute would miss his helpless body. The chute drifted closer to the trees, and its canopy snagged a limb, leaving him suspended just above the main thoroughfare in a small village. Still hanging in his harness, he watched as a mob of townspeople began running toward him.

He released the latches on his harness and dropped onto the muddy street. A surge of villagers knocked him down and began pummeling him with fists, clubs, or whatever they had, hitting wherever they found an opening. Someone knocked him hard on the head. Above the din, he could hear a distant whistle—a police officer, salvation from the relentless bludgeoning. The crowd stepped back, still encircling him menacingly. Under direction from the constable, several boys stepped forward and began cutting away Jim's clothes—his flight suit, his T-shirt, the red polka-dot boxers Sybil had bought him during his last shore leave. The officer pointed at Jim's leg, and for the first time, he looked at his body. The ejection had completely shattered his left knee; the leg was now bent 60 degrees to the side. He tried to move his left arm; it didn't respond. Jim had forgotten to grab his right wrist with his left hand as he pulled the ejection lever. Consequently, his left arm had flailed freely during his exit from the cockpit, doing untold damage to his shoulder, which seemed dislocated if not shattered. He thought the force of the exit had also broken his back.

He heard jets overhead, and his spirits momentarily rose. Then he saw villagers concealing the parachute that would have caught their attention or at least indicated that Jim had landed safely. Now, nobody would know if he had survived—not his wingmen, not his squadron, not his government, not his wife, not his four boys. Nobody.

As the mob dragged Jim through the street—naked, bloodied, crippled, and humiliated—he steeled himself for what would come. He knew it would get much worse.

Still, he'd never imagined anything as horrible as the floor of this cell. Nearly eight hundred days had passed since he'd involuntarily parachuted into North Vietnam, and he saw no prospect of release. He wondered if he would exist like this, a maimed, blinded animal, for the rest of his life.

The night of October 25, 1967, found him lying on his floor as usual, inhaling the room's stench—his stench—almost oblivious to the mosquitoes that feasted upon him, when suddenly he heard a key turning in his cell door and guards entered his squalid world. They removed his blindfold and cuffs; they ordered him to roll up his bamboo sleeping mat and gather his few belongings. They helped him to his feet and motioned for him to follow. He hobbled along after them, swinging his left leg outward with each painful stride, trying to maintain his balance.

A guard blindfolded him again for a short ride in a jeep; about eight blocks, he estimated. The blindfold remained fixed in place when the jeep parked and the guards led him toward the sound of a gate opening. He heard voices below him; he guessed there were stairs ahead. He felt for the first step with his stiff leg, found it, and swung his body down to it carefully. He felt for the next step but lost his balance and toppled headfirst, landing in a heap. His drinking cup noisily clattered down the stairs after him. Several hands pulled him to his feet and ushered him to his right. He sensed light, and the hands shoved him toward it. When guards took off his blindfold, he found himself in a dimly lit, windowless concrete box, approximately 9 feet long by 4 feet wide. Another guard entered and clapped 15-pound irons around his ankles, then locked the door and left the prisoner alone.

When Jim surmised nobody was coming back, he picked up his enameled cup and placed its rim against the wall. He pressed his ear against its bottom and with his free hand sent five taps through the wall, rhythmically sounding out "shave and a haircut."

He heard two taps from the other side, completing the classic jingle. "Two bits."

With his knuckles working like a woodpecker's bill, he sent a sequence of two taps, then five; four taps, then three. "JS," for Jim Stockdale.

In reply, he heard two taps, then five; three taps, then two. Interpreting the taps as fast as telegraph operators once translated Morse code, he knew that navy commander Jim Mulligan, "JM," occupied the adjacent cell.

During his nineteen months of imprisonment, Mulligan had earned a reputation similar to Stockdale's. He took a hard line against the Camp Authority, refusing to cooperate in any manner—at least until Pigeye used his ropes. Mulligan had helped Stockdale run the camp's underground resistance and had suffered for it, but the beatings and solitary confinement never deterred him. The Camp Authority considered him a leader and therefore a problem.

Now the prison commandant—known as Cat—had locked these two troublemakers away together, along with other prisoners that Stockdale and Mulligan heard shuffling into nearby cells during the night. The next morning they would discover nine other American stalwarts imprisoned with them: senior officers Jeremiah Denton, Harry Jenkins, and Howie Rutledge; troublemakers Sam Johnson, Bob Shumaker, and Nels Tanner; and young antagonists George Coker, George McKnight, and Ron Storz.

Stockdale remembered Rabbit, one of Cat's underlings, issuing a threat over the Hanoi Hilton's speaker network several months earlier. In shrill tones, he'd denounced the leaders of the American resistance and promised he was preparing "a dark place" for the "darkest criminals who persist in inciting the other criminals to oppose the Camp Authority."

The Camp Authority, he knew, saw him as the ringleader of those "criminals." He feared he and his most loyal lieutenants had now been brought to that dark place, a dungeon designed to break their bodies and crush their souls, meant to punish and neutralize the eleven POWs Cat considered the most subversive.

Jim Stockdale and his ten compatriots had arrived at Alcatraz.

BLACK SEA AND AMERICAN FIREPOWER

Even at 43,000 tons and nearly three football fields in length, the USS *Ticonderoga* rolled with the swells of the South China Sea. She had cruised the waters of the Pacific Ocean for more than twenty years now, surviving a 1945 kamikaze attack off Taiwan and steaming victoriously into Tokyo Bay six months later. In the summer of 1964, *Ticonderoga* had deployed to monitor a new conflict in Asia—one between Communist North Vietnam and the American-allied government in the South. Should the growing unrest finally draw America into war, she would respond with her force of more than fifty modern aircraft.

The carrier's flight deck resembled the busiest of airports, as if the substantial traffic and activity at O'Hare or LaGuardia were compressed onto a 2-acre expanse of concrete surrounded by a 52-foot cliff. Idle planes sat chained mere feet away from the ship's narrow landing strip. In between aircraft recoveries, taxiing jets laden with fuel and bombs jockeyed toward the two forward catapults that sent aircraft screaming off the bow, bathing everything behind them with heat, noise, and thick exhaust. Among the jet blasts and spinning propellers scurried men in grease-smudged pants and shirts of every color. Some lugged heavy chains, others pushed carts of ordnance, all shared a common mission.

Commander Jim Stockdale landed amid this chaos on August 4,

1964. He taxied to a stop, shut down the engine of his Vought F-8 Crusader, and climbed out of its single-seat cockpit. He stepped down the ladder to the deck and gazed west into the sunset. Then he watched distant lightning flicker to the north, over the Gulf of Tonkin. Hungry after a long day of patrols, he headed below deck for dinner, away from the noise and commotion.

The ship's wardroom was testament to the adage that if a navy man gave his life for his country, he'd die clean and well fed. Stewards served dishes of hot food to officers seated at linen-covered tables. A mess officer made sure everyone maintained decorum. If an aviator had already flown his missions for the day, as Jim had, a hot shower might follow the evening meal. Later, each would fall asleep in shared staterooms. Squadron commanders—known as skippers—like Stockdale often rated a room to themselves. Regardless of their rank or roots, these naval aviators—most of whom had yet to see age thirty-five, and many younger than thirty—shared a certain confidence.

That armor was forged by surviving flight after flight and beating the grim statistics of midcentury military aviation. At the outset of flight training, many instructors warned students that their aircraft would try to kill them. Many planes succeeded. In 1956 alone, naval aviation lost 776 aircraft and 535 lives. One study gave career aviators a 23 percent chance of dying in a crash. Another offered even odds that they'd eject before they retired, an unpleasant prospect given the severe injuries pilots often sustained when blasted out of their cockpits and into an unforgiving airstream. Then the pilot could only hope his parachute would open correctly and prevent a tragic freefall.

Yet despite these risks, a certain breed of man still volunteered, men who believed they could meet any challenge and hungered for the chance to prove it. Jim Stockdale knew too many who'd died amid smashed metal and hot-burning wreckage, but he believed that he would avoid that fate; *he* would return. Through a combination of heavenly grace, raw talent, and navy training, he controlled his airplane and his destiny. Those that perished had made some mistake, had committed some error, had not lived up to the standard. Stepping into a jet cockpit on the pitching deck of an aircraft carrier required trust in self and machine as well as a belief in the former's dominance over the latter. He, just like everyone else in the wardroom, thought he could control the uncontrollable.

After dinner, Jim retired to Fighter Squadron 51's briefing room, where fewer rules of etiquette applied. These rooms were the domain of the ship's aviators and seemed like both an office and a fraternity house. In the room's red lighting, Jim relaxed as pilots often do—by talking about flying. Suddenly, he heard propellers turning on the flight deck: A-1 Skyraiders. Just as he began wondering why *Ticonderoga* had decided to launch aircraft at this late hour, an officer from the ship's Combat Information Center opened the ready room door and asked Jim, "Are they ready to go?"

He explained that two U.S. destroyers in the Gulf of Tonkin expected an imminent attack from North Vietnamese torpedo boats; the American ships were presenting a show of force as they gathered intelligence. Two days earlier, Jim had defended one of these destroyers, the *Maddox,* from three such boats, firing the navy's first shots in the escalating conflict with North Vietnam. This evening, *Ticonderoga* again received orders to scramble her Combat Air Patrol—the two Crusaders from Jim's squadron that remained armed, manned, and ready on catapults 1 and 2. Jim knew both CAP pilots were relatively inexperienced, and this mission's sensitive nature called for a veteran. Jim had the cooler head of a senior officer and the fresh experience of his recent attack on the torpedo boats. Besides, he didn't want to miss a fight. So he buckled his survival gear over his flight suit, grabbed his helmet, and climbed the ladder to the flight deck. He opened the metal hatch and stepped out into the din and darkness of nighttime flight operations. Toward the bow, Jim saw swarms of men wearing reflective coats and holding lighted wands to direct the launch of his squadron's two aircraft. He dashed across the darkened flight deck to the closest Crusader, climbed to the cockpit, and relieved its startled pilot. "Unstrap and get out," Jim ordered. "I'm getting in!"

As deckhands finished harnessing the Crusader to the catapult, Jim looked to his rearview mirror and admired the lean body of his aircraft. Behind the cockpit lay a monstrous turbojet engine that would send him racing through the sky faster than the speed of sound. Missiles hung beneath the plane's swept-back wings. Quite literally, he sat perched on a rocket's nose, about to join the fray. James Bond Stockdale—call sign 007—had never wanted to be anyplace else.

The square-faced forty-one-year-old had wanted this job since his boyhood, when his father, a retired navy chief petty officer, had taken his seven-year-old son east from Abington, Illinois, to Annapolis, Maryland, to witness midshipmen on parade at the U.S. Naval Academy. He heard the drums. He felt the spirit of the storied institution in its eighty-five-year history, its revered graduates, its regimented students, its unmistakable purpose. Four years later, Jim's father took him to see the celebrated polar explorer Rear Admiral Richard E. Byrd deliver the 1935 graduation address at Iowa Wesleyan College. Fresh from an Antarctic expedition, Byrd had worn his service dress whites that day. The high-collared uniform, appointed with gold naval aviator's wings and rows of ribbons across the left side of the chest, captivated young Jim. He promised himself that one day he, like this admiral and adventurer, would accomplish something great.

Occasionally, a father's dreams for his son coincide with his son's own aspirations; this became the case for Vernon and Jim Stockdale. Father and son hoped that the academy would accept Jim into the brigade after he graduated high school. Jim's father provided the encouragement, Jim did the work, and in June 1943 he joined the Class of 1947.

Regular performance reports ushered him quickly up the ranks after graduation. The reports graded him on an extensive list of qualities related to running an organization and carrying out his duties as an officer. The navy had developed Jim into an exceptional aviator, but it had first taught him to lead men. Those lessons in leadership had in no way diminished his love of flight and of the open sky. By the time he had begun his present tour as squadron commander with Fighter Squadron 51—the Screaming Eagles—he had already excelled as an aviator and officer in the eighteen years since he entered the fleet. He'd even served as an instructor at the elite navy test pilot school at Naval Air Station (NAS) Patuxent River, Maryland.

From the dark cockpit, his blue eyes watched for the catapult officer's signals. Jim saw him spin his hand rapidly and pressed the throttle forward, feeling the Crusader's engine strain against the catapult, which would soon accelerate his plane from a standstill to 150 knots. Those jarring three seconds of his flight would be the only ones when he'd relinquish control. Jim signaled the officer with his external lights, and moments later catapult and engine launched pilot and jet into the black void at deck's end. Aloft, Jim climbed northwest toward the fight.

Shortly after 9:00 P.M., he neared the sector the two destroyers were patrolling and descended through clouds and rain, firing several bursts from his four 20mm cannons to ensure each barrel worked smoothly. According to reports coming through his radio, the two ships had identified contacts on their radar that the crew suspected were hostile torpedo boats.

Once below cloud level, Jim spied two wakes glowing with phosphoresce on the dark sea; he traced them to *Maddox* and *Turner Joy.* He dropped lower, to 1,000 feet, darting over the waters around the ships, searching for the reported boats. He canvassed the entire area but saw nothing. Around 9:30 P.M., *Maddox* fired illuminating star shells to the east, where her radar had detected inbound contacts. *Turner Joy* began shelling with no results. Then a new cry went up: "Torpedo in the water!" During the next hour, the *Maddox* reported twenty-two enemy torpedoes, yet *Turner Joy* reported none. The ships maneuvered across the sea, zigzagging to avoid the feared torpedoes, firing at suspected targets that seemed to appear and disappear on their radars, and directing the aircraft overhead toward the same. The executive officer aboard *Maddox* observed Jim's daring maneuvers and thought the aviator either insane or the finest pilot he'd ever seen.

By the time *Turner Joy* and *Maddox* ceased firing, the destroyers had sent more than three hundred rounds into the night. Inside his cockpit, Jim wondered what kind of circus he'd joined. While frenzied men aboard the ships had reported wakes, searchlights, muzzle flashes, torpedoes, and enemy boats, Jim had seen absolutely nothing. Perhaps unbeknown to the crew, the peculiar atmospheric conditions over the gulf were capable of causing false radar contacts, and the stormy murkiness of that August night—a radarman aboard USS *Maddox* called the night "darker than the hubs of hell"—had added to the confusion.

Exhausted, irritated, and low on fuel, Jim winged home to *Ticonderoga.* He found the ship's wake on the vast sea and lined up behind its distant runway of lights, which steadily grew larger in his view. He finessed his throttle and controls until he thundered over the carrier's stern. His wheels squeaked onto the deck, and he felt his tailhook snag an arresting cable. When the jet had decelerated and stopped safely, he climbed out of the cockpit, still mulling the night's strange turns.

He walked into the ready room, and his squadron mates asked, "What the hell has been going on out there?"

"Damned if I know," Jim said. "It's really a flap. The guy on the

Maddox air control radio was giving blow-by-blow accounts . . . turning left, turning right, torpedoes to the right of us, torpedoes to the left of us—boom, boom, boom! I got right down there and shot at whatever they were shooting at."

"Did you see any boats?"

"Not a one," he answered. "No boats, no boat wakes, no ricochets off boats, no boat gunfire, no torpedo wakes."

After he filed his debrief, baffling reports from *Maddox* and *Turner Joy* began filtering into the ready room. The destroyer captains first claimed their guns had sunk or damaged several boats. Then they began to question their equipment and their men; they second-guessed the entire incident. No witness aboard either ship had definitively seen anything. Shortly after midnight, the commander of the two destroyers, Captain John Herrick, cabled a telling flash message that advised, "Review of action makes many recorded contacts and torpedoes fired appear doubtful. Freak weather effects and overeager sonarmen may have accounted for many reports. No actual visual sightings by *Maddox*. Suggest complete evaluation before any further actions." When Jim learned of Herrick's last communiqué, he tossed his helmet at the ceiling and stormed off to bed, annoyed that he'd just risked his life for absolutely nothing.

Ever since Jim and his wingmen first dueled with and damaged three torpedo boats on August 2, President Lyndon Johnson saw conflict in the Gulf of Tonkin as an excuse to escalate U.S. involvement in Vietnam. Even as uncertain and conflicting accounts of what had transpired two nights later arrived in Washington, President Johnson and Secretary of Defense Robert McNamara decided to retaliate for what they considered two North Vietnamese provocations: one on August 2 and one on August 4. In their living rooms, thirteen hours after the second incident, Americans watched their president condemn the attacks and announce the nation's response. "[America's] reply," he said, "is being given as I speak to you tonight. Air action is now in execution against gunboats and certain supporting facilities in North Vietnam which have been used in these hostile operations."

As Johnson spoke, viewers could envision a deluge of bombs avenging the two reported attacks, when in fact the bombs had yet to fall. Jim Stockdale had been rousted out of his bunk only several hours earlier, as August 5 dawned on the waters off Vietnam, to lead the first wave of aircraft off *Ticonderoga;* the planes had launched less than an hour before Johnson's speech. In a move that foreshadowed the disconnect that would persist between battlefield pilots and Washington strategists throughout the coming war, President Johnson announced the attacks before bombs had been dropped. His words helped alert the North Vietnamese to the American warplanes that were at that moment approaching their coastline, led by the skeptical yet duty-bound aviator who'd been involved in both Gulf of Tonkin incidents.

In the years following, the government never ascertained exactly what transpired on the Gulf of Tonkin that night of August 4, when the supposed second attack took place. For his part, Jim Stockdale maintained that he'd seen nothing but "black sea and American firepower." Given the twenty-year collision course charted by Washington and Hanoi, however, if the August incident had not escalated the conflict, another incident almost certainly would have. Regardless, President Johnson used the episode to pass the Joint Resolution on Southeast Asia—widely known as the Gulf of Tonkin Resolution—on August 7. The resolution, which passed unanimously in the U.S. House and almost so in the Senate, authorized the president to send combat forces into Vietnam without a declaration of war.

The Gulf of Tonkin Resolution and the military escalation that followed led the United States into a long war—one never officially declared—that would drastically affect millions of Vietnamese and American lives. It was a war that would leave Jim Stockdale and hundreds of other U.S. servicemen languishing in North Vietnamese prisons, some without their families' knowledge, while their country became ensnared in a long, costly conflict originally meant to end in quick victory.

WELCOME TO THE HANOI HILTON

On December 7, 1964, Lieutenant Commander Bob Shumaker thundered westward across the California coastline in his F-8 Crusader, the sun rising at his back. Spread throughout the clear sky around him was Fighter Squadron 154—the Black Knights—and beyond them the rest of the USS *Coral Sea*'s air wing. With a thrill of excitement, these aviators winged over blue waters toward a Western Pacific deployment. Thirty miles offshore, the aircraft converged on the carrier, their home for the next seven months. Bob flew along the carrier's starboard side, then peeled off into the landing pattern. Once the ship's arresting wires trapped his Crusader, he stepped out of his cockpit and onto the flight deck, rejoining the brotherhood of men at sea. For the next several months, he would spend most of each day within 100 yards of his fellow aviators. He and his squadron mates would become inseparable, sharing a ready room, staterooms, heads, and wardroom dining tables. He would miss home, as would they all, but at sea he did his job, he served his country. Bob would choose no other life, no other company. His education and smarts rivaled those of any Ivy League graduate or Wall Street financier, men who could see their families each night, who possessed considerably more substantial means, and whose chances of dying on the job hovered around nil. In the navy, though, Bob had found a code by which to live. He and his shipmates heard a call to duty and they answered, volunteering despite the risks and hardships of aviation. They also craved the rush of adrenaline the way their white-collar counterparts needed their morning coffee. Thus drawn by the adventure of the open sea and sky, the *Coral Sea*'s fraternity of aviators willed the great ship westward into sunset after sunset, toward the test they all sought, in the air against the enemy.

After he landed his Crusader on the deck that December morning, Bob walked below and settled himself into his small, shared stateroom. He laid his light 5'10" frame on the narrow bunk and contemplated the wife and newborn son he'd left in San Diego. He'd married Lorraine Shaw less than a year before. At twenty-nine and with subtle freckles, he'd looked nearly as young as the twenty-one-year-old Canadian schoolteacher he'd met on her first trip to California, less than two years earlier. Their cross-continent romance budded so quickly and quietly that when Lorraine told her mother that she planned to get married, Rose Shaw had asked, "To whom?"

Lorraine began her service as a navy wife in Monterey, California, in January 1964, while her new husband finished his master's degree in aero-electronics at the Naval Postgraduate School. The scientific discipline suited Bob Shumaker perfectly. The numbers, formulas, and logarithms of the world simply lined up clearly in the mind of the bright-eyed, soft-spoken Pennsylvanian. He solved complex equations like a high schooler handling simple addition; he'd graduated eighth out of 681 in the Naval Academy Class of 1956. By the time he earned his diploma and received his officer's commission, his classmates and nearly everyone else called him Shu. Six years later, the same summer he met Lorraine, NASA selected the distinguished graduate for the Apollo astronaut pipeline. He made the cuts from the original list of nine thousand applicants to the thirty-four finalists. Then doctors uncovered some enlarged nodes in his chest, remnants of a long-ago bout with mononucleosis. Shu considered it inconsequential; NASA's physicians did not.

Disappointed but not discouraged, Shu returned to Monterey and earned his master's degree in June 1964. Then he received orders for NAS Miramar, so Shu and Lorraine packed their scant belongings and drove down the California coast via U.S. Route 1. Once they'd settled in San Diego, Lorraine gave birth to Grant Shumaker on November 13, 1964—three months after the August Gulf of Tonkin incident had escalated America's involvement in Southeast Asia. At the birth of his first son, Shu felt the excitement of fatherhood along with the responsibility of raising a child he considered a gift from above. He deployed aboard the *Coral Sea* just one month later.

On that last morning together, Lorraine and infant Grant had driven him to the hangar of Fighter Squadron 154. When they arrived, Shu had quickly exited the car; he'd told Lorraine a long good-bye would be too difficult. The car door closed with a metallic *thud,* and Shu walked off toward his duty. Lorraine and Grant suddenly found themselves alone in an unfamiliar city. At age twenty-two, Lorraine began her first real tour as a navy wife. Hers would last longer than that of any other wife in U.S. Navy history.

Since the August 5, 1964, raid led by Jim Stockdale, America's carrier air forces had stayed out of North Vietnam. President Johnson had promised his constituents, "We are not about to send American boys 9,000 or 10,000 miles away from home to do what Asian boys ought to be doing for themselves." Yet by 1965 more than 20,000 U.S. soldiers were serving in South Vietnam as "military advisers"—troops technically designated for training or support, not combat. On February 7, Communist guerrillas killed eight of these American advisers and wounded more than one hundred during an attack on the U.S. base at Camp Holloway, deep in the interior of South Vietnam. President Johnson found himself caught between the fear of this conflict escalating into outright war and provoking North Vietnam's Chinese and Soviet allies on the one hand, and the fear of hawkish opponents impugning his anti-Communist commitment on the other. Embarking on a middle course of gradual escalation that would mark his prosecution of the war, Johnson immediately ordered U.S. forces to execute Operation Flaming Dart, a very limited reprisal against North Vietnam, which he viewed as sponsoring the attacks. Undeterred by Flaming Dart, the guerrillas bombed U.S. barracks in Quy Nhơn three days later, killing twenty-three military personnel. Johnson responded with a larger operation, Flaming Dart II, which commenced on February 11.

The *Coral Sea* had taken up her post off the coast of North Vietnam in January of 1965, and on the day Flaming Dart II began, Bob Shumaker arrived in his squadron's ready room for a combat briefing. He found himself and three other Black Knights tasked with escorting a single reconnaissance plane on a mission over Đồng Hới, a town just north of the demilitarized zone (DMZ) that separated North and South Vietnam. Shu felt uneasy about the assignment, which he felt needlessly risked four pilots for the sake of one reconnaissance plane that needed no escort. Nevertheless, with the frustrated resignation that would become familiar to American airmen during this new war, he sat through his preflight briefing and then returned to his stateroom. There, he quietly placed his gold wedding band and his USNA '56 class ring in his desk safe. He locked away those memories of home and, with firm resolution, walked down the passageway and climbed the ladder to the flight deck. When Shu stepped into the cockpit of his waiting plane— number 403—his crew chief had no doubt he'd see his pilot return.

Less than an hour later, Shu's jet streaked low over North Vietnam at 2,000 feet. Suddenly, the plane shuddered, rolled upside down, and dove for the ground. Shu toggled his radio, intending to report "403, mayday, I'm hit!"

He managed "Four-zero" then ran out of time. He yanked the ejection handles. Small charges blew the canopy off the jet, and the ejection seat shot him into the sky. His chute opened at what he estimated was 35 feet above the ground. Had he waited to complete his mayday call before ejecting, he would have crashed with his plane.

As it was, he spent less than five seconds in the air. The ground rushed up to him and he tried to execute the roll landing he'd learned in training, but the low-altitude ejection made it impossible and he hit the earth hard on his tailbone. Slowly, he recovered from the shock of his ejection and assessed his surroundings. He'd landed in a deserted field of scrub and waist-high grass. In the roughly ten seconds from the moment his Crusader took the hit until he landed, he had instinctively followed his training. On the ground, his first conscious thought developed. A life insurance salesman had visited the Shumaker home in California shortly before Bob deployed. The man had offered the family additional coverage. Shu declined. There on the ground in North Vietnam, he wished he'd bought it.

Shu felt pain in his back slowly growing but ignored it and turned his attention to his current predicament. He quickly loaded his revolver with .38 caliber slugs, then began burrowing into a nearby thicket, hoping to hide until nightfall. With darkness cloaking him, he planned to trek the 5 miles to the coast and somehow orchestrate a rescue.

For the next hour, he watched from his hiding place as North Vietnamese soldiers and civilians canvassed the field, calling in French for the English-speaking pilot, *"Anglais, Anglais!"* Shu thought he had evaded the search parties until one last North Vietnamese soldier happened to look through a small tunnel in the brush that led directly to Shu's eyes. The two men stared at each other, and the soldier leveled an AK-47 at the fugitive. Shu considered firing his .38, but the soldier had the drop on him—and as one man with six bullets surrounded by foes with automatic weapons, he knew his odds.

Bob Shumaker, the second American aviator captured in North Vietnam.

An hour earlier, Shu's Crusader had roared over the waves firmly under his control. Now he huddled in the scrub brush of a third-world country, dirty, outgunned, unable to speak the language. With no realistic options, he raised his hands. During the August 5, 1964, retaliatory raid ordered by President Johnson and led by Jim Stockdale, Lieutenant Ev Alvarez had become the first U.S. aviator captured in North Vietnam. Shu had now become the second.

Soldiers quickly bound his hands, blindfolded him, and stuffed him into a jeep. Then he began a three-day journey that would take him from Đồng Hới to the North Vietnamese capital of Hanoi. Every pothole the driver hit sent pain shooting up Shu's injured back, making the trip all the worse. The jeep stopped before entering each town along the way, and a political officer would hustle into the village and gather crowds of citizens to receive the prisoner. The guards would take Shu out of the truck and parade him through mobs of shouting townspeople who rained blows on the captive, likely the first American they had ever seen. With his hands cuffed, Shu simply tried to maintain his footing and get through one humiliating onslaught so he could face the next.

After three nights of traveling blindfolded through villages and farmland, Shu detected the noises of an urban area. The jeep made a number of turns that seemed to lead deeper into a city until it rumbled to a halt. Soldiers lifted Shu out and set him on his feet. He heard gates open and walked forward along a bricked path. The gates shut behind him, and he heard another pair swing open. Hands on his arms and back pushed him forward. He heard his footsteps echo off walls and a ceiling; he had entered a tunnel. The echoes faded as he emerged 70 feet later and again detected open space around him. The air smelled musty. He felt the guards direct him to the left. He stepped onto a hard floor and heard his steps echo again in a smaller corridor until he emerged into another open space. He turned right and was shoved through a doorway. Then the guards removed his blindfold.

He looked around at a Spartan room with white walls and a smooth concrete floor. He guessed he was somewhere in Hanoi. In fact, he stood near the city's heart. He had arrived at one of the darkest spots in Southeast Asia: Hỏa Lò Prison.

When native Vietnamese forces surrendered to the French in 1883, the conquerors quickly consolidated their power and claimed the territory's people and resources for France. The vigorous application of colonial justice soon filled jails with so many rebels and dissenters that the penal system needed additional space. In 1896, the French regime began constructing a new prison in central Hanoi, near the existing Court of Justice and Intelligence Department. The government cleared forty-eight small houses from the neighborhood of Phú Khánh to build a 42,349-square-foot detention facility. Phú Khánh residents had been known for their pottery kilns, or hỏa lò—pronounced "wah low." So although the administration gave it the official name of Maison Centrale (literally the "central house," but meaning "prison"), the place quickly became known as Hỏa Lò Prison. It received the name for another reason as well, though. Hỏa lò had an alternative translation: hellhole.

When Hỏa Lò began receiving inmates in 1898, the compound's yellow and gray stone wall—built nearly 2 feet thick—stretched around a trapezoidal plot between several of Hanoi's busiest thoroughfares. A hedge of green glass shards covered the top of the 13-foot-high bulwark. Live electrical wires ran above the glass. Several trees arched over the walls and shaded the security moat between the outer wall and the inner buildings. Inside, the terra-cotta roofs of cellblocks and administration offices rose above the walls. From the outside, Hỏa Lò looked as much like a walled government compound as a prison.

Its interior, however, revealed its purpose. Colonial jailers at Hỏa Lò had clamped Vietnamese prisoners in stocks on long wooden platforms in mass holding rooms, pressing twenty-five nearly naked men together with little concern for their toilet or exercise. Authorities dispensed food and water frugally—and prisoners found both of deplorable quality. Wardens sent the condemned into solitary confinement in the southeasternmost cellblock, where they spent their last days chained to bunks in dirty, claustrophobic cells. In the courtyard, jailers frequently employed the guillotine. As the years passed, conditions grew worse. Wardens became more callous, and overcrowding soon added more misery to the inmates' dreadful existence. In 1913, the population had reached six hundred inmates. By the end of French rule in 1954, the place held more than two thousand; many of those prisoners suffocated in impossibly cramped cells.

Like the American airmen who would one day inhabit these same cellblocks, the Vietnamese inmates learned to retaliate. In January 1930, they declared Hỏa Lò's first hunger strike. United, they protested the food they received, and the wardens begrudgingly improved their rations thereafter. For the next twenty years, prisoners won similarly small but important victories through unified resistance. On several occasions, the French purged the prison population of its leaders, either killing them or exiling them to other facilities. Less overt but equally important defiance came in the form of covert communication. The Vietnamese developed invisible ink from stolen medical supplies and stashed notes throughout the prison. The authorities knew their control depended on isolating prisoners; the prisoners knew their lives hinged on maintaining contact with one another. Some of those same prisoners would return to Hỏa Lò as wardens themselves when the cells began to fill with Americans; North Vietnam's prime minister and its general secretary had also served long prison terms during the 1930s and 1940s. The North Vietnamese would not forget the lessons of their own captivity.

In this new conflict, North Vietnam would use Hỏa Lò Prison as part of its plan to defeat—or more precisely *outlast*—the United States and whatever U.S. ally might hold power in the South Vietnamese capital of Saigon. The North's three-pronged strategy included a committed military campaign, international diplomacy and political choreography, and proselytizing—influencing the minds and hearts of citizens and soldiers in North Vietnam, South Vietnam, and the United States. General Võ Nguyên Giáp advocated "using the enemy against the enemy," and the Ministry of National Defense directed the Enemy Proselytizing Department (EPD) to gather intelligence from any American POWs. The government would also use prisoners for propaganda and attempt to indoctrinate them with Communist dogma. The Ministry of Public Safety, an organization similar to the Soviet KGB, would run the prisons and shared responsibility for interrogating prisoners with the EPD. They were to extract information and propaganda statements, then deliver the results to the Ministry of National Defense, for military use, or to the Office of the Prime Minister, which would broadcast the material through national and international print, television,

Hỏa Lò Prison, the "Hanoi Hilton," looking east by southeast. The main gate is top, center.

and radio. These groups—collectively called the Camp Authority—aimed to use POW statements to win sympathy and erode domestic and foreign support for the Americans. North Vietnamese leaders considered antiwar propaganda vital, and they would place heavy pressure upon the Camp Authority to obtain it.

When he arrived at Hỏa Lò Prison, Bob Shumaker knew none of this. He just found an old, dirty colonial garrison. There in his holding room, he could only speculate that elsewhere in the facility, jailers had locked away Ev Alvarez, who Shu knew was the first aviator taken captive. Indeed, Alvarez was locked in Room Twenty-four, less than 100 feet away.

Since Shu had worn a blindfold throughout his drive into Hanoi, it took his eyes some time to readjust. Observing his new room more closely, he found it not unpleasant and, in fact, fairly spacious—perhaps 12 by 15 feet—more like an office than a prison cell. A desk even stood along one wall. On the tile floor, he found a woven bamboo bedroll, along with a toothbrush and toothpaste tube, a wash rag, coarse brown toilet paper, a bar of brown soap, a mosquito net, and a thin blanket. A guard soon entered the room and took his flight suit, leaving Shu what seemed like civilian clothes: khaki pants and a shirt. He also received a pair of sandals made from tire treads. The guard said, *"Xô,"* Vietnamese for "bucket," and pointed to a corner. There, Shu found the most demeaning item of all, his "bo," a three-gallon pail that he quickly deduced would serve as his personal latrine.

Roughly six hours after Shu arrived, a guard outfitted in green fatigues and sandals similar to his own opened the door and motioned the captive into the courtyard outside. As he left, Shu noticed the number "19" by his door. The guard pushed him down a short open-air passageway of dusty terra-cotta tiles to a large room with French doors, heavy curtains, and concrete flooring much like his own room. Its door was numbered "18." When he entered, he found three officers seated behind a table covered with blue cloth. Above them, a lightbulb dangled from a plaster ceiling that also held a meat hook. A low concrete block sat before the officers; Shu gathered they intended that to be his seat. He squatted down onto the block and looked up at his captors. The interrogators did not state their names, so Shu privately assigned nicknames. He dubbed the apparent ringleader Owl, for his round face, short body, and deepset eyes. Owl introduced himself as commandant of Hỏa Lò Prison and pulled up his sleeves to show Shu ghastly scars from his own imprisonment in Maison Centrale.

Shu began by stating his basic identifying information, "Shumaker, Robert H.; Lieutenant Commander; 548955; May 11, 1933." The interrogators smiled and thanked him, then inquired about his squadron, his training, his airplane, his ship, his family, and his opinions. It reminded Shu of a high school quiz. If Owl expected answers, however, he was disappointed. In response, Shu just asserted his rights under the 1949 Geneva Convention Relative to the Treatment of Prisoners of War. The treaty, signed by North Vietnam, the United States, and 102 other countries, defined the rights of POWs and outlined rules to ensure their humane treatment. It also prohibited captors from extracting anything more than a prisoner's name, rank, service number, and date of birth. Shu had given everything he intended to give.

When he invoked Geneva protection, Owl scoffed, "You are not a prisoner of war. You are a war criminal! And we will try you before the Vietnamese people."

Owl explained that, in North Vietnam's view, the Geneva Convention did not apply to the present conflict—war had not been declared between his country and the United States. Even if it had, he said, the Geneva Convention granted no protection to pilots who had attacked civilians, which he accused Shu of doing. The soft-spoken engineer maintained his characteristically calm composure and simply took note that trial was a possibility. Whether the North Vietnamese honored the Geneva Convention or not, he planned to stick by the U.S. military's Code of Conduct, which governed the behavior of servicemen captured by an enemy.

After learning how POWs struggled against Communist interrogators and harsh conditions during the Korean War, the Department of Defense had decreed that its men needed better preparation and guidelines to follow in captivity. So on August 17, 1955, in an executive order, President Dwight Eisenhower set forth the Code of Conduct for Members of the Armed Forces of the United States. Its words would inform every American act of resistance in North Vietnam.

ARTICLE I

I am an American fighting man. I serve in the forces which guard my country and our way of life. I am prepared to give my life in their defense.

ARTICLE II

I will never surrender of my own free will. If in command I will never surrender my men while they still have the means to resist.

ARTICLE III

If I am captured, I will continue to resist by all means available. I will make every effort to escape and aid others to escape. I will accept neither parole nor special favors from the enemy.

ARTICLE IV

If I become a prisoner of war, I will keep faith with my fellow prisoners. I will give no information or take part in any action which might be harmful to my comrades. If I am senior, I will take command. If not, I will obey the lawful orders of those appointed over me and will back them up in every way.

ARTICLE V

When questioned, should I become a prisoner of war, I am bound to give only name, rank, service number, and date of birth. I will evade answering further questions to the utmost of my ability. I will make no oral or written statements disloyal to my country and its allies or harmful to their cause.

ARTICLE VI

I will never forget that I am an American fighting man, responsible for my actions, and dedicated to the principles which made my country free. I will trust in my God and in the United States of America.

Shu had every intention of adhering to the Code. Since he never expected to be taken prisoner, however, he had to work to recall those specific points and phrases that provided the standard by which U.S. POWs could always measure their actions and others could in turn hold them accountable.

The Code, like the Geneva Convention, established the Big Four—name, rank, service number, date of birth—as the only information properly obtainable from a prisoner of war. However, since the North Vietnamese knew that Shu had not surrendered freely and had no interest in cooperating, they saw little reason to extend Geneva Convention protection to an active combatant in an undeclared war. As it dawned on Shu that North Vietnam would make propaganda coerced from POWs a key component of its war effort, he would come to believe he had the right—the *duty*—to continue fighting this war tooth and nail, from cells, interrogation rooms, or wherever the enemy might confine him.

At present, Shu's fighting was confined to Rooms Eighteen and Nineteen. After Owl's initial failed attempts to get additional information, he switched to lecturing Shu on the history of Vietnam. He explained the long and unhappy colonial legacy left by the French and Japanese, lamenting his people's struggle for rights and basic security. As recently as 1945, when it celebrated its newly won freedom from imperial Japan, Vietnam had looked to America as an ally. Now, as Owl saw it, the United States seemed bent on becoming his country's new master. In fact, when Vietnam marked its liberation from Japan, Hồ Chí Minh, the leader of the Việtminh—the League for the Independence of Vietnam— had gratefully acknowledged assistance from America's Office of Strategic Services (OSS), the World War II precursor to the CIA. As Hồ Chí Minh himself had worked in Boston and New York during 1911, he had great hope for an alliance with the United States. President Franklin Roosevelt's statements of support for former colonies like Vietnam further encouraged Hồ Chí Minh and other Vietnamese leaders. Then France set about reestablishing control over its former colony. The brief peace ended, and the First Indochina War began. Roosevelt's successor, Harry Truman, needed France to counterbalance the Soviet threat in Europe, and he believed the French military offered the only roadblock to Communist domination in Southeast Asia. Thus, Truman committed himself to the French cause, even as his advisers expressed doubts about anyone's ability to suppress Vietnam's growing nationalism.

The Eisenhower administration held the course, believing that the Việtminh did the bidding of America's Cold War adversaries in Moscow and Beijing. By the end of 1954, America had spent more on France's venture in Indochina than it had on France's portion of the postwar Marshall Plan; the United States bore 80 percent of the costs of the Indochina War. One U.S. diplomat quipped, "We are the last French colonialists in Indochina."

In Room Eighteen, Owl extolled Việtminh general Võ Nguyên Giáp, who had secured independence with a victory over French troops in the northwestern valley of Điện Biên Phủ. The resulting Geneva Accords of 1954 declared a cease-fire and divided Vietnam—temporarily— into two halves. An internationally supervised election scheduled for 1956 would unify the country under a single government. By then, however, Owl explained that neither the regime in Saigon nor its French or American patrons had any interest in staging national elections. All parties knew popular ballots would hand power to the Communist Việtminh. Thus, Vietnam remained split, and North and South Vietnam had consequently come into being as two distinct entities.

During the lectures, Shu sat silently on his concrete block, amazed that Owl and others spent day after day delivering three-hour history lessons from the desk. "They must have cast-iron bottoms," Shu thought to himself. "They *must* have."

As his fruitless efforts to reeducate Bob Shumaker continued, Owl explained that under North Vietnam's direction, South Vietnamese factions—Communist and not—that opposed the American-backed regime of Ngô Đình Diệm founded the National Liberation Front (NLF), a Communist-led political organization. They called their military wing the People's Liberation Armed Forces (PLAF); Diệm had dubbed the PLAF the "Việtcộng," a truncated and pejorative form of the term "Vietnamese Communists." Owl praised the resistance and its opposition to what he viewed as a puppet regime in Saigon. He told Shu the NLF would triumph, aided by North Vietnam, which was pumping men and materials southward along a jungle transportation network that the United States nicknamed the "Hồ Chí Minh Trail" after North Vietnam's head of state and chairman of its Vietnamese Communist Party. With that lifeline, the NLF had gained significant control of more than 40 percent of South Vietnam, despite heavy U.S. aid and thousands of advisers. Hanoi hoped the insurgency's success would overwhelm the southern regime and precipitate a U.S. exit by turning American public opinion against the war.

Instead of exiting, however, President Johnson reaffirmed his country's involvement in Vietnam. For nearly two decades, the United States had staked part of its Cold War credibility on this fight, and he would not abandon the cause now. In a speech that spring of 1965, Johnson said, "To withdraw from one battlefield means only to prepare for the next. We must say in Southeast Asia—as we did in Europe—in the words of the Bible: 'Hitherto shalt thou come, but no further.'" He concluded, "We will not be defeated." Yet secretly Johnson had long harbored serious reservations. "It looks like to me that we're getting into another Korea," he confided to an aide the previous year. "I don't think it's worth fighting for and I don't think we can get out. And it's just the biggest damn mess that I ever saw." Despite those worries, Johnson forged ahead and decided to send combat troops into South Vietnam.

On March 9, Owl informed Shu that 3,500 U.S. Marines had landed at Đà Nẵng the day before. "We're finally going to win this war," Shu thought. "I'll be home by Christmas." Now more optimistic, Shu feigned interest in the lessons but never trusted his interrogator. Besides, an enemy gulag seemed the worst of all places to begin questioning his government.

As March progressed, Owl returned to his interrogation. Shu's training had taught him not to answer anything beyond the Big Four, but Owl's questions came unrelentingly. Shu gradually began responding but deftly avoided providing any substantive answers, instead adopting a facade that he hoped would convince his enemy that they'd captured the most dimwitted aviator in the U.S. Navy. He told them his responsibility aboard ship extended only to tending pool tables. When they asked him about the most vulnerable spot on an F-8 Crusader, Shu pointed to a spot between his eyes; a bullet would kill the pilot. He figured that wouldn't reveal anything new.

Taking a different approach, the interrogators began asking about the economic status of the Shumaker family. Shu suspected blackmail and stonewalled. When they asked how many chickens his father owned, Shu couldn't resist any longer. "Twelve," he said. In reality, Shu's father, Alvah, had earned a law degree at Harvard and ran a successful litigation practice—but Alvah's education did not mean that the Shumakers had never worked a farm. In fact, the family lived on 250 acres in Pennsylvania with forty dairy cattle. They had four hundred chickens.

Shu divulged none of that family history, and to his private amusement, his response satisfied the interrogators. He had begun to notice that they often appeared under pressure to deliver answers to their superiors. The quality and substance of the answers seemed less important, and so Shu slowly began talking, feeding the North Vietnamese a diet of falsehoods made all the more believable by his soft voice and mild, earnest manner.

After that session, he returned to the solitude of Room Nineteen, amused by his performance. However, he soon realized—with horror and regret—that he'd broken the Code of Conduct. Though he'd lied, he'd given up more than the Big Four. He'd started down a dangerous path of compromise. Shu resolved to stonewall them thereafter.

The interrogations—quizzes, as he thought of them—persisted, usually twice a day, over the following weeks. During one interrogation, Owl told Shu that North Vietnamese air defenses had downed thirty-five American aircraft in a single day. The report sounded preposterous, and initially Shu dismissed it. Then he returned to his cell, alone. He'd had no outside news for weeks now, and with little else to occupy his mind, he began turning over the statement, examining it from every perspective. He began to wonder. Could it have been possible? Were their defenses good enough to bring down thirty-five aircraft? If so, what did that mean for America's prospects—and for his own?

The dearth of information was an unexpected shock. At home and even aboard *Coral Sea*, news poured in from television programs, radio broadcasts, conversations, and firsthand experiences. Once in North Vietnam, that flow of trusted information ceased. All he heard was propaganda from interrogators; he supposed some statements might be partially true, he just couldn't tell which ones. He would never wish a fellow aviator to meet his fate, yet he realized that new POWs offered the only trustworthy news sources—and he grew desperate to communicate with an American. Surely, he thought, repatriation would come soon. New POWs came sooner than any release.

Each day, Shu surveyed the courtyard from the crack beneath his door, hoping to see an American and establish contact; he felt certain other pilots would join him in Hỏa Lò. He eventually saw another POW regularly emptying his bucket—his honey pot—in the same bathhouse he used himself, one just off the courtyard. After dumping and scraping out his bucket, this new American would participate in the prison's charade of personal hygiene by washing himself with the cold, less-than-clean water that trickled out of the latrine's spigots. No inmate ever felt clean in Hỏa Lò Prison.

While the bathhouse proved fairly useless for cleaning, it did offer rare minutes of privacy away from the guards. Shu devised the first of countless note-drop procedures he would use in the years to come. In Room Nineteen, he found an old ink spill in a desk drawer. He added water to the dried puddle and reconstituted enough ink to wet the end of a bamboo shard. He neatly tore a rectangular section of toilet paper and poised his pen above it. He paused and considered his words, then wrote, "Welcome to the Hanoi Hilton."

Thus one of the most famous nicknames in prison history came into being. During the coming years, hundreds of downed airmen would receive similar greetings when they arrived at Hỏa Lò. In time, the Vietnamese name became lost in the Western world, where people would simply refer to the prison as the Hanoi Hilton.

The meticulous engineer needed to know if the drop had been successful, so he added a second sentence. Dipping the bamboo in the ink again, Shu wrote, "If you get note, scratch balls as you're coming back."

The next day, May 15, 1965, he hid the note in his pants before his walk to the latrine. Once inside and out of view, he rolled the paper into what looked like a miniature cigarette, then tied it with a string from his clothes. He wiggled a loosened piece of concrete from the brick wall, revealing a small nook. He stashed the note and replaced the concrete, leaving a length of string exposed as a marker.

Back in his room, Shu pressed his temple to the floor and peered under the door, training his eye on the path to the bathhouse, anxious to see if his plan worked; three months had passed since he'd last communicated with an American. Luckily, nobody had checked the latrine before the next POW entered. The prisoner's guard remained outside, paying little attention. Five minutes later, the man came walking out of the bath, wildly scratching his crotch: He'd found the note. Shu had at last established friendly contact. When he returned to the latrine the next day, Shu found that the POW had used a burned matchstick to scratch a response: "Storz, Capt. USAF."

Unlike most downed aviators who would arrive in Hanoi, thirty-one-year-old Air Force Captain Ronald E. Storz did not fly jets, or any other large aircraft, for that matter. He piloted a Cessna L-19 forward observation plane. On April 28, 1965, he had been flying low over Sông Bến Hải, the river which flowed along the DMZ. When ground fire disabled the plane's engine, he was forced to make an emergency landing on the river's north side. The North Vietnamese quickly took Ron into custody, and he became the eighth American aviator to arrive at the Hanoi Hilton.

Ron's parents had emigrated from Germany to the United States before World War II, and when America entered the war, Ron saw his father volunteer to serve in the U.S. Army, willing to take up arms against his own homeland because he believed passionately in America's principles. The army rejected him, however, and he had to confront the public prejudice that came as his new country went to war against his old country. Max Storz lost his job, and to keep the family of seven fed, Ron's mother worked as a maid. The government confiscated the family's firearms; they stopped speaking German entirely. Yet their wartime experience never diminished their love of America, and they instilled that patriotism in their children.

Before long, that passion for country drove eighteen-year-old Ron to enlist in the U.S. Air Force. He worked hard for three years and received his commission as an officer in 1954. By the fall of 1964, Ron had become a flight instructor. He and his wife, Sandra, had a five-year-old son and a newborn daughter. That autumn, between flying and being a father, Ron read two books about prisoners of war in World War II, one by a German, one by a Brit. Their stories of survival fascinated him, and as he read and reread the books, he contemplated what he would have done in their situations. In late fall, Ron learned a friend had been ordered to Vietnam and would miss the birth of his first child. Even though he knew it would mean an early separation from his own wife, son, and newborn daughter, Ron volunteered to take his place.

On November 2, 1964, at the family's home in New Hampshire, Ron knelt in front of his son, Mark, and pulled him close. Keeping with the long tradition of fathers leaving for war, he explained to his young son, "With me away, you're going to have to take care of the family and be the man for your mother and your baby sister." Mark would never forget how the penetrating yet soft blue eyes of his father looked at him that day. Ron left for Vietnam, thirty-one years old and promising to return soon. As Sandra watched him leave, she thought, "I'll never see him again in this life." She quickly dismissed the premonition; surely he'd be home within a year.

On June 6, Bob Shumaker was nearing his fourth month of isolation in Room Nineteen when Owl surprised him with paper and a pen. The Camp Authority was at last permitting him to write home. He wrote two pages to his young wife in clear cursive. He explained how he'd thought about their every experience, reliving even their disagreements, and how he treasured the time they'd had together.

By good fortune, Shu was among a handful of aviators the U.S. military had clandestinely trained to use a cipher that remains classified to this day. It was, and is, intended precisely for situations such as captivity. Now, in his first letter home, he used his training to arrange his words and letters, encrypting the initials of confirmed POWs to inform U.S. intelligence whom the North Vietnamese held. Mentally composing the encrypted letter before writing it took tremendous focus, but in Room Nineteen, Shu had no distractions.

By the time Shu had written his first letter, seven other prisoners had joined him and Ron Storz in the Hanoi Hilton. With other sections of the prison full of Vietnamese civilians or being otherwise utilized, the growing American population forced the North Vietnamese to end Bob Shumaker's solitary imprisonment. After four months—133 days—of loneliness, Shu watched his door open to reveal an American POW. From behind, a guard nudged Captain Carlyle "Smitty" Harris, USAF, into the room, then closed the door. At the sight of each other, wide smiles broke across the two pilots' haggard faces. Several minutes later, guards ushered in Lieutenant Phil Butler from the USS *Midway*. Air Force Lieutenant Bob Peel followed to round out the new foursome. Shu grinned at his roommates until his cheeks hurt. Together with other Americans for the first time since their shootdowns, the men talked for nearly three straight days.

After the euphoria subsided, Butler told Shu about Operation Rolling Thunder, which President Johnson had launched in early March. He explained that the president intended the eight-week air offensive against North Vietnam to cut the insurgency's lifelines without a costly ground campaign. The air operation had extended long past the eight-week mark; nobody saw an end in sight. More captives would arrive, and Shu suspected that the Camp Authority would separate Room Nineteen's residents at the earliest opportunity. While he and his new roommates could converse safely in their shared room, camp policy strictly forbade communication elsewhere. Shu—the senior officer in Room Nineteen—knew they would need to exchange information covertly in the days ahead. Demonstrating exactly why the North Vietnamese would want to isolate their captives, the men of Room Nineteen collaborated and devised a plan to maintain contact.

	1	2	3	4	5
1	A	B	C/K	D	E
2	F	G	H	I	J
3	L	M	N	O	P
4	Q	R	S	T	U
5	V	W	X	Y	Z

The foursome already knew Morse code, but that required sending and receiving short and long transmissions, called dots and dashes. Telegraph or signal lamp operators did this quite easily, but the men knew distinguishing between longs and shorts would prove difficult for prisoners tapping with their hands. Besides, the entire world used Morse code, including the North Vietnamese. Harris suggested an alternative. Back in the United States, he'd attended the Air Force Survival, Evasion, Resistance, and Escape (SERE) School and a course led in part by a former POW from the Korean War. During a coffee break, Harris had overheard him explain how prisoners in Korea used a code that the instructor called AFLQV, which stood for the first letter in each row of a five-by-five alphabetic grid. The phrase "American Football League Quid Victorious" served as a mnemonic to remember the grid. Harris explained that a combination of taps represented each letter of the English alphabet (except *K*, for which *C* substituted) and related to the letter's position in the grid. A prisoner's first set of taps represented the letter's horizontal row. Then he'd pause briefly. His second set would denote the letter's vertical column. The group decided that the code's simple grid and the numerous ways one could transmit it suited the POWs' situation in North Vietnam perfectly. The four men in Room Nineteen committed it to memory. In the conflict that was to come, few things would prove more valuable—not just to those four, but to every single American who would arrive at the Hanoi Hilton.

3

DEAD OR ALIVE?

In July, Bob Shumaker noticed a new POW shuffling to and from the bathhouse in New Guy Village, as the prisoners in Room Nineteen had taken to calling the four cells, two main rooms, and courtyard near Hỏa Lò's southeast corner. The new captive wore the red-and pink-striped pajamalike uniform that had begun to replace the oxfords and khakis issued to the initial wave of prisoners. The Americans called the striped outfits their "clown suits." As the new POW crossed the courtyard, he heard a soft voice call from Room Nineteen, "Go fishing." In the privacy of the bathhouse, he searched the drain and noticed a matchstick lying over the metal grate. When he picked it up, he found a dangling note attached. It bore the words, "If you read this, spit as you depart the latrine door." Bob Shumaker had established contact with Commander Jeremiah Denton, Naval Academy Class of 1947. He was the thirteenth American to arrive at Hỏa Lò Prison and the new highest-ranking U.S. officer in Hanoi.

Shu found Jerry's first reply shocking. Jerry had used a wetted burned matchstick to scribble a note explaining that the North Vietnamese had put him in leg irons; he stashed it in the bathhouse nook. "What the hell for?" Shu asked in his next drop. He had heard interrogators threaten POWs with harsh treatment, but Shu hadn't realized they actually went through with it. He wondered how a captive could have brought such punishment upon himself. He would learn the answer as he came to discover the defiance of Jerry Denton.

Thirty-seven years before he arrived in Hanoi, Jerry Denton received his first airplane as a gift for his third birthday. His father, a hotel manager, presented him with a blue-and-gold airplane on wheels, which he rode around the Fisher Hotel in El Paso, Texas, where his family lived. He thought little more of the navy or of aviation until he saw the 1937 film *Navy Blue and Gold.* As he watched actors Lionel Barrymore and Jimmy Stewart navigate a football season at the U.S. Naval Academy, he realized the navy—and its academy—might help him rise above his parents' station and provide him a path to success. As a high school senior—and as quarterback of McGill Institute's football team, captain of its baseball and basketball teams, and its "Most Popular" student—he sought the required nomination to the academy from his U.S. representative. He did not receive a response.

With his dream hostage to bureaucracy, he enrolled at Spring Hill College, where his freshman class elected him president. The following year, he still hadn't heard from Annapolis and decided to enter navy boot camp. One day, his commanding officer called him off the field and into his office. "Denton," he boomed, "you're going to Bancroft Hall!" The words meant nothing to Jerry until the officer explained that Bancroft Hall housed the Brigade of Midshipmen at the Naval Academy. Midshipman Denton walked onto the Yard in June of 1943, along with Jim Stockdale of Abingdon, Illinois, and Jimmy Carter of Plains, Georgia.

Jerry forsook Navy football so he could devote his weekends to courting his Mobile sweetheart, Jane Maury, who attended Mary Washington College in Virginia. They were married in the Naval Academy Chapel the day after he graduated. The couple left the chapel and walked beneath the Arch of Sabers, six swords held aloft by Jerry's classmates. The ceremony initiated Jane into a world where she would see her husband excel as an officer and an aviator. Like so many others, Jerry was led to aviation by his unrelenting competitiveness and high aspirations. In the fleet's new Grumman A-6 Intruder, he would find status, freedom, and invincibility. All that ended on July 18, 1965.

Just two days before taking command of Attack Squadron 75— the Sunday Punchers—aboard the USS *Independence,* Jerry worked the throttle to ease his aircraft onto the catapult located at the ship's waist. He looked to his right, past his bombardier-navigator, Bill Tschudy, and toward the ship's island, marked with a large white "62," signifying *Independence*'s place as the navy's sixty-second aircraft carrier. A dark-suited civilian emerged from the island, a small delegation trailing him; Jerry knew it was Secretary of Defense Robert McNamara. The visiting secretary made his way through the heat and noise of the flight deck toward Jerry's plane. When McNamara arrived planeside to observe the launch, Jerry began his final preflight sequence, wondering if McNamara's visit portended a successful mission.

Jerry returned his attention to the task at hand. He watched the yellow-shirted catapult officer, known as the shooter, signal him to rev his engines. He felt the plane buck as the turbojets came to life. He checked his control surfaces and, finding them all functioning, snapped a salute to the shooter. The man returned Jerry's gesture, then pointed his arm forward, down the deck. The catapult engaged at his signal and sent the Intruder thundering off the deck and into the sky.

The flight of twenty-eight planes from *Independence* soon crossed into North Vietnam, and Jerry led them toward the heavily defended Thanh Hóa Bridge—the "Dragon's Jaw"—roughly 75 miles south of Hanoi. Once they arrived over the target, Jerry dove for the bridge first. Just as he released his bombs, his jet suffered a mortal wound; he suspected a bomb had immediately detonated upon release, although he would never know for certain. The plane soon sustained a second hit. The radio failed. The hydraulic controls failed. The Intruder began rolling to the right. Jerry rose out of the seat and jammed his foot onto the left rudder pedal with such force that he snapped a tendon in his leg. When the stricken craft rolled upright, he hit Bill Tschudy's shoulder and signaled: Time to go. Jerry yanked the ejection loop at the top of his seat. Seconds later, Tschudy did the same. Both men's parachutes deployed after they rocketed out of the aircraft, and the two flyers floated helplessly down into North Vietnam.

Upon Jerry's arrival at the Hanoi Hilton, guards escorted him down a dark hallway of four New Guy Village cells just south of the main gate. As did most new arrivals that summer, he heard a soulful "Yankee Doodle" whistled in welcome, courtesy of POW John McKamey. The slamming door of Cell Four ended the serenade. Jerry looked around at the bleak room, which had two concrete bunks with leg stocks attached. Unlike portable leg irons, the stocks had wooden bottoms affixed to the foot of a bunk, with two semicircular indentions carved into the wood. A hinged iron bar with corresponding indentions would close over the prisoner's ankles, locking him firmly into the stocks and rendering him immobile. Judging by the wear and sweat stains on the bunks and stocks, Jerry surmised that French jailers had put the draconian devices to good use in the past. Surely, he thought, the North Vietnamese wouldn't place Americans in such dated confinement. He noticed rust had eaten away at one of the steel locking bars, and he began working on the rusted piece of metal, attempting to break it off near the hinges. He hid his work for six days and finally broke off the bar. When he felt safe, he began using it to try to pry open the thin iron bars keeping him from escaping through the cell's large window. When that proved useless, he started chipping away at the concrete holding the window frame in place. Eventually, he had made a hole and believed he could quickly finish pulling out the frame once he had devised an escape plan.

As he worked on the window, he whistled "Anchors Aweigh," hoping for a response. He got one. A New Jersey–accented voice whispered, "Hello, Yank . . . what's your name?"

"This is Jerry Denton, U.S. Navy," he said. "Who are you?"

"Guarino, major, air force," said Larry Guarino, a POW who'd arrived in Hanoi that June.

"Oh . . . yeah, I've heard of you. The Vietnamese released your name as captured."

"No kidding? That's great news, Jerry." It meant that Guarino's wife would know he'd survived and that one day the North Vietnamese would have to account for him. With good reason POWs often doubted that Hanoi released their names and wondered if their families knew they were still alive.

"What kind of airplane were you flying?" Guarino asked.

Jerry chuckled and said, "That's what they would like to know!"

Guarino thought to himself that Jerry would be tough to break. Then he said aloud, "I bet you're from Canoe U," meaning the U.S. Naval Academy.

"That's right," Jerry said. "Well, don't worry, we'll hack 'er." Then he asked, "How many men have been repatriated so far?"

Surprised, Guarino replied, "Never heard of anybody being repatriated."

"How's the mail been coming through?"

"Don't be ridiculous, Jerry. We don't get any mail up here."

"Well, don't worry about it, we'll hack 'er."

For several days, they talked and sang to one another through the open windows until an officer reprimanded them. The two protested: They *had* to talk. There was nothing else to do.

"You are absolutely forbidden to speak or make any sounds," he ordered. "You must only sit and ponder your crimes against the Vietnamese people!"

The two learned to save much of their conversation for the guards' usual midday siesta. The postlunch break gave the prisoners precious hours to communicate without harassment.

Unluckily for Jerry, guards inspected his cell on July 28. When they discovered the loose iron bar and the damage to the window frame, they hauled him to neighboring Cell Three, pushed him onto the sleeping platform, and immobilized his right ankle in the stocks. Since he'd badly injured his left leg upon ejection, the guards left it free. The gesture seemed humane at first but soon led to his free leg rubbing against the rough metal atop the stocks. Within days, his foot had a raging infection. He also confronted the challenge of using his latrine bucket with one leg bound. He called to Guarino, knowing that guards had locked one of his legs in stocks some days earlier. "Larry," Jerry called. "How do you take a crap in those stocks?"

"Ah, heck, that's a long story, Jerry," Guarino answered. "You don't want to hear that."

"Yeah, I'm interested," Jerry said. "How the hell do you do it?"

Guarino shared his trick of rotating his locked leg and standing on his knees while placing the bucket under his rear end. Somewhat irritated, he asked Jerry why he'd wanted to know; he thought Jerry was poking fun at his predicament. He laughed at Jerry's reply.

"Because," Jerry said, "I've been in these stocks for three days, and I couldn't figure it out!"

By the end of July, Bob Shumaker and his band in Room Nineteen had established contact with Jerry and Guarino via note drops in the latrine. Shu had made certain that his group shared the tap code with them, and for the first time the code successfully passed to other

Americans. Jerry soon learned most of the known prisoners' names and that Guarino ranked senior among the eleven captured air force pilots; Jerry ranked senior among the seven navy men. He convinced Guarino that the situation called for a single commanding officer. Guarino deferred to his higher-ranking fellow captive, and Jerry assumed command of the eighteen Americans in Hỏa Lò and set about organizing their joint unit.

Guarino had stolen a pencil during a quiz—as all POWs had now taken to calling interrogations—and Jerry asked him to stash it in the latrine. The next day, Jerry found the pencil and used a scavenged razor blade to sharpen it. He began composing policies on toilet paper and hiding them in the latrine's nook. Thus POWs using the New Guy Village facilities learned his basic operational plan, which would evolve into several main points. Above all, the POWs should follow the Code of Conduct. More specific to their situation, they should communicate by all means, learn the names and locations of all POWs, complain about their food, and gather materials like wire, nails, and paper. They should not attempt escape without outside help, nor should they antagonize the guards. They were always to remain vigilant and faithful. To advance the latter cause, a weekly devotional period was announced by the whistling of "God Bless America."

A hierarchy soon formed among the POWs; orders and information replaced jokes and innocuous communication. To combat the camp's rampant dysentery, Jerry ordered everyone to wash their hands as often as possible. He also asked them to assemble the names of confirmed prisoners so he would know whom the North Vietnamese held and their conditions. Should the jailers kill any of them, Jerry wanted to hold North Vietnam accountable. He always encouraged his troops to follow the Code of Conduct and not give interrogators more than their names, ranks, service numbers, and dates of birth, if they could help it. Firmly under Jerry's command, the POWs began an organized campaign of resistance against the North Vietnamese Camp Authority.

At home in America's military communities, the families of aviators flying over Vietnam lived in perpetual worry. Wives feared a dark government sedan pulling into their driveway and a senior officer, his wife, and a chaplain walking to their door. One glimpse of this triumvirate would indicate that something terrible had happened. They might no longer have a husband; their children's father might never return. Every ring of the telephone, every knock on the door, every car pulling into the driveway sent a chill up the spines of the women who anxiously awaited word from Vietnam. Jane Denton was one such woman.

The night before Jerry catapulted off the *Independence* on his final flight, Jane and their three youngest children watched the sun set behind the screen of a Virginia Beach drive-in. Soon, *Mary Poppins* began playing. Sometime during the movie, in the dark of the car, a dreadful feeling gripped Jane. For the first time since Jerry's departure two months earlier, she lost her composure. Hoping the film would distract her children, she began to cry silently. Hot tears streamed down her face; she wiped them away surreptitiously. In her nearly twenty years as a navy wife, she'd never experienced dread such as this. She wondered if something had happened to Jerry. The feeling persisted throughout the night.

The next day, July 18, 1965, Captain Stu Nelson, his wife, Barbara, and the family's priest drove to the quiet Denton home on Watergate Lane. One of Jane's five sons answered the door. As the captain waited, he walked upstairs and called, "Mother, Captain Nelson is here." Jane knew at once why he'd come. Stunned, she walked down the stairs. "He's all right, he's all right," the captain said as soon as he saw Jane. He explained that Jerry had gone down over North Vietnam but had in all likelihood survived and been captured. Jane knew her husband's job involved risk, but she'd never considered that he could become a prisoner of war. She did her best to accept the news bravely and sought comfort in her seven children, the small devoted army that would defend her against despair. The official Western Union telegram followed shortly thereafter, its yellow paper and black type impersonally conveying the country's condolences and offering hope that Jerry might survive.

As it had asked of Lorraine Shumaker, Sandra Storz, and all the wives of missing airmen, in its telegram and subsequent letters the government requested that Jane keep Jerry's status secret. POWs' families were urged not to tell anybody except immediate family about the situation. Beyond that, they, too, were to disclose no more than their husbands' names, ranks, service numbers, and dates of birth to anyone. They were to respond to all press inquires with "No comment for the press at this time." As navy officials explained to Jane, public statements might agitate the North Vietnamese and lead to their harming Jerry or other POWs. They also worried that the North Vietnamese might use any new personal information against the POWs or against the Denton family itself; wives received instruction to correspond about children in only the most general terms. The military was less concerned about the public simply learning the North Vietnamese held Jerry as a POW. Official navy communiqués told Jane her husband was being well treated, and the navy expected that treatment to continue. "If present conditions do continue," one navy letter stated, "the prisoner will probably not have to undergo brutal torture." Jane should not intercede, but rather trust the State Department's diplomacy and hold on. The "Keep Quiet" directive, as it became known, struck her as odd, but she lived in the order-bound world of the U.S. military, and she, like other POW wives, would abide by the rules.

Despite the policy, the tight-knit naval aviation community quickly learned of Jerry's capture and delivered food to sustain the eight Dentons while Jane was preoccupied with worry over Jerry. She called her sister, who arrived the next day. Jane's youngest, ages six and two, went to stay with friends; the older five stayed at home and tried to help their mother. Other relatives and neighbors arrived to make sure Jane did not endure her troubles alone. She wished the help, comfort, and food could be directed toward her missing husband. He needed the charity far more than she.

The next day, two letters from Jerry arrived, letters he'd penned from *Independence,* comforting letters that spoke of his upcoming promotion to squadron commander. Shortly afterward, Jane received the expected news that the navy had ended its search. Four days later, she learned her husband had at least survived: North Vietnam announced his capture, and the national news broadcast his photograph. Jane thought he looked awful and immediately worried his captors had mistreated him. That afternoon, she bought a newspaper that she knew featured Jerry's photo on the front page, but she kept it folded until she reached St. Nicholas Catholic church. In the back pew of the empty sanctuary, she opened the paper and stared at her husband's face in black and white. She prayed. Then she returned home to her family, firmly resolved to find a way to help.

On July 26, Jane arrived in Washington, D.C. She'd mourned for eight days, and it was time to work on bringing Jerry home. In the course of two trips to the capital over the next three weeks, Jane met with officials at the State Department, Department of Defense, White House, and American Red Cross. She asked hard questions about the treatment of POWs in North Vietnam. She asked how—and when—the government would negotiate the prisoners' returns. President Johnson's liaison to the House, Henry Wilson, assured her that the most important people in the government were doing all they could for Jerry and the other missing servicemen. "Confidentially, I'll tell you the president himself is personally concerned about your husband's care," he told her. Then he added, "Mrs. Denton, I've been in this city four and a half years and if there's one thing I've learned, it's that if you try pushing too many buttons, you can mess up the whole switchboard." He promised to do all he could and encouraged Jane to go home and take care of her family. Jane did as instructed, trusting that the government would keep Jerry safe and bring him home soon.

Jane Denton with four of her seven children.

When she arrived back on Watergate Lane, a box of Jerry's personal items from his stateroom aboard *Independence* greeted her: letters he'd saved, photographs of her and the children, his wallet, his rosary, his wedding ring—all packed into his worn briefcase. Seeing these items nearly broke Jane's heart, yet they were parts of Jerry coming home, and she treasured them.

Life continued in Virginia Beach, and Jane fought to remain strong for her seven children. In early September, they returned to school. In Michael's first-grade classroom, the teacher asked each child about his or her father's occupation. Michael replied that the Vietnamese had captured his daddy. At home, he warily asked his mother if he'd violated the military's Keep Quiet policy. That same evening, thirteen-year-old Bill started to cry softly at dinner. Jane asked if something had happened at school to upset him. Nothing had. Knowing the answer already, she asked if he was worried about his father. He began sobbing.

Later that month, Jane Denton and Janie Tschudy, the wife of Jerry's bombardier-navigator and fellow POW, attended a briefing by Navy Commander John Thornton, a veteran POW from the Korean War. Thornton did not sugarcoat his description of imprisonment under a Communist regime. For more than two hours, he described a lack of medical treatment, a diet of seaweed and birdseed, and savage beatings. He told a story of a Catholic POW who—like Jerry—wore a St. Christopher's medal around his neck. The North Koreans singled him out, asking why his god, his saint, didn't rescue him. They mocked him incessantly and beat him mercilessly. He did not survive.

Despite the gruesome detail, Jane wanted to hear it all. She needed to know what Jerry might face in Hanoi, even though some had tried to assure her that North Vietnam's sensitivity to world opinion would keep them from exercising such brutality. Still, Jane had her doubts and thought that by learning about the most brutal treatment that might befall her husband, she could somehow share his pain. That night, she wrote in her diary, "I wish I could really know what Jerry's going thru because in knowing I would share a little more of his suffering. I'm so comfortable and well-cared for and he is not only suffering but I can't even really fully know how much. But I suspect the worse and pray for the best and I'll never forget for a minute."

The following night at dinner, she dissolved into tears—something she'd avoided doing publically since Jerry's capture. Her dinner guest, Polly Taylor, said she'd been proud of—and somewhat surprised by— the strength Jane had shown. She confessed that before, she'd thought of Jane as reserved and largely dependent upon Jerry, but as Jane had faced these trials, Polly had seen her as a rock. That night, Jane again opened her diary and wrote, "I like to think that someone thinks of me that way—dependent on Jerry and sort of in his shadow—yet able to take, alone, the blows I must take with some strength and guts . . . I keep reminding myself that I must take care of everything here at home, in other words, hold up my end."

The veteran navy wife resolutely concluded, "And I must do it."

As unlucky as her circumstances seemed, Jane was far more fortunate than many other wives who received the news that the North Vietnamese had downed their husbands' planes—she at least knew Jerry was alive. More often than not, Hanoi chose not to release the names of captured aviators, sentencing families to anguish in limbo, wondering about the fate of their beloved pilot. So it was for Sybil Stockdale, who received the dreaded news in her home in Coronado, just across the harbor from San Diego, California.

On the evening of September 9, 1965, she had lain down for a short rest after putting her three youngest boys to bed. Sleep had come easily—unexpectedly so. Then voices from downstairs roused her from her light nap. She looked at the clock: 10:00 P.M. Why would someone call so late? She listened for a moment, orienting herself, identifying the voices—her best friend, her oldest son, and someone else. Then she walked downstairs. Her friend, Doyen Salsig, whose husband commanded the aircraft carrier *Ticonderoga*, met her on the way.

"What are you doing here?" Sybil asked.

Doyen pulled her friend close to deliver the news every wife feared. "There's been a message," Doyen said. "Jim is missing."

Sybil heard the words and her mind raced. "She'd said Jim was missing," Sybil thought. "Missing! How could he be missing? It was impossible for a person to be missing. You couldn't be missing if you were alive. You'd have to be *somewhere* in the world."

Sybil finally voiced her confused thoughts. "Missing?" she asked. "How can he be missing?"

Gently, Doyen said, "His plane was shot down and they think he got out, but they're not sure. There's a chaplain downstairs telling Jimmy. He has all the details about what they know so far. His name is Parker. He's a lieutenant."

Sybil, forty years old and eighteen years a navy wife, listened to the young chaplain's voice tremble as he related the details. "Poor young man," she thought as he stammered away. She wondered if he'd ever delivered news like this. The chaplain explained that roughly twenty-four hours earlier, over North Vietnam, another aircraft had seen Jim's plane descending in flames. A parachute had deployed, but the radio beacon never activated, and Jim's wingmen had not observed any signs of life on the ground. A violent ejection could have killed him as easily as ground fire aimed at his helpless figure as it hung beneath the chute. He might have survived the ejection and the descent only to be killed on the ground. Or perhaps the North Vietnamese had captured him and, at this very moment, had him locked inside a village jail. Nobody really knew. So the navy had classified Commander Jim Stockdale as missing in action.

No tears came to Sybil's eyes. No sobbing, no pleading, no crumpling to the floor, just the slow onset of shock. She began to tremble. Doyen brought her sherry; Lieutenant Parker excused himself.

During all of this, fourteen-year-old Jimmy had disappeared to his room, escaping the formality of the chaplain, avoiding the sight of his shaking mother, who seemed momentarily at a loss. Before long, his mother descended the steps to his basement room. He lay on his bed, listening to music from the radio. Sybil rubbed his back, and they sat together quietly reflecting. Jimmy asked her if he still had a father. His mother searched her intuition but found no hint of her husband's fate. At last, she bid Jimmy good night and climbed the stairs to her room. She fell into the half-empty bed, pondering when—*if*—Jim would share it with her again. She decided to pray, but wondered what for. For Jim to be alive? For him to escape? For her boys? For her own sake? She asked God to grant them all strength. She didn't know what God, fate, or the North Vietnamese had in store, but Sybil knew that she and Jim would need more strength than either had called upon before.

The next morning, she told her younger sons the news. She held eleven-year-old Sid in her arms until he could cry no more. She doubted five-year-old Stanford really understood; three-year-old Taylor certainly did not. After breakfast, the older boys went off to school, and Sybil contemplated her new life, feeling more asleep than awake as she fielded phone calls from officials and friends in the military community. She could at least take some comfort in previous briefings she'd received, in which the navy had assured wives that North Vietnam would treat prisoners well. Briefers had explained that as long as the families kept quiet, the men would receive good treatment.

Sybil opted to believe Jim had survived, and she wanted him to come home to a strong wife and family. So she resolved not to drink away her sadness or spend her days crying and worrying. She endeavored to live with the uncertainty as best she could and make him proud. Her children resolved to do the same. Nothing touched Sybil more than little Stanford, who stopped her as she was washing clothes one day. "Mom," he said earnestly. She looked down into his blue eyes, which so reminded her of his father's. "I'm so sorry about Dad."

"Thank you, sweetheart," Sybil said softly, wrapping him tightly in her arms.

As condolence calls turned from a steady flow to a slow trickle, Jane, Sybil, and other wives of captured or missing airmen had to march on. Bills arrived in mailboxes, mortgage notes came due, and fatherless children needed their mothers' attention, not to mention breakfast each morning and dinner each night. Sybil had to fight just to receive her husband's paycheck. He wasn't classified as killed, so she couldn't receive any death benefits. Yet he was still missing, so what would the navy do with his pay? She called her navy contacts daily for two weeks, receiving only rote assurances that they would resolve the issue soon. On the last Friday of the month, with their mortgage payment almost due, Sybil lost her patience. "I've waited long enough!" she shouted at the base's financial director. "I'll give you until Monday to find out about that pay for me or I'm going to call the admiral in Washington who's head of all navy personnel!" Two hours later, the base called to say that she'd receive Jim's pay in time to meet the mortgage. After paying the bank, she began carefully saving as much as possible, knowing that if—God forbid—Jim never returned, she'd need far more than his benefits and pension to support her family.

As September turned to October, Sybil received a phone call from Captain Bob Baldwin at the Pentagon. Jim's old friend had come across a Soviet *Pravda* article written by a correspondent in North Vietnam. Baldwin read part of the article to Sybil: "[We saw] a tall, fair-haired, sturdy fellow [who] sat on a bench with his back leaning against the automobile. It was an American prisoner, Captain James B. Stackdel."

"That *must* be Jim," she thought, although Jim wasn't particularly tall and she couldn't be sure. For months, she would cling to the faint hope provided by the article. As weeks and months passed without word from North Vietnam, her dread grew: Was her husband alive?

During 1965, the majority of the public backed the government's actions in Vietnam. President Johnson had the tacit support of the press and Congress—he counted only ten senators, around seventy representatives, and a handful of journalists in the antiwar camp. In November 1965, however, signs of dissent started to emerge. Outside the Pentagon, 40 feet from Secretary McNamara's office, a Quaker named Norman Morrison, a young father of three, lit himself on fire to protest U.S. involvement in Vietnam. At the month's end, more than twenty thousand antiwar protesters marched on the White House. Trouble stirred within the Johnson Administration when General William Westmoreland, commander of U.S. forces in Vietnam, requested more troops. Westmoreland originally had estimated the war would require 275,000 U.S. troops in 1966. Now he increased the number to 410,000 and warned he'd need an additional 200,000 for 1967. The numbers shocked the president, but he forged ahead. While most Americans still backed escalation, some inside the government—including McNamara himself—began to quietly question the American mission. *Can we win this war?* they wondered. *How will we get out?*

Each week more names were added to the rolls of the lost, missing, and captured, feeding the country's emerging undercurrents of worry and doubt. By the end of 1965, more than 2,100 Americans had lost their lives in North and South Vietnam during the past two years. In the first two weeks of November, North Vietnam captured seven more U.S. aviators. At home, their families continued to prepare for Thanksgiving in oblivion—until the military sedan arrived. On November 13, fourteen-year-old Chris Jenkins saw it pulling into his driveway. He stopped washing his breakfast dishes and watched silently as the commanding officer of NAS Lemoore stepped out. A chaplain and the wife of Chris's father's second-in-command followed him to the door. Chris knew they would tell him that his dad—Harry Jenkins, skipper of Attack Squadron 163—had been shot down or killed. If the commanding officer and chaplain had been delivering the news to another Squadron 163 family, his mother, Marj, would have filled out the triumvirate.

The visitors knocked. Chris called from the kitchen, "Mom, the CO and chaplain are here with Mrs. Foster." In the living room, Marj heard him and knew what their appearance meant. She opened the door and asked, "Is he dead or alive?"

"Let's come in and discuss this, Marj," said the commanding officer gently.

"No," she said. "Is he dead or alive?"

"Marj, let's go inside," he repeated.

"Dead or alive?" she asked, blocking the doorway. He repeated the entreaty, and she again refused. "No," she said. "Tell me."

"We think he's alive," the CO said. "He's classified missing in action."

With that, Marj stepped back to allow them in; Chris listened from the kitchen. Harry's wingman had seen the commander's A-4 Skyhawk aflame from cockpit to tail. It exploded the instant Harry ejected. When the wingman circled back, he saw Harry on the ground surrounded by North Vietnamese troops. The squadron's pilots trained their guns around their besieged commander and, for a time, held off the swarming soldiers. The first rescue helicopter on scene went down; the second salvaged the crew from the first helicopter but did not reach Harry before the North Vietnamese. The captured aviator disappeared into the jungle as his squadron mates watched helplessly from on high.

4

I SUBMIT

Harry Jenkins arrived at Hỏa Lò Prison at dawn on November 23, 1965, two days before Thanksgiving. He quickly found himself in Room Eighteen, sitting on a stool below a single lightbulb and a hook. Across from him sat a chain-smoking North Vietnamese officer who looked to be in his midforties; he spoke English well. The lieutenant colonel, dubbed Eagle by the other POWs, had read about Harry's 132 missions over North Vietnam in *Stars and Stripes,* the U.S. military's newspaper. He considered Harry a war criminal and paid no attention to his suggestion that the North Vietnamese must abide by the Geneva Convention.

Still, Harry would offer nothing beyond his name, rank, service number, and date of birth. When Harry made his intractability clear, Eagle departed from the relatively benign interrogation routine that other POWs had experienced in the previous months. He had three guards take Harry to Room Nineteen, which Bob Shumaker had vacated in August. Since Shu's five-month occupancy there, the North Vietnamese had added a rough coat of plaster to the walls that formed large globular knobs that would both increase the damage when a body collided with a wall and muffle screams and other sounds. Prisoners now called it the Knobby Room.

Soon Harry watched as a short but powerfully built soldier joined him in the room. The man seemed around thirty-five or forty years of age and moved like a gymnast. His eyes appeared devoid of emotion. On his head, he wore a pith helmet covered in camouflage netting. Harry had become the first senior officer to meet Pigeye, the man who would extract more screams from the Americans in Hanoi than any other individual, but Harry did not yet know this guard's nickname or what he was capable of.

Under Pigeye's direction, the guards sat Harry on the floor, his feet straight out in front of him. They placed his legs in a pair of antiquated irons with horseshoe-shaped loops that fit tightly around his ankles; a weighted closure bar rested across his shins. Just as they used the prison's original French leg stocks, the North Vietnamese also used French leg irons that would prove too small for many Americans, especially a 6'5" figure like Harry. They became instruments of torture, not just confinement; they often stopped blood flow and cut into skin. After squeezing Harry's ankles into the cuffs, Pigeye paused. Eagle gave Harry a final chance to answer a question about his father's occupation. In Harry's mind, disclosing that fact—as innocuous as it may have seemed—would violate the Code of Conduct and lead to progressively greater revelations. He refused to cooperate.

On Eagle's command, Pigeye yanked Harry's arms behind his back. Employing aspects of a centuries-old torture technique known as strappado, Pigeye grabbed his victim's wrists, wrapped them in rags to help prevent scarring, and began winding a rope around them, cinching it tighter and tighter. Next, the guards similarly wrapped his upper arms and tied ropes between them. They stuck their feet into Harry's back for leverage as they ratcheted his arms ever closer together, bending his shoulders backward and bowing them toward each other. Harry felt as if his sternum would snap, his pectorals would tear away from his rib cage, and his shoulders would pop from their sockets. His upper arms and elbows nearly touched each other; he never imagined a human could achieve this position or feel this much pain. Harry craned his neck toward the right and saw shades of red, white, and purple covering his swelling hand. The ropes pulling his upper arms together conspired with the ropes binding his wrists to strangle circulation. His hands lost feeling; he felt sure he would lose them. Then Pigeye pushed his bound arms forward like a lever, driving his head between his outstretched thighs. No training, no briefing, no experience, no imagination had prepared Harry for such agony. The pain became a ferocious devil unleashed inside his body. He screamed. Then he passed out.

"If God had wanted you to fly, He'd have given you wings," Clistie Jenkins had once told her four boys. Only one listened, while two became air force pilots and Harry became a naval aviator. He had never aspired to do anything else. His father's floral business served the White House, and young Harry saw Franklin Delano Roosevelt often as he delivered flowers to the Executive Mansion. On those trips, he also met a decorated naval attaché, and he forgot any other future career he had entertained. He wanted to fly for the navy. On Saturdays, thirteen-year-old Harry would often visit NAS Anacostia, just across the Potomac River from Washington, D.C. He became a weekend fixture, and eventually a young aviator approached him and said, "I see you here a lot."

"I want to be a pilot," he replied.

"You do?" remarked the young officer. "You sure? Have you ever been flying?"

Harry hadn't.

"Then how do you know you want to be a pilot?"

"I know I want to be a pilot like I know my name," Harry said.

"Well, you want to go for a ride?"

The aviator gave the teenager a helmet and flight suit and told him to keep his helmet on and not to speak to anyone as they walked from the hangar to an airplane. Minutes later, Harry was soaring over the nation's capital. He kept his stomach despite the plane's twists and dives, and when they returned to the hangar, the young pilot said, "If you're convinced this is something you want to do, bring me fifty cents each Saturday and I'll teach you to fly."

In the following months, Harry did extra chores and sold *Liberty* magazines at ten cents per issue so he could afford lessons. He had his first solo flight on his fourteenth birthday. The pilot rode alongside him, relaying Harry's calls to the tower but never touching the controls. As a present for his birthday, his instructor returned all the fifty-cent fees Harry had paid him.

As a high school senior, Harry turned down an appointment to the U.S. Naval Academy, instead enlisting in the Naval Aviation Cadet program at the University of South Carolina. There, he'd receive his degree, his officer's commission, and his wings within four years instead of the usual six or more; he didn't want to miss World War II.

Much to his disappointment, the war ended before he earned his gold wings. He would forever maintain that the Japanese capitulated because they heard he was coming.

By 1965, he commanded an attack squadron at war, a post many still consider the pinnacle of an aviator's career. Harry set a fine example as skipper of Attack Squadron 163—the Saints—aboard the USS *Oriskany*. He flew his share of undesirable missions, including tanker duty and stand-by. Always competitive, he made sure to stay at least one trap (a successful carrier landing) and one mission ahead of everyone else. He built a reputation as one of the most daring pilots on the ship. When the time for his change of command drew near—when the executive officer (XO) would take over the squadron and Harry would take command of a full air wing—Harry joked to his XO, "I'm having too much fun being squadron skipper. Why don't you go find your own squadron somewhere else?" Several weeks later, on November 13, 1965, the squawk box in the Saints' ready room grimly promoted the XO. "Your boss is down," it announced.

Harry still fumed that he got bagged. As he parachuted into North Vietnam, he thought, "Boy, God, you messed this up. No way

Harry Jenkins, commanding officer of Attack Squadron 163—the Saints—aboard the USS *Oriskany*.

I deserved this." He always thought the other guy would get shot down—the guy who flew too slow, who didn't have the skills, who didn't have the right stuff. Not him, not an attack squadron commander, not an aviator with 132 successful missions behind him. No, aviation should not have led him here to Hanoi, to Room Nineteen, to this medieval torturer.

When he came to, the aches he found radiating from his every joint reminded him that it most definitely had.

Pigeye stripped him of his pride and showed him a side of military aviation he'd never considered. Harry sat on the cold floor, bound by rope, angry at fate, and seething at the men who did this to him. He soon lost the capacity for anger; pain consumed him. Yet he refused to divulge anything more than required by the Code of Conduct. So Pigeye ran another rope around Harry's bound wrists, which were still behind his back. He tossed the rope over the meat hook in the ceiling and yanked Harry's arms skyward, jerking his entire body off the floor. Harry shrieked. He prayed fervently for death, which he preferred to breaking the Code. He longed for the relief that his last heartbeat would bring, but death would not come. Harry passed out a second time.

When he regained consciousness, he'd been lowered back to the floor. He still refused to answer any questions, so Eagle ordered him to stand on his knees. When after some time Harry still wouldn't comply, Eagle ordered him to spread gravel on the floor and then kneel on the tiny rocks. Once Harry had done so, Eagle left. After three hours, Harry's kneecaps showed through his broken, bloody skin. By then, thirst had replaced pain as his worst tormentor. Sweat had soaked his flight suit and drained his body of its fluids; he desperately wanted water, and he called for a guard. Pigeye returned. He looked over his victim, ignoring Harry's cries for water. He waited for the American's total surrender. Twenty minutes later, he had it. "I submit," Harry rasped.

Pigeye called for the interrogators. They returned but didn't release Harry from the torturous ropes. As he writhed in pain, they asked him—again—about his father's occupation. He finally gave more than the Big Four. He said, honestly, "My father grows flowers."

"Everybody grows flowers," they said, not believing him.

Hurt, broken, and now irritated, Harry decided to lie. He said his father ran a farm.

On the second page of a large handwritten ledger, sixteen rows and twenty-two columns to a page, the interrogators dutifully recorded "farmer" as his father's occupation. The name Everett Alvarez Jr.—the first U.S. airman to arrive at Hỏa Lò—anchored the first row of the first page of the ledger. Robert Harper Shumaker, the second American captured, appeared in the second row. So the rows continued, listing U.S. servicemen in order of their arrival at the Hanoi Hilton. The staff also assigned each prisoner a Vietnamese name; Harry became Dư. The columns of each page listed the biographical information that the Enemy Proselytizing Department expected the interrogators to obtain: full name, date of birth, home state, ethnicity, education, service number, branch of service, rank, squadron, ship or base, spouse, spouse's maiden name, spouse's address, father, mother, father's occupation, parents' address, and condition upon capture. The ledger would contain few blank spaces. Under torture, even the strongest could not hold out forever.

For six days, the guards perpetuated the cycle of questions, torture, and answers. Each time, Harry would reach a point where he would do anything—*anything*—to escape the pain. Then he'd give as little information as he could and try to recoup his strength for the next round. He could never beat the ropes. In his own view, Harry had repeatedly broken the Code of Conduct he'd sworn to uphold and loathed himself for it. He felt certain that everyone else had resisted.

When the interrogators were finished with him, they threw the shamed aviator into a dingy cellblock in another section of the prison. Harry lay there wondering about the God his mother had promised would always protect him. He'd seen no sign of the Lord's grace; God had not made his presence known. Harry began to wonder if God really existed. With that despairing thought, he fell asleep.

That same evening of November 29, 1965, found Jim Stockdale lying beneath a mosquito net on a 27-inch-wide concrete slab above the dirtiest cell floor he'd ever seen. His 6-by-8-foot cell was one of eight in Heartbreak Hotel, the low one-story edifice across the courtyard from the main gate of the Hanoi Hilton. Heartbreak had become a regular first stop for new POWs, and it typically had the effect its name suggested. A walking space only 22 inches wide separated the two sleeping slabs in each cell, but nobody in Heartbreak had a roommate, as the Camp Authority still aspired to isolate POWs. Leg stocks taunted Jim from the end of his bunk. He watched assorted vermin passing through a small drain to the gutter outside. His latrine bucket sat near the drain, and since the cell had a metal feeding chute near the door, he surmised guards could keep inmates locked inside their cells indefinitely. Equally demoralizing, a sheet listing the camp regulations antagonized him from the inside of the cell's door.

"The criminals are under an obligation to give full and clear written or oral answers to all questions raised by the camp authorities," it read. "All attempts and tricks intended to evade answering further questions and acts directed to opposition by refusing to answer any questions will be considered manifestations of obstinacy and antagonism which deserves strict punishment." The typed regulations went on, criminalizing refusals to bow or stand at attention when a guard or officer entered a prisoner's room; the North Vietnamese almost never used the term "cell." They also forbade any communication among the prisoners— "criminals," in their parlance. They offered special incentives to anyone willing to turn in violators.

Above the door and its regulations, each cell had a barred transom through which inmates could communicate when guards weren't present. Unfortunately, the transoms also allowed the stench of the eighth cell to pervade each room. Jim remembered his first visit to Cell Eight, just after arriving in Heartbreak. A guard he'd nicknamed Dipshit had flung open Jim's door and yelled in Vietnamese, pointing to Jim's bucket, bar of soap, and wash rag. Then he pointed at the hallway. Jim collected the rag and soap, put his crutches under his shoulders, and grabbed the pail, which still contained a previous occupant's waste. He made his way into the hallway and was directed toward Cell Eight. On his way, he spied a grinning American face peering down from above a door. The lift Jim's spirits gained from seeing that smile disappeared when he saw the makeshift bathroom into which Dipshit pushed him. Cell Eight looked just like his own cell except that it had a water pipe opposite the door, and it reeked of excrement. Jim nearly slipped on the floor and recoiled when he realized a glaze of filth and urine covered it; guards often used the room as a latrine. He emptied his bucket in the room's drain and undressed. "Syb, you would hardly know me now," he thought, looking at his thin, dirty body. Who would have thought all this could happen? He began shivering and chose to forgo the drizzle of cold water coming from the pipe. On the wall, one POW had scratched "Smile, you're on 'Candid Camera.'" At the least, Cell Eight did give new captives their first taste of the humor that would help them cope with their situation.

That night of November 29, when Harry Jenkins arrived in Heartbreak, Jim heard guards drag the new prisoner through the corridor and shut him in one of the four padlocked cells across the hallway. When the guards left, Jim called through the transom to the new inmate. He heard no response and went to sleep. He'd try to learn the man's identity in the morning. Hours later, Jim woke up; the new guy snored like a bear. Jim realized he had heard that snore just months earlier aboard his ship, the *Oriskany*, and he knew only one individual who could muster such bunk-rattling noise.

The next morning, the cellblock's designated lookout, Air Force Captain George McKnight, watched from the crack beneath his door as the guard completed his rounds. When he saw the guard's feet leave the cellblock, George whistled "Mary Had a Little Lamb," the all-clear signal. The residents of Heartbreak pulled themselves up to their transoms as they were able. "Harry Jenkins," Jim called out to the new resident. "Jim Stockdale!"

On the *Oriskany*, Jenkins had served under Stockdale, who had commanded the carrier's entire air wing. Everyone aboard called Jim "CAG," an acronym for "Commander, Air Group." The Navy had redesignated "air groups" as "air wings" in 1963, but "CAG" had stuck. Hearing the familiar voice, Harry pulled himself up to his transom. He remembered that Stockdale had been flying one of his squadron's A-4 Skyhawks when he bailed out over North Vietnam in September. "Oh, hi, CAG!" Harry quipped. "I came up here to see what happened to that plane I loaned you; you never brought it back!"

CAG expected such a crack from his happy-go-lucky squadron commander; Harry's sense of humor was legendary. He did not expect the grim story Harry told next. Harry shared his tale with the cellblock's six other residents and learned he had become the first senior officer to experience the Camp Authority's new torture regime and the rope trick, as POWs began calling Pigeye's trademark device. The Enemy Proselytizing Department apparently had come under pressure to produce more statements for North Vietnam's propaganda campaign, and they'd sanctioned the use of alternative means to obtain them. While the prisoners did not know the official reasons behind the new tactics, the experience that Harry described shocked the men in Heartbreak. If the Camp Authority had tortured a senior officer like Harry, would they be next? These aviators, actors usually in control of their roles, found themselves in someone else's terrifying play.

Harry testified to the torture's effect and confessed what he'd given up. Silence followed. Then Stockdale spoke up, "Don't feel like the Lone Ranger." Nobody had been able to follow the letter of the Code, he said; they could only do their best for as long as possible. A solemn moment passed. Then Harry, a renowned lover of chocolate, cracked a smile and said, "Hey, just think what they could've gotten out of me for a Hershey bar!"

When Howie Rutledge arrived in Heartbreak Hotel several days later, he'd faced an experience in Rooms Eighteen and Nineteen markedly similar to Harry's. In fact, the thirty-seven-year-old commander's arrival in Hanoi fell just short of a miracle. Minutes before his capture, he'd shot and killed a villager who'd threatened him with a machete. Incredibly, the North Vietnamese had not executed Howie on the spot. Howie's reaction came in part from some bravado; he belonged to a circle of old-school aviators simultaneously envied for their skill and disliked for their swagger. He was a fighter pilot's fighter pilot, and he arrived in Hanoi thinking he had the mettle to withstand whatever the North Vietnamese might bring. His training and bearing didn't even get him through the first day.

His interrogation began with him sitting buck naked on a stool, parts of his body still caked with dirt and blood, with one leg not entirely in joint. A burly officer calmly asked for his name, rank, service number, and date of birth, all of which he provided. Then the officer asked for his ship and squadron. Howie balked and explained the Geneva Convention.

"You are not a prisoner of war," the interrogator replied. "Your government has not declared war upon the Vietnamese people. You must answer my questions. You are protected by no international law."

After Howie had refused several more questions, the officer closed his notebook and leaned toward his prisoner. "Commander Rutledge," he said, "you are a criminal, guilty of high crimes against the Vietnamese people. If you do not answer my questions, you will be severely punished."

Guards escorted Howie back to Room Nineteen to reconsider. After thirty minutes, they returned him to Room Eighteen, where the officer repeated his questions, yelling at him when he refused to divulge more than the Big Four. The pattern continued for much of the day, and Howie believed he and his training were winning.

Like most naval aviators, Howie had undergone SERE instruction in Warner Springs, California, or Brunswick, Maine. The escape and evasion techniques he and most aviators learned—how to hide in foliage and survive on berries and small animals—proved of little use in Vietnam since downed aviators often found themselves badly injured and descending into groups of waiting North Vietnamese.

SERE training also included resistance elements, which at first proved helpful as the interrogator harangued Howie. His course had prepared him for this exact situation: foreign officers demanding confessions, personal biographies, and military secrets. He knew to fall back on the Code of Conduct and to make interrogators work for every piece of information. In training, though, the interrogators had limits and Howie knew he'd return home at week's end. His SERE instructors had also taught him that if he showed an iron will to resist, his captors would spend their time working on softer prisoners. Once their torture program had begun, however, the North Vietnamese went after every American viciously—and for as long as it took.

By evening, the interrogator stopped making idle threats. Howie refused a final battery of questions and found Pigeye waiting for him upon his return to Room Nineteen. The interrogator ordered Howie to the floor, where a guard stomped on his swollen, dislocated leg, forcing it flat onto the smooth concrete. Despite the momentary explosion of pain, Howie was silently thankful to have his leg back in joint. The U.S. military's meticulously developed resistance training then became irrelevant as Pigeye wrapped Howie with his grimly effective ropes and beat him with bamboo rods. He forced Howie to break the Code of Conduct and answer the interrogator's fifth question: What was his branch of service? He said United States Navy. The officer asked no further questions, leaving Howie baffled as well as broken. Howie, like Harry Jenkins before him, was dragged into Heartbreak Hotel feeling he had failed his fellow Americans.

Shortly after arriving in his new cell, he heard a voice drift through his transom, asking, "Hey, new guy who just moved in, what's your name? What ship are you from?"

Revived by the presence of another American, Howie grasped the bars of the transom and pulled himself up. He looked out and saw the faces of other prisoners peering out from above their doors. He might have been momentarily defeated, but he no longer felt alone. He learned the voice he'd heard belonged to Jim Stockdale, who briefed him on the cellblock's lineup. Then, to his new comrades, Howie whispered his confession. "I feel like a traitor," he said.

"Welcome to the club," Harry Jenkins responded from across the hall. The two commanders had never met before, but when Harry learned that Howie was celebrating his birthday the very day Harry got shot down, he began to claim that he'd *volunteered* to take Howie's November 13 flight so Howie could sleep off a hangover. He would never stop razzing Howie with the joke, which quickly became legend among the POWs.

As Harry and Howie shared their wrenching stories and as Jim Stockdale and the others listened and forgave, the POWs' stance toward taking torture began to form. They would share what had happened to them and confess what they had surrendered—that is, how they broke the Code. Then their fellow POWs would forgive them. They would resist as best they could, for as long as they could, but no man could defy the Camp Authority's new methods indefinitely.

One day in December, Pigeye opened the door to Jim Stockdale's cell. He brushed his forearms and tapped his wrists, signaling for Jim to don his gray long-sleeved shirt and dark pants—his quiz suit, as he called it. Once Jim had dressed, Pigeye led him into a rainy Heartbreak courtyard and toward the main gate. Jim followed on crude crutches, still healing from three operations North Vietnamese doctors had performed on his knee—all unsuccessful as far as he could tell. While his leg remained stiff and grotesque, his left shoulder had been healing slowly. Before he reached the main gate or New Guy Village, Pigeye ushered the battered aviator into a room off the courtyard. A small lamp lit the room, numbered "24." At a table sat a young English-speaking officer with prominent ears: Rabbit. In the shadows, Jim spied a senior officer of his own age. Jim bowed to them as required and sat on a stool placed before the table. Rabbit began asking innocuous questions about Jim's health, food, and clothing. In response, Jim protested North Vietnam's violation of the Geneva Convention and griped about his accommodations, diet of watery pumpkin soup, and nagging injuries. His attitude roused the senior man, who moved toward the table and began lecturing in Vietnamese. Rabbit translated.

"You have no right to protest. You are a criminal and not entitled to Geneva Convention privileges," he said evenly. "It is true that my country acceded to the Geneva Convention of 1949, but we later filed an exception against those captured in wars of aggression. You are nothing but a common criminal, guilty of bombing schools, churches, and pagodas, crimes against humanity."

Indicating Jim's injured left leg, he said, "You have medical problems and you have political problems, and in this country, we take care of the medical problems only after the political problems are resolved."

When he'd finished his diatribe, the senior officer left, and Rabbit told Jim he'd just upset an influential member of the general staff, a man Jim would soon know as Cat.

Later that month, an air force lieutenant colonel named Robinson "Robbie" Risner moved into Heartbreak Cell Two, next to Jim. An ace in the Korean War, Risner had been shot down on September 16, seven days after Jim, and replaced him as the ranking American; Risner had received his officer's commission shortly before Jim. He was returning from a camp outside the Hilton, known as the Zoo, where he'd learned the tap code that had been developed in Room Nineteen months before and had been spreading ever since. Whispering through the transom when guards weren't present, Risner taught it to Jim. The two men practiced tapping on their shared wall, each pressing his ear to his drinking cup to amplify the other's taps. As Jim's skill improved, he began "buying a word," as he called it, by tapping twice when he'd guessed the word being sent; Risner would then move on to the next word. If he realized that he'd guessed wrong, Jim would send three quick taps—the error signal—and Risner would back up and repeat the word. Practice soon became genuine conversation, which turned to the most pressing question on every POW's mind.

"When do you think we'll go home?" Jim tapped, abbreviating his transmission as "WN DO U TK WE GO HOME" to speed the process.

That winter, Risner tapped back an answer on which most POWs agreed: "This spring."

Not everyone in Heartbreak picked up the code as readily as CAG. George McKnight was having trouble grasping what his neighbor tapped through the wall. His exasperated instructor finally risked punishment and just yelled the instructions. "You idiot! Tap the row then the column! It's a five-by-five alphabet matrix, and use *C* for *K*!" After that, George became quite adept.

On Christmas Day, Pigeye again called Jim Stockdale from his cell and led him across the courtyard to a carpeted ceremonial room. When Jim entered the room on his crutches, he saw Rabbit alongside the senior officer he'd upset earlier that month. Major Nguyễn Văn Bài—known to the POWs as Cat—directed the entire American detention program. In contrast to most guards, he wore well-pressed uniforms or fashionable suits; the slender, well-read forty-year-old claimed to have taught university courses before coming to Hỏa Lò. He spoke French and, when he chose to, English. That day he wore a new-looking suit and waited at a table with a tea service spread before him.

"Stockdale," he said, using Jim's English name instead of Đán, as the North Vietnamese usually called him. "You and I are the same age, we are both lifelong military officers, we both have sons the same age. But we are from different social systems. There is a wall between us which will always be there . . . but you and I must try to see through it. We must join together and bring this imperialist war to an end. Together we can do much to bring that about. You must help me make the other criminals realize that it is in their interest as well as ours to stop the war. You will help me. You do not realize it now but you will."

As Cat continued, Jim realized this canny operator recognized him as a leader among the Americans and hoped he would help convince the other POWs to cooperate with the North Vietnamese propaganda program. He broke into a cold sweat.

When Cat finished, he handed Jim the first letter from home he had seen since his capture. Jim was sure it was just one of many that Sybil had sent but the Camp Authority had chosen not to deliver. Cat then sent him back to his cell, saying, "Now go back to your room and think about what I have told you, Stockdale. You are very old and you are not well. You must think of yourself. You must think of the family that wrote you that letter. You must help me end this war."

Back in his cell, Jim let his crutches fall to the ground and vaulted himself onto his slab to read the letter. "Dearest Jim," the October 3 letter began. "It is early morning here and the world is waiting for the sun to rise. The world seems very special in these moments before dawn. It seems to be pausing and waiting to hear birds begin to sing." Jim drank in the reassurance of his wife's words as he read how she loved him, how she had hope for his swift return. He learned all was well at home. The next day, Rabbit allowed Jim to write his first letter back.

In early January, Cat requested that Jim return his favor. Pigeye escorted him into a room in New Guy Village that he'd not seen before, though he noticed the number "18" by the door. Inside, a table covered with blue cloth sat in the room's center. He saw a meat hook hanging from the ceiling. Rabbit entered, scowling. "It has been decided that you must write to your government and explain to them the true story of the Vietnamese people's willingness to fight for four, eight, twelve years to defeat you imperialist aggressors," he said. "You must recommend to your government that this illegal and immoral war must be stopped."

Rabbit slid paper and pen across the table to Jim and ordered him to another cell in New Guy Village to compose his letter. Jim was relieved Rabbit hadn't somehow discovered what he considered his great secret—his role in the Gulf of Tonkin incident. He knew that if Rabbit had learned that he'd witnessed no torpedo boats attacking American destroyers that night of August 4, 1964, he'd be tortured and forced to write out that admission, suggesting that President Johnson finagled himself the power to wage war in Southeast Asia based on an event that never happened; Jim had been an eyewitness. The fear of being made to expose that secret had weighed on Jim from the moment he fell onto North Vietnamese soil.

Back in the cell, Jim wrote nothing. Instead, he recalled the words his father spoke when he left his son at the Naval Academy, two decades ago, "Do your best to be the best midshipman here." Jim resolved not to write, a fact Rabbit discovered when he returned late that evening. He walked into the cell, looked at the blank paper, and said, "You will learn." Thirty minutes later, Jim, Rabbit, Pigeye, and an officer nicknamed Mickey Mouse assembled in Room Eighteen; Mickey Mouse would soon assume command of Hỏa Lò Prison. Jim saw that Pigeye held a long metal rod, leg irons, and a coil of hemp rope.

"You are insolent and obdurate," Rabbit said. "This is your last chance. Write the paper."

Jim shook his head.

The iron bar clanged to the floor and Pigeye sprang toward Jim, felling him with a hard blow to the head. Pigeye beat him soundly before employing the rope trick, wrapping Jim's body with cords and drawing them tight. Then he yanked Jim's arms behind him, eliciting a scream as his unhealed left shoulder reacted. Another guard locked Jim's ankles in cuffs attached to the long bar and slid the cuffs apart, forcing Jim into a spread-eagle position. Pigeye kept pulling on the ropes and then hopped barefoot onto Jim's back, pressing Jim's face toward the floor as he pulled his victim's arms higher. Rabbit shouted, "Down, down!" and Pigeye pressed harder. Jim yelled and screamed—maybe someone would hear him—then a guard shoved a rag in his mouth. The pain intensified. Rabbit pulled out the rag and shouted into his ear, "Keep silent, keep silent!" Pain, claustrophobia, and the futility of resistance coursed through Jim Stockdale as he fought the ropes. Through the fog of agony and confusion, he again became aware of Rabbit's voice.

"Do you submit?" he was asking. "Are you ready to comply?"

"Yes," Jim managed. "I submit."

When his hand had sufficiently recovered from the ropes, he sloppily wrote out Rabbit's letter to the "U.S. Foreign Secretary of State," decrying America's unjust war and extolling the virtue of the Vietnamese people, their cause, and their humane and lenient treatment of POWs. Pigeye collected the letter and returned Jim to his cell, where the beaten commander laid down his crutches and sat dejectedly on the bed slab. He could not sleep that night. He understood what Jenkins and Rutledge had undergone and how they felt afterward. Pigeye and Rabbit had broken the POW leader just as they'd broken so many of the sixty-six Americans now in Hanoi. *How to live this down?* Jim wondered. *What to do now?*

T-O-R-T-U-R-E

That same fall of 1965, a truck carried Bob Shumaker out of Hỏa Lò Prison—the Hanoi Hilton—his dungeon for the previous seven months. It drove him to a remote camp in the countryside where the North Vietnamese held him for three uneventful weeks. Then guards loaded him into another truck, blindfolded him, and sent him back toward the capital. He rode down country roads alongside other silent POWs until their convoy rolled onto the smoother streets of a city. Urban hubbub replaced rural quiet, and Bob guessed he'd returned to Hanoi. When the trip ended, guards cleared the prisoners from the truck and ushered them inside a compound. Shu immediately smelled something foul. He heard the rustling of livestock, and the scratching of chickens. He trudged along dirt pathways until guards pushed him through a doorway and down a hushed corridor. They shoved him inside a room and removed his blindfold. He saw Smitty Harris looking back at him.

As soon as their door closed, the two men heard taps coming through the wall. They recognized the code they'd practiced in Room Nineteen. They tapped back and quickly learned they had arrived at a facility opened that summer, 5 miles southwest of the Hanoi Hilton and known to the North Vietnamese as Cu Loc. The Americans there called it the Zoo. The incoming taps explained that the odor Shu'd detected outside came from Lake Fester, a swimming pool filled with garbage, dirty water, and small fish that guards raised for food. At least eight buildings surrounded the pool and had received nicknames like Barn, Stable, Pig Sty, and Chicken Coop, which reflected the compound's menagerie. POWs had nicknamed other buildings the Auditorium, Pool Hall, Office, and Garage. Shu had landed in the Office. He and Harris found their cell filled with dust; trash littered the hall outside. Their room smelled musty; they heard others smelled worse. Odors from their latrine buckets and unshowered bodies soon added to the room's aroma, which they only escaped during a daily fifteen minutes of exercise and when they bathed once every four days. During the remaining hours of each week, Shu tried to communicate or keep his mind occupied as he paced the small cell—a walk POWs derisively called the Hanoi Shuffle.

To pass time, Shu fashioned a piano for his roommate. On a 2-foot-long piece of toilet paper, Shu used a burned match to draw several octaves of keys. A guitarist himself, Shu wrote out music across a longer piece. Harris happily played the keyboard during the day, and the two men envisioned how the live performance might sound. Each night, they used improvised plugs to conceal the rolled piano and music inside a hole in the wall. One day, Shu and Harris tapped to Ev Alvarez in the neighboring cell, asking, "How you feel, Alvy?"

"Bad," Hanoi's first POW responded. "Must be that time of the month."

"Cheer up," Harris sent. "I'll play you a tune."

At the end of the day, Shu and Harris tapped to Alvarez, "Did you like our music?"

"Not bad for ragtime," Alvarez tapped back. They all needed the laugh.

The two musicians enjoyed their time together until a guard forgot to lock their cell door and Shu accidentally leaned against it, spilling into the hallway. He and Harris contemplated making a run for it but decided to stay put. Shu might as well have run. The Camp Authority accused him of trying to escape and moved him to a room inside the old theater known as the Auditorium. They left him in absolute blackness. Shu could not see his own hands as he felt his way around the room's edges, brushing away spiderwebs. He heard the scurrying of rats and insects; he smelled human waste somewhere in the room. Days passed. No light appeared. The smell and crushing loneliness both grew more unbearable. His only human contact came when a guard emptied his latrine bucket and brought him his miserable ration of food, much of which he forfeited due to a fast-developing case of dysentery. His honey bucket would overflow with waste and vomit, attracting more rats and adding to the squalor. After days without light, he began suffering vertigo, spells of dizziness that sent him spinning and crashing into the floor, where he would retch again, unable to prevent himself from worsening the conditions in that awful, pitch-black room where he seemed destined to die. He had no idea whether the Camp Authority had condemned him to spend days, months, or even years there. His captors gave no indication of his fate. In the end, he stayed there for nearly three weeks, puzzling over this alarming change in Hanoi's detention program. If the North Vietnamese treated the Americans this inhumanely, would they ever allow them to return home to tell the tale?

After sentencing Shu to the darkness of the Auditorium, the Camp Authority also relocated his roommate Smitty Harris. Ron Storz, the first POW Shu had contacted in Hanoi, filled the vacancy in their old Office cell. On the other side of one of the cell's walls, Ron found Robbie Risner, the most senior POW in Hanoi. Although Risner would not become one of the eleven troublemakers who would, in two years, be exiled to the prison nicknamed Alcatraz, most everyone recognized his wise leadership and will to resist. Ron Storz, who was destined to join that special clan at Alcatraz, would try speaking to him through a vent, but Risner could never understand him. Frustrated, Ron reverted to tapping and asked, "Have you tried boring a hole through the wall yet?"

In fact, Risner had discovered a loose rod about 2 feet in length and half an inch in diameter. He had tried to drill through his wall with it, but a double row of bricks had stymied his effort each time. He suggested Ron search his drainage grate and fashion his own drill. Ron stuck his hand into the drain and grabbed hold of a metal rod. He began pulling and twisting, hoping to break it free before a guard caught him. He succeeded and began drilling away from his side of the brick-and-plaster wall. By that afternoon, he'd bored a hole through the mortar to Risner's cell.

"I'm really down in the mouth," Ron told Risner once they could understand one another. "I have nothing. They have taken everything away from me. They took my shoes, my flying suit, and everything I possessed. They even took my glasses. I don't have a single thing."

"Ron," Risner replied, "I don't think we really have lost every-thing."

"What do you mean?"

"According to the Bible, we are sons of God," Risner said. "Every-thing out there in the courtyard, all the buildings and the whole shooting match, belongs to God. Since we are children of God, you might say that all belongs to us, too."

"Let me think about it, and I'll call you back," Ron said. After some time, the junior officer called back to Risner. "I really feel a lot better," he said. "In fact, every time I get to thinking about it, I have to laugh."

"What do you mean?" Risner asked.

Ron exclaimed, "I am just loaning it to them!"

Since the moment of his capture, Ron Storz had loathed the North Vietnamese. He hated them for taking his liberty, and he fiercely de-fended the little control he still had. He refused to bow or stand at at-tention for the guards, as the camp rules stipulated. To him, it would have symbolized the United States submitting to Communism. One day, he refused to stand at attention when guards entered his cell, and they began poking his legs with a bayonet, trying to force his feet together. Afterward, he spoke to Risner about the confrontation. "They cut my legs with a bayonet, trying to make me put my feet together," he ex-plained. "I am just not going to do it."

"Ron, I'm afraid we don't have the power to combat them by physical force," Risner said. "I believe I would reconsider. Then, if we decide differently, we all should resist simultaneously. With only you resisting while everybody else is doing it, you are bound to lose." Ris-ner knew that if he had told Ron to stand firm, he would have resisted until it killed him. In that first year of imprisonment, Risner and other seniors recognized that Ron Storz had more mettle than most.

After that incident had passed, Ron and Risner returned to their task of riddling the walls of the Office with holes. Like a pair of carpen-ter bees, they bored holes between their own cells, then from their cells to others. They'd then pass along instructions to other POWs about how to drill their own; sometimes they'd pass along tools, too. Each new hole brought the gifts of verbal conversation and the sight of another American. POWs would stand back from their holes so that their neighbors could simply see them. For men in solitary confinement, just glimpsing another captive lifted their morale for days.

As a result of the holes, communication began to hum between cells inside the Office and then spread throughout the Zoo. A prison bureaucracy developed, and Ron and Risner became central to its function. At great risk, Ron would transcribe new directives from Risner onto toilet paper and send them to other sections of the Office by pushing them through holes. To communicate with the broader camp, he'd stash notes in common areas such as the bathhouse. When prisoners transferred to other buildings and camps, Risner's directives went with them. Unfortunately, it wasn't long before a guard caught Ron breaking the Camp Authority's cardinal rule of no communication.

Unless a cellmate or nearby prisoner acted as lookout, inmates had little, if any, warning before a guard slid back a peephole cover or flung open a cell door. They lived under the constant threat of interruption and discovery. So it happened that on October 24, 1965, a guard burst into Ron's room unannounced and found him transcribing two contraband notes. The guard confiscated the two sheets of tissue that served as paper. One listed POW names. The other contained directives such as "gather all string, nails and wire; save whatever soap or medicine you get; familiarize yourself with any possible escape routes; become acquainted with the guards." It also included a map of the Zoo and Robbie Risner's name.

Ron lunged toward the guard and ripped the nearest document from his hand and stuffed it into his own mouth, fending off the incensed guard until he had swallowed the pulp. The guard ran off with the other sheet, and Ron went to the wall he shared with Risner. He sent the emergency signal—one heavy thump—and Robbie came to their hole. "They searched and found everything," Ron said. "I ate the list of names, but they got the policies. Get rid of anything you don't want them to find." They both promised to deny everything under interrogation.

Before anyone questioned Ron, the guards put him in isolation for three days and nights as punishment for consumption of evidence and, because of the map, for planning an escape. He had no company, no food, no water, no sleeping mat, no blanket, and no mosquito net. He suffered terribly, perhaps from the mosquitoes most of all. When the North Vietnamese finally interrogated him, they told him Risner had confessed and given up Ron. He knew they were lying and held fast. The North Vietnamese had also told Risner that Ron had confessed and implicated *him*. Risner caught their lie; he knew Ron would have died before he implicated someone else. The guards exhorted both men to sign confessions and admit to their criminal acts, but they refrained from outright torture. The two air force men refused, and the guards eventually returned them to their adjacent cells, where they resumed tapping.

"Remember, I'll never confess to anything," Risner sent.

"Roger, I won't either," tapped Ron. "God bless you."

With those three closing words, communicated with three letters, "G-B-U," Ron sent his commanding officer a message much deeper than it might appear. GBU had become the sign-off phrase of choice for POWs, and its meaning extended beyond "May God bless you." It also meant "I know you've been tortured, I understand your situation, and I know what you're going through." It told a brother POW "I know it's not easy, but we'll make it" and "Remember you're not alone; we're all pulling for you." Four years later, "GBU" would also be the last message Ron Storz would ever receive from a fellow American.

By the winter of 1966, the Camp Authority had returned Robbie Risner to the Hanoi Hilton, where he began a long stint in isolation. Leadership fell to Jerry Denton at the Zoo. If the North Vietnamese had hoped that removing Risner would weaken resistance, his successor would disappoint them. When Jerry took command as the new senior ranking officer at the Zoo, he broadcast his hardline stance vis-à-vis the Code of Conduct. POWs should not give written or tape-recorded statements during their frequent and often brutal quizzes. They should concede absolutely nothing beyond the Big Four unless the North Vietnamese forced it out of them, as yielding anything else without taking torture made POWs vulnerable to exploitation and violated the Code of Conduct.

While the Code bound the POWs to follow the orders of their commanding officer, some of Jerry's subordinates voiced their disagreement with his strict policy. They saw little need to risk physical harm when they could provide their captors completely innocuous or even fabricated information; besides, many were injured or ill and needed to recover, not invite more afflictions. They advocated playing each quiz by ear, being smart, and giving some information where it mattered little. If those tactics failed and the interrogators wanted something significant, then they would stop talking. They saw flexibility in their pledge "I am bound to give only name, rank, service number, and date of birth." To Jerry, those compromises seemed dangerous and divisive— and would jeopardize all POWs. Ultimately, however, each man would have to square his actions in prison with his own conscience. Could a POW hold up his head proudly before his family and countrymen when he was finally repatriated? The common aspiration of returning with honor began spreading through the POW ranks.

During the last months of 1965, rations at the Zoo dwindled and men became dangerously thin. Hanoi's winter lows, which typically only dipped into the fifties, proved sufficient to chill them severely; colds and respiratory ailments became common. Often, however, what the guards heard as sickly coughs or loud sneezes, Jerry and the POWs recognized as expressions like "Bullshit," "Horse shit," or "Fuck Ho!" POWs directed the latter message to Hồ Chí Minh. The disguised comments helped buoy lagging spirits.

Jerry spent those winter months in solitary confinement, and for the first time since his arrival, he faced real hunger. One day, he found his bowl of soup waiting outside his cell. It sat on the dirt, cold and collecting grit blown about by the wind. Jerry had once carefully picked debris out of his soup, but now the famished prisoner seized the bowl and gulped it down, neither examining nor caring what it contained. A group of civilians—Jerry guessed they were politicians—visited him during that time and found him huddled in his cell.

"Well, Denton," one said, "do you know that you are eating shit?"

Jerry didn't answer; he wondered if he was referring to the debris lacing his soup.

"So you want to continue eating shit?"

Jerry struggled to his feet and said, "Well, I hope there is some protein in it."

The man nodded and said, "You should be reasonable, or you will continue to eat shit!"

By mid-November, Jerry estimated he weighed only 120 pounds, but his indeterminate sentence bothered him more than the weight loss or cold. His morale sank lower as the Hỏa Lò torture program spread to the Zoo. One day, he heard guards beating young Lieutenant Ed Davis in a neighboring cell. Jerry recalled young Davis tenderly crooning "Fly Me to the Moon" during easier times in New Guy Village—now this. When the beating ended, Davis used a nail to send tap code to Jerry, describing his pain and the ropes that still bound him. Davis tapped a final word: "agony." Then Jerry listened to him writhe and scream on his floor. That night, the lieutenant gave a verbal biography to his interrogators, revealing his background, education, and military service. The next day, Jerry heard him sobbing and used a nail to send code asking Davis how he felt.

"Commander," the lieutenant tapped back earnestly, "I've been doing some soul-searching. If I had it to do over again, maybe I could have just held out five minutes more."

Jerry felt immeasurable pride in his men's will to resist. On December 4, guards took Davis to another camp. Jerry could only hope he'd survive.

As torture became widespread, Jerry laid out new rules. "We will die before we give them classified military information," he whispered down his cellblock. "[When they press for biographical information], take all you can. When you think you have reached the limit of your endurance, give them harmless and inaccurate information that you can remember and repeat if tortured again."

With Pigeye busy at Hỏa Lò, however, less-effective heavies applied the duress at the Zoo. Statements could take several days or even weeks to obtain, and the POWs quickly learned to approach quizzes the way experienced gamblers approach Las Vegas poker tables; hating the dealer only clouded one's judgment. Jerry tried to remain unemotional so he could outwit his opponents. If these aviators hated anything, they hated losing.

They also hated latrine duty, and Jerry Denton loathed it more than most. The infection caused by his first stint in Hỏa Lò's draconian leg stocks had never fully subsided. Nearly four months after the incident, his blood-and-pus-covered foot still stung every time he took a step, and the guards at the Zoo picked a period of particularly ugly inflammation to assign Jerry a most unpleasant duty. Each night, prisoners placed their full latrine buckets outside their cells for selected inmates to collect and consolidate into several larger pails. The waste from the Zoo's fifty-six residents made its way from each cellblock to the edge of a field, where one POW would carry roughly twenty buckets of human slop 50 yards to a dump, two at a time. On this night, the guards had tapped Jerry as the anchor man in the relay. Limping to the dump, struggling with two heavy buckets, Jerry stepped on a sharp rock that felt like a knife in his foot. The indignity of the task had already infuriated him; the pain stoked him even more. When he returned from the dump, he stepped on yet another rock. He'd had enough. Thoroughly pissed off, he threw down the two empty pails and yelled in French, *"Fini, fini!"*

The supervising guard patted his pistol and gestured for Jerry to pick up the buckets. Jerry glared at him and yelled, "Bullshit!" He stormed across the Zoo's grounds, straight past a startled second guard, and back to his cell. He slammed his door shut. Minutes later, he heard someone discreetly close the lock. The following day, doctors finally treated his infection.

By April 20, 1966, Jerry's leadership and general stubbornness—particularly his persistent refusal to sign a confession admitting his crimes—had earned him a visit with Pigeye in Room Nineteen of the Hanoi Hilton. Inside, Jerry watched the practiced torturer efficiently stack two four-legged stools, one on top of the other. Then Pigeye helped Jerry to the top of the stack, a precarious 5 feet above the tile floor and annoyingly close to the single lightbulb that lit the room. Cuffs bound his hands behind his back. Then Pigeye left.

Hours passed. Nobody entered the room. Jerry sat balanced atop the stools, staring straight ahead. More hours passed. Discomfort began growing in his legs and back, increasing by the minute. Eventually, Jerry noticed he had to urinate. His pride would not allow him to soil himself, so he deftly collapsed the stools while managing to land feet first. He looked around for a bucket, a pot, something he could use to relieve himself. He saw nothing. Then he noticed the chest-level peephole in the door and dragged one of the stools to the threshold. Since cuffs still locked his hands behind his back, he opened the peephole with his nose. He stepped onto the stool, pulled his pants down from behind, and urinated into the courtyard. Fortunately, no guards passed by. Thus relieved, he confronted the challenge of re-creating his previous position. Stacking the stools and climbing on top of them proved impossible to accomplish by himself, so he scraped his cheek against the knobby plaster wall, scattered the stools, and staged an accident. When Pigeye returned to check on his prisoner, he made no mention of the puddle outside. He silently stacked the stools once again and returned Jerry to his perch.

The setup prevented Jerry from sleeping, forcing him to endure the burning bulb throughout the first night and the second day. He was offered neither food nor water. The hours passed with excruciating slowness, and Jerry's mind began suffering as much as his body. Sometime during the second night, the plaster knobs on the walls became faces. Jerry's weary eyes and sleep-deprived brain conspired to render devils and angels from them. The devils screamed; the angels sang. Jerry realized his companions were hallucinations, so he held tightly to one coherent and driving thought: He would choose death from starvation over writing a confession.

Somehow, he struggled through that second night atop the stools. Then he forced himself to ignore the cries of his empty belly throughout the third day. Still, he could not sleep. On the third night, he received a visit from Rabbit, the English-speaking political officer Jim Stockdale had met in December. Rabbit seemed to hope that this slow torture and sleep deprivation had softened his cagey prisoner. Perhaps Jerry Denton would see the wisdom in compromise.

"I tell you man to man, Denton," Rabbit said, playing the good-cop role of which he seemed fond, "they are going to torture you tomorrow if you do not write a confession. I know you will not give in to starvation. I have told them that. They will hurt you very badly. Maybe they will kill you."

For the first time, Jerry heard a North Vietnamese officer say "torture." Prior to Rabbit's slip they'd always referred to their techniques as "punishment." Regardless, Jerry held his ground; he would not write.

"Denton, my government will probably not even use the confession," Rabbit reasoned. "Maybe no one will ever read it. My government knows that it is humiliating for you to write a confession, even if the confession is forced and not credible. They hope the suffering will cause you to act more reasonable, but they will probably not publicize your confession. You have everything to gain and nothing to lose if you write. Your treatment will greatly improve; you will even get a roommate. Aren't you lonely after ten months alone?"

In fact, Jerry felt desperately lonely. His refusal to cooperate had earned him three hundred days without any caring contact other than taps through a wall and occasional whispers. He wanted to lay eyes on an American perhaps more than he wanted to eat or sleep. Yet Jerry would not allow Rabbit to sway him. The young officer sighed and said, "We will allow you to rest sometime tonight. You have until morning to change your mind."

Rabbit had offered Jerry a way out, but Jerry would not grasp a branch offered by an enemy. What Rabbit might have seen as senseless and stubborn, Jerry considered a principled obligation under the Code of Conduct to which he clung like a drowning man clings to a lifeline. It gave some small sense of order to Jerry's otherwise out-of-control world.

Soon, Pigeye arrived to escort Jerry to Cell One in New Guy Village, the cellblock where he had begun his ordeal those ten months earlier. Rabbit appeared four hours later, offering him crackers and tea. Jerry refused what he thought would be his last meal. Once he was resigned to death, his fear evaporated. No punishment for communication could top his recent treatment—or what the North Vietnamese had surely already planned for the next day—so he pulled himself to the barred window and brazenly called out, not caring if guards heard him. He hoped to find another POW nearby. He found Jim Stockdale in Cell Three.

"I'm going in there to die," Jerry confided to his old Annapolis classmate. He didn't think he'd survive his impending rendezvous with Room Eighteen. For a long time, the two commanders talked with each another about the coming day. Jerry sincerely believed that the Camp Authority would kill him when they attempted to extract a statement; he had resolved not to give them one. Whispering out his window to CAG, Jerry said, "Tell [Jane] I love her, but that I want her to remarry." He also explained the Catholic concept of martyrdom and wondered aloud if God might consider this a religious battle—a faithful Christian facing down godless Communists. That night, with CAG listening, he prepared himself for an honorable death.

Pigeye retrieved Jerry the next morning and brought him to Room Eighteen. He cuffed Jerry's wrists behind him, then began pounding Jerry's face and body with his fists. Jerry tried to take the blows without emotion, without falling, but he could not. The punches sent him spinning around the room and tumbling to the floor again and again. Another guard would drag him to his feet and Pigeye would simply resume the beating. Every punch and every drop of blood that flowed from his nose fueled Jerry's anger and resolve.

He caught his breath as Pigeye repositioned him on the floor. He noticed rope in Pigeye's arms as the torturer pulled down his subject's sleeves. Jerry knew what would come and planned to lose his arms before his honor. The two guards began lacing his upper arms with rope, digging their feet into Jerry's back to pull the ropes tight against the muscle and bone.

The tightening ropes quickly cut off circulation to his lower arms and hands. Starved for oxygen, his muscles tried desperately to keep cells alive by converting stored sugars and starches to acids, creating a condition Pigeye would soon use to great effect. Pigeye and the other guard began cinching Jerry's upper arms closer together. His shoulders began to strain; his sternum seemed likely to crack. His chest bowed backward almost unbelievably—the terrible sensation surpassed anything he'd known. He wanted it to stop, but Pigeye had more. The guards worked Jerry's bound upper arms closer together, until his elbows touched. Excruciating pain shot from his arms until they became numb. At that point, Pigeye loosened the ropes. Jerry's arteries rushed blood back into his starved lower arms. The built-up acids in the strangled tissue poisoned the reawakened nerve endings, creating a condition called allodynia and making Jerry feel a blinding pins-and-needles sensation.

Jerry did not submit. Now sweating from the effort, Pigeye placed a long concrete-filled iron bar across his captive's ankles. The two guards slipped off their sandals and balanced themselves on the bar barefoot, rolling it along Jerry's legs. Pigeye occasionally paused and gazed into Jerry's eyes to gauge his lucidity. "Okay?" he asked.

Jerry spat back, "Okay," and the guards continued rolling the bar across his shins. Next they grabbed the cuffs that still bound Jerry's arms behind his back. They lifted his arms skyward, nearly tearing the muscles around Jerry's shoulder sockets. They alternated between these methods until their victim began crying uncontrollably. He prayed to black out—he wished for the relief it would bring—but Pigeye would not allow him the luxury of escape. He knew how to keep prisoners lucid enough to experience unabated pain; he'd take them to the brink of passing out, then ease up. When Jerry closed his eyes and feigned unconsciousness, Pigeye just lifted his eyelids and grinned.

Jerry eventually reached a point where instinct began overpowering

conscious thought. Pain consumed his mind. He would do anything to
end this agony. Conscious only of his desire to escape the present, he
whispered, *"Bào cào, bào cào,"* the Vietnamese words for "to report" or
"to submit," which the Camp Authority required POWs to use. Jerry
capitulated. Then Pigeye let him pass out.

He awoke on the floor of Heartbreak Cell Eight. He watched water from
the room's pipe mix with blood and flow down his naked body and
into the drain. Pigeye stood over him and ordered him to wash. Back
in Room Eighteen, Mickey Mouse awaited the broken prisoner. When
Pigeye had seated Jerry before him, Mickey Mouse asked, "Now, Denton, you are ready to write a confession of your crimes against the
Vietnamese people—and make a tape recording of it?" Jerry nodded.
Guards produced a notebook and closed Jerry's hand around a pen. He
tried to write as Mickey Mouse dictated. The torture session had so
addled his brain that he only traced slow spirals across the paper. He
could not even repeat Mickey Mouse's words—"heinous crimes . . .
Yankee imperialists . . . aggressors"—into a tape recorder.

 After a night of rest, he again sat before his interrogator, pen in
hand. He wrote his confession. Then, with hot coffee warming his
throat, he managed to repeat the words aloud into a tape recorder. He
described "vicious, revolting crimes [against] the innocent people and
civilian buildings of the Democratic Republic of Viet Nam." Then he
praised "the brave and determined workers of an antiaircraft battery
[who] shot down my aircraft" and "the kindness of heart of the Vietnamese government and people." When the interrogators had finished
with him, Jerry shuffled back to his cell, defeated and despondent.

 For three nights after that April 1966 torture session, Mickey Mouse
discussed the war with Jerry. The persistence he showed in attempting
to make Jerry understand the North Vietnamese perspective mystified
the American commander. Did he really think a forty-year-old academy-
educated navy veteran who had been imprisoned and tortured for ten
months would buy his line? He didn't understand Mickey Mouse's tactics or the urgency he displayed in making his arguments. Then Jerry
went to visit Cat.

 "Denton," began Cat, "you are going to meet with some members
of the press. Use your head, Denton. This interview is very important.

Be polite and do what you are told. Remember what punishment you have received in the past. I need not say more."

"I'll be polite, but that's all," grumbled Jerry.

Cat returned the captive to his holding cell in New Guy Village. Once the cell door closed, Jerry agonized about whether he should take more torture before submitting to the interview. However, he knew he had still not recovered from his bouts with the stools and Pigeye's ropes. This was a losing battle. He prayed to God. Then he sought counsel from his neighbor, Robbie Risner, whom the Camp Authority still kept in New Guy Village. The two men prayed and debated throughout the night. Risner suggested Jerry stop subjecting himself to torture and just try to neutralize the interview by not giving up any real propaganda.

"I'll go," Jerry finally decided, "and blow it wide open." He would not parrot Cat's Communist line; he would state the truth.

On May 2, 1966, Pigeye watched as guards bound and blindfolded Jerry before he escorted his captive to the Plantation, a detention facility a mile north of Hỏa Lò, near the Ministry of National Defense. The complex included a large French home the North Vietnamese frequently used for press and propaganda activities. The building offered a glimpse of Paris in tropical Hanoi, with rug-covered hardwood floors, ornate decorations, and crown molding. Beginning the next spring, the North Vietnamese would use the camp to show foreign visitors how well they treated their prisoners. A row of cells called the Show Room displayed what the Camp Authority claimed were typical facilities. The glimpses presented to these international delegates in no way represented the dismal conditions under which most uncooperative POWs lived

Pigeye shut Jerry in one of the mansion's powder rooms, then handed him a beer. Jerry had wanted few things so badly, but he feared it might damage his emaciated body and weakened mind, so he regretfully poured it out when the guards turned away. He knew that he'd need all his faculties to execute the plan he'd hatched for the interview. Soon Pigeye pulled him from the room and ushered him down a well-appointed hallway toward a set of French doors. Through the glass panels, Jerry saw Cat, Mickey Mouse, and Rabbit sitting in the room, along with a number of North Vietnamese officials. A Japanese reporter sat in the room's center and motioned for Jerry to enter. Jerry stepped into the blinding klieg lights, blinked hard, and thought of yet another way to retaliate.

Two weeks later, on May 17, 1966, television viewers in the United States watched the scene unfold in grainy black and white. Among them were Jerry's father and stepmother, his wife, Jane, and the seven Denton children, who had been notified of the interview just before the air date by Commander Bob Boroughs at Naval Intelligence, one of Jane's most helpful Pentagon contacts. Together in their Virginia Beach home, they

Jerry Denton at the televised 1966 interview during which he blinked TORTURE in Morse code.

watched Jerry walk from the shadowy hallway into the brightly lit room where the reporter waited. He seemed subdued, his face expressionless, his eyes glazed. His hair was cut short, and his face appeared haggard. He wore a drab suit buttoned to the neck. When he bowed, his shoulders hunched forward like those of a meek child. He walked slowly to an empty wooden chair and sat across from the journalist.

The captured aviator looked around, seemingly confused and blinded by the bright lights. He began blinking noticeably, sometimes quickly, other times slowly. He rolled his head back and forward. His eyes looked toward the ceiling, then toward the floor. He hunched his shoulders forward and clutched his hands timidly between his thighs, almost as if he were cold despite the hot studio lights. On her television screen, Jane saw a man shockingly different from the proud commander she'd kissed good-bye more than a year earlier.

"Those bastards!" Jane shrieked. "He looks terrible!" The startled children looked at their mother in near disbelief; they'd never heard her use such language. Several of the children shouted at the image of their father, some cried, and others watched in silence.

Jane recalled reading a newspaper with Jerry and their son Don six years prior, in 1960. The article recounted the public apology of U.S. Air Force Captain Francis Gary Powers, who became a Soviet captive when a surface-to-air missile downed his U-2 spy plane over Siberia. At his 1960 trial in Moscow, he confessed to committing a crime against the Soviet Union; he stated that he was "deeply repentant and profoundly sorry" for his actions. After Powers had served two years of a ten-year sentence at Vladimir Prison outside Moscow, the Soviets released him to the United States in exchange for a high-ranking KGB colonel.

"Isn't it too bad that he wasn't able to stand up and say something," Jane had stated more than asked at the time.

Her son had responded, "Don't you know that they can make you say anything?"

"Yes, but wouldn't it have been great if he had found the courage to say something?" Jane said.

Now she watched her husband face the same frightful situation: imprisoned by a Communist regime, forced to do their bidding and read their script. Did she want her husband to find the courage to speak his mind? What would happen to him if he did? How would he live with himself if he didn't?

Jerry continued to blink his eyes, almost deliberately. Long blinks followed by short blinks, short blinks followed by long blinks. He looked dazed as he fielded several innocuous questions.

"Denton," the reporter then asked, "what is your feeling toward your government's action?"

Jerry summoned all his courage and executed his plan. "I don't know what is going on in the war now because the only sources I have access to are North Vietnam radio, magazines, and newspapers," he answered, boldly defying Cat's instructions that he condemn America.

"What do you think about the so-called Vietnamese War?" the

reporter asked next, arriving at what the officers observing off-camera expected to be the coup de grace, the payoff for all their indoctrination. Jerry paused slightly. Jane wondered what choices his mind weighed. She knew nothing of the torture he'd just received or the punishment a wrong answer would earn him. He had made his choice.

"I don't know what is happening, but whatever the position of my government is I support it—fully," he began, his voice gathering strength with each word. "Whatever the position of my government is, I believe in it, yes sir. I'm a member of that government and it's my job to support it and I will as long as I live."

Because of what he'd just said, he didn't think he was going to live much longer.

At home in Virginia, Jane gasped. In contrast to her husband's other statements, this one rang strong and purposeful. She knew it would anger the North Vietnamese; she rightly worried about what would befall Jerry when the camera lights faded and the journalist departed.

Jane's oldest son was haunted by the consequences of so bold an answer, but a sense of pride overpowered the dread. In the clutches of a foreign regime, in a situation where, for all he knew, not a single person outside Hanoi would ever see or hear his statement, Jerry Denton courageously supported his government and country. On television, the young Dentons saw their father live out the principles for which he'd always stood. Then, less than a minute later, the interview ended and his image disappeared. His family wondered when they would see him again. They wondered if he'd survive.

When U.S. intelligence agencies reviewed the video before it was aired, they appreciated more than just the commander's courageous statement. He had also covertly relayed information about the conditions in Hanoi. The blinks that seemed so strange to television viewers were, in fact, very deliberate. Unbeknown to his captors, Jerry had blinked in Morse code.

Long blink (T), three long blinks (O), quick blink, long blink, quick blink (R), long blink (T), quick blink, quick blink, long blink (U), quick blink, long blink, quick blink (R), quick blink (E).

"T-O-R-T-U-R-E."

MY DEAREST SYB

As Jerry Denton suffered in preparation for his spring press interview, Sybil Stockdale kept her vigil on A Avenue in Coronado. Unlike Jane Denton, Sybil had yet to receive confirmation that her husband remained alive. Each day, she opened the mailbox with a complicated sense of anticipation, dread, and resignation. Perhaps she'd find news that Jim had survived; perhaps she'd learn the worst—that she'd become a widow—but at least she'd know. After six months, however, she had begun expecting an answer less and less. Then, on Friday, April 15, 1966, she pulled a stack of letters and flyers from the mailbox and began sifting through them. Her heart nearly stopped. She saw Jim's handwriting. She found a letter—no, *two* letters—postmarked Hanoi. She held both gently, afraid they might disappear. She noticed the second letter was addressed by a different hand. Maybe something had happened to Jim; maybe he couldn't write, maybe he had died. Still, a letter with his handwriting! Shaking with emotion and not wanting to open them alone, Sybil drove to her friend Gala Arnold's house. Gala ushered Sybil into her study and waited in the hallway while Sybil opened the letters. First, she opened the letter addressed by someone else; if it contained bad news, she wanted to hear it first. Inside she found a letter from Jim, dated February 3, 1966.

"My Dearest Syb," it began. "On this chilly afternoon I am so glad to be permitted to write my monthly letter and let you know that I am still OK." Sybil, of course, had received none of those previous letters. "One thinks of Vietnam as a tropical country but in January the rains came, and there was cold and darkness, even at noon. Keeping warm takes energy, and I lost some weight. February already brings the promise of spring, and I think I will gain it back as the temperature rises . . .

"Every night I remember each of you individually; and I know you do the same for me. I live for the day of our reunion, which I suppose will be soon after the war is over. I have no idea how that is working itself out. Let us think positively."

He closed the letter "All my love, Jim."

Sybil's eyes welled with tears of happiness (he was *alive*), tears of sadness (he was so far away), and tears of relief (at least she'd heard from him). Then she opened the first letter, dated December 26, 1965. "I have not seen an American since I was shot down," it reported before musing, "Perhaps solitude builds character; I sometimes think of how such experiences gave depth of insight to Dostoevsky and the other writers."

At the end, he again closed "All my love, Jim."

He had survived. He still had his wits, he still loved her, and Sybil knew he would not stop fighting. Now she had to bring him home.

On the night of May 1, 1966, a navy attaché telephoned Sybil to inform her that North Vietnam had announced Jim's capture; the next day's *San Diego Union* would carry the story. With no small amount of apprehension, she wondered what the story might say—and what photos it would show, if any. Anxiously, she placed a call to the newspaper office and learned the next day's editions would arrive from San Diego via ferry at the Coronado dock. Sybil drove to the pier at 2:00 A.M. but found the ferry had no newspapers. A dockworker told her they'd arrive on the 4:00 A.M. ferry instead. She returned two hours later and heard the boat's foghorn before it came into sight. Once the ferry docked, she watched a truck receive the fresh stacks and followed it to the local newspaper office, where she asked the manager for a copy. With a curious look, the man silently handed her a morning edition. She tore through the pages until she saw Jim, grim and scruffy but alive. The photo caption read CDR JAMES STOCKDALE . . . HELD BY REDS? The article indicated North Vietnam had also released the names of four other pilots captured in 1965.

On May 10, Sybil flew to Washington, D.C., accepting an invitation from Naval Intelligence officer Bob Boroughs. They met the next morning in his Pentagon office, where he tried to restore Sybil's confidence in the government, as he had for Jane Denton and as he would for other wives who visited him at the Office of Naval Intelligence, where he worked with the Interagency POW Intelligence Working Group. POW wives would find few men kinder or more helpful than the endearingly disheveled officer who reminded many of a gumshoe detective. In Boroughs, Sybil found someone who offered compassion as well as information. Wearing a suit rather than a uniform, Boroughs received her graciously and shared what he could as they reviewed Jim's two letters, which Sybil had forwarded to the Office of Naval Intelligence in April. Sybil told Boroughs that one phrase, "there was cold and darkness, even at noon," seemed to reference *Darkness at Noon*, Arthur Koestler's book about the Soviet gulag system. Boroughs, in turn, reported that Jim's odd request for Sybil to "say hello to our old football mates Bobby Tom, Baldy, and Red Dog" likely referenced three downed aviators from *Oriskany:* Harlan "Baldy" Chapman, Ed "Red Dog" Davis, and Harry Jenkins, who shared a last name with CAG's Naval Academy teammate Bobby Tom Jenkins. Boroughs thought that Jim's references indicated these three men had survived. As air wing commander aboard *Oriskany*, Jim himself had declared Ed Davis killed in action after his August 1965 downing, so when he got to Hanoi and found Davis alive, he'd been particularly concerned about getting news of his survival back to the United States.

Before Sybil left the Pentagon, Boroughs broached a related subject. He wondered if Sybil might cooperate with Naval Intelligence in covert communications and intelligence gathering. Would she help them send a secret message to Jim?

"That sounds dangerous," she said. "What if he gets caught?"

"That's why I want you to think it over carefully before you give your answer," Boroughs replied.

"Well, I don't know," Sybil answered. "What guarantees are there that Jim would be protected if he got caught?"

"None," Boroughs leveled. "He'd be on his own."

"And I'd be responsible for having involved him."

"That's right," Boroughs said. "But I think you have to consider whether or not he'd want you to involve him."

"I guess he's already answered in part by sending those messages out in his letters."

"Yes, I think you could say that. But I don't want you to give me [your] answer now. Think about it, because you're right, it is a dangerous business, and you are taking his life into your own hands, so to speak."

If she involved Jim in the navy's scheme, she'd enlist her husband as a spy, an assignment far more dangerous than being a prisoner of war. Foreign governments executed spies.

While in Washington, Sybil had also scheduled a meeting with the U.S. State Department, the other federal channel she felt ought to help her husband. When she mentioned this to Boroughs, he asked her to learn more about State's efforts on behalf of the POWs. The agencies did not always cooperate closely, and the more conservative Pentagon was often suspicious of the more liberal State Department. Boroughs explained that in the absence of a declared war, State led the handling of the POW issue, and Sybil detected in his words doubts about State's efficacy. She thought it particularly odd that State and the Pentagon operated separately.

The next day, Sybil visited the State Department office of Ambassador-at-Large Averell Harriman, who oversaw POW matters. Few in Washington could match Harriman's pedigree. He served Franklin Roosevelt during World War II, had been ambassador to the Soviet Union and Great Britain, served as Democratic governor of New York, and twice ran to be the Democratic presidential candidate, losing each time to the more centrist Adlai Stevenson. In a thick-carpeted office, one of Harriman's assistants, Philip Heymann, assured Sybil that the ambassador had lent his considerable experience and talent to the POW issue but that security protocols prevented him from disclosing details. He noted again that Sybil was fortunate to have someone as experienced as Harriman on the case. Sybil only cared if he could bring back her husband. She departed her meeting unsatisfied and somewhat skeptical; her faith in the Johnson administration began to ebb.

Much like their husbands, military spouses were expected to follow orders without question, and so the growing ranks of POW wives continued respecting the government's instructions to remain silent. They didn't want to cause harm to their husbands. Outside family, the military community, and sometimes church congregations, most people didn't know about the nightmare these women faced. Since the government would not share information about families of men listed as prisoners of war or missing in action, even within the military community, these women knew little of each other. They often suffered alone.

Most affected navy families tended to live near San Diego, Lemoore, and Virginia Beach, as those were the bases for the fighter and attack squadrons that sustained most of the air losses. Within those small communities, families of captured or missing personnel slowly began finding one another. Several months after her trip to Washington, Sybil hosted a luncheon for the wives of servicemen classified as prisoners or missing. Lorraine Shumaker, Phyllis Rutledge, and nine other wives spent an entire late-September afternoon commiserating in the Stockdales' Coronado home. They shared their frustrations with the military, related scraps of information they'd gleaned from one source or another, and vented their indignation over North Vietnam's refusal to honor the Geneva Convention. The regime had published no list of captives, had not allowed International Red Cross inspections of their prison camps, had not accepted packages for captives, and had not allowed prisoners to write home with any regularity, if at all—and to their knowledge, the U.S. government had done nothing about it. Their anger flashed and swelled that afternoon on A Avenue.

The Vietnam War had resurrected the terms "POW" and "MIA," and it gave birth to a new generation of POW/MIA wives. Part widow and part woman-in-waiting, yet still a mother and military wife, these women faced daunting circumstances. Sadly, neither their friends nor their government knew how to treat them. The public scarcely knew they existed. Across the country, though, they began finding one another, creating a network of families who had drawn the same indefinite fate. In time, they would rally the nation to bring their loved ones home.

7

LORD, I JUST NEED YOUR HELP

The same month that Sybil received her first letter from Jim and that Jerry Denton prepared to blink his desperate message, thirty-five-year-old Sam Johnson walked through the humidity of a tropical afternoon. Sweat beaded on his forehead and soaked through his air force flight suit. On the nearby Mun River, he saw natives hunting tigers from canoes while jets roared overhead. "What a strange situation and foreign world this is," he thought. "I really couldn't be any farther from home."

The Texan's boots fell lightly on the expansive concrete tarmac at Thailand's Ubon Royal Thai Air Force Base. Tall and handsome, Sam looked every bit the fighter pilot. In his right hand, he held his flight bag and helmet. He breathed the thick air and contemplated his upcoming flight, his twenty-fifth night mission for the 8th Tactical Fighter Wing. For more than a year now, the air force and navy had attacked the infrastructure that fed the Communist insurgency, which had only grown despite countless sorties and the more than 200,000 U.S. troops now stationed in South Vietnam. Further hampering America's ability to beat back the Việtcộng and win over the South Vietnamese civilian population, conflict had recently broken out between South Vietnam's prime minister and the generals who ran the country's four military regions. When the prime minister tried to assert control over the military, protests and violence spread throughout the country. South Vietnam seemed destined for a simultaneous civil war of its own making. U.S. officers and diplomats were aghast. They wondered how this would affect public support and what it portended for America's mission in Southeast Asia. Sam carried those same questions with him as he walked across the tarmac toward his waiting McDonnell-Douglas F-4 Phantom II.

Suddenly, another member of the 433rd Tactical Fighter Squadron—Satan's Angels—caught his attention. "Major, we've got a communication link to the States," the man yelled from the hangar. "You want to talk to your wife?"

When the technician patched him through and Shirley Johnson answered the phone, Sam found her slightly upset by a recent letter he'd sent that described the heavy antiaircraft defenses he'd encountered on a recent mission near Điện Biên Phủ in North Vietnam. He did his best to reassure her; it did little good. He should be more careful in his next letter, he thought.

Husband and wife moved on to the more pleasant subject of their three children: Bobby, fifteen; Gini, twelve; and Beverly, nine. They talked about the difficulty of their separation. They'd both volunteered for this lifestyle, but that didn't make it any easier to bear. Sam promised to send her a tape-recorded message when he returned from the evening's mission so she could hear his easy drawl. He assured her that he'd fly safely and promised that he'd always love her. The couple said their good-byes, and Sam again confronted his mission.

Sam would always do the job assigned to him—and perform it well. Yet somehow he had become trapped in a ground war, nearly devoid of the air-to-air battles for which fighter pilots like him were prepared. Relatively few North Vietnamese MiGs patrolled the skies; U.S. aircraft had downed fewer than fifteen planes in more than a year of combat. Truck parks, depots, and bridges comprised target lists; Sam worried about surface-to-air missiles and ground artillery, not hostile jets and opposing pilots. Indeed, he missed the old rush of aerial combat.

In 1953, just one year after earning his wings, the twenty-two-year-old novice found himself dogfighting over Korea, flying an F-86 Sabre that he nicknamed *Shirley's Texas Tornado* after his new bride. On May 23, Sam and his Sabre knocked their first North Korean MiG out of the sky. Sam emerged from the fight undamaged but nearly out of gas. He climbed to 40,000 feet, then cut his engine and glided back toward his base with a scant 50 pounds of fuel in his tanks—around seven gallons. He relit the engine as he neared the field and burned his last drops of fuel as he taxied to the flightline. Sam received an earful from his commanding officer for nearly running out of gas, but no punishment came—after all, he'd downed the MiG.

After the war, Sam made his way to Nellis Air Force Base in Nevada, where the air force's aerobatic team, the Thunderbirds, invited him to become their solo pilot—an honor that no pilot could refuse. Sam, just twenty-six, joined them for the group's fifth season, demonstrating the capabilities of the F-100 Super Sabre in grand fashion. Sam relished the solo role, especially his show-opening, low-level passes, often performed upside down, just above the ground. He occasionally made the opening pass at supersonic speeds, which thrilled audiences but often shattered glass in the vicinity. Sam loved being a showman, and as lead solo, he could argue the air force had no finer pilot.

Sam Johnson after downing a North Korean MiG and before joining the Air Force Thunderbirds as a solo pilot.

When his tour with the Thunderbirds ended, Sam earned an assignment to the USAF Fighter Weapons School—the air force equivalent of the navy's future Top Gun program. He also took his skills to Lakenheath Air Force Base in England, where he laid down a challenge to his fellow flyboys. He'd buy a case of beer for any pilot who could outmaneuver him in the sky. Nobody ever claimed his case. Wiping away the Thai humidity on this day in 1966, Sam again wondered how the *hell* he'd ever become ensnared in a ground war.

•   •   •

After saying good-bye to his wife, he caught up with his weapons systems officer and backseater, Lieutenant Larry Chesley. Young Chesley did his best to conceal his excitement about flying with a pilot as accomplished as Sam Johnson. Once they arrived at the waiting jet, both men turned their full attention to the preflight check.

As they strapped themselves into the Phantom's cockpit, Sam and Chesley reviewed their mission one last time. Intelligence had discovered the North Vietnamese using a new road to bring supplies south to Việtcộng guerrillas. Panther One and Panther Two, as their two-plane flight had been designated, were to attack a ferry crossing, then seek out targets of opportunity along the road. No enemy guns, intelligence had reported. Air force pilots called simple missions like these milk runs.

It was 5:30 P.M. on April 16, 1966, when Sam ignited Panther One's two engines. He fed gas into the combustors and heard the whine of the compressors as their blades spun ever faster, pushing air through the engine. He felt the rumble through his seat. The tower directed Panthers One and Two toward the runway for takeoff. The flight received a final clearance and a friendly "good evening" from the tower. Sam pressed his throttle hard and the big plane responded, speeding down the runway until its wings bit into the air and lifted it off the ground. In his element and in control, the Korea veteran, Thunderbird, father, and husband rushed over the two hundred miles between Ubon and his target.

As he entered North Vietnam, Sam skimmed low over jungles and fields to avoid its air defense radar. While much of the country's military technology was outdated, North Vietnam's Soviet-provided air defenses had already downed two hundred American warplanes. Flying above the 17th parallel required all the seriousness and focus the combat veteran could muster.

Still, Sam couldn't help smiling beneath his oxygen mask as he watched glowing tracer rounds from North Vietnamese small arms harmlessly floating toward his near-supersonic Phantom. Suddenly much larger red tracers streaked upward from the dark ground. North Vietnamese antiaircraft guns had discovered the flight.

"Two, go right!" Sam barked at Panther Two. The duo split to evade the deadly fire. Sam, in Panther One, circled around a nearby hill. Then he put the hostile guns in his sights and pulled the trigger.

Nothing happened. Again he pulled the trigger. Nothing. His gun had jammed. He double-checked the switches and kept his finger on the trigger, all the while trying to track the guns on the ground and dodge the flak bursting around him. Then a vibration pulsed through the Phantom. The jet began porpoising, bucking up and down. Two more hits jarred the plane. Sam looked around and saw nothing but red, white, and orange. Nearly every warning light, including the right-engine fire light, glowed urgently. Sam doused the right engine and gave the left full power. The stick ripped itself from his hand and lurched forward. The Phantom plunged into a hard dive. Sam strained against the pressing g-forces to reach the stick. When he finally grasped it, he found it jammed. He pulled, pushed, and pulled again, but the stick would not yield and the fighter plummeted toward the ground.

"Larry, get out!" the pilot shouted to his backseater. "Repeating—get out!" He heard no response from behind him.

"Larry, get out!" Sam yelled again. Silence answered.

Scarcely five seconds had passed since the Phantom had taken its fateful plunge, but Sam had no time left. He pulled hard on the yellow and black ejection ring, and the seat's rocket wrenched him from the cockpit. The wind ripped off his helmet and gloves; he prayed it wouldn't shred his parachute. With immense gratitude, he saw the chute billow open above him. Below, he watched Panther One spiral toward the dark ground. He thought only of Chesley. Moments before the plane crashed into the ground, Sam saw a white chute open below him. He felt relief. Chesley had ejected. Then Panther One exploded. At the Johnson home in Texas, Shirley was on her knees gardening when she heard the sedan pull into the driveway. She looked up to see three figures step out. One was a chaplain. The officials told Shirley that Sam's plane had gone down and only one chute had been seen. The Johnsons entered a long season of uncertainty. They wouldn't hear from Sam for four years.

As he drifted through the night sky toward the dark unknown below, Sam's mind raced. How did his plane fail him? How did one of the finest combat pilots in the U.S. Air Force get shot down? With a few lucky shells, a North Vietnamese gun battery had smashed his sense of control and confidence. He hoped he had enough left to survive what awaited him on the ground.

The ground! He shook himself back to the here-and-now; only seconds remained until he would land. He tried to reach the chute's risers, which would allow him to direct his landing, but his arms wouldn't work. The ejection had dislocated his right shoulder, broken his left, and fractured his left arm in several places. He looked right. His arm twisted in the wind, hanging completely loose. He attempted to grab it with his left arm but couldn't. Both arms hung limp and useless; he could barely move his right hand. Helpless, he drifted lower and implored the Almighty for a soft landing; he'd already lost his arms, he couldn't lose his legs, too. The heavens answered, and Sam touched down gently between the plowed rows of a rice paddy.

A full moon illuminated the well-tended furrows, and as he looked around he saw the outlines of jungle-covered hills beyond the fields. The chatter of antiaircraft guns quickly reminded him that a hostile army surrounded him.

Sam knew there'd be no rescue—not this far into North Vietnam, not at night, not with tracers lacing the sky. Were his arms of any use, he might have drawn his .38 pistol or raised Panther Two on his radio. While neither would have significantly improved his situation, they would at least have provided some comfort. Instead, he could only sit there, his arms flailing uselessly every time he tried to use them.

Within minutes, two figures attired in loose dark clothing materialized on the field's edge. They came straight at Sam, one brandishing a pistol, one holding a machete. He thought his short stay in North Vietnam would end with a beheading, but instead of decapitating him, the two men used their machete to free him from his parachute. He discovered that he couldn't stand. His legs jellied and momentarily seemed as useless as his arms. The two men helped him to his feet, then gently pushed him toward the field's edge. They made no move to smash his radio or confiscate his pistol. They seemed genuinely kind, and a new, crazy thought flashed through his mind. They would rescue him! They would take him down hidden jungle trails and stow him away on canoes until he reached some secret extraction point. In his condition, the trek would prove taxing, but he would survive. He'd end this mission wrapped in the crisp sheets of a hospital bed, warm, with his broken arms set and mending at his side. He'd have a phone call with Shirley, the promise of another mission.

With adrenaline flowing through his bloodstream, Sam charged across the rice paddies with his two presumed saviors. The moon lit the scene: two quick-moving Vietnamese followed by a loping Texan, bent awkwardly forward at the waist, trying to hold his useless arms against his body. They entered the woods at a sprint and began climbing—toward rescue, Sam let himself think. They fell into single file along a narrow jungle trail.

A sharp yell suddenly punctured the quiet. Sam's escorts froze and responded in Vietnamese as they pushed Sam to the ground. His companions began fumbling for his flight vest, radio, and pistol—all of which they had allowed Sam to keep on his person up until that point. A North Vietnamese officer appeared and finished the job with quick efficiency. The officer gestured, and the two black-clad North Vietnamese turned their backs, ran down the hill, and never looked back. Any last hopes of reaching safety disappeared as they fled. They had, either purposely or inadvertently, led Sam into a North Vietnamese Army unit. Soon the entire unit began beating him, their welcome to North Vietnam.

Sam had a fight on his hands—one that would require an entirely different set of resources than those he relied upon as a fighter pilot. As the soldiers tied him to a stretcher, he knew his survival would depend on his will, spirit, and character; the preceding half hour had stripped away everything else.

Sam grew up an only child. With a father and mother who both worked, he learned to fend for himself at a young age and developed a particularly stubborn independence. In high school, he competed in late-night drag races down U.S. Route 75 in Dallas. He ran with a gang called the Lakewood Rats and earned a night in jail for shooting out streetlights. During his fifteenth summer, he found a job stringing Western Union wires across the northern panhandle of Texas. He lived with other linemen in a railroad car and survived as the only boy in a crew of grizzled workers who, on evening visits to local saloons, taught Sam to hold his beer and to acquit himself in a fistfight. The rough Texas upbringing molded him into the young man who would excel in the elite circles of fighter pilots. Now, as soldiers carried him farther into the jungles of North Vietnam, he hoped that his scrappy boyhood preparation would see him through whatever came next. With that thought, he passed out.

He jolted back to consciousness when his stretcher-bearers dropped his litter onto the hard dirt floor of a small hut. His broken shoulders screamed. His eyes adjusted to the dim interior, and he saw a family as well as two armed soldiers. The soldiers glared at him; the family tried to show him compassion. An elderly man approached Sam with a spoon of soup. Sam cringed at the smell. His host insisted. Sam felt obligated to accept the hospitality, and his stomach needed food, so he allowed the man to feed him. He forced down the foul-smelling broth. His second sip made him vomit, and he passed out again.

The next night, several soldiers took him to a larger house on the outskirts of Đồng Hới, although Sam did not know the village's name. The windows of the house were blacked out with blankets. Inside, he found a dozen locals standing in the main room, partially encircling a man seated at a table. An empty stool waited before him. Once Sam took his seat, the man behind the table began talking. A second man translated. "You are not entitled to military treatment," he said. "You will be tried by the Vietnamese people as a war criminal . . . You are a pirate! You are imperialist criminal! You must repent!"

The leader began asking questions. Sam answered each one, "I don't know." As the ad hoc trial progressed, Sam's injuries and fatigue overwhelmed him and he slipped into a defensive unconsciousness. His body fell to the ground and his broken arms erupted with pain, immediately reviving him. A torrent of rifle butts fell upon his body. Then the men—the jury, as Sam thought of them—placed him back on the stool. When the group tired of the fruitless routine, the man who seemed to serve as judge declared, "You are guilty! You have been sentenced to die!"

The words would have terrified Sam had exhaustion and shock not dulled his senses, but when the men ran Sam outside, marched him into the woods, and placed him in front of a fresh trench, the terror came. He peered into the newly dug pit and realized the villagers had prepared it for his body. For the first time, he felt real fear. He turned around to face three soldiers with AK-47s. The riflemen slammed fresh magazines into their weapons. They opened and closed the chambers. On an officer's order, they placed the guns against their shoulders and took aim.

Sam's mother had marched him to church every Sunday of his boyhood, but Sam had never really called upon the Lord until that moment. He started praying hard, harder than he'd ever prayed. "Lord, I just need your help," he asked, not knowing whether his prayers would bring rescue or simply comfort in his final moments. He entrusted his fate to God; he would abide by his will. The officer barked the order to fire. Sam closed his eyes. The soldiers squeezed the triggers of their guns. Sam heard *Click, click, click.* The soldiers had not loaded rounds; their hammers clicked harmlessly into empty chambers.

Sam let out a laugh; he couldn't help himself. The soldiers kicked him into the trench and began stomping on him. As their boots and sandals pounded his broken body, Sam knew he would face a difficult road as a prisoner of war—although had he known he would ultimately spend 2,494 arduous days in such captivity, he might have wished the soldiers had used live rounds. Still, from that moment forward, he never feared the North Vietnamese. He would always believe the Lord had protected him that dark night and would never leave his side.

While the Lord may have been with Sam in the woods outside Đồng Hới, Commander Jim Mulligan did not feel his presence when he arrived at the Hanoi Hilton that same spring.

The forty-year-old naval aviator awakened slowly. With his eyes still closed, he could imagine he'd only experienced a nightmare. He hoped that when he opened them he would find the clean sheets and secure walls of his bunk aboard the USS *Enterprise*. Even before he could will his eyelids open, though, he felt the pain and knew he would not awake in his stateroom. His arms were bound together tightly. His entire body throbbed. His head hurt. He reached for it with his conjoined arms. His hands found a sticky lump: blood. When he focused on opening his eyes, he realized someone had blindfolded him. He pulled himself into an awkward crawling position, but he couldn't feel his hands. He felt ropes biting into his forearms, strangling his wrists. Crawling along with his knees and bound hands, he found an exposed rod. He looped the blindfold's long end around it twice, then drew it taut with his hands. He finally pulled the cloth over his head. When his eyes adjusted, he saw the concrete cell of a prison. Iron rods barred a large window that looked onto an exterior wall, capped with green glass shards and electrical wires. He spied a sparrow in a tree and, like a superstitious sailor, took the bird as a good omen. He heard the sounds of a city: people, trucks. He surmised that he had arrived in Hanoi. Although he didn't yet know it, he had specifically arrived in New Guy Village, having become the seventy-first American to check in at the Hanoi Hilton.

His memory cleared as he assessed his injuries. In his A-4 Sky-hawk's last moments, it had received a hit to the nose, ramming a section of the instrument console into his chest; his ribs still ached. He found his entire left arm unresponsive; the rough ejection from the smoke-filled cockpit had jerked it from its socket and twisted it backward. He looked at his bloodied, swollen, stockinged feet. He remembered villagers stripping him of his boots, along with his flight suit, wallet, and rosary. He recalled rocks and pebbles shredding his socks and feet, and stepping in piles of fresh dung as he struggled to keep pace with his captors, who had yanked him along gravel roads and rough footpaths. Twice during their march, the North Vietnamese had paraded their half-naked captive through violent mobs, which left him further humiliated and covered with bruises. After he endured those gauntlets, only his dirty boxer shorts remained. Every inch of his body hurt, but nothing hurt worse than his arms.

While on his way to Hanoi in an army truck, Jim—still blindfolded—had begun working at the relatively loose rope that bound his wrists together. A soldier caught him and furiously pulled the rope tighter until it dug into Jim's wrists. Soon, he could not feel his hands. When the truck stopped to refuel along the roadside, Jim heard a crowd gathering. Then he smelled gas. Moments later, the gasoline poured over Jim's forearms, a soldier's idea to entertain onlookers. The rope had cut bloody rings into his skin, and the gasoline burned like straight alcohol on the open wounds. It seemed as if someone had hooked his arms to a high-voltage current. Jim had never known such pain. He began sobbing; he lost control of himself. Mercifully, he passed out. When he regained his senses nine days later, he found himself lying on the floor of Hỏa Lò Prison. It was March 31. POWs would later tell him that he'd spent many of those lost days raving mad, crashing around a cell in Heartbreak Hotel. During that time, the gasoline-soaked ropes had tightened as they dried, burrowing into the bloody flesh of his forearms. The pain returned with his consciousness. He realized that he had turned forty just four days earlier and muttered to himself, "If life begins at forty, I'm off to a helluva bad start."

Like every other resident of Hỏa Lò Prison, Jim Mulligan never expected to find himself in such a situation, but he believed his faith and character would see him through. Devout Roman Catholics who lived in Lawrence, Massachusetts, his parents had worked long hours in the town's mills, and while his parents passed on their strong work ethic and religious convictions to Jim, it was his French-Canadian grandparents who instilled within him a deep sense of patriotism. During the 1940 ceremony when his grandmother became a United States citizen at age eighty, she pointed to the nearby cemetery and in broken English told the magistrate, "My husband is buried over there and he's not a citizen. This country has been good to my family and me. I want to be a citizen when I lie next to him." Jim never forgot this moment and dreamed of serving the country his grandparents loved so dearly. He became an Eagle Scout and at age seventeen enlisted in the Navy's V-5 aviation cadet program. At the end of World War II, he was still waiting for flight school. Two years later he'd earned his wings, and by the time he received his college degree in 1955, he had a wife, Louise, and four sons. When he deployed aboard the USS *Enterprise* in November of 1965, Jim and Louise had two more boys.

Like many other aviators in 1966, Jim believed in the stated American cause of containing Communism. He'd grown up with a staunchly anti-Communist father and grandfather and had been stationed in the Caribbean during the Cuban Missile Crisis, defending his country and family from the warheads of Khrushchev and Castro. He never forgot his experiences. Still, even though he hated all things Communist, he objected to the conduct of the war in Vietnam and the political rules that limited him as an aviator. He could attack munitions moving south, but not when they were being unloaded from foreign ships onto North Vietnamese docks; he could attack truck parks, but not factories. It seemed Washington had to approve every target. The eight-week Rolling Thunder campaign announced in March 1965 had now lasted fifty-four weeks. Targets were limited, and campaign intensity varied; Jim thought Hanoi would only understand force applied consistently and convincingly—and he judged Johnson and McNamara unwilling to do this. He did not conceal his opinions well, nor did he really care to. Before he was shot down, he worried that another month of flying handicapped missions and he would no longer be able to keep those views to himself. Of course, the only people who would appreciate his untempered opinions even less than his superior officers were the North Vietnamese.

By the time Jim Mulligan's Skyhawk went down over North Vietnam in March 1966, the Camp Authority no longer considered torture a last resort; it was a first option. On Jim's first conscious night in the Hilton, two khaki-shirted officials unlocked and entered his cell. Jim met Rabbit and Pigeye, who were fast becoming two of the most hated members of the prison staff. They ordered him to his feet, and Pigeye took the rope dangling from Jim's still-bound wrists and led him out of the cell, toward the dim corridor between Rooms Eighteen and Nineteen. They pulled him into Room Eighteen and sat him on a small stool before a panel of three other officials, Cat, Mickey Mouse, and an officer known as the Pro. Jim recalled a survival instructor telling him, "One, you're smarter than those people. Two, don't ever let them know what you know." With his training in mind, Jim readied himself.

Rabbit opened the session. He said, "You must remember that you are not a prisoner of war—you are a criminal of war in the eyes of the Vietnamese people. You must obey all the regulations of the camp if you expect to receive the humane treatment offered by our people." Rabbit listed Jim's alleged crimes—bombing churches, schools, and children. He explained that Jim would pay dearly for his crimes against Vietnam.

"Bat shit," Jim said.

"You must answer all the questions of the camp authorities," Rabbit continued.

Jim interjected, saying, "My name is James Alfred Mulligan Jr., commander, 504324, born on 27 March 1926."

Piqued, Rabbit raised his voice. "You are impolite," he said. "You have bad attitude. You have no rank in Vietnam. You are a criminal of war!"

Jim's injuries and fatigue conspired against him. He lost his balance and fell to the floor. Pigeye immediately returned him to his stool. The adrenaline initially summoned by the interrogation began to wear off, and the pain from Jim's injuries resurfaced, circling his wrists and spreading up his arms. His shoulder throbbed. Jim regrouped and pronounced, "I am an American prisoner of war and I demand medical treatment for my wounds, as guaranteed by the Geneva Convention."

"Keep silent," commanded Mickey Mouse. "You are a criminal of war, you have no right to make demands of Vietnamese people. You will receive humane treatment when you admit your crimes to the Vietnamese people and to the world."

The Pro resumed the questioning, shouting, "Where were you captured? What was your target? When were you shot down?" Jim just repeated the Big Four. Even as his arms throbbed, he did not plan to submit.

Before too long, Rabbit tired of the game. He stood and announced, "You will stand at attention on the wall, and my guard will punish you if you fail to obey. You are a very sick man. You will not receive the humane treatment when you have bad attitude. You will get nothing until you are polite and repent your crimes."

The officers filed out; Pigeye stayed. Jim stood against the wall. The preceding hours had exhausted his body, and the stinging in his arms increased at an alarming rate. It had far surpassed any level he'd thought he could tolerate. He didn't understand how the pain could grow, but it did. Tears came to his eyes. Pigeye just sat nearby, calmly smoking a cigarette and watching, detached and knowing. When the position became unbearable, as Pigeye knew it would, Jim submitted. Pigeye walked into the hallway and called for Rabbit, Cat, the Pro, and Mickey Mouse. The foursome filed back into the room and retook their seats. They looked at Jim, saw his tears, his grotesquely bound fore-arms, his scabbed feet, his brown shorts, his filthy, almost-naked body. Jim thought he must be the ugliest American in North Vietnam.

"Untie the ropes," Jim begged. "Untie the ropes."

"I will have my guard remove the ropes when you tell me that you will read the statement on the document we have prepared for you," said Mickey Mouse. "You will make the recording and confess your crimes to the American people and the world."

"Take off the ropes," Jim begged again. "Please take off the ropes. I can't stand it anymore. I'm done. I'm finished. I'll do what you want, but please take off the ropes."

The officers told Pigeye to take off the ropes. He could not; the strands had become embedded too deeply in Jim's skin. Pigeye left and returned with a knife. Jim sobbed with defeat, exhaustion, and agony as Pigeye cut the ropes away from his skin. The ropes tore away sicken-ingly, taking dead skin and dried pus with them. The newly opened sores began to bleed, and the sensation of freed circulation struck him ferociously. It soon subsided, and Jim at last felt relief. Broken, he faced his next task. He prepared to betray his country and break the sacred Code of Conduct. He had been weak. He had not outlasted the North Vietnamese. He hated himself.

The ropes had rendered Jim's hands useless. He could neither feel nor use them to any effect. Anticipating this, Rabbit had produced a typed document for Jim to review and recite into a tape recorder. It begged forgiveness for criminal acts and condemned the war. To encourage Jim's cooperation, Rabbit showed him an assortment of alleged confessions made by other prisoners. "You must confess your crimes and repent like the others," Rabbit said. Jim wondered what hell they'd endured before they'd broken. Being in their company made Jim feel no better as he began reading the script aloud. His first recitation proved unsatisfactory. His exhausted brain couldn't function. Rabbit had Pigeye fetch coffee and sugar. Since Jim's arms were useless, Rabbit had to help pour two cups down the aviator's throat. Jim's mind cleared, and soon Rabbit had the confession he needed.

With the quiz almost over, Mickey Mouse said, "I am the camp commander of this camp. I will have for you the regulations of the camp, which you must follow. If you do not follow the regulations of the camp my guard will punish you . . . You must now stand and bow to the authorities before you return to your room. You must remember to be polite and bow to all the Vietnamese army men and people. You greet everyone with a bow. Do you understand?"

Jim answered, "Yes, I understand."

Mickey Mouse gave Jim a copy of the camp regulations, and the panel of officers smiled as he bowed to them before leaving Room Eighteen. After Pigeye locked his cell, Jim shuffled to his bunk. He lay down, surrounded by dirt, rats, and cockroaches. Not long ago, he had slept soundly, with a full stomach, between clean sheets aboard the *Enterprise*. Now he found himself in a situation so degrading that he still had difficulty believing it was real. However, he knew his pain, his hunger, and his crushing sense of failure were all very genuine. "I'm broken," he sobbed quietly into his bamboo mat. "I'm a traitor. I've disgraced my family, my country, and myself." Why couldn't he have been killed in his Skyhawk's crash? He wished the villagers who'd shot at him as he parachuted to earth had found their mark. He wished the infections in his wounded feet or his arms would poison him. "Lord, forgive me," he prayed. "Please, Lord, help me." Tears streaked his face as he fell asleep.

I LOVE A PARADE

Every summer, Sybil Stockdale took her four boys—plus Jim whenever he could secure leave—to Sunset Beach in Connecticut, where her parents kept a cottage overlooking Long Island Sound. She'd come here every summer since she turned five. As a young girl, she enjoyed the break from chores on her family's New England dairy farm. As a teenager, she'd had her first date in the nearby village. Sunset Beach had become a place of memories, a retreat that renewed her strength.

During the summer of 1966, Sybil watched many sunsets from the seawall that separated the family's house from the sound. As she sat there one night, her father approached, placed his hand on her shoulder, and gently said, "Sybil." His tone caught his daughter's attention; he'd been watching the news on television. "The news isn't good, Sybil," he said, "but I'm sure they won't go through with it . . ."

"What, Father? What is it that they said?" she asked.

"They said they're going to try the prisoners with war crimes trials," he explained, "but I'm sure they won't go through with it, Sybil. I'm sure they won't." Together, they watched the sun set over Long Island Sound. As they listened to the boys playing on the shore in the fading light, they wondered how Jim—how all of them—had become participants in this surreal drama. She wondered how their family would survive. That night, Sybil lay in bed debating how to tell the boys about the trials. They'd endured the prospect of their father's death once already—how could they face it again? She wondered how she would bear the horror of Jim, blindfolded and bound, being executed by a North Vietnamese firing squad. She prayed, "Dear Heavenly Father, please don't let it happen, and if it does, I'm going to need extra help only you can give me."

The next morning, she told her boys not to worry about the reports of war crimes tribunals; they needed to stay brave for their father. She tried to maintain a confident facade, but she secretly carried dread in her heart. Everywhere she went, she felt neighbors pitying her. After a week of soldiering on, she finally broke down. At home, sobbing in her mother's arms like a child, she cried out, "I can't stand it! I can't stand it. What am I going to do?"

"It's no good to hold it in all the time," her mother said gently. "I think letting it out some will help you hold up for the boys. You've got to hold up for the boys, you know. You don't really have any choice. That's what Jim would want you to do."

Thousands of miles away, the voice of Hanoi Hannah tried Sam Johnson's nerves. If the Texan had had two good arms, he would have torn down the speaker in his cell at the Zoo to protect his very sanity from the happy singsong voice of Trịnh Thị Ngọ—known as Hanoi Hannah by Americans. North Vietnam considered proselytizing a vital part of its strategy, with Radio Hanoi—the Voice of Vietnam—broadcasting English-language propaganda to U.S. troops in the South, an attempt to undermine their will to fight. Through speakers at the Zoo, Hannah's musical selections and propaganda also reached an unappreciative Sam Johnson and his fellow POWs.

"You will be tried for your crimes," Hannah kept repeating from the speaker in Sam's cell that late-June day in 1966. "You will never go home. The just cause of the Vietnamese people will never be defeated. Even now the tribunal is being assembled. Your crimes will be punished." Was she telling the truth or was it just empty bluster?

"It's just for show, guys," Sam insisted, trying to reassure his cellmate, Jim Lamar, and their neighbor Jim Stockdale. "More Communist garbage. If they tried to try us as war criminals, the American people would react, and they know it." Sam tried hard to believe his own words.

On June 29, he heard heavy artillery fire erupt near the prison. Then air raid sirens blared as aircraft roared overhead. Sam and the other POWs peered through cracks in their shutters to glimpse the battle until guards rushed into the cellblock and yelled, "Under bed! Get under bed!" Lying beneath their improvised bunks, they listened to bombs explode and felt the floor vibrate. Even amid the bombardment, the men could find reason to laugh. For months, they had subsisted on an unvarying diet of thin soup—usually cabbage—and over the noise of the air raid, one POW could be heard imploring the American planes, "Bomb the cabbage patches!"

Air raids throughout North Vietnam had claimed 2,000 lives per month that spring, leaving the public clamoring for revenge. After the heavy June 29 raids near Hanoi, North Vietnam's citizenry erupted with fury. The POWs, who had all confessed their alleged crimes to the Camp Authority, were the public's most proximate targets.

One week after the attack, Sam Johnson and Jim Stockdale watched some of their fellow POWs being assembled in the courtyard of the Zoo. The two friends tapped back and forth between their cells, guessing what the activity meant for those being gathered and for those being left behind. In the courtyard, they saw guards using hemp or cloth to fasten rubber flip-flops to the feet of thirty POWs who were clad in newly issued drab long-sleeved shirts and pants. Most of the shirts bore stenciled identification numbers on the back or chest. Numbering lifted the hopes of desperate POWs throughout the Zoo that the time for their release had finally arrived. It had not.

Guards blindfolded and cuffed the prisoners, then herded them into waiting trucks, which soon lumbered out of sight and into the coming twilight. Sam, Jim, and other injured POWs were left behind to wonder about the fate of their friends. Men like Howie Rutledge and Harry Jenkins, whose names the North Vietnamese had not yet released to the United States, also remained. Later that night, Hannah would narrate the fate of their fellow POWs.

Bob Shumaker was one of the POWs chosen for the excursion and spent the ride from the Zoo to their unknown destination tapping by finger and toe with the other blindfolded POWs in his truck; mostly, they just shared their names. When the caravan eventually stopped, guards ordered the Americans out and into the epicenter of Hanoi.

Earlier that day, Ron Storz and thirteen other prisoners from a remote camp nicknamed Briar Patch arrived in Hanoi's Hàng Đẫy soccer
stadium for a relative feast of water, rice balls, and bananas. The image
of fourteen Americans in the large stadium reminded one POW of an
ancient spectacle in Rome's Coliseum. "Well, the Christians are here,"
he said as he looked around at the empty seats. "Where are the lions?"

As evening neared, guards loaded the Briar Patch prisoners back
into trucks, and they rumbled east into the heart of Hanoi to meet
POWs from the Hilton and the Zoo, like Bob Shumaker. The trucks all
met at a common point and commenced unloading. As each POW
stepped from the truck, a guard took off his blindfold. Shu was handcuffed to Smitty Harris and pushed into a two-column formation, four
rows from the front. They looked around and observed a total of fifty
POWs in the roundabout in front of the Hanoi Opera House. Shu's attention quickly turned from the building to the boisterous, jeering mass
of Hanoi citizenry that had begun to line the east-west thoroughfare of
Phố Tràng Tiền (Tràng Tiền Street). Most POWs had never ventured
outside their prison walls without a blindfold; Shu's first sights of the
angry city were terrifying.

As officers and guards finished forming the columns, the prisoners began to understand the night's plan. One POW quipped, "A parade! A parade! Oh boy, I love a parade!"

Then Rabbit's familiar voice rang out. "You must remember that
you are all criminals and that tonight you are being taken to your public interrogations so that all the world will know your terrible crimes . . .
Today you will see the fury and hatred of the Vietnamese people. They
will try to kill you. We cannot protect you. Show proper attitude for
your crimes. If you repent, you will see our lenient and humane treatment. If not, the people will decide what to do with you." The parade
would serve as a symbolic public tribunal. Rabbit was the prosecutor,
the people of Hanoi his jury.

Behind Shu and Smitty Harris stood twenty more rows of handcuffed twosomes, including Jerry Denton and Bob Peel. Mickey Mouse
and Pigeye had punished Jerry for the defiant answers he issued in his
May press interview with a vengeful all-night torture session in his
Heartbreak Hotel cell, but they judged him sufficiently convalesced for
the evening's march. Ron Storz and Air Force Captain Wes Schierman
paired off just behind Jerry Denton and heard Rabbit's final counsel.

"Now I give you advice: Do not look to the right or to the left, do not look behind you. Do not speak. Walk straight ahead . . . Bow your heads in shame for your crimes."

American POWs begin the Hanoi March, July 6, 1966; Bob Shumaker is in second row, on left.

The procession began around 7:30 P.M., as dusk descended upon the capital, only slightly reducing the summer heat and humidity. The POWs were sweating before even taking a single step. On an order from the guards, the column began moving along the darkening streets.

As the parade began, 8 feet separated each of the twenty-five two-somes from the one behind it. Most POWs stood at least a head taller than the uniformed guards that flanked them. When the guards began moving the assemblage west, across the roundabout and toward Tràng Tiền, they noticed prisoners holding their heads up in defiance. They began yelling, "Bow! Bow!"

Over the growing ruckus, Shu heard Jerry Denton roar, "You are *Americans*! Keep your heads up." His command spread through the columns, and heads snapped back up. Rifle butts descended on those who refused to bow, but the men did their best not to submit before the citizens of Hanoi. By the end of the march, however, many heads would bow, not out of submission but to dodge all manner of projectiles.

Suddenly, Shu noticed a truck engine start. From the direction of the sound came a blaze of light. Floodlights affixed to a flatbed truck lit up the marchers like entertainers on a Las Vegas stage. Squinting through the dazzling lights, the POWs saw reporters and cameras on the truck, which kept close to the curb and moved slowly along with the marchers. The floodlights revoked the last cover the prisoners had: darkness. Now the Americans might as well have been marching at high noon.

The two columns of POWs progressed down Tràng Tiền, and citizens crowded the sidewalks to gawk and vent their anger at America and the bombings that were disrupting—and in many ways destroying—their lives. They lived on shortened rations, often no more than the POWs received. They had no certainty that they or their family would live through the next night. Many families had lost members to American bombs or bullets. While their military retaliated with artillery and rockets, the North Vietnamese people felt a sense of disconnected helplessness. They almost never saw the face of the enemy who flew over their country, showering them with ordnance. They were angry. They had been calling for blood, and in a calculated move, their government had thrown them fresh meat. The July 6, 1966, march presented Hanoi with the first look at those responsible for their sadness, frustration, and outrage. Hanoi's citizens did not waste their chance. All along the 2-mile-long parade route, the sidewalks filled with men and women of all ages, shaking their fists and spewing hatred at the foreigners trudging through their streets. The noise echoed across Hanoi.

The parade passed Hồ Hoàn Kiếm, the lake at the city's heart, where the public congregated in the mornings and evenings. They marched within two blocks of Hỏa Lò Prison itself, although the men had little idea of their whereabouts. At regular intervals, party officials stood in the crowds, leading chants and generally riling up the populace. As particular POWs passed, the officials would make the chants personal and used English so the Americans would understand. "Alvarez, Alvarez, son of a bitch, son of a bitch," they'd yell.

Tens of thousands turned out to witness the spectacle, and the crowds swelled as word of the march spread throughout the city. The miserable POWs slogged along as Rabbit walked ahead, helping to incite the onlookers. "Down with the imperialist American aggressors!" the people chanted. "America get out!"

Emotions intensified, and the guards struggled to control the increasingly unruly crowd. A militiawoman stepped from the sidewalk toward the POWs; a guard pushed her back. "No," she said in Vietnamese, "I'm not going to hit them. I only want to take a close look at the face of that tall lanky guy over there. I keep thinking of how unbelievably vicious and boastful he must have been before he was shot down."

Another man yelled, "There, brethren of the capital; there, right before our eyes, is the 'might of American air power!'" Indeed, these pilots had once exuded pride. Here in the unruly streets of Hanoi, however, they seemed humbled and vulnerable. The people tried to strip what pride these men had left. In its first mile, the parade served the purpose that the government intended. The Communist Party had promised its people trials but likely realized the disastrous consequences of actually trying and sentencing U.S. airmen. Perhaps staging the public march was a middle course. During the second mile, however, the North Vietnamese soldiers lost control of the populace.

No POW could say who felt the first brick or who received the first punch, but the blows began landing on POWs as the march reached the intersection of Nguyễn Thái Học and Hàng Bông. Two trolleys arrived near the intersection at the same time as the column, and passengers poured out to join the melee. Guards turned their rifles and bayonets away from the prisoners and toward the mob. Curses and screams cascaded from all sides; citizens began slipping through the line of guards and assailing the captives with fists, feet, stones, and whatever weapons they could fashion. As the guards and prisoners neared the march's end, they faced a full-fledged riot.

Jerry Denton locked eyes with a woman carrying a basket of rocks. She glared at him, then moved into line behind him, walking directly in front of Ron Storz. Jerry saw several rocks sail past his head harmlessly. Then the woman adjusted her aim. Jerry took a rock to the skull and fell forward, his handcuffs yanking his partner, Bob Peel, down with him. The shackled pair got to their feet just in time for Jerry to receive a sharp punch to the groin.

Jerry spied the man who had delivered the shot preparing another assault. Jerry and Peel readied themselves. When the assailant came at them again, Jerry jabbed him with his free hand. Then Jerry and Peel punched at him with the fists of their conjoined arms and connected. Jerry spied a familiar officer nicknamed Spot watching the scene with concern and shouted over the growing din, "If that son of a bitch comes out again, I'm going to kill him." Spot, easily recognized by the white birthmark or napalm scar on his chin, knew enough English to understand Jerry's threat. When the man prepared to attack Jerry and Bob again, Spot grabbed him by the shirt and hit him with his pistol, then threw the man onto the sidewalk.

In the row behind Jerry, someone smashed a shoe against Ron Storz's face. Blood erupted from his now-broken nose, but he could do little to tend it. One hand fended off more would-be assailants; the other hand was cuffed to his friend Wes Schierman. An elderly woman walked into the street and pulled off her *nón lá,* her country's traditional woven conical hat. She began weakly hitting the Americans with the hat's peak as they plodded by. The POWs thought her effort was almost comical until they noticed the tears in her eyes.

By the time the besieged column neared the gates of Hàng Đẫy Stadium, riotous crowds had swarmed the street. Guards and prisoners alike had to battle their way down Phố Hàng Đẫy to reach the shelter of the arena. Many prisoners crawled on their hands and knees through the final yards while guards yelled, "Quickly, quickly," as if their prisoners needed encouragement. The POWs had always worried about meeting death alone in a Hỏa Lò torture room. Now they faced death together at the hands of a civilian mob.

The front of the column reached the haven of the stadium some forty-five minutes after the march began. The guards held the gates against the throngs, keeping the middle open just wide enough to allow the Americans and guards to squeeze through to safety. Finally— miraculously, many POWs thought—the last of the column slipped through the opening and the guards shut the gates against the crowd. The Hanoi March had ended.

At least one American pilot thought he came closer to dying during the march through downtown Hanoi than he did when the North Vietnamese downed his aircraft. With similar thoughts in their minds, the other POWs collapsed on the cinder track that circled the stadium's soccer field, nursing their bloodied faces and bruised limbs. They heard the mob outside begin to dissipate. They looked up at stars that many had not seen for months.

Newly arrived POW Cole Black asked, "Man, do you guys do this every night?"

"Nope, just on Saturdays," veteran Chuck Boyd deadpanned. The response drew laughter from the marchers. For a short half hour, they found peace. They savored being alive, if not free.

After the guards finished dispersing the crowd and secured the stadium, they, too, savored the precious minutes of peace. These men—most younger than the pilots they guarded—had run the same gauntlet as their captives. They had feared for their own safety, and they, too, had survived. Soon, though, the men resumed their roles of prisoners and guards. The guards loaded the Americans into trucks and sent them back to their respective camps. Upon receiving the returning POWs at the Zoo, the wardens unshackled the marchers and led most of them to their rooms. On Bob Shumaker's way back to his cell from the truck, his guard led him straight into a concrete wall, knocking him out for the night. Shu never determined whether his collision with the wall had been intentional.

Jerry Denton's escort was a young officer with the nickname JC, as whenever POWs saw him they'd say, "Jesus Christ, he's going to give us hell." He also seemed to think everyone should treat him as if he were, in fact, Christ almighty. On the walk back to the cellblock, JC delivered at least one brutal slug to Jerry, presumably for his refusal to bow during the march.

Jerry returned to his cell conscious, despite JC's drumming. Soon a new guard came and led him outside for a singular event the POWs would term the Garden Party. Guards led several prisoners to the far end of the Zoo, near the cesspool of Lake Fester. Mosquitoes and a pungent smell filled the air. Jerry's escort stopped and unwrapped the two grimy cloths that had bound his sandals to his feet during the march. He stuffed one filthy rag into Jerry's mouth and tied the other tightly around his eyes as a blindfold. He then forced Jerry against a tree and cuffed his hands behind it. Others experienced the same treatment. For much of the evening, guards milled about talking, joking, and throwing savage punches at the helpless prisoners.

Alone with his thoughts, Jerry tasted the dirt and grit of the rag. Every part of his body ached, his groin worst of all. He imagined himself as a pitiful sight, although he hadn't actually seen his face in months. He wondered how he looked, then realized nobody cared. Eventually—as always—his thoughts turned to communication. He heard at least two men tied nearby, one on each side of him; he thought of them as crucified thieves on Calvary. He gave two coughs, then five—"J." Next, he gave one cough, then four—"D." "JD" for Jerry Denton. He heard responding coughs from his left: "JC." For a moment, he thought Jesus Christ had divinely answered. Then the mental haze created by the night's trauma lifted, and he realized "JC" stood for POW Jerry Coffee. Despite the pain and the rag stuffed down his throat, Denton smiled.

After Jerry had spent the night bound to the tree, a guard finally opened his cuffs and removed his gag and blindfold. Denton blinked and squinted in the morning light to restore his vision. He stepped in the direction of his cellblock, but the guard prodded him toward the camp office. Inside, he found the camp commander—an officer nicknamed Fox—waiting with JC. JC ordered the guard to wipe the blood and dirt from Jerry's face. He complied with a thoughtless sweep. JC shocked Jerry and the guard by ordering a more thorough cleaning. Jerry wondered what the officers had in mind. With JC acting as interpreter, Fox asked for Jerry's opinions on the previous night's march.

The North Vietnamese rarely offered prisoners the opportunity to express themselves, and Jerry made sure not to waste this one. "You fools!" he exclaimed. "It's the biggest mistake you've made. Parading prisoners in the streets is a return to barbaric times. I have nothing but contempt for your utter cowardice. The spectacle of helpless prisoners being paraded through the streets will bring a wave of criticism from the world."

JC translated for Fox and then asked if Jerry had finished. He had.

Through JC, Fox said, "I have something to say to you, and I request that you remember it for a long time. These words are important. Do you understand?"

Jerry indicated that he did.

"The march was not the idea of the Army of Vietnam. The march was the idea of the people." In North Vietnam, "the people" meant the Communist Party. Fox had just told Jerry that he disagreed with the party. As Jerry returned to his cell, he wondered about the divide between the army and the party. Always optimistic, he tried to discern how that division might somehow portend release. It held no such indication, but on only one other known occasion would a North Vietnamese official come so close to offering an American prisoner a sincere explanation of any sort.

•   •   •

At home, networks aired footage of the Hanoi March for the nation to see. Nobody watched with more interest than the families whose loved ones were listed as POW or MIA. Each scoured the black-and-white newsreels that showed downed pilots walking stoically through the crowds on Tràng Tiền. Some saw their husband, son, or father and learned for the first time that he'd survived. Sandra Storz watched the film closely but never saw Ron. She still wondered what had happened to him; she still hadn't received a letter or sign of any type.

In Virginia Beach, the Denton family watched for Jerry but didn't spot him either. Still, they were also oddly relieved by the sight of POWs walking—some proudly—and surmised the men retained at least a modicum of health. Further, Jane believed the families' best hope lay in exposing North Vietnam's illegal treatment of POWs, and the footage of servicemen being paraded through Hanoi served that purpose quite well.

The event sparked outrage across the United States. In the Senate, seventeen prominent doves—men Hanoi typically viewed as allies—protested the march and the threatened trials. Democrat Senator Richard Russell and Republican George Aiken both predicted that the U.S. military would level North Vietnam should trials occur; Russell said the country would be made "a desert." President Johnson joined the condemnation with only slightly more measured words. On an international level, Ambassador-at-Large Averell Harriman rallied allies and organizations like the International Committee of the Red Cross to make North Vietnam honor the Geneva Convention.

The initial relief Jane Denton and her children felt upon seeing the footage proved short-lived, however. The next night, Jerry's namesake eldest son and a date arrived at the beach for a cookout. Nineteen-year-old Jerry had brought an unread copy of the morning paper and tossed it on the sand as he set up the grill. After a while, he glanced down and noticed a photograph on the front page, which showed two POWs struggling to support each other as the mob besieged them. He became acutely aware that as he enjoyed this summer evening by the sea, his father languished in a miserable cell on the far side of the world, possibly never to return. His date shared his sentiment. This reality wasn't going to go away, young Jerry thought. They didn't stay long at the beach.

• • •

The North Vietnamese knew that numerous international parties, particularly those not aligned with or not dependent upon the United States,
sympathized with them. In the aftermath of the march, they began to
realize that staging war crimes trials would jeopardize this standing, regardless of their supporters' relationships with America. Several weeks
after the July 6 parade, Hanoi softened its stance. On July 20, 1966, Hồ
Chí Minh conspicuously omitted the term "war criminals" from several diplomatic cables. On July 21, a French reporter found no party
member willing to confirm plans for trials; the next day the reporter
had learned more and announced that the government had postponed
them. By the month's end, Hồ Chí Minh had told another reporter no
trials were in view. The POWs knew none of this and entered the dog
days of summer 1966 still no closer to freedom.

SUPERMAN!

Early in that summer of 1966, Jim Mulligan served as one of the ranking American officers at the Zoo, alongside Jerry Denton and Jim Stockdale. He ran the cellblock known as the Barn, and even though he'd
only arrived in Hanoi three months earlier, in late March, he'd already
become a problem case. The gruff New Englander had argued vocifer-
ously with the Camp Authority on behalf of his men, kicked doors
when he heard Americans being beaten, and yelled at misbehaving
guards. His abrasive methods, as much as his commander's rank, signified to the North Vietnamese his role in the resistance. Accordingly,
Rabbit called Jim Mulligan to a special quiz in late June, just before the
Hanoi March. He entered the interrogation room, mindlessly rubbing
his forearms, which were still healing from the gasoline-soaked ropes
that had bound them during his initial trip to Hanoi. He sat down upon
a small stool and faced Rabbit and a senior officer. The senior man announced a new program to reeducate the prisoners; Rabbit translated
with enthusiasm.

"It is time to make your choice," Rabbit proclaimed. "A small group
of you will understand [the reeducation program] and cooperate. They
will receive good food and exercise, probably be released early. The vast
majority will be in middle."

He explained those in the middle would try but fail to grasp the lessons because of their Western heritage. Nevertheless, the Camp Authority would show them leniency. They would release them when the war ended.

"And we know a small minority will resist the program and lead others in resisting the program," he said, almost sneering. Jim felt Rabbit meant his words for him in particular. "They will be cast off and kept in small cells alone, with bad food, no exercise. They will die here. It will be your choice.

"Only you decide which group you will join," he emphasized. "Do you understand?"

Jim nodded.

"Soon the program will begin over the radio of the camp. You must pay attention to what we tell you over the radio. You must study, you must learn, you must think of your own situation. Do you understand?"

Jim said yes.

Through Rabbit, the senior officer asked if Jim wanted coffee.

"Yes, thank you," he said, "but I cannot accept it for myself while the other Americans do not have any."

Rabbit replied, "In that case, all of you will get coffee tonight from him as his gift . . . You may return to your room, but remember it is up to you to make your own choice. The treatment you receive from us only depends on you." That night, the POWs all enjoyed hot coffee. The program began the next day.

From its apparent inception at the Zoo that spring, the Make Your Choice campaign quickly spread to the other detention facilities. After the Hanoi March, it arrived at the Briar Patch, where the Camp Authority had assembled a particularly volatile group of troublemakers. One notable dissident was Air Force Captain George McKnight.

Shortly after capturing McKnight in November 1965, the Camp Authority handed him a letter from his mother that implored her son to cooperate with his captors. His interrogators at Hỏa Lò thought the letter might help tame their combative new prisoner. When they showed him the letter, however, George ripped it apart. His attitude had not improved since. The former boxer had earned a reputation among POWs as having mastered giving guards the "fuck you" look.

Before he deployed to Vietnam with the 602nd Special Operations

Squadron, he had read a book entitled *The Smoked Yank*, published in 1888 by Colonel Melvin Grigsby, a U.S. soldier who had been captured by Confederate troops during the Civil War. Grigsby recounted his capture, the horrific conditions inside the infamous stockade at Andersonville, Georgia, and his daring escape through South Carolina. Colonel Grigsby was McKnight's great-grandfather, making the story particularly memorable. A century later, George would find his experience as a POW in Vietnam worse and better, different and similar. By comparison, the stories of Andersonville almost made the camps around Hanoi seem humane. Intentionally or not, the Confederates subjected their POWs to torturous conditions, though they rarely employed the

George McKnight *(right)*, one of the toughest resistors among the American POWs.

personal torture meted out by Pigeye. The prisoner death rate for Andersonville's 45,000 cumulative inmates—nearly 30-in-100—far outpaced the 9-in-100 rate for the 725 known military prisoners held in North Vietnamese and NLF camps during the Vietnam War. (An unknown number of Americans did perish after their capture but before they officially entered the prison system, so nobody will ever know the exact number of POW deaths.) As inspiring as it was, however, Colonel Grigsby's account had not prepared his great-grandson for what he would find at the Briar Patch.

McKnight had arrived at the remote camp on April 21, 1966, but his nightmare wouldn't truly begin until after the July 6 Hanoi March.

That April, as a military truck carried him into the countryside, farther and farther from the community of POWs in the Hilton and the Zoo, George felt as if he were being driven off the map. The truck stopped 35 miles west of Hanoi, outside the village of Xóm Ấp Lô. He entered the secluded prison camp there and soon learned why the POWs had nicknamed the compound the Briar Patch. It had neither running water nor electricity, so bedtime came early. At sundown on his first night, George crawled under his mosquito net and tried to ignore the sounds of rats running through the cellblock. He drew some comfort from his netting, which at least kept bugs and vermin at bay—until the rodents began chewing through it. George heard softer noises, like those from insects, but he could see nothing in his pitch-black cell. He heard a guard approach and saw the beam of a flashlight beneath the door. When the door opened, the guard cast his beam inside, and George looked around in horror. The walls seemed to writhe in the light. Cockroaches covered them from floor to ceiling.

Roaches terrorized him at night; the camp commander—nicknamed Frenchy for his accent—tormented him during the day. George, along with many other POWs, admired the commandant's calm, handsome countenance, wavy dark hair, and charm, yet they soon came to fear his lightning-quick descents into violent hysteria. POWs at the Briar Patch considered him genuinely insane. In crazed fury, he'd scream at his captives over the camp loudspeakers. When they suffered his tirades in person, POWs noticed a burning madness in his eyes. Frenchy wanted to break Americans, and he did, keeping Hanoi's propaganda engine supplied with forced confessions and antiwar statements. He reigned supreme in this remote camp, commanding a staff of thugs like the aptly nicknamed Slugger, who wound up guarding troublemakers like Ron Storz, Bob Shumaker, and George McKnight. The Briar Patch seemed to have become a repository for American and North Vietnamese hard-liners alike.

George quickly learned that no prisoner could escape the deliberate and effective demoralization that accompanied the Make Your Choice initiative. Interrogators began pressing Americans to choose the path of cooperation and lenient treatment or the path of resistance and punishment; they sought to separate the potentially cooperative from the stubbornly intransigent. The Camp Authority offered each prisoner what it claimed was a final opportunity to cooperate and avoid the limitless misery that guards and solitary confinement inflicted. Most chose resistance—punishment be damned—but the North Vietnamese did not make their choice easy.

Those brave yet unfortunate Americans who continued to make what Frenchy considered the wrong choice found themselves beaten and put in solitary confinement. Even then they had to endure the screams of fellow POWs under torture and contend with Frenchy's incessant drills—he feared imminent attacks and drilled his guards and prisoners constantly. He forced Americans to run up a nearby hill, dive into muddy air raid trenches, then crawl into individual boxes, where he'd lock them for hours while guards dug more air raid trenches beneath the bunks in the cellblocks. Worst of all, the POWs felt as if they had disappeared. At least in Hanoi they had felt positive U.S. intelligence knew their position. George worried that if he died out here—and that seemed quite likely under Frenchy's administration—nobody would ever know.

In late July, Frenchy prepared McKnight to make his final choice. For thirty-four nights, he cuffed George's hands behind his back at sundown and shoved him into the 4-foot-deep air raid trench beneath his bed. There he stayed for the next twelve hours. His 6'2" frame barely fit the damp confines of what seemed like a grave. Worms and bugs crawled across his body, and mosquitoes feasted upon him. His immobilized hands could do nothing to help. The slightest itch became torture, and no amount of screaming or pleading would convince guards to exhume him before his twelve hours had expired. He passed each minute in blackness and near-silence. The dirt walls seemed to creep ever closer, and he desperately combated intense claustrophobia. During the day, he lay on his bed listening to the screams of fellow POWs and dreading sunset. When it came, guards forced him back into the trench.

During those hellish weeks, George thought often of a particularly influential priest at his high school. George had an unhappy childhood in Alaska, due in part to a particularly difficult relationship with his father. His grandfather served as his father figure until George left Alaska to attend Catholic preparatory school in Washington. As a freshman, George met a priest who mentored many students. He made an exceptionally strong impression on George through his faith and kindness. Through a combination of inspiration and discipline, he built the future pilot's character and faith. Whenever George found himself in trouble inside a Hanoi quiz room or lonely in a trench, he retreated to the Lord and, even more so, to the memory of the priest. Imagining his reunion with his mentor when he returned home, he resolved to weather the present trial to make him proud, and he hoped that if he didn't survive, the priest would know he'd died with his honor intact.

The example of Ron Storz also sustained him. In the previous weeks, George had seen Ron sentenced to nearly identical punishment in an outdoor trench he passed on his daily walk to the latrine. When George shuffled by, Ron would lift one of the boards covering his pit and whisper "God bless America" or flash a thumbs-up with his manacled hands. When his own dark, dank walls threatened to break his resolve, George remembered Ron's example and redoubled his effort.

After thirty-four nights of confinement in the trench, however, George McKnight had been reduced to an animal that only wanted its suffering to end. Eventually he wrote the confession Frenchy demanded: He had maliciously bombed civilians and hospitals as he carried out a war of imperial aggression. He begged the Vietnamese people for forgiveness. He promised to make the right choice. Nobody could resist torture forever, as every prisoner discovered. Their adversaries had unlimited time and unlimited options; everyone could be broken eventually. As George bitterly wrote the propaganda, he fell back on his doctrine of "pain then brain." When his body couldn't take more abuse, George used his wits to carry on the fight. As he wrote his coerced statement calling for the war's end, he inserted a sentence that began "The only reason the undersigned really expects this letter to be appreciated is . . ."

Together, the first letters of the first seven words spelled "T-O-R-T-U-R-E."

He hoped that if the letter ever made it to the United States, someone would notice the code. If he ever made it home himself, he'd use his hidden message to prove he had only violated the Code of Conduct under extreme duress.

Yet even after incorporating his hidden message, George believed he had failed miserably. He had broken the Code of Conduct, surrendered information, and written statements disloyal to the United States. In his own view, he had disgraced himself, his priest, and the air force. Back in his cell, he tapped to his neighbor, air force POW Jon

Reynolds. He told him that he could never return to America; Reynolds shared his feeling and planned to flee to Canada if the North Vietnamese ever released him. McKnight suggested they then meet up in Australia or South Africa, where they could dwell in shameful exile.

Ron Storz proved no less intractable at the Briar Patch than he had at the Zoo. Above all things, Ron still hated to bow. He stubbornly refused to comply with the rule and received numerous beatings for it, often delivered by Frenchy with bamboo rods. Instead of becoming cowed after a year of captivity, Ron had only become more hateful and stubborn. He would concede nothing to interrogators, and at the end of each quiz, he'd emphasize that they'd made no progress. When an interrogator threatened him by saying, "Your fate is in our hands," Ron shot back, "My fate is in God's hands."

Even before arriving in Vietnam, Ron had aspired to become a minister after the war. Since boyhood, he always held a strong belief in God. The Camp Authority had—quite surprisingly—returned to him a silver cross and chain he'd received from an Episcopal minister in New York. He valued nothing more and always wore it. During one confrontation in the prison yard, a guard yanked the cross from Ron's neck. Fury seized him and he grabbed the guard's arm, ripping the cross out of his hand. A second guard reared back to swing a bamboo pole toward Ron, but he stepped toward the guard, blocked the pole, and shoved him back. Before the situation led to a full-out brawl, POW Wes Schierman jumped between the guards and Ron; everyone backed away from each other. Ron seethed. The stunned guards didn't know how to respond. As punishment, Frenchy kept Ron on a stool for seven days, pressing for a confession and allowing him almost no sleep. Guards administered regular beatings with bamboo. During one interlude, Ron experienced the only kindness ever shown to him at the Briar Patch. A guard nicknamed Jim entered Ron's interrogation room and found him off his stool, sprawled on the floor. Instead of kicking him and returning him to the stool, the guard adjusted Ron's head and said gently, "Sleep, Storz."

Ron's reprieve did not last. Frenchy soon returned him to the stool and completed the weeklong treatment; he nearly killed Ron with his combination of stool, bamboo, and ropes. After seven days, Frenchy threw an utterly spent Ron Storz into a cell with Schierman, his partner from the Hanoi March. Schierman began nursing Ron back to health. When he pulled up Ron's sleeve, he found his arm had turned green. He discovered infected boils caused by the camp's filth and their own poor hygiene. He suggested they call a medic.

"No," Ron said, "I've decided I'm going to leave them. If it kills me, maybe the V will back off and stop torturing all of us."

Ron believed God had sent him into North Vietnam for a purpose, and in a den of wolves he had become shepherd to this flock of brother POWs. While Wes admired Ron's devotion, he dissuaded his friend from sacrificing his life to an infection. Ron eventually relented and let his cellmate treat his boils. Wes washed Ron's arm with the hot water guards provided daily—out of necessity, not courtesy. Given the camp's remoteness, guards had to purify water by boiling it. POWs nearest the fire, like Wes and Ron, got the hottest water. The water drew up the infections inside the boils, and Wes popped them with bamboo slivers. Then he squeezed out repulsively large amounts of white pus. With the pus gone, he saw congealed green plugs inside the boils. POWs always had long fingernails, and he used his to fish out what looked like a cigarette filter from each of Ron's boils. Wes shouted, *"Bào cào,"* and Frenchy soon appeared. Instead of flying into his usual rage, he looked at Ron's arms and grunted. He returned with a medic, who applied ointment, then used a piece of broken bottle glass to grind an antibiotic sulfa pill. He sprinkled the powder into the wounds, then wrapped Ron's arm in a bandage, which would remain, as POWs' bandages usually did, until it rotted off. Slowly, Ron began to recover as he prepared for the next inevitable round of torture.

As George McKnight and Ron Storz slogged through the summer of 1966, new prisoners continued joining the population at the Hilton. On August 22, 1966, bombardier-navigator George Coker became the 121st arrival, having ejected from his crippled A-6 Intruder less than a month after turning twenty-three. George would become one of the youngest airmen taken captive during the war. Within weeks of his appearance in Hanoi, the North Vietnamese likely wished he'd stayed with his doomed aircraft. Perhaps only Ron Storz hated his captors with as much ferocity as George Coker. George and Ron's defiance antagonized the North Vietnamese to an extent the Camp Authority may have never anticipated. From the moment they first mistreated him—which was almost immediately—George hated the North Vietnamese, and he hated them more with each ratchet of his cuffs, each blow to his body. He vowed never to cooperate in any manner, for any reason. His torturers and the camp officials became his mortal enemies; he wanted nothing more than to kill them. George would describe himself as "two inches taller than Napoleon." He actually measured shorter, but his small size did not hinder his quick ascension up the Camp Authority's list of incorrigibles.

At an early age, George Coker learned fear. On a walk in downtown San Diego, his older siblings let their six-year-old brother fall behind. He became lost and terribly afraid. He would never forget the incident. He had night terrors and for the rest of his life would harbor a fear of getting lost. Yet despite his fear, he had hitchhiked from New Jersey to Seattle during college. He also feared heights, yet he chose to fly. For his entire life, George had stared fear in the eye and beaten it.

Nothing had ever scared him more than Father Joe, one of his teachers at St. Benedict's Preparatory School in Newark, New Jersey. Once, George used a poetry assignment to ridicule the priest. After reading George's submission, Father Joe stalked down the aisle toward George's desk. George saw something hideous in the glowering face and massive figure, but he checked his fear and mustered the courage to stare down the priest. When he reached George's desk, Father Joe backhanded him across the face, then grabbed him by the neck and belt. He strode to the door and tossed his student through its large glass window. With a tremendous shattering of glass, George flew out of the classroom and landed in the hallway. He couldn't have been happier: He was on one side of the door and Father Joe was on the other. The experience had showed him that he could confront fear—even taunt those whom he feared—and survive.

As a prisoner of war, George maintained a fierce devotion to his Catholic faith, reconciling his vitriolic wrath with Matthew 5:39. In the verse George had memorized at St. Benedict's, Jesus had admonished, "Whosoever shall smite thee on thy right cheek, turn to him the other also." George reasoned that he had turned both cheeks more than once. He also drew strength from the biblical story of Abednego, Meshach, and Shadrach, the faithful triumvirate who were cast into Babylon's fiery furnace for refusing to worship the idols of King

Nebuchadnezzar. George aspired to emulate their bravery, and just as they had trusted God to save them from the flames, so George trusted the Lord to deliver him from the godless Communists of North Vietnam and Hỏa Lò Prison.

George's enemies may have hated him as much as he hated them. When they compared notes, they found he lied in every interrogation. If he told them one thing under pressure on Tuesday, he'd tell them something different on Saturday. One day, the Camp Authority received a package from Mr. and Mrs. John Coker of Linden, New Jersey. They called George to quiz. "You have a package from somebody," they announced. "Where do your parents live?"

George had already given them at least three bogus answers and said, "I don't know, they move a lot."

"Is it possible they live in New Jersey?"

"Yes, that's possible," George conceded. George never would have divulged his real hometown. The former New Jersey state wrestling champ maintained that the North Vietnamese had no damn business knowing anything beyond his name, rank, service number, and date of birth anyway. He believed that conditions could not get any worse, so cooperation had no upside. He persisted in answering his interrogators' questions with lies until eventually they stopped asking.

Less than two months after he arrived in Hanoi, the personal war between George Coker and North Vietnam escalated. The Camp Authority wanted statements, and George wouldn't give them. On one late October morning, a guard woke George at 6:00 A.M. and posted the aviator against a plaster wall inside a room in the Office, one of the Zoo's main cellblocks. The guard poked him in the ribs until he raised his hands above his head. He indicated George should remain thus. He stood at the wall, arms raised, until 6:00 P.M. George again spent the next day with his arms over his head, glaring at whichever guard sat nearby or looked in through the peephole. So it would continue, the guards promised, until he agreed to write.

Once, when his guard left, George heard the call-up sequence coming through the far wall: "shave and a haircut." He tapped back twice: "two bits." He discovered that Jerry Denton occupied the neighboring cell. Jerry's cell provided a view of the cellblock door, so the two navy flyers tapped until Jerry saw the guard returning. His warning thump sent George springing back to his spot, hands over his head. During the rare moments when guards would leave George unattended, the two would often resume their conversations.

During his long days of standing, George wondered about a peculiar 4-foot-square hole in the floor. He finally learned its purpose when a guard told him, "When air raid comes, you get down there."

At his next opportunity, George tapped to Jerry, "Do you do anything special for an air raid?"

Jerry tapped back, "I use my blanket."

The joke caught George entirely off guard, and he laughed for what seemed like hours, imagining Jerry—eighteen years his senior—uselessly sheltering himself beneath a threadbare blanket as bombs rained down upon the camp.

At the outset of his ordeal, George had steeled himself for the physical contest. How could his legs—one of which had been injured in his ejection two months earlier—and his arms survive such duress? As the days began to pass, however, he realized the torture would test his mind more than his body. He learned to drift away mentally, to take his mind outside his physical being, away from the wall, away from the Zoo, away from North Vietnam. He thought about his family. He remembered church hymns and poems and recited them again and again. He offered elaborate silent prayers. He staged grand debates with himself about theology and life's meaning. He did anything to distract his mind from the reality of his situation—standing against a wall for twelve hours each day, forever hungry, hands raised above his head by exhausted arms, weary legs shaking beneath him. Inevitably his mind would return to the present. Upon each return, he found his condition worse than ever. His sporadic communication with Jerry Denton provided his only pleasure.

The battle of wills stretched into a second week, then into November and past Thanksgiving. Every day, the disbelief of the staff grew—if this bullheaded American would only write a simple statement, it would end—but the North Vietnamese knew that nobody could withstand such hardship indefinitely, and eventually George's mind began to slip. Where once he could drift away for half-hour blocks, he could now only take himself away for a few minutes. He couldn't think about surviving the next twelve hours or even the next hour. He had to concentrate on surviving the next sixty seconds, and then the next.

By December, his mental escapes became more fleeting, and soon he couldn't remember his family. He couldn't recall his squadron mates or his voyage on the *Constellation*. For a time, he held on to the Catholic liturgy, but that, too, faded. As the weeks wore on, memories of sports and Scouting offered his only relief. On the field and mat at St. Benedict's, he had learned not to quit—*Benedict's hates a quitter*—but sports, too, eventually faded. Only the Scout Oath, the promise he recited every week as a boy, remained. Even as his prospects dwindled, the twenty-three-year-old forced himself—over and over—to repeat the first line of the oath: "On my honor, I will do my best." He would not submit.

On Christmas Eve 1966, the North Vietnamese called a truce. The victor slept for two straight days and emerged fortified for whatever lay in store.

When George Coker began his battle in Hanoi, only one future inmate of the infamous Alcatraz prison still eluded North Vietnam's detention system: Tennessean Charles "Nels" Tanner. October 1966 found Nels aboard the USS *Coral Sea*, flying missions over North Vietnam from the carrier's offshore post at Yankee Station in the South China Sea. Until age eighteen, Nels had never seen the ocean. Now, sixteen years later, it completely surrounded him.

The Tanners hailed from the western Tennessee town of Covington, where rows of cotton stretched along two-lane roads, shared by tractors and cars alike. There, Totsie Tanner delivered her second son, Nels, in 1932. Nels loved the family's rolling farmland, which they had settled generations before. At age eight, he met Sara Ann Sage. Thirteen years later, a justice of the peace married Nels and Sara Ann in Hernando, Mississippi. Nels was twenty-one; Sara Ann was eighteen. They paid for the ceremony and license with two dollars she had saved. Thankfully, Nels soon began receiving a navy paycheck, eventually accompanied by flight pay.

In his cabin aboard *Coral Sea*, his thoughts turned to his upcoming flight. By October 1966, more than 350 planes had gone down over North Vietnam. While pilots still joked about the outmoded People's Army of Vietnam, that army had learned to bring down U.S. aircraft quite effectively. It could happen to him. Writing letters home always helped banish those thoughts, so he sat down at his metal desk and, on a plain memo pad, wrote to his twelve-year-old daughter, Cyndi. In rough but careful cursive he shared news from his life aboard ship and expressed pride in her grades at school. He signed the note "Love, Daddy" and dated it "Wed Oct 5."

Four days later, before Cyndi received the letter, she watched her mother open the door to their La Jolla, California, home. Two navy commanders stood in the doorway. Sara Ann Tanner instantly knew something had happened to her husband. The officers explained that on October 9, Nels and Ross Terry, the radar intercept officer in the backseat of their stricken F-4 Phantom, had ejected over North Vietnam. Another aircraft reported their two parachutes drifting into a storm of small-arms fire. The navy had received no signals from the ground; the crew's survival appeared doubtful.

Cyndi's mother called her into the foyer and told her that her father had been shot down; the navy considered him missing in action. Sara Ann explained that his wingman had seen a parachute, but Cyndi heard nothing after the words "shot down." She dashed between the men on the doorstep, across the lawn, and down the street, tears streaming down her face. She raced along the centerline, thinking she could run away, somehow make this not real. One of the officers who'd delivered the news found her and brought her home. Two days afterward, Commander Roger Boh, a former commanding officer and close friend of Cyndi's father, took her to dinner and a movie for her thirteenth birthday. As it always did, the navy community came together to support a family in distress.

Still, something had changed, perhaps permanently, in the household. An emptiness filled Cyndi, her mother, and her six-year-old brother. With so little information—and no word from Hanoi—they didn't allow themselves much hope. What little hope they had, they kept to themselves, not wanting to hurt the others with useless conjecture. Within two months, the family returned to the Tennessee farming community of Covington, where Sara Ann could raise her children surrounded by their extended family, away from the memories in San Diego. In the small town, the Tanners found kindness but no real understanding. Most of Cyndi's classmates thought her father was in the state penitentiary.

Fortunately, both Nels and his radar intercept officer had survived the hit and the subsequent ejection. Then, through some combination of prayers and luck, the pair had drifted safely through the flak. When Nels's feet touched the ground, the last of the men fated to become the Alcatraz Eleven had arrived in North Vietnam.

Two days after he lost his aircraft, Nels arrived at Hỏa Lò Prison and entered a room marked with the number "19." Nels had memorized a portion of the Geneva Convention, which he quoted to the officer present.

"You are quite right," the officer said, seemingly impressed, "but we don't intend to ever abide by any of it!"

Minutes later, Nels watched a short but powerfully built man enter the room. He wore a pith helmet covered with camouflage netting; he carried a coil of rope and manacles. Pigeye, who handled the torture at the Hilton, clamped the manacles on Nels's wrists and used a wrench to fasten them. He used the rope to lace up Nels's arms, then jerked them back so suddenly and violently that Nels heard cartilage and bone pop. Pigeye soon had Nels consumed by pain. During the ensuing interrogation, a North Vietnamese MiG pilot stepped into the room. He claimed that he'd downed Nels's F-4 two days earlier. The officers behind the table demanded that Nels agree. When he didn't, Pigeye drew the ropes tighter. Despite the torturer's methods, Nels never would agree that the MiG had downed his plane—he refused to grant the enemy pilot any credit or his interrogators any satisfaction. The pilot left, and the session continued, the interrogators moving on to other questions.

After they'd completed their initial interrogations of Nels and Ross Terry, the North Vietnamese locked them together in Heartbreak Hotel. The guard set Nels's right ankle in one side of the stocks affixed to his bed slab. Then he handcuffed Nels and fastened one wrist in the other side of the stocks, pulling his torso forward into a horribly uncomfortable position. The guards arranged Terry in the same manner.

The two men spent the next several nights thus contorted. When nature called, they maneuvered themselves as best they could to use their buckets. If they could not, they would wallow in their own waste. During the days, they agonized in separate quiz rooms at the hands of torturers and interrogators. The officers checked off their list of information for the Hanoi Hilton's guest register. Nels realized death would provide the only escape—the only way to avoid surrendering—and after the sessions, he began to contemplate suicide. He found a sharp piece of iron in his Heartbreak cell, but since torture had virtually paralyzed his arms, he couldn't even grab the shank, let alone use it to slash his wrists. Soon interrogators began seeking confessions that their government could use to inflame their citizenry, the kind of confessions Nels feared they could use in a war crimes tribunal. He clung to the Code of Conduct and fought like a cornered tiger, but nobody ever bested Pigeye's methods.

The torturer laid Nels on his stomach and tied a rope between his feet and neck. If Nels let his feet fall, the rope would choke him. Then Pigeye applied nylon straps taken from captured parachutes. The green straps improved upon the traditional ropes he regularly used; they proved stronger and could induce compliance more quickly. Because of this method, some POWs would begin calling Pigeye "Old Straps and Bars." Pigeye went to work with his tools, methodically dislocating Nels's shoulders until Nels gave in and provided a propaganda statement, incapable of bearing the pain any longer. Even after enduring such torture, he viewed himself as a failure. Both he and Terry believed they'd broken the Code; they'd made disloyal statements. The two aviators felt utterly shamed when they returned to Heartbreak Hotel after first crossing that line. They had failed their country and their fellow prisoners. They had faced a challenge and proven unable to meet it. Then a POW in a neighboring cell relayed a message from Robbie Risner that helped to restore their self-respect. Risner had said, "We have all broken. Now blow smoke up their ass."

Nels considered writing the confession Cat and Rabbit wanted, but he couldn't write. His hands and arms were still paralyzed. His arms hung uselessly at his sides, much like those of Sam Johnson. Ross Terry would have to feed Nels for weeks.

Unable to face another day of torture, Nels hatched a plan one evening. "Ross," Nels said, "if we give them a lot of phony names and ridiculous incidents, maybe they won't catch it. Maybe they'll accept it and leave us alone."

That next day, Nels and Terry sat defeated across from their tormentors, wishing they were anywhere but that quiz room. Cat explained what he needed and walked out. Rabbit directed Terry to write and rewrite statements with his own barely functional right hand until Rabbit felt the time had arrived to tape-record them. The two airmen read their scripts into a microphone, then received criticism from Rabbit, often for mispronouncing words in order to indicate their insincerity. Then they'd read again, still hoping to slip in one clue or another. Rabbit had a solid command of modern English, so he caught most of their distortions and hidden clues. He only missed one thing.

In Nels's statement, he had testified, "During the briefings [aboard *Coral Sea*] I was sick at the thought of dropping such horrible weapons as fragmentation bombs, CBU, and napalm on innocent people. I was afraid to disobey so I went to fly my missions. Some pilots had refused to fly. I remember Lieutenant Commander Ben Casey of VHA-2 and Lieutenant Clark Kent of VAW-11 who refused to fly their missions on the first day we got to Vietnam. They were court-martialed on the ship and discharged most dishonorably."

Rabbit paid no heed to the seemingly normal names Ben Casey and Clark Kent and failed to notice the hidden subterfuge. At the time,

Nels Tanner, author of the incendiary *Superman* confession.

Ben Casey was a popular television medical drama, and Clark Kent was the hero's alter ego in *The Adventures of Superman*. The North Vietnamese released the letters, and Cat then sent Nels and Terry for an interview with a Japanese television journalist. At the interview, they pounced upon a spread of food set before them. They indulged as if the North Vietnamese were starving them—that proved a simple act considering their measly diet of soup and sewer greens, as they called the mysterious stringy vegetables. The journalist politely waited as the two famished men stuffed their mouths with bananas, cookies, and so much coffee that it trickled onto their chins. When he realized the orgy wouldn't stop, the journalist proceeded. The POWs answered questions with their mouths full, but they followed the script, and Rabbit seemed happy as he watched from a nearby seat.

In Covington, the Tanner family was watching the nightly news together when suddenly grainy footage of two unidentified Americans—being interviewed with their mouths full of food—played across the screen. Having received no additional information from Washington or Hanoi about their husband and father, they were shocked when they recognized one of the unidentified Americans as Nels. By God, he had survived! Joy rushed into the void that had been their lives. After seeing Nels alive, they believed that his country grit would give him the edge to survive. His family never realized how hard he'd have to fight.

For several months, Nels received no indication that anyone had noticed his message. He assumed his Ben Casey–Clark Kent statement had either gone unnoticed or never reached the West. Cat had him moved to the Zoo, and he settled into life as a POW in North Vietnam. Then the April 14, 1967, issue of *Time* magazine delivered a special report on American prisoners in Southeast Asia. One article discussed North Vietnam's use of POWs for propaganda. It mentioned Nels's statement, noting, "One artful dodger who beat the system was Lieut. Commander Charles Tanner, 34, from Covington, Tenn., who solemnly declared that two fellow pilots on the U.S.S. *Coral Sea* refused to fly their missions, were court-martialed and dishonorably discharged. The officers' names, subsequently trumpeted by Hanoi: Lieut. Commander Ben Casey and Lieut. Clark Kent."

The people and press in the United States found the joke highly amusing, but Hanoi lost face internationally. On April 16, 1967, a cadre of agitated guards burst into Nels's cell at the Zoo and dragged him to a waiting truck. He soon found himself back in Hỏa Lò, sitting before a panel of officers that included Cat and Rabbit. Another officer, nick-named Eel, asked Nels to list Hollywood stars. When Nels asked for clarification, Eel shouted, "Just name some! Write down names of all movie stars you can think of."

Nels, not knowing that his confession had received worldwide attention, wrote a long list of names but omitted Ben Casey and Clark Kent.

The English-speaking Cat often chose to speak Vietnamese and use an interpreter, so through Eel, he asked, "Do you know any comical characters?"

"Comical characters?" Nels asked. "Could you mean funny characters?"

"You know what I mean! Comical characters!"

Nels provided a list of comedic actors, but Cat cut him off. He was infuriated. Through an interpreting Eel he shouted, "You know what I mean! You know, Superman!"

"Oh," Nels replied. "You mean comic strips."

"No, I mean comical characters, Superman and Ben Casey, movie stars. Terry has told us all. He told us you are a liar!" Nels didn't believe Terry had told them anything. "We have here a letter from the Communist Party of the United States," Cat continued, waving a letter. "My friends in your country have written me and told me of your *deceit*!"

For what seemed like hours, Nels sat on a stool and listened to Cat rant, with Eel translating. He was furious about Nels's trick and incensed that his prisoner had embarrassed him, Rabbit, and North Vietnam. Cat's anger didn't seem to be abating, and Nels began to fear for his life. Then suddenly Cat left. Guards dragged the American to an unfamiliar section of Hỏa Lò. Life would become much worse for Nels Tanner.

YOUR ADORING HUSBAND

In the autumn of 1966, Commander Bob Boroughs and two Naval Intelligence specialists visited Sybil Stockdale in Coronado. Sybil had discussed Boroughs's proposal with her eldest son, Jimmy, who had echoed her own thoughts, saying, "Sounds like one of the only ways we'll ever have to fight back." With her son's affirmation, Sybil agreed to involve her husband in intelligence gathering after Boroughs promised to reveal whatever Jim's messages might contain. She knew her husband would have wanted her to participate since, as Jimmy observed, it would let him retaliate in some small measure. The intelligence officers visiting Sybil supplied his weapon: a Polaroid photograph. The photo showed a woman around the age of Jim's mother wading on the beach in Coronado; Jim would instantly know it wasn't his mother. If he immersed the photograph in water, the backing would peel off. Inside, he would find instructions to use in providing intelligence to the United States. Everything depended on Jim knowing to soak the picture.

Sybil had to devise clues to plant in her accompanying letter—enough hints to make Jim think twice about her words and the photograph. She concocted a situation that would seem entirely plausible to censors but entirely absurd to Jim. Then Sybil devised the tip-off sentence, the line that told Jim to soak the photo. Once everyone agreed on the language, they tested the package—letter and Polaroid—with Jim and Sybil's close friend Captain Budd Salsig. When he recognized the clue, they felt satisfied Jim would also. In the photograph's hidden message, Naval Intelligence told Jim to begin any encoded replies with "Darling" and close them with "Your adoring husband." Those were two phrases her fighter pilot of a husband would never otherwise use. All of this hinged on Hanoi giving the package to Jim. He'd only sent two letters in twelve months, and neither indicated he'd received anything from Sybil. Boroughs hoped a letter mailed in the fall might reach Jim as a gesture of Christmas charity.

On October 9, 1966, Sybil Stockdale rode her bicycle along Coronado's quiet streets to the U.S. Post Office. She stood before the mailbox and glanced over the letter one final time. In her excitement and apprehension, she had forgotten stamps. Embarrassed, she put stamps on the envelope, kissed it for luck, and started it on its long journey to Hanoi and her husband, whom she had just made a spy.

After eight months in Hanoi, Jim Mulligan had still not been permitted to contact his family, but he thought an officer nicknamed Lump might offer him a chance. The Massachusetts native had met Lump at the Zoo in early November 1966. Lump spoke English with a French accent and began his conversation with Mulligan by showing rare compassion. He observed Jim's deteriorating physique and within a week had decreed that he should receive a banana and vitamins with his meals. The two men, both around forty years of age, talked of classical music and Boston. Although Jim knew little about the Boston Pops, or any classical music, for that matter, he let Lump believe otherwise and cultivated the relationship to his advantage. He let the conversation progress, hoping for a favor, an opening, a first chance to write home—a letter from loved ones. He wondered if his wife, Louise, and six boys even knew he had survived.

Finally, the two men began talking of their families. Jim lowered his eyes sadly. He expressed his deep loneliness and his hope that he would be allowed a letter from home at Christmas; the prisoners knew the Camp Authority routinely withheld mail. Jim also wished he could send a letter to his wife. His appeal began as a charade, but real tears soon welled in his eyes. Lump listened sympathetically. Several days later, on November 16, the peephole in Jim's door opened. Lump peered in and handed the commander three sheets of paper, a pen, and ink. He told Jim to write a draft, which he would then collect and submit for review.

Jim would not waste his opportunity. As he poised pen above paper, he looked at his ghastly forearms, withered from hunger and scarred from the gas-soaked ropes that had bound him during his first days in captivity. God, how he longed to tell Louise everything—but those words would have to wait. He recalled his survival school instructor telling him that he would be smarter and better trained than his captors; he could outsmart them. With careful forethought, Jim began writing, "My darling wife and children, My captors are allowing me to write a letter home. BIG DEAL! I hope that it arrives before Christmas."

Then he continued, smartly, deliberately, carefully. He wrote, "If I had a deck of cards I could play that famous game of solitaire." Then, he added, "Life is very much like the religious retreat I made a few years back only it is much more quiet here and I have more time for thinking and meditating." From those clues, Jim knew Louise would understand that he spent his days alone. Then he passed along information about other Americans. "I get piles of whole grain rice, plenty of warm soup, and a pot of water, and now estimate my weight at 150 pounds," he wrote. He'd included three sets of three words in which the first letters spelled out "POW," and he'd almost perfectly estimated the number of men in captivity at 150; by year's end, the exact number stood at 151. He also wrote, "Give my best to Father Gallagher. You know, he is some athlete, he got six hits out of seven at bats." Father Gallagher was the chaplain on the *Enterprise,* and Jim hoped to convey that he had found six of seven downed aviators from the carrier. Then he mentioned a fictitious tennis match and commented on a squadron mate being *"rough in missing* his forehand shots"—*Enterprise* aviator Jim Ruffin was still missing. Importantly, he instructed his wife to give his love to Uncle Mark and Aunt Ginny, a reference to their friend Admiral Clarence A. "Mark" Hill, to whom he hoped Louise would pass his letter.

Two days later, Lump returned with the original letter completely unedited. Jim had apparently included enough niceties to gain approval from the censors. He began recopying the letter on the official paper Lump supplied. Dusk had arrived when Lump opened the peephole to collect the finished letter. "Why do you have no light?" he asked.

"Because one of the officers of the camp said that I had a bad attitude and must live in darkness," Jim answered.

The next morning, Lump would send a guard to reinstall the lightbulb. That night, Jim cried himself to sleep in the dark cell, the letter having stirred memories of a home he wondered if he'd ever see again.

The following day, Lump granted Jim thirty additional minutes outside to bathe and wash his clothes. POWs cherished almost nothing more than time spent under the open sky, outside their cramped cells. Jim felt the sun on his pale skin and drew strength even from its faint winter warmth. He watched sparrows fly about the yard and thought of Matthew 10:29, which he'd memorized as part his Catholic upbringing: "Are not two Sparrows sold for a farthing? And one of them shall not fall on the ground without your Father." God controlled all that transpired on earth—even something as insignificant as a bird falling from the sky. Certainly, Jim believed, God's hand also guided him. He knew that the Lord had some divine purpose for sending him through this trying time. He prayed, "Lord, grant me increased faith . . . Please send me home to my family and my country a better man than when I came here. Thy Will be done. Amen."

Before being shot down, Jim Mulligan had smoked more than two packs of cigarettes each day. He'd regularly burn through a pack before noon. When he arrived in Hanoi, he received only one or two smokes per day. When they realized he wouldn't cooperate, the Camp Authority cut off his supply. That December, however, they offered him cigarettes again. "You are too poor," he responded, "Give them to your army and people." He'd decided not to reacquire the habit—and, out of spite, not to do anything his enemy suggested. The officers present in the quiz room overlooked his refusal, and Lump moved on to preparations for the impending Christmas holiday. "Where should the tree be placed?" he asked. Skeptically imagining what a North Vietnamese Christmas tree would look like, Jim suggested the far corner. Then Lump made his grand announcement: "We permit you on the occasion of Christmas to send a message over the radio to your family."

Jim's mind filled with images of ropes binding his arms, of Pigeye cutting them off that first conscious night in Hanoi. He remembered what it had cost to make that first tape and how despondent he'd felt afterward. Never again, he'd resolved. "I can't do that," he said nervously, expecting torture. His heartbeat quickened; his hands began to sweat.

"Why cannot you do this?" Lump asked. "Some of your compatriots have already sent the Christmas message to their families. They will be played over the Voice of Vietnam and you yourself will hear them over the radio of the camp . . . If you send a message over the radio the authorities of the camp may give you a letter from your family on the occasion of Christmas."

Jim desperately wanted a letter from his family; he hadn't received one since he arrived. He wouldn't be party to blackmail, however, and Jerry Denton's order barring recorded statements was still law. "No," Jim answered. "I am too sad about my family. I cannot send a message over the radio." Lump eventually gave up.

On Christmas Eve, Jim went to quiz with Lump and Fox, the Zoo's commandant. After politely enduring a lecture about the history and kindness of the Vietnamese people, Jim asked hopefully, "Will I get a letter from my wife?"

"If your wife writes, the camp authorities will give you the letter," Lump replied.

"Bullshit," Jim thought, but he bowed politely and returned to his cell. There, he composed a Christmas greeting, which he sent via tap code to the eighteen men living in the cells of the Zoo's Pool Hall. He tapped, "Remember at Christmas as we celebrate the rebirth of Christ that upon our release, we also will be born again into a free world, better men than when we came here. God bless! Happy Christmas!" He went to sleep, still longing for his family and for a proper Catholic service, and thinking his barren room seemed very much like that barren manger in Bethlehem.

The North Vietnamese permitted several prisoners to write home during the 1966 Christmas season, and in Virginia Beach, Louise Mulligan watched as other wives joyfully reported news from their husbands in Hanoi. She did her best to celebrate with those lucky families, but she longed to hear from her Jim. At least, she thought,

North Vietnam had released Jim's photograph that summer. Other wives still wondered about the fate of their husbands. By the end of 1966, Cat had granted only 47 of 151 prisoners the privilege of writing home.

At last, the U.S Post Office in Jacksonville, Florida, forwarded an envelope postmarked Hanoi to the Mulligans' new home in Virginia Beach. Louise and her six boys—now aged three to fifteen—couldn't have imagined a better Christmas present. They read and reread the words their father had written with Lump's permission in November. The four pages would have to sustain them for twelve more months until his next letter arrived.

Louise's upbringing in Lawrence, Massachusetts, had prepared her well for the hard times she now faced. Her parents both worked in the local mills during the Great Depression. Their divorce only added to the family's hardships. Louise, like her future husband, Jim, had lived in tenement housing. Jim wore his toughness near the surface, while Louise kept hers cloaked. Even so, as Louise assumed command of her family in 1966, nobody could mistake her iron determination. She would fight for Jim and hold her family together.

As she watched news reports of Operation Rolling Thunder passing the eighteen-month mark, however, she admitted to herself that the likelihood of a near-term homecoming was dim for her husband and the other U.S. airmen in Hanoi. Aircraft had dropped roughly 500,000 tons of bombs onto the North with little apparent effect on Hanoi's leaders. In the South, America had 385,000 troops deployed and, to date, had suffered more than 8,000 casualties. Yet South Vietnam seemed bogged in turmoil, America seemed no closer to victory, and both casualty and budget concerns began to percolate at home. Still, the majority of Johnson's constituents supported the war. The president maintained that more bombs and the influx of military aid would eventually drive North Vietnam to the negotiating table. He would not cease bombing as a precondition to peace talks, as Hanoi had insisted. Nor would he acquiesce to North Vietnam's demand that the NLF have some role in South Vietnam's future. Johnson would not, under any circumstances, accept a Communist influence in Saigon. On the other side, Hồ Chí Minh, Prime Minister Phạm Văn Đồng, and Vietnamese Communist Party general secretary Lê Duẩn proved equally stubborn. Confident in eventual victory, they hunkered down to outlast the United States and its fragile ally in Saigon. The stalemate dragged into 1967, and the more than 150 U.S. POWs faced another year in Hanoi. At home, their wives dutifully soldiered on, continuing to keep quiet.

When they'd first arrived, most POWs had believed their stay would last less than six months. Surely, they thought, their government would negotiate their release or quickly win the war. Instead, Jim Stockdale—CAG—now faced his second lonely Christmas in solitary confinement. To mark the occasion, the Camp Authority gave him a letter from Sybil, the value of which they never realized.

Since June 1966, Jim Stockdale and Sam Johnson had lived at the Zoo, adjacent to one another in solitary cells and largely isolated from the camp's communication chain. Jim at least enjoyed a relatively spacious three-bed cell, and the wall between his cell and Sam's hummed with taps. The former air force Thunderbird and the former navy test pilot amused themselves by signing off in the evenings with abbreviated phrases like "GN ST" for "Good night, sleep tight" and "DLTBBB" for "Don't let the bed bugs bite." However, humor and friendship could not prevent the onset of depression. At Christmastime, melancholy and despondency rolled into the cells like a thick fog.

Holidays—birthdays and Christmas in particular—were the hardest times to endure. On these days, Jim could not help recalling memories of home and family. He knew there was a fifteen-hour time difference between Hanoi and Coronado, and he pictured what his family might be doing without him at each minute. He knew they could not fathom the extent of his tribulations. They didn't know the torture he endured for them, for his country, and they might never find out. He bore the burden of fighting this battle alone. If he died, who would know? Those thoughts plagued him that Christmas Eve, until he at last managed to fall asleep on his hard wooden bunk. The cell's infernal lightbulb would burn throughout the night so guards could monitor him through the door's peephole.

Shortly after he'd fallen asleep, a guard burst into the cell and summoned him to a late-evening quiz. Jim soon sat in an interrogation room across from an officer he'd never seen before. When he observed the man's bulging eyes, long neck, and high cheekbones, he realized that Sam Johnson had described such a man; Jim guessed he sat across from

Chihuahua. Stockdale had prepared himself for one of the propaganda-laced holiday speeches for which the Camp Authority was known, and Chihuahua did not disappoint.

"On the occasion of your religious holiday, in accordance with the humane and lenient treatment of the Democratic Republic of Vietnam, you are provided sweets," the political officer began. "Did you notice the ashtray on the table? Our artisan fashioned it from the wreckage of a war criminal's F-105 Thunderchief. Your imperialist air pirate was brought down by our brilliant gunners in Nghệ An Province. It was the fifteen-hundredth American aggressor aircraft to be destroyed by our people."

Jim tried to discern the accuracy of those figures. He doubted them strongly, but in the absence of reliable information, they troubled him. As Jerry Denton had told the world in his televised interview, the POWs lacked access to any news other than that reported by Radio Hanoi, suspect statements from the Camp Authority, and tidbits provided by new captives. Jim offered no reaction to Chihuahua's statement.

"In honor of your religious holiday, we also offer you a banana," the officer continued. Jim grabbed the proffered fruit, peeled it, and devoured it.

Chihuahua then reached into a desk drawer and produced an envelope. As Jim reached for it, bright lights flashed on behind him; a movie camera began to whir. Chihuahua produced a microphone and said, "In accordance with the humane and lenient policy of the Democratic Republic of Vietnam, on this occasion of Christmas, my government presents you these letters from your wife—one from last September and one from last October. Also, here are two photographs—one of your wife and children, and one of your mother." Jim had fallen victim to a staged propaganda stunt, but he snatched the letters and photos the way a greedy child might grab a chocolate bar.

"What do you have to say about your Christmas letters and photographs?" Chihuahua asked, sticking the microphone in Jim's face. Jim looked at the Polaroid photo of an older woman standing in the surf. Before he could think, Jim blurted out, "That's not *my* mother!"

Nobody seemed to notice what he'd said. The lights switched off. The room's attention turned to the next prisoner, and a guard returned

Jim to solitary. Once locked into his cell, he turned to the pictures and Sybil's letters. The first photograph showed his smiling wife at Sunset

Photo received in December 1966 by Jim Stockdale, showing Sybil with their four sons at Sunset Beach.

Beach standing behind his four sons. They looked healthy and happy, a young family enjoying the summertime. It was yet another season of memories he would miss.

Then Jim returned to the photograph of his mother. Could it be her? She seemed older, much thinner, and her hair had changed color. He began reading the first letter and arrived at a bewildering paragraph. "I surely do hope you have received the pictures I have sent in my last two letters," his wife had written. "And speaking of pictures, I am enclosing one of your mother in this letter as we had a most unexpected surprise last week. Your mother arrived in a taxi. She said she had decided on impulse to fly out and stay with us a few days and treat herself to a good long soak in the water. I took the enclosed picture while she was here."

His mother's behavior confused Jim even more than the Polaroid had. Jim knew air travel and swimming both terrified his mother. She did not like surprise visits, and she detested taxicabs. The whole situation seemed preposterous. He tapped his frustration to Sam Johnson, but that helped little.

He began wishing he'd never seen the photograph. In his fragile mental state, it tormented him. It became an upsetting presence in the cell, and when guards began daily shakedowns shortly after Christmas, Jim wished they'd take away the damned photograph of someone else's mother. Each day, though, they left it. Although he hated to destroy anything from home, he finally resolved to shred the Polaroid into his honey bucket. Just as he started to rip the picture into pieces, however, he hesitated. "What would James Bond do?" Jim asked himself. He decided to soak the photograph. He urinated into his half-full water jug until the mixture neared the brim. He dropped the photo into the jug, half-hoping it would just disappear. After half an hour, it still floated there mockingly.

Jim lifted it out and noticed that its backing had begun to peel, but it revealed nothing. He laid it on a bunk and went to retrieve his honey bucket, which would serve as the trash can. When he returned, he noticed dark marks materializing on the Polaroid's back. He took the square photo to the crack below the door, where a beam of light streamed into the otherwise dimly lit room. He squinted at the tiny markings. He was thunderstruck. The markings were letters. He'd found the message explaining that Sybil's letter was written on carbon paper, as all future letters bearing an odd date would be. To send coded letters back to the United States, Jim was to write a normal letter, then place it on a hard surface. On top of it, he should place the carbon paper, then a cover sheet. He was to write his secret message on the cover sheet with enough pressure to transfer the carbon but not enough to indent the actual letter. The instructions suggested writing the carbon message perpendicular to the horizontal lines of the letter. By writing the salutation "Darling" and the closing "Your adoring husband," he would indicate the letter was encoded. The instructions told him to soak any photograph containing a rose and urged him to be careful; using the carbon could lead to charges of espionage. The instructions ended with two words of encouragement, "Hang on."

Suddenly, he understood Sybil's hint that his mother needed a good soak. He realized how solitary had worn away his intellect—but it hadn't eroded his survival instinct. He heard the gong that heralded the guard's next round. He tore the photograph into pieces and mixed them into his honey bucket. He heard footsteps. He reread the words once more, then threw the instructions into his mouth as the door clicked open. Ignoring the foul taste of water and urine, he chewed the secret message as he stood nose-to-wall during the inspection. He heard the guard open his bucket lid to check for contraband. He offered a quick prayer of hope. Then he heard the guard let the lid slap shut without comment, and he offered a quick prayer of thanks. The guard completed his search, ordered Jim to bow, then left.

Jim had not received a letter since Christmas 1965; now he knew his family and his navy had not forgotten him. In fact, they *trusted* him to understand the message and serve as a spy. In this way, he could fight back against his captors. If he could share the barbarity of Hanoi with the world, he could destroy the North Vietnamese ruse of humanitarianism. He could disclose the names of prisoners. Purpose returned to his life. He just needed to get permission to write home.

Jim told Sam Johnson the news, and over the next few days, they tapped through the wall to refine their list of verified prisoner names. They developed a mental list of forty. In their isolation, they did not know that there were more than one hundred others. In anticipation of sending the names home, Jim began reviewing the list each day, committing it to memory. On January 2, 1967, Jim received his chance to write. The officer known as JC entered his cell with several sheets of paper and indicated that a visiting Women Strike for Peace delegation had offered to carry POW mail home to the United States. Jim's spirits soared. "Act quickly," JC said. "I must pick up soon."

Jim threw a blank sheet onto a wooden bunk. "Darling," he began to write, using the salutatory signal as instructed. He rushed through the perfunctory letter, making sure to write nothing that would risk the censor's disapproval. As instructed, he closed the letter with "Your adoring husband, Jim." Finished, he flipped over his letter and rotated it 90 degrees. He covered it with Sybil's original letter written on carbon paper. Then he placed a blank sheet on top of the stack and began, "Experts in Torture Hand and Leg Irons 16 hours a day." Next he started on his list of names, "Alive here are . . ."

As he finished, he heard a door open outside. He stuffed the cover sheet into his mouth, chewing and swallowing the written evidence of his subterfuge. He stuck Sybil's carbon letter back into its place under the bed board. JC walked in as Jim wrote the last lines of his home address on the envelope. The officer took the encoded letter and left.

Jim was surprised when JC visited his cell just two weeks later carrying paper, pen, and an envelope. As he knew from a recent Hanoi Hannah broadcast, another visitor had offered to ferry mail from prisoners back to the United States. Most POWs had little affection for antiwar delegations like Women Strike for Peace or pacifists like Reverend A. J. Muste, but their visits to Hanoi did serve one positive purpose from their perspective. Jim started writing a letter for Reverend Muste to carry home—and unwittingly aid Naval Intelligence.

"Darling," he began and covered the blank pages with words for Sybil and his boys. As before, he rushed through the pleasantries and utterly fictitious descriptions of his condition, anxious to begin writing his second carbon-coded message. He concluded the letter "Your adoring husband, Jim." He then started on his secret message, listing the new names he'd learned in the past two weeks. Then he added the forty original names in case the Women Strike for Peace delegation hadn't delivered the first letter. Next, he assumed the role of a true spy. He implored the military to attack the radio infrastructure that he believed kept the North motivated and fighting—and tormented the prisoners to no end. He wrote down information gleaned from interrogation sessions: what questions the interrogators asked, what information most interested them. He also did his best to estimate positions of POW camps.

The cell door suddenly opened, and two guards burst into the room. Horrified, Jim looked up from his position by his bunk. He held the pen in his hand, poised over a sheet of paper that could convict him of espionage. The small pile of papers—a cover sheet, Sybil's letter, and his new letter—surely looked suspicious, but he resisted his first instinct to eat the incriminating letter. Maybe he could play this out.

The lead guard positioned Jim nose-to-plaster against the cell's wall while he began teaching a new guard how to shake down a prison cell. As the guards did their job, Jim began to pray. He closed his eyes and saw the bright stained glass of the Naval Academy Chapel, which depicted Christ serenely walking across a blue sea below gathered storm clouds. He wondered if this vision of Christ appeared as a simple memory or as an omen the Lord would soon call him to heaven. Given the content of the letter lying on his bunk, he worried it was the latter.

The lead guard's rough touch interrupted Jim's vision, and he spun around to face the two jailers. One reached for Jim's waist and snapped the string holding up his pajama bottoms. Both guards laughed as the thin pants pooled at Jim's ankles. They practiced a body search on the half-naked aviator, then made him bow. The two left the prisoner alone, humiliated, but immensely relieved. Jim found his stack of papers undisturbed.

Before another guard could enter unannounced, Jim finished his writing, gobbled up the cover sheet, and folded his letter. He wrote out the address, and JC returned to collect the envelope. "Go, Muste," Jim thought. "Go, man, go! Praise the Lord and pass the target list!"

The ring of the doorbell called Sybil Stockdale out of her kitchen, where she'd been packing lunches for her boys. Pulling her robe tight, she opened the front door. A postman handed her a package, special delivery. Inside, she found an envelope with Jim's handwriting. She opened it quickly, her heart beating wildly. She saw the date—January 2, 1967—only nine days earlier. Her eyes sped through the letter, basking in his words but wondering what carbonized secrets the pages contained. Jim had begun with "Darling" and closed with "Your adoring husband." Sybil knew he'd deciphered the secret message in her October letter. She read the letter to her boys; tears welled in young Sid's eyes. As soon as the boys left for school, Sybil called Bob Boroughs at the Pentagon. He chuckled gently at her exuberance and told her where to send the letter. He renewed his promise to tell Sybil what Jim had encoded, even if the truth might hurt. Several days later, Boroughs arrived in San Diego. He didn't chuckle when he met Sybil. He took her to the local Naval Intelligence office, where he led her to a small room containing a folding chair placed before a large shelf. Boroughs said the folder on the shelf held Jim's encoded message. He left Sybil by herself to open it. In now-visible carbon, she read the words Jim had written from his dark cell in Hanoi: "Experts in Torture Hand and Leg Irons 16 hours a day." She looked over his list of names and recognized several men whose wives lived in California. She noted that the navy had incorrectly declared Ed Davis, another man on Jim's list, killed in action. Sybil returned to the horrifying first words. She pulled the room's wastebasket closer; she felt nauseous. She'd harbored suspicions about North Vietnam's treatment of POWs, and she certainly didn't believe the platitudes in Jim's letters. Now she stood face-to-face with her husband's true situation. "Oh, my God," she thought. "My own dearest, beloved Jim. 'Hand and Leg Irons 16 hours a day.' Oh, God." Surely, she thought, her government would act.

The following month, Reverend Muste's delegation forwarded Jim's second letter to Sybil. She opened the package and immediately saw the salutation and closing that told her she would be calling Boroughs again. The letter's last sentence read, "You're doing a *swell* job." She basked in the words that confirmed she had made the right decision; Jim wanted to take the risk.

In Washington, the information in Jim's letters filtered through the intelligence community. Yet the government did not act. President Johnson and Ambassador Harriman chose not to risk jeopardizing negotiations with North Vietnam by confronting them with unpleasant accusations, nor did they want to give families of missing servicemen unconfirmed information that might spark false hopes of survival. Thus families like the Jenkinses, Johnsons, Storzes, and Rutledges continued to wonder what fate had befallen their husbands and fathers. Along with other POW/MIA families, these women and children still dutifully followed their orders to keep quiet, not cause trouble, and trust the administration.

11

BACK US

"Đán! Đán!" the guard shouted, using the Vietnamese name the Camp Authority had assigned Jim Stockdale. "Roll up, roll up!" The command startled Jim from his sleep, which he'd managed to find despite the late-January chill. He heard other doors opening and closing down the Barn cellblock at the Zoo; the Camp Authority must have a big move planned. The guard indicated he'd return in several minutes and expected to find Jim ready. Jim pulled himself off his bed and stuffed his belongings—his porcelain drinking cup, Sybil's letters on the priceless carbon paper—into his bedroll. An officer and guard appeared at the door. "You will move far away to another camp," the officer said. "Keep silent—any communication and you will be severely punished. Leave bucket." The guard tied a blindfold around Jim's head and pushed him down a corridor to a waiting truck. With some difficulty, several guards manhandled Jim and his badly healed, stiff leg into the truck bed; Jim estimated his weight had fallen from 170 pounds to around 125, making their task somewhat easier. Inside the truck, guards reiterated orders not to communicate.

Jim heard a distinctive postnasal drip nearby, the same condition that caused the most unmistakable snoring he'd heard in Hanoi. On the truck-bed floor, his bare foot touched another foot—whether of a friend or guard he couldn't say. He gambled, and with the ball of his right foot, he tapped "shave and a haircut."

The other foot readjusted itself, toe-to-toe with Jim now. A strikingly large toe tapped back "two bits." Jim's foot pressed two times, then five; four times, then three: "JS." The toe responded: "HJ." It was Harry Jenkins, commander of Attack Squadron 163—the Saints—part of *Oriskany*'s Carrier Air Wing 16, which Jim had commanded. He hadn't seen his close friend since he'd created such a ruckus with his snoring in the Hilton's Heartbreak Hotel cellblock in November of 1965; that was after Harry had become the first senior officer to undergo torture. Even though he hadn't actually laid eyes on his friend in more than a year, Jim had found a discreet message from Harry scratched into a baseboard in the Zoo's bathhouse several weeks before the move: "Hi CAG, Saint."

When the truck came to a halt, guards unloaded the blindfolded Americans and pressed them through a gate toward a facility where Jim could hear cell doors opening, closing, and locking. His turn came, and a guard thrust him into a well-lit cell with four bunks. Surprisingly, the place seemed new. Fresh whitewash covered plastered walls; even the wooden bunk beds seemed newly made. Jim knew the underlying smell, though. He recognized the sounds, and later even the particular taste of the water. He'd returned to Hỏa Lò Prison, the Hanoi Hilton. The Camp Authority had now opened its northern section, partitioning the old rooms where Jim knew French jailers once held scores of Vietnamese convicts. The new architects had hoped the partitions would stifle the prisoner communication network that seemed to persist despite the Camp Authority's vigorous efforts to squash it. Within minutes, the new American residents rendered the construction efforts worthless.

CAG occupied the cell nearest the cellblock entrance, and, acting as sentry, he constantly looked under his door to monitor when guards came and went. When he saw the guard leave that first night back in the Hilton, he sounded the all-clear signal: two thumps on his wall. He found that the wall reverberated beautifully. By thumping the walls or simply beating out code on their chests, the men began identifying themselves. Jim Stockdale, Jerry Denton, George Coker, Harry Jenkins, and Sam Johnson all thumped their names and locations. During the interchange, a short, English-speaking officer burst into the cellblock, furious about the noise, which he knew to be communication. Unable to pinpoint the source of the thumps, he slid open the peephole of every cell door to deliver an agitated reprimand. The five men he scolded nicknamed the short popeyed man Bug. As soon as Bug left the cellblock, CAG recognized Sam Johnson's familiar thumping: "GN GBU." He and Sam were back with others, back in the Hilton, back with leaders and friends like Harry and Jerry. He'd only heard of George Coker—who reportedly looked like the actor Jimmy Cagney and acted like the pugnacious star as well. He knew he'd get to know Coker now that his long isolation had ended. CAG would remember that night of January 26, 1967, as among the happiest of that trying period in his life.

The next morning, the Hỏa Lò guards took the new arrivals one by one to dump their buckets and wash up. CAG went first and walked into a courtyard he'd never seen. Within days, a creative air force POW named Dave Hatcher would endow each building around the courtyard with a lasting nickname based on the Las Vegas casinos frequented by pilots stationed at the nearby Nellis Air Force Base. With approval of senior officers, he named this new northeastern section of Hỏa Lò and its collective buildings Little Vegas. Along the dirt courtyard's eastern edge, parallel to the prison's moat and exterior wall, Jim saw two long buildings—each subdivided into eight cells—with arched windows near the eaves; these would become Stardust (to the south) and the Desert Inn (to the north); Jim and the others had spent the previous night in Stardust. A third large, pale stucco building formed the courtyard's northern border; it became known as Thunderbird. Along the western edge of the courtyard sat a four-room shed called the Golden Nugget. The four-roomed Riviera cellblock marked the area's southern boundary. In the middle of the Little Vegas courtyard stood the ten bath stalls of the Sands, where CAG found water trickling from pipes over large metal sinks. Studying his surroundings as he walked to and from the Sands under the two almond trees that partially shaded the area, CAG realized that the North Vietnamese were preparing a large number of cells for long-term residents; they weren't planning to send him home anytime soon. His spirits, so high the night before, abruptly sank. Within days, a total of fifty-four Americans had arrived in Little Vegas, most coming from the Zoo or the Briar Patch.

•   •   •

In Stardust, the Camp Authority corralled ten of its worst offenders, men identified as leaders, subversives, and general rabble-rousers. They were Commanders Stockdale, Denton, Jenkins, Rutledge, and Mulligan, along with Major Sam Johnson, Lieutenant Commander Bob Shumaker, Air Force Captains George McKnight and Ron Storz, and twenty-three-year-old troublemaker Lieutenant (Junior Grade) George Coker, whom CAG took to calling Cagney. Three months later, an eleventh troublesome POW—Lieutenant Commander Nels Tanner—would join these ten problem cases and for the first time, the men who would become known as the Alcatraz Eleven would be together under a single roof.

The move into Little Vegas ushered in a period of relatively mild treatment and slightly more food. Optimists like Jerry Denton attributed this leniency to North Vietnamese plans to send them home; extra rations were fattening them up for repatriation. Realists like Jim Stockdale expected another long season in Hanoi.

Shortly after their arrival, Sam Johnson noticed workers wiring each cell with a speaker. He felt a pit in his stomach; he'd escaped the Zoo but not Hanoi Hannah. Sure enough, Hannah could soon be heard everywhere, providing the latest news and antiwar propaganda, grating on the nerves of Sam and every other POW forced to listen. Some days prisoners endured broadcasts for up to five hours, wincing as American antiwar activists uttered critical statements similar to ones POWs had made only under torture; the baffled prisoners wondered what had gone wrong at home. Hannah rested only on Sundays, when classical music or the high-pitched singing of North Vietnamese children was substituted.

The Camp Authority still played statements made by POWs, albeit with less frequency. While some POWs did provide laughs—one referred to Hồ Chí Minh as "Horseshit Minh" throughout a reading—Jim Stockdale saw the danger in POWs reading propaganda of any type. He realized the men needed rules and a common understanding of how to follow the Code of Conduct in the face of an adversary who disregarded the Geneva Convention.

So Jim helped the Americans regroup. Since Robbie Risner remained quarantined in New Guy Village, Jim took command, aiming to bind his men together in their opposition to the Camp Authority and set community standards by which they could live. Disagreement still surfaced about how strictly men should adhere to the Code of Conduct, as the prisoners had found dogmatic obedience to the Code unrealistic, if not impossible. Jim realized they needed practical guidance—and a shared understanding of right and wrong—that fit their new circumstances. Only then could they feel the sense of unity that shared sacrifice would create.

At the week's end, Cat summoned Jim to quiz. He found Cat and Rabbit waiting in a room just off Little Vegas. "My officer has told me of the impolite manner in which you and your four cronies behaved the night you were brought to this place," Cat began, referring to their encounter with Bug. "You and those with you that night are establishing yourselves as the blackest criminals in the Democratic Republic of Vietnam, and you have been separated.

"Let me warn you," he continued, "do not tamper with our work with the other criminals. Things can go very bad for you very quickly. I can have you made into a domestic animal, if necessary. But I do not want to do that. I think you have a certain understanding of the world that could make you a force for peace. Do you have any other requests?"

"Yes," CAG answered. "I have been alone for a year and a half. I want a cellmate."

"We will study," Cat answered. "It will depend on your attitude. Obey camp regulations. Do not communicate. Go."

Apparently, Cat soon decided sequestering Stockdale's band together in Stardust only allowed them to collaborate more, so he redistributed some of them throughout the buildings of Little Vegas. The Camp Authority moved Jim out of Stardust and into a chilly, dusty cell in Thunderbird, where a recent arrival, young Navy Lieutenant Dan Glenn, became his cellmate. They moved Ron Storz to the same cellblock. In his Thunderbird cell, Number Six in the building's western section, Jim formulated his new doctrine. Limping around his room, he considered the challenge of writing fair and simple rules for applying the broadly written Code of Conduct to their daily lives. How could the Americans, as a unified group, defeat Cat's programs? How could Jim fashion rules that all POWs could physically and mentally uphold? With Pigeye nearby and many POWs sick or injured, could everyone realistically avoid disclosing more than the Big Four?

Jim carefully developed his policy and created a memorable acronym. With his cellmate watching for guards, he whispered the new orders under his door or out his window, where the words would drift to the next window or be heard by POWs in the courtyard. "BACK US," he began, then explained the doctrine behind the acronym. Across the hallway, Ron Storz picked up CAG's whispers and passed them along to others. As Ron liked communicating, his cellmate Wes Schierman spent much of his time peering beneath the cell door, monitoring the hallway for telltale shadows that heralded a guard's approach; since guards often wore sandals, they could approach in virtual silence. Until Schierman whispered, "Stop!" Ron would pass along the BACK US directives, becoming the first link in a chain that would hold the American POWs together.

Bow: Don't bow in public. Prisoners should resist bowing to anyone outside of prison. The Camp Authority required POWs to bow to them inside the camps, but Jim thought reversing that policy would only bring needless reprimand and hardship. He recognized that the North Vietnamese would not, however, beat them before the world's cameras and risk smudging their carefully crafted image as humane captors.

Air: Stay off the air. No prisoner should read anything over the camp speakers or on North Vietnamese radio or television, nor should any prisoner tape-record propaganda statements. He set a minimum price of one week in irons—that is, a POW must endure a week in irons or undergo some equivalent punishment before making any statements.

Crime: Admit no crimes. Every American, if forced to make a statement following torture, should avoid using the word "crime." In part, this would blunt propaganda that reached the outside world, and it might also encumber North Vietnamese prosecutors in any war crime tribunals. Foremost, Jim wanted POWs to remember they were soldiers, not criminals.

Kiss: Don't kiss up or kiss them good-bye. POWs should show no gratitude to the Camp Authority or attempt to curry favor. Nor should they kiss them good-bye, as the saying went, when they left Vietnam. Jim did not want POWs reconciling with their captors at homecoming. The Camp Authority had treated the POWs atrociously. The world should know it, and the prisoners should not forget it.

Unity over **S**elf. The POWs must remain united against the Camp Authority. To CAG, nothing was more important than supporting the man in the next cell, and beyond him, every member of the POW community. The Americans had to toe the same line, and face the same consequences, in order to uphold their Code, support their fellow soldiers, and preserve their unified battle line. The Camp Authority knew that playing to prisoner self-interests could undermine their cohesion; the POWs could not let that happen.

From Thunderbird, a corps of willing lieutenants—such men as Sam Johnson, Ron Storz, and George Coker—helped disperse CAG's orders to POWs throughout Little Vegas, often sending code across the courtyard, sometimes window to window, by using hand signals. They also stashed notes in bowls of rice or in the bathhouse. Fortunately for the resistance, the Camp Authority used some Little Vegas cells as temporary holding places for recent arrivals. These new POWs would quickly learn Jim's orders and then carry them to such facilities as the Zoo, Sơn Tây, and the Plantation. The BACK US code soon united POWs across the prison system.

Questions about the policy often returned from CAG's troops, making their way back to his cell by whispers, taps, and notes. He and other seniors clarified that POWs were allowed to break the BACK US principles—that is, they should *submit*—before torture claimed their lives or sanity. When they had to give in, they should collect themselves and try again, like a boxer rising up from the canvas. Everyone was told to plan and memorize a false story before going to quiz so interrogators couldn't catch their lies months later. Nobody should discuss other prisoners; doing so might contradict the fabrications of fellow POWs. CAG also reminded his subordinates throughout the system that the Code obligated every senior officer to step up and lead. Like the values and duty that first drew these men to the military, the BACK US directives endowed a POW's life with purpose. They restored his spirit. Once again, he had a standard to uphold, a goal to achieve, a reason to fight.

After Cat discovered his Superman stunt, Nels Tanner was transferred to Stardust. He arrived on April 16, 1967, meeting for the first time many of the men with whom he'd face Alcatraz. After a month's stay in Stardust, guards moved Nels to a section of the Hanoi Hilton that few Americans had seen: the Mint. French architects had called this corner of Hỏa Lò *le cachot*—the dungeon. Nels was led out of Stardust and into the Vegas courtyard, north past the Desert Inn, and back inside through a large doorway in the courtyard's corner. Guards pushed him through two more doorways, into the recesses of the cellblock. He found three cells there and surmised they were used for problematic prisoners like himself. The guards thrust him into a narrow stall that measured roughly 3 feet by 7 feet. A crude wooden bed protruded 2 feet from the wall, leaving him only an alley of flooring 6 feet long and 1 foot wide. Wooden leg stocks were affixed to the bed's end, for use should isolation in the miserable cell prove insufficient torment by itself. The cell's window opened above the pigsty that occupied the northeast corner of the walkway between the interior and exterior walls of Hỏa Lò. Twice each week, the camp butcher slaughtered some of the pigs there. The animals squealed out their life just feet from the cell's window, and the acrid smells of death and intestines wafted into the Mint. Each slaughter reminded inmates that their status rated only marginally higher than that of the pigs. The window also offered Nels a glimpse of the sky, and he could hear pedestrians on Phố Hai Bà Trưng, just beyond the prison's exterior wall. If he'd had a rock, he could have easily tossed it into the street, where the sound of happy voices reminded him how life was passing him by.

Locked away in the Mint, Nels wondered why the guards hadn't just shot him. He concluded that since the world knew he lived, killing him would ruin North Vietnam's guise of humane treatment. What the prison staff did do, however, proved almost worse. First, they slapped him into tight-fitting cuffs that immediately chafed his wrists. Always resourceful, Nels improved his situation by picking the lock on the handcuffs with a piece of copper wire he found on the room's floor, but he could not escape the torment of the leg irons. The guards had placed his ankles in iron horseshoes secured with a weighted metal rod. His ankles would bear the 15 pounds continuously for 123 days. The Camp Authority forced no other prisoner to live in irons for so long. Vigilant guards effectively stifled his communication, and Nels could only tap sporadically with prisoners who occupied the neighboring two cells; he was never allowed a trip to the bathhouse. He usually felt alone, except for bugs and rats.

Nels soon had difficulty deciding what he feared more: the isolation of his cell or daily beatings in the interrogation rooms. His only escape from either was the five minutes it took for him to empty his waste bucket in the latrine each day. When the guards would drag him out of the Mint, out of the Little Vegas section of the camp, and into

Room Eighteen or Nineteen in New Guy Village, a series of officials would berate and abuse him without mercy. The cycle repeated every day from April into May and then into June: solitary misery in the Mint followed by agony at quiz. The routine never relented. Nels pleaded for it to stop. He had written an apology, what more did the Camp Authority want?

"Apology?" responded an officer one day. "Apology! You have embarrassed my government so much, there is no apology enough, and there is no punishment enough for you!"

So despite his pleading, the guards worked on Nels for the rest of the day. That night, they returned him to the confines of the Mint. Once the guards left, Nels tapped the wall five times: "shave-and-a-haircut." His neighbor, naval aviator Jerry Coffee, responded with: "two bits."

"I tell you, Jerry," Nels commed, "as I bobbled back across the courtyard to the Mint here, I held my head a 'lil higher. The asshole couldn't have paid me a nicer compliment."

Even with the American leadership together in Little Vegas, winter and spring of 1967 had passed without major altercations between the Camp Authority and the POWs. Then in May, Rabbit's voice came over the speakers. Jim listened to him recite familiar rhetoric, commanding the pilots to atone for their crimes and extolling the magnanimity of North Vietnam. "You are criminals," Rabbit said. "You must work for us. You must pay for your keep. You have obligations to the DRV. You must atone for your crimes and thereby enjoy the historic lenience and generosity of the Vietnamese people." Rabbit went on, saying they must reject the influence of those individuals who continued to incite resistance. CAG took that line personally. Toward the end of his speech, Rabbit issued a chilling admonition. He told the prisoners that the Camp Authority was preparing a special place for the "darkest criminals, who persist in inciting the other criminals to oppose the Camp Authority." In time, Jim and ten others would call that place home.

Then Rabbit announced his government's new early release policy. "Those who repent, [who] show true repentance in actions as well as words, will be permitted to go home even before the war is over," he said. In Jim's opinion, Rabbit had fired a direct shot at the Code of Conduct and the Unity over Self tenet of the BACK US guidelines. With his offer, Rabbit might divide the POWs, encouraging them to compete against one another to secure a ticket home—perhaps by turning each other in or issuing propaganda statements. Jim wouldn't tolerate it. Like an opposing party responding to the president's State of the Union address, he immediately sent his rebuttal through the network. He dubbed Rabbit's offer the FRP—Fink Release Program. "No early release," he ordered. "We all go home together."

The next day, the Camp Authority began conducting short quizzes that POWs called attitude checks. The sessions did not involve torture but rather let the interrogators gauge the mindsets of their captives. When one POW returned from a session, he let Jim know that the Camp Authority planned to partition POWs into three categories: "the willings, the partial-willings, and the diehards." That was how they would identify candidates for early release.

One day, as 1967's spring turned to summer, a guard opened Jim's cell and signaled that he needed his long-sleeved quiz suit. Under escort, he hobbled across the Little Vegas courtyard to Cat's private quiz room. Cat and the Camp Authority knew Jim led the POWs, but they could never officially recognize that fact; their regulations forbade prisoner communication and organization. Acknowledging the existence of the American underground would mean admitting their personal failure to crush it. At this meeting, Cat extended what he perhaps considered an olive branch. He slyly suggested that the men could escape the heat of their cells, enjoy fresh air, and have more bath water if they would help Hanoi's citizenry clean up the debris created by U.S. bombing. Would Jim, just this once, announce this opportunity over the radio?

Jim would not read over the air, had no interest in helping the people of Hanoi, and suspected a propaganda stunt. He pictured the headlines in world papers: "American prisoners of war go to the aid of North Vietnamese patriots as Yank bombs rain on the city of Hanoi." He envisioned five cameras for every shovelful of dirt. "No," he said. "I will not."

Jim's response must have disappointed Cat, but it seemed not to surprise him. "Well, I am sorry," Cat said with some resignation. "I just want you to remember that I gave you a chance to do something good for your fellows, under my own auspices."

During the guards' noon siesta, after Jim had been sent back to his cell, he lay on the concrete floor, appreciating its coolness. He heard someone whistle "Mary Had a Little Lamb," the all-clear signal, and he began whispering a new directive under the door, "No repent; no repay; do not work in town." His words had already spread throughout Little Vegas by whispers, taps, and notes when a North Vietnamese voice came through the speakers that evening, inviting prisoners to work in Hanoi. "Criminals will be given an opportunity to atone for their crimes in a meaningful way," the speaker announced. "They will be allowed to help the Vietnamese people clean up the debris of bomb damage. Work parties are to start among volunteers and the work will afford you the opportunity of fresh air and exercise. A bath will be available to each volunteer after returning from the bomb-site area. You will be approached individually." For the next week, the Camp Authority tried to find cooperative recruits. Not a single POW agreed.

Outside Hỏa Lò Prison, Operation Rolling Thunder entered its third summer. On the occasion of Hồ Chí Minh's seventy-seventh birthday— May 19, 1967—the North Vietnamese captured eleven downed naval aviators, adding overcrowding to the many problems in Little Vegas. The POWs knew the swelling numbers of new prisoners meant an escalated bombing pace—a tidbit that restored some hope even as it led to less food and more crowded conditions. Harry Jenkins, one of the POWs confined in Little Vegas, considered the raids a good sign; the United States would finally make Hanoi submit. Naturally good-spirited and renowned for his sense of humor, Harry pronounced most everything a good sign. If another year passed without release, he had one year less to wait for repatriation. More torture meant that U.S. battlefield success required more propaganda. Every piece of fruit signaled homecoming, every bombing halt indicated peace. Harry's unflagging positive spin inspired even the most despondent of prisoners. While he offered encouragement to others, Harry suspected—correctly—that North Vietnam had still not released his name as captured; he'd never been allowed to write a letter to his family. He secretly believed they would never send him home.

As more POWs arrived, the Camp Authority reshuffled Little Vegas. On May 21, they pulled Jim Mulligan into a quiz room where Jerry Denton joined him. Just seeing each other excited both men, who had spent most of their sentences without companionship. Both aviators sat down before Greasy, the junior officer currently administering Little

Vegas. He announced, "The camp is very crowded with American prisoners. The camp commander permits you to live together. You must
obey the regulations of the camp and not communicate." The news
stunned Jim and Jerry, but they were grateful. "Thank you," Jim said,
and they followed a guard to an 8-by-4-foot room with two stacked
bunks in Stardust. For the first time since their arrival, they would live
with another American. Mosquitoes filled the room and thick woven
mats covered the window, but Jim offered a prayer of thanks and fell
asleep contentedly after a real conversation, happy for companionship.

Inside their room, Jim Mulligan soon discovered the downside of
cohabitation. For months, dysentery and worms had given his digestive
tract fits, but the pungency of his diarrhea affected only him. With
Jerry in the room, Jim was embarrassed every time he used his bucket.
"Hell, Jim," Jerry said, "forget it; we're lucky to be alive. All of Vietnam
smells, not just this cell."

In their new arrangement, one of the men could communicate
while the other cleared. Jim spent long stints on the floor, checking
beneath the door for guards and flashing messages with his hand to the
cell across the hall by moving his hand in and out of the light coming
from under the door.

At the same time, Jerry whispered through the mats covering the
window and tapped to other Stardust cells. They soon established contact with an aviator from the *Enterprise*, Eugene "Red" McDaniel, who'd
been shot down on May 19; Jerry knew McDaniel from Virginia Beach.
Via neighboring POW Scotty Morgan, McDaniel briefed Jerry on the
war's progress.

General William Westmoreland now had 448,000 troops at his
disposal in South Vietnam. They were backed by a massive logistical
system, an array of advanced aircraft, and stockpiles of modern and
deadly munitions. Westmoreland pursued a search-and-destroy strategy that rapidly inserted well-supported U.S. fighting units throughout
the countryside. The general used enemy body count as one measure of
progress, and Communist casualties did pile up, but North Vietnam
would pump 100,000 fresh troops into the South during 1967 and each
year thereafter. "Born in the North to die in the South" became a frequently used expression among North Vietnamese. Efforts to win over
peasants were also largely unsuccessful, and some cynical U.S. officers
summarized the reality by saying, "Grab 'em by the balls, and their

hearts and minds will follow." Bombs and herbicides displaced thousands of farmers, pushing them into poverty and inadvertently creating support for the insurgency. So despite the mounting Communist casualties, the Americans made little real progress.

Operation Rolling Thunder had now entered its twenty-sixth month, and bombs continued to rain on North Vietnam, but strategic targets like dikes, manufacturing centers, and urban areas remained largely off-limits. Johnson still wanted to avoid an all-out war in North Vietnam, which might upset relations with China and the Soviet Union. Aviators were growing tired of risking their lives for what they considered low-value missions like attacking roads, troops, and trucks. North Vietnam's defenses continued to take their toll on American flyers, as McDaniel's arrival attested. He was the 212th POW to arrive at the Hilton.

McDaniel and Jerry's conversation about the war stretched too long to avoid notice, in Jim Mulligan's opinion. "Jerry!" Jim hissed. "Get off the goddamn wall!"

Ravenous for new information, Jerry didn't stop. McDaniel asked if Jerry knew Jim Mulligan. "Hell yes," he said. "He's lying on the deck clearing under the door for me right now."

"Tell Jim his wife is in Virginia Beach and knows he is a POW," McDaniel said through Morgan. "Father Gallagher says they are all praying for him aboard *Enterprise*."

Then he told Jerry that his family was doing fine, particularly his son Billy. "Your son is burning up Little League," McDaniel said.

"Hot dog!" Jerry exclaimed, just as the cell peephole flew open. An angry guard accused Jerry of communicating. Minutes later, he returned, told Jerry to dress for quiz, and led him out of the cell. Jerry wouldn't return for nine days. He spent the first several days with hands cuffed behind his back and ankles in leg irons, kneeling in a bathhouse stall, baking in the sun. Beatings, hunger, and grotesquely swollen ankles drove a doctor to order him inside Riviera, where he developed a high fever and spent several days and nights blindfolded, in rear cuffs, sitting on a stool. Every time he fell asleep, he'd wake up on the floor, a fresh bump on his head. On July 8, guards at last returned him to Stardust with Jim Mulligan.

The pair lived in relative peace, although in oppressive heat, for the next month. Then one day in August, Jim heard a guard open the peephole on their Stardust cell door. He saw the face of a guard nicknamed Pimples, who motioned for Jim to approach. When Jim walked over and leaned toward the open peephole, Pimples spit in his face. Jim didn't hesitate for a second and hawked a glob of phlegm into the guard's right eye.

"You son of a bitch!" Jim yelled.

"What's wrong, Jim?" Jerry asked, hearing the shout.

"Pimples got me up and spit in my face, so I got him back right in the eye."

"Jim, it's time to take a crap, whether you have to or not, because they're going to come back and punish us. They'll be here in minutes; the comm purge"—the campwide communication crackdown—"must be on good. Pimples didn't come here to do that; he was sent here."

They both used their bucket; they figured they'd be in stocks soon, which made bowel movements much trickier. Thirty minutes later, just as Jim finished his business, guards arrived and locked the two friends in stocks, as expected, Jerry on the top bunk, Jim on the bottom. One night soon thereafter, the guards placed their shared latrine bucket out of reach. Jim heard Jerry wake up and moan, "Jim, I have to piss so bad I can't stand it." With the bucket out of reach, Jim drank the last drops of water in his cup and handed it up to Jerry.

"Use this," he said. "It's the only thing I can reach. Besides, I don't want to get wet down here."

When the guards first clamped them in stocks, Jerry Denton had counted the days until September 2, which marked Vietnam's National Day; he knew the independence celebration often included pardons. "We'll be out in twenty-five days," he predicted.

"Oh, I don't think it will be that long," Jim replied.

"Yep, it'll be that long," Jerry had said. He turned out to be correct.

Late in the summer of 1967, Cat decided it was finally time to destroy the American resistance in Little Vegas, and the Camp Authority began to target Jim Stockdale and his network. To counter his directives, they needed to find out what they were and how they spread through the cellblocks, and to quash the POWs' organization, they needed to neutralize its leader. During one quiz, Cat sauntered around the table to Sam Johnson, leered at him, and hissed, "We will make a domestic animal out of Stockdale." Sam sensed the Camp Authority's fury as well as Cat's fear—the American resistance was confounding his plan,

his *orders*, to harness POWs for Hanoi's purposes. Like detectives building a case, the Camp Authority began extracting information about the
communication network from POWs. Unlike in Western investigations,
however, these suspects had no rights and their interrogators had no
limits. During 1967, many POWs experienced what they would recall as
the worst summer of their lives; for eleven, that summer would be a
prelude to their stay in Alcatraz.

On August 6, guards pulled Nels Tanner from his hole in the Mint.
At quiz, Rabbit told him, "Now you will pay for your Clark Kent and
Ben Casey crimes. You will act the part of Clark Kent and Ben Casey in
a movie to help our effort."

"No, I won't," Nels said.

Rabbit called Pigeye, who arrived with nylon straps. Pigeye pulled
Nels's sleeves down his arms to prevent the straps from cutting his skin
or leaving other marks. He spoke soothingly in Vietnamese as he
wrapped the lengths around Nels. While Nels did not understand the
language, he imagined Pigeye told him he would hurt very badly but
only for a short while. Pigeye and Nels both knew nobody could resist
for long when he'd received orders to break a prisoner fully. Pigeye began, and his tortured captive soon agreed to play the role.

Rabbit pressed his advantage. "You must reveal your organization,"
he declared to Nels. "You must tell who is in charge. You must tell his
policies and how he communicates them."

When Nels didn't respond, Rabbit grew angry and shouted, "We
know it is Stockdale! You must admit it. You must tell us his policies
and how they are communicated."

Nels still refused to give up CAG, and Rabbit sought a lesser victory, torturing Nels to confess he communicated with his neighbor in
the Mint. "You have communicated with the man in the next cell,"
Rabbit said. "Admit it! You have talked with him, in the next cell!"

Twisted by Pigeye's ropes, Nels finally submitted. Afterward he
collapsed on his bed and tapped to that neighbor, Jerry Coffee. "Oh,
God, Jerry," he tapped, "I'm so sorry! They worked me over with ropes.
Made me say how I knew Stockdale's policies. I told 'em from you . . .
I'm so sorry, Jerry! I wish I could have been stronger."

Coffee understood what torture could do, and he forgave Nels
immediately. Soon he would face the same questions as the Camp Authority ruthlessly pursued the American leader.

In a different room, five guards tried to coerce Bob Shumaker into appearing in the same propaganda film. The film, eventually released under the title *Pilots in Pajamas*, was produced by an East German documentary crew interested in making Communist propaganda and reinforcing North Vietnam's image as a benevolent captor. Using a large hook in the ceiling, the guards hoisted Shu into the air by his wrists, which they had tied behind his back. Shu couldn't believe his shoulders could handle the strain. He quit worrying about his shoulders when the guards used an iron bar to shove a rag down his throat to silence his screams, nearly suffocating him. The torture session left him coughing blood, bruised, and unable to walk; he crawled back to his cell. He thought he'd avoided participating in the film, but the director simply assigned Shu the role of a badly injured pilot. With no more strength to resist, he played the part.

Shu's resistance did, in fact, foil the filmmakers' original plans. The final script of *Pilots in Pajamas* noted, "Lieutenant-Commander Shumaker also refused to speak [to us]. We certainly would have liked to become acquainted with this pilot's pilot. Because after all Shumaker, before being sent to Vietnam, was a back-up man in the American Astronaut group. But we know why he refused. His camp commander told us. Upon capture Schumaker [sic] fell down on his knees and cried for his life. We understand: The man is ashamed of himself." Shu, who could barely swallow after his torture session, would have offered a different explanation.

After being tortured throughout the brutal summer of 1967, Shu almost envied pilots who had lost their lives at shootdown. Most of those in CAG's inner circle found themselves wishing for death on at least one occasion during that horrific summer as interrogators and their henchmen plied them for propaganda, information, and confessions. Yet Pigeye wouldn't let them die. He waited for them to confess, to write, to read, to perform. To give up Jim Stockdale.

Air Force Captain Ron Storz spent much of the summer in Thunderbird, serving CAG devotedly by passing along his policies and never neglecting an opportunity to defy their captors. He consequently attracted special attention from the Camp Authority and became another victim of the 1967 Stockdale Purge, as POWs called the campaign. By late August, Cat and Rabbit had begun torturing Jim's suspected closest confidants to learn more about the network and to build their case against him. They slowly began to isolate him by removing these accomplices from Thunderbird.

Ron Storz and George McKnight were put in a Desert Inn cell along with two other uncooperatives, Georgia-born marine aviator Orson Swindle and air force Captain Wes Schierman. When Swindle found himself together with Ron and George, he said, "Look, you guys, I've heard about you and I just can't tell you how much I admire you. But I've got to tell you something: I betrayed you up here. I gave them a statement and didn't take torture for it." He had tears in his eyes as he spoke. Swindle had endured ferocious beatings and rope sessions en route to Hanoi and had been starved and sleep-deprived upon his arrival. When Pigeye showed him the ropes, he'd submitted, too weak to take more.

"Orson," Ron said, "don't worry about that."

"Hell," George McKnight responded, "you're looking at the Ernest Hemingway of North Vietnam. When those bastards have you in the ropes, you're going to write!"

Orson laughed and felt better. Now the foursome faced the Camp Authority together.

Throughout his imprisonment, Ron Storz had loathed bowing to guards. He'd perfected giving only the slightest bend or nod possible, and from time to time he would simply not comply. That August, he rallied his three roommates to his cause. They all refused to bow. After several days, Greasy, the supervisor of Little Vegas, had had enough. He ordered his guards to begin taunting the four POWs early on the afternoon of August 21. Then he led the guards into the cell that night to deliver the real retribution. The squad locked each American in stocks, Ron and George on the top bunks and Swindle and Schierman on the bottom ones. They started on Ron, gagging him, tying him with rope, and administering a savage beating. A guard stuffed a rag down Ron's throat with a sheath knife to muffle his cries. The guards worked themselves into a manic frenzy. The blows fell harder. George began yelling on his friend's behalf, crying, "He's no more guilty than I am! If you punish him, you must punish me!" The guards climbed up to his top bunk and rammed a rag down George's throat as well. Then they jumped on his stomach like two men on a trampoline. From their bunks below, Schierman and Swindle realized that if the abdominal trauma didn't kill him, the rag would. George had begun to suffocate. "Stop! You're going to kill him!" they shouted. "Stop it! Torture! Torture! Torture!"

The guards turned their fury on the men locked onto the lower bunks. By this time, other POWs had joined the commotion, yelling and banging on their cell doors in protest. For another half hour, the guards continued their frenzied beatings. When one realized the rag had nearly killed George, he pulled it out. George gagged as his starved lungs sucked in oxygen. The melee lasted until the prisoners simply had nothing left; they could only manage weak grunts as fists and feet pummeled them.

Around 10:00 P.M., the guards herded the foursome into the Little Vegas bathhouse. They put them in leg irons, then tied them in contorted positions with ropes. They left the four men to face North Vietnam's mosquitoes. As the insects assaulted their bodies, faces, ears, and nostrils, they could do nothing but futilely puff bursts of air at the tiny assailants. The mosquitoes feasted on their victims for the next two days. Afterward, the interrogators brought the four battered men to quiz rooms and tortured them for information about Jim Stockdale and the network.

Ron Storz spent the following days recovering on the floor of the Tết Room, an unoccupied utility room between Stardust and the Desert Inn, named in honor of the Vietnamese New Year. He brazenly communicated with occupants of cells that shared common walls; he reported that guards had broken several of his ribs but that he was coping. When a guard caught Ron tapping, he hogtied him. Furious that the North Vietnamese still refused to treat him according to the Geneva Convention, Ron began the first American hunger strike in Hỏa Lò. The Camp Authority relented after three days, likely because they knew that if Ron starved to death, the remaining POWs could hold them accountable when the war ended. With the hunger strike, Ron had discovered his signature method of resistance, his way to influence an otherwise uncontrollable situation.

The staff soon returned Ron to Thunderbird and instructed him to spy and report on "the two black criminals, Stockdale and Johnson." After several days, the Camp Authority gave him a pen and paper to write an indictment of his commanding officer. Simmering with hatred and defiance, Ron took the pen and jammed it into his left arm.

A SNAKE YOU CAN'T KILL

Shortly before the Camp Authority tried in vain to enlist Ron as a spy, Jim Stockdale had been moved down the hallway from Thunderbird Six West to Thunderbird Six East, a larger room in the eastern portion of the cellblock, adjacent to the latrine that separated Thunderbird from the Mint. The navy commander had resigned himself to another stay in solitary when he heard keys rattle in the lock. The door opened, and guards shoved in a stooped, skinny prisoner. Jim grinned, recognizing his friend Sam Johnson. He smothered him in a bear hug before Sam could put down his bedroll and honey bucket. They regarded each other through stinging tears. Jim took in Sam's sallow cheeks and thin frame; his shoulders still hung limply by his sides. Sam saw that Jim's hair was graying rapidly, although it remained as thick as ever, and his tired face made him look twice his age. At least they were together.

The two cellmates immediately began turning their room into a communication hub. Since they shared no walls with other cells, the two whispered directives under their door or out their window, where their voices would carry along the narrow space between Thunderbird and the outer north wall. They'd also use burned matches to write messages on toilet paper, often using dots as code, and hide the notes in bowls of rice being distributed to other inmates or stash them in hiding spots in the bath stalls. Prisoners repeated their orders and distributed their notes throughout Hỏa Lò. Since the Camp Authority still used Little Vegas—Thunderbird in particular—as a temporary facility for new arrivals, Jim and Sam always had new POWs to educate. Their system hummed along until late summer, when the Camp Authority began removing conspirators from Thunderbird. Sam and Jim would listen helplessly as guards rushed into the cellblock and marched out suspects. Slowly, Thunderbird emptied, cell by cell. Jim and Sam became more isolated and more worried. Increasingly, they had to communicate with others via the bath stalls. One would watch for guards while one carefully hid notes or whispered to neighboring bathers. Riskier still, Sam and Jim sometimes whispered loudly down the Thunderbird hallway, hoping to contact prisoners sequestered on the western end.

Despite the purge, each newly arrived POW would soon hear a whisper or find a note in his rice that explained the BACK US guidelines. Eighty-two new aviators joined the colony between May 1 and mid-September 1967, and they all knew the orders came from a senior officer called CAG whom they'd never actually seen. With so many people knowing his edicts, Jim knew he would eventually find himself in real trouble. In August 1967, he finally did.

A young navy pilot, who had only recently joined the POW ranks, faced an interrogation and stubbornly refused to answer any questions about his background or mission. When interrogators asked why he wouldn't respond, he cited the rules of his commanding officer. The interrogator blinked in apparent disbelief—there were no ranks among the prisoners! The Camp Authority held all power. The interrogator immediately summoned Cat, who oversaw the application of ropes and fists until the young man broke. He surrendered the rules and gave up Jim's name. At last, Cat seemed to feel as if he had the evidence or proper cover he needed to go after the crippled, half-starved commander. By breaking Jim Stockdale, Cat aimed to decapitate the American resistance.

Shortly after 8:00 P.M. one August night, Jim and Sam's Thunderbird cell went dark. Lights went out in the hallway and along the exterior wall outside their window. Jim heard hushed voices and soft footsteps outside their door; he sensed the guards were waiting for him to whisper to the neighboring cells. Jim didn't take the bait, and after a period of silence, the peephole flew open with a loud *slap.* A flashlight's beam cut through the dark. A sharp command for silence followed. Seconds later, Rabbit stormed into the room. In the confusion, he and Jim collided. Rabbit sprawled backward into another guard.

"You attack me!" Rabbit screamed. "You will be punished!"

Rabbit slammed the door and left Jim and Sam to ponder their fate. Minutes later, the camp restored power and Rabbit reappeared. "Roll up, Ðán," he commanded. As Jim gathered his pitiful possessions, Rabbit said, "You are instigating a revolt! You and Sông"—Sam—"are threatening to overthrow the Vietnamese government. You are going to be punished."

The accusation astounded Sam. How could two starving prisoners with one good arm between them present any threat to the government of North Vietnam? It didn't matter. Jim bid good luck to Sam and hobbled after Rabbit, who led him to the Mint, the worst cellblock of the entire Hanoi Hilton, not just the Little Vegas section. With Jim securely stowed in Cell Three of the Mint, Rabbit returned for Sam, pulling him out of Thunderbird and shoving him into the Mint's Cell One. Several days later, unable to find any prisoner willing to occupy the Mint's middle cell and spy on the nefarious duo, the Camp Authority moved Sam to the center cell and placed another agitator in his former end cell: Commander Howie Rutledge, who'd already logged one stay in the Mint for an earlier communication infraction. The guards locked all three troublemakers in leg irons. Not that it mattered—the cells were so small, the inmates could scarcely move anyway.

Howie had not forgotten the stench of the Mint. Oppressive heat and humidity combined with the foul smell of the pigsty outside and honey buckets inside made Mint residents constantly fight their gag reflexes. If Howie stood in the cell's center—that is, if he stood on the wooden bunk—only 6 inches of space separated each shoulder from the closest wall. When he lay down, his body nearly stretched the length of the floor. Howie couldn't escape his physical surroundings—nearly two years in Hanoi had taught him this well—but he could control his mind. If he didn't, he'd go mad. So like other POWs, Howie enforced order upon his existence. Each morning, he walked the six-step circuit around his cell, humming old spirituals, pausing after every fifth hymn to offer a prayer. He usually offered prayers for his children, his wife, and his mother. Then he'd recite scripture, those verses he could recall. Some verses he remembered accurately; others he cobbled together as best he could. Such improvised liturgy shepherded him through long days of isolation. Guards constantly patrolled the cellblock's small vestibule, where they could hear telltale taps or open a door's peephole at any moment. With only three cells to monitor, they made communication exceptionally risky.

To sustain himself, Howie relied heavily upon his previous three weeks of happy cohabitation with air force Captain George McKnight in the Desert Inn. The stint together began with McKnight tossing shreds of toilet paper into the air like confetti and the two men toasting each other with their cups of water. By the end of three days, they both had sore throats from talking so much. George's abiding faith had helped Howie remember the value of scripture and prayer. Prior to his weeks with George, Howie had spent 540 straight days in solitary confinement. He had not had a roommate since arriving in Hanoi in November of 1965, when he and Harry Jenkins earned the distinction of being the first senior officers to meet Pigeye. Whereas George McKnight had spent thirty-four days half-buried in his Briar Patch cell's bomb shelter, Howie had spent twenty-eight days locked in the Zoo's Outhouse, surrounded by darkness, insects, and human waste. By the time he had signed a statement—*I am a Yankee imperialist aggressor*—Howie could not even remember how many children he had.

In fact, he and his high school sweetheart, Phyllis, had four, Sondra, Johnny, Peggy, and Barbara—all in Oklahoma, not sure whether he was dead or alive, and certainly not aware of what he actually faced. When Phyllis had turned eighteen, Howie broke navy regulations to marry her; rules forbade students from marrying before they'd graduated flight school, but Howie had avoided getting caught. As their life together progressed, aviation often took priority over family. Howie had become a fixture at the Officers' Club—time he perhaps should have spent at home. During his days in Hanoi, regret preyed upon him. He lamented not spending more time with his family, and he resolved to do better when he returned. He also vowed to renew his faith. He grew up in a Southern Baptist family, but within months of marrying Phyllis, he had stopped attending church—"too busy," he'd always say. In the Outhouse and Desert Inn, Howie crawled back to the Lord. Church became not a weekly event but an hourly one. In their shared Desert Inn cell, George McKnight helped oversee Howie's spiritual reawakening and enabled him to reach back to his childhood to recall scripture, prayers, and hymns. Without the opportunity to renew his belief in God with George, he could not have endured the Mint.

As he smelled the pigsty and sweated in the heat, he also pined for the less-religious aspects of the companionship he'd enjoyed with George. The two men had discovered the rare pleasure of cursing. Since most staff could not understand English, Howie and George expressed themselves by smiling kindly at guards while unleashing torrents of obscenity. It provided immense enjoyment and a rare sense of victory. Before long, though, both agreed their swearing had slipped out of hand, and they decided to spend a full week counting their curses. At week's end, the cellmate with the fewest curses would win a banana. They didn't have a banana, of course; they would have to steal one. As for the morality of stealing, Howie figured they were concentrating on cursing that week—lessons about thievery could come later.

Suspecting the nature of their exchanges with guards, Bug called Howie to quiz. "You have been given very good treatment, very humane," he told the prisoner. "Look, now you have a roommate. You should show gratitude and cooperative spirit."

Howie fired right back, "I spent a year and a half in solitary confinement before I got a roommate! That is the worst form of mental cruelty. Your government signed the Geneva Convention, yet you do not treat us as we are entitled to be treated, as prisoners of war. You are in violation of international law!" Bug did not appreciate the outburst. He soon separated Howie and George and hauled Howie back to the Mint.

In his new cell, Howie started communicating with his neighbor, Sam Johnson. Unfortunately, a guard soon caught him with his ear to his cup, tapping on the wall. The guard cuffed Howie's hands behind his back and locked him to his bed. For five days, he lay flat, cooking in the late summer heat. He sweated through his daily ration of water before noon. Successive hot days without bathing led to boils erupting on every part of his body; many oozed foul-smelling pus. Howie counted sixty that measured an inch or more.

The boils tormented him relentlessly and robbed him of precious sleep, which offered his only escape from the wretched conditions. Curing the boils became an increasing priority in his daily prayers. He found himself in a constant state of misery that had no foreseeable end. Fi-

Howie Rutledge in training at Naval Air Station Pensacola, Florida, 1949.

nally, as he wondered how he could survive any longer, a doctor administered antibiotics to kill the infections. The boils slowly began to heal.

If Howie, Sam, and CAG had been in contact with the underground network humming outside their isolated corner of Hỏa Lò, they would have learned that boils afflicted nearly all the prisoners during the summer of 1967. Ever competitive and always desperate for entertainment, the POWs initiated a contest. With the help of cellmates—when available—they counted their boils and tapped their tallies through the walls. They learned that twenty to forty boils had erupted on the average body. One fair-skinned midwesterner ran away with the title; he counted 243.

Sam Johnson's boils numbered above average, but nobody outside the Mint could have known. The Camp Authority usually permitted the three residents to leave their cells only once a day—and only one by one—to visit the latrines just outside their cellblock, an excursion of less than forty steps. Such endless drudgery took its toll. Sam found it harder and harder to find refuge in God. He never saw other Americans. Days passed without him using his voice. He felt his mind slipping. In federal prison, regulations once limited a prisoner's stay in solitary to nineteen consecutive days—a longer stay could have devastating long-term effects. Sam had passed that limit many times over by 1967. Six days would pass without his ever seeing the sun, which boarded windows effectively blocked. Once a week the guard might allow Sam and his two friends to leave the Mint—still only one at a time—and walk to the bath stalls in the Little Vegas courtyard. Only then could they see the daytime sky. They never saw stars.

Unbeknown to Sam, his wife, Shirley, gazed at the stars on his behalf. On lonely nights back in Texas, she imagined her husband locked away in a Hanoi jail, behind walls and a roof that barred him from seeing the nighttime sky. She would step outside their Texas home and quietly look up toward the heavens and think of Sam, hoping that he had somehow survived. These peaceful moments became her daily gift to him; she could do little else.

On the East Coast, Sandra Storz still waited for word from Ron. She lived near Pease Air Force Base in New Hampshire with her parents, who helped her raise her eight-year-old son and three-year-old daughter. In more than two years, Sandra had received no news from Hanoi or Washington regarding her husband's death or capture; he was still missing. So the package that arrived on her birthday surprised her. On July 29, she opened a large envelope from the U.S. Air Force. Inside, she found a letter asking her to identify the captured pilot in the enclosed photograph from April 1965. It was Ron. Suddenly, she had a new reason to hope.

In San Diego, Howie Rutledge's seventeen-year-old daughter, Sondra, became one of the first POW family members to become a public advocate for American prisoners in Vietnam. She was as outspoken as her father, and government rules about POW families keeping quiet did not sit well with her. As the domestic antiwar movement gained momentum, she felt it was her duty to remind citizens that even if they opposed the war, they shouldn't forget about the servicemen in Vietnam.

The brother of Sondra's close friend Virginia Nasmyth had been a POW since September 1966, and with the help of California congressman Bob Wilson, Sondra and Virginia set up a small office outside San

Diego with two lamps, two phones, and two thick phone books. They started at *A* and began dialing numbers. When people answered, Sondra would say, "We're just calling to remind you to remember our POWs and have concern for our prisoners in Vietnam." Sometimes their calls would spark conversation, sometimes the young women would just receive a polite "thank you." Only rarely did the line go dead. Night after night, the two high schoolers diligently made their calls, building public awareness and hoping their work would help America's POWs.

While Phyllis Rutledge would never become as outspoken as her daughter, she would join thirty-two other San Diego–area POW/MIA wives to form the League of Wives of American Vietnam Prisoners of War. By the end of 1967, the women had new stationery and a post office box. They went to work, sharing information and slivers of hope and commiserating with one another. They weren't yet bucking their orders to say nothing publicly—the Keep Quiet policy the wives regarded with increasing contempt—but with Sybil Stockdale as its leader, this League of Wives began to call attention to America's POW and MIA families. The group started to draw San Diego families together for support, press the government to release more information, and serve as an example for POW/MIA wives in other regions of the country. Their small band would grow and become part of a larger national movement, positioning these women to shape the entire world's dialogue about American POWs—and eventually affect the policies of the North Vietnamese Camp Authority itself.

Oblivious to the stirrings of public concern for POWs and his wife's role in spreading awareness, Jim Stockdale soldiered on in the Mint alongside Howie and Sam. The guards considered Jim the most dangerous criminal in their custody. When he stepped outside the shadows of the Mint, wobbling and squinting as his dilated pupils adjusted to the sunlight, guards adopted what he called the Ted Williams shift. Just as baseball teams would shift defensive postures when the great Red Sox slugger came to bat, the North Vietnamese blocked the other POWs from Jim's influence by clearing the baths and all surrounding areas when they let him out of his cell. His only time outside the Mint—his walk to and from the Little Vegas baths—offered him few signs of other Americans.

One day on the short walk to the bath, the guard gave him a razor and indicated he should shave. Jim welcomed the chance to clear his salt-and-pepper stubble—more salt than pepper now that he'd reached age forty-three—even though the dirty water and lack of shaving cream made the process distinctively uncomfortable. Afterward, as Jim left the stall and started for the Mint, the guard yanked him in the opposite direction, toward the Riviera cellblock and Cat's quiz room. Jim entered the room warily and bowed slightly to a young interrogator named Vy who sat behind the desk. Vy informed Jim that visitors wanted to interview him. He warned that severe punishment would accompany any misbehavior. Jim said little. Before Vy dismissed his prisoner, he leaned across the table, beckoning Jim to move closer. In a hushed voice, he said something Jim would never forget. "You have made a lot of trouble for the general staff officer," Vy warned, referring to Cat. "He is very, very angry. Criminals at camps miles away all know your rules. The general staff officer says that you have set back the Camp Authority two years."

Even as the guard blindfolded him for the excursion to the interview, Jim's spirits soared. Vy had reaffirmed his purpose.

Jim's next battle took place at the Plantation, where Jerry Denton had blinked his T-O-R-T-U-R-E message the previous year. When guards unloaded him from the truck and removed his blindfold, Jim found Cat, Vy, and several men dressed in Western clothes: Russians seeking material for a novel. Jim gave them the minimum and did so hostilely, refusing to look at them. Instead, he fixed his eyes on Cat, glaring at him as he responded to the Russians' questions. Cat spoke to Vy, who rose and walked around the table to Jim. He leaned over and whispered, "The general staff officer says you are to quit looking at him. You are not to look in his direction."

Jim mentally chalked up another small win.

At last, the Russians gave Jim a chance to ask any questions. "Yes, I have a question," he said, looking for an excuse to chat and to annoy Cat. "How are the Russian-U.S. track meets coming?"

Jim saw befuddlement and irritation on every face at the table. In broken English, one Russian scoffed, "Do you mean sport?"

"Yes," Jim said. "I remember seeing a great track-and-field contest between the Soviet Union and the United States at the stadium of Stanford University in 1962. Are they still being held?"

"No, they have been stopped because of the American imperialist war of aggression in Vietnam."

"What was the name of that great Russian high jumper of those years?" Jim asked, amusing himself and wondering when Cat would end the small talk.

"Valeriy Brumel," the Russian replied.

"That's all!" Cat broke in. "The conference is finished."

With several victories tallied that day, Jim returned to the Mint and relayed the day's events to Sam and Howie; he was grateful for their presence on the other side of the wall. While the three couldn't see each other, their secretive taps and whispers sustained them. For that short time, they at least had each other.

One morning in early September, Jim leaned his cup against his cell wall and tapped the letters "GM" to Sam—short for "good morning." Before Sam could respond, Jim heard a loud whoop from the alleyway outside the Mint. A guard had been peering through the window from the watchtower and caught him in the act. As Jim knew, the Camp Authority apparently needed to catch a prisoner breaking a rule before they could punish him. Now that they had caught Jim, he suspected torture—punishment, as the North Vietnamese called it—would soon come. Indeed, the guard came into the Mint and hastily unlocked Jim's leg irons. He shoved him out of the cell and across the courtyard to Cat's quiz room, tucked on the southern side of Little Vegas, just across from Stardust. Greasy met them and pushed Jim onto a floor covered with dirt, debris, and remnants of recent torture sessions. On went the blindfold and handcuffs.

"Why fool around with nonsense like that?" Jim shouted, referring to his small communication infraction. "Let's get on with it. Let's talk about 'BACK US.' 'We all go home together.' 'No repent, no repay.'"

Greasy wasn't yet ready for the interrogation. He ignored the argument and tied a rope tightly around Jim's neck. He handed the loose end to the guard.

For half an hour, the guard beat the navy commander across the dirt courtyard and back again. Every time Jim fell, rocks, sticks, and scrub brush would add to his cuts and bruises. Prisoners in the cells surrounding the Little Vegas courtyard could only listen helplessly as they heard the blows. Covered in dirt and blood, Jim backed away from the hail of fists and boots until he hunkered against the wall of the Desert Inn. The guard pulled him into a standing position and delivered two powerful blows to each kidney, then aimed the capstone punch at Jim's solar plexus. The punch emptied Jim's lungs. He slumped to the ground, defeated. He spent the rest of the day lying in irons on the quiz room's floor. His pain had no single source. It seemed to originate in every nerve and it consumed his body throughout the night.

At 10:00 A.M. the next day, the Camp Authority began a formal interrogation and torture session with a panel of North Vietnamese military officials presiding. They hoped the event would yield a confession and at last break the leader of the American resistance. Guards hauled Jim across the Heartbreak courtyard and into Room Nineteen, the Knobby Room. There, he confronted a panel of six officers he'd never seen. To his rear stood several guards, each armed as if the debilitated commander might try to escape. Off to the side, Jim saw Pigeye and a lumbering apprentice known as Big Ugh. He knew it would be an unpleasant morning.

"I have not been here long," began the lead officer at the table, a senior man called Mao, "but I have heard a lot about you and it's all bad. You have incited the other criminals to oppose the Camp Authority."

With that, Pigeye began the show with a hard slap to Jim's jaw. He received hearty encouragement from his audience and brought out the ropes. Pigeye looped one length around Jim's neck and under his injured left leg. Then he jerked the rope savagely, forcing Jim's head down toward his left knee. The leg began to bow. Pigeye pulled harder and harder, viciously bending the leg in a direction it could not go. Everyone inside the room reacted to an audible *pop*. A new pain, a worse pain shot from Jim's knee through his entire body. Pigeye had not only inflicted immediate hurt, he had crippled Jim for life. With nothing left and absolutely no prospects for relief, Jim gave up the fight.

"I am a war criminal who has wreaked destruction on your country," he testified mechanically after he had recovered. "I have violated the good treatment you have given me by urging others to oppose the camp authority. I confess my guilt and I beg the authority for mercy."

Pigeye had untied the ropes, but the acute throbbing hadn't stopped. It emanated from his knee and half the other joints in his body. The interrogation had ended. The satisfied officers filed out as

Jim lay on the floor, broken physically and, for the moment, spiritually. He would not leave the room for three weeks. A full month would pass before he regained his ability to stand. During those weeks, Greasy and Vy returned time and again to ply him for statements and information of every sort. Whenever Jim resisted—which still happened regularly— Pigeye and Big Ugh were called to employ their ropes. To increase their captive's discomfort, the guards neglected to empty Jim's honey bucket. With his bucket full, he would urinate through the crack under the door or defecate on the floor. He existed like a sick animal, writhing in its own waste, inhaling its own stench, having no control over its lot.

For companionship, he had the countless bugs that thrived in the prison's squalor. Ants crawled over his body, biting him at will. From his position on the filthy floor, he watched as the ants slowly devoured the carcass of a beetle nearby, its stiff legs and brittle belly facing up toward the ceiling. As the ants carried away the beetle's remains, Jim couldn't help but draw the parallel to his own plight, his body and spirit confined and slowly consumed by this awful place. His captors seemed too cruel to let him die, however. Unlike the beetle, he could find no escape.

In a happier time, Jim was a lieutenant commander, fresh from deployment, taking graduate courses at Stanford University. One day in 1962, he ventured into the Philosophy Department. He heard a resonant voice say, "Can I help you?" The voice came from Philip Rhinelander, a Harvard-educated attorney and World War II navy veteran who taught "Philosophy 6: The Problems of Good and Evil." Rhinelander had immediately liked the square-jawed graduate student and allowed him to join his class midterm, provided Jim report for weekly tutorials at his home. Thus Jim began a course of instruction that proved every bit as important to his survival as anything he learned in the navy. Philip Rhinelander introduced him to Job and Epictetus.

The Old Testament tells of Job, a faithful and wealthy man in southern Israel. He has always honored the Lord and lived without sin, but Satan craftily challenges God that Job would forsake him if he lost his bounties. To prove Job's devotion, God allows Satan to unleash a series of calamities upon this devout believer. When misfortune befalls Job, his friends urge him to forsake God, but Job refuses. He had accepted God's blessings without question; he could accept his tragedies as well. Then, as the trials never seem to end, Job finally questions God.

The Lord forcefully explains to Job that man must always stay faithful to God's larger vision and trust that he plays a role in the Lord's plan, a plan man can never fully comprehend. From that point, Job keeps faith, and in the end, God restores his blessings. While in Hỏa Lò, the story of Job helped Jim to stop wondering, "Why me?" He didn't search for some past transgression that had caused his condition. Like Job, he would learn to trust in God.

While Job taught Jim Stockdale to accept his fate, Epictetus showed him how to endure it. When Jim and Rhinelander said good-bye at the semester's end, the professor gave his pupil a copy of the *Enchiridion*, a handbook for the teachings of Epictetus, a former slave in Ancient Greece who became a leading Stoic philosopher. "As a military man," Rhinelander told Jim, "I think you'll have a special interest in this. Frederick the Great never went on a campaign without a copy of this handbook in his kit." As Jim would in North Vietnam, Epictetus had a knee shattered in battle and left untreated by his captors. The philosopher understood that a man's most important and desperate struggles often lay inside himself, that physical discomfort could never equate to the deep, lasting emotional anguish brought on by a failure to fulfill one's duty. Epictetus taught that to uphold his charge and avoid that inner misery, every man must play his role in life as best he can. He cannot choose his role, however. That responsibility lies elsewhere. In that sense, Jim understood that his own thoughts and actions posed the real danger. During his long days in prison, he divided his mind into two compartments, as Epictetus taught: one for things he could control and another for things beyond his power. He could always control his attitude, his opinions, his goals, and his actions. He could *not* control what Rabbit or Cat might do, when the war might end, or from where he would fight that war. Other powers dictated those things for him. In Hỏa Lò Prison, Jim found solace and strength in the lessons of Epictetus and Job. He accepted his circumstance yet resolved to fight on.

He wasn't always alone. His men endeavored to support their commanding officer during his hardest times. On one of the long days he spent on the floor, Jim heard a prisoner snapping his washcloth in the nearby bath area. He listened intently as the snaps spelled out G-B-U-J-S: "God bless you, Jim Stockdale." The message reminded him of why he endured, why he resisted. Jim's resolve stemmed not so much from faith or patriotism or family, but rather from his duty to his fellow POWs. The snapping rag, this message from his troops, rallied his spirits and readied him for his next match with Greasy and Vy.

In the weeks since the formal interrogation, the two officers had continued to interrogate Jim in Room Nineteen. From their questions, he soon deduced that the authorities planned to piece together a picture of the American chain of command for a formal indictment. In particular, they wanted a list of the "central committee" in the Stockdale organization. Jim protested that no such committee existed. "I issued the orders," he said. "They were carried out. The men to whom I addressed the orders had no choice but to obey them; that is military law."

Still his interrogators demanded names. Big Ugh wrapped ropes around his arms. Over CAG's continuing refusals, his tormentors chanted, "Who? Who? Who?" The ropes squeezed and contorted their victim until he complied. After CAG at last uttered *"bào cào,"* he asked for a pencil, paper, and time. When he regained his abilities, he began writing, "James Stockdale. Jeremiah Denton. Harry Jenkins . . ." He listed POWs in order of rank until his list held 212 names.

The extensive list astounded the staff. They had no idea that Jim—or any prisoner—had memorized the names of so many POWs; the detention system now held a total of more than 270. It reminded the Camp Authority that if a POW died in captivity, from causes natural or otherwise, Americans would know it, and one day reckoning might come. Jim's long list also confounded the officials, who still insisted a central committee must exist. Jim did his best to explain, saying, "This is our organization. It is a lineal responsibility list. It is like a snake you can't kill—the head will always grow back: Take me out and Denton will take over; take Denton out and Jenkins will fill in."

Still under pressure to identify a central committee, Jim looked down the list, past the names of navy commanders and air force lieutenant colonels, which were equivalent military ranks. When he reached the last of these senior officers, he drew a line. Everyone above the line, he explained, served on the central committee. That satisfied the cadre only temporarily. They came back, demanding more information about the senior leaders. CAG wrote statements that read like glowing performance reviews. "Jeremiah A. Denton, Jr., Comdr., USN, served under

my command . . . has carried out all of my orders in a forthright manner, and thereby opposed the camp authority. He organized communications in his cellblock so as to execute my orders . . ."

He continued praising Denton as well as Jenkins, Rutledge, and
Mulligan; he reasoned the Camp Authority already knew these men
were troublemakers, and by giving up their names, he could protect
junior officers like Coker, McKnight, and Storz. The cadre wanted more.

"You are obscure," they charged. "You have not given details on
what these people did, and when they did them."

"I would not know such details," Jim answered. "I issued general
orders. The details are up to my subordinates. That is our military
custom."

The interrogators still demanded incriminating information. "You
have not said which of these men has the capability of doing damage to
the Democratic Republic of Vietnam," they complained. To the end of
his report on each senior man, CAG simply added, "He also has the
capability to do damage to the Democratic Republic of Vietnam."

"Now you must beg the mercy of the Vietnamese people," they
told him and presented a typed statement as an example. CAG wrote
and signed a propaganda statement, interlacing oddly worded phrases
like "I want to thank you for saving my life from death" to indicate his
insincerity, and the matter seemed finished.

Sometime around October 1, guards entered Room Nineteen,
which had housed their arch criminal for the past three weeks. They
lifted him from the floor and half walked, half dragged him back to
Little Vegas. They shoved him into the first cell in Riviera. He fell face
forward onto the hard floor and collapsed. A guard called Drut ("Turd"
spelled backward) cuffed Jim's hands behind him, then cinched on a
blindfold. The guards left him alone, unable to see, unable to stand,
barely able to sit upright. He could only move by sliding like a worm
along the smooth concrete, which would soon be covered in his own
filth. With his hands cuffed behind his back, he could not even swat at
the mosquitoes. Nor could he send messages to other POWs. He had no
idea when or if this existence would end. There in his dark Riviera cell,
on the edges of the Little Vegas courtyard, Jim Stockdale became Job,
seemingly forsaken by his country and his God. Drawing inspiration
from the biblical story, Jim refused to abdicate faith in either. He humbly accepted his role and the reality of his present situation, yet he

would never stop believing that he would ultimately triumph. He didn't know how long he would remain in Hanoi and tried not to speculate; it was beyond his control. He locked those distracting thoughts away; they'd only divert the precious focus he needed to complete the task at hand: leading his men until they returned home, their honor intact. He readied himself for the worst and forced himself to recognize that his deplorable condition would not change until his captivity ended— either with a ticket home or with his death on the floor of Riviera One.

Over in the Mint, Sam Johnson continued his own depressing existence. The only human voice Sam or Howie Rutledge heard came from the hostile guard who delivered two daily meals and escorted the captives 40 feet to the latrine. Every morning, slivers of daylight passed through the boards covering the high barred windows. Two spiders occupied the corners of the window, spinning intricate webs that, to Sam, became art. Each morning he gently tugged down the webs, carefully leaving the artists with a blank canvas so he could pass the next hours watching them weave new masterpieces. "Howie," Sam whispered to his neighbor, "I got a construction job going on in here. It's pretty interesting. Watch the spiders in your cell. It passes the time."

"Yeah," responded Howie. "And you can eat 'em, too. It's pure protein. Not bad. Try some." The idea proved tempting, but Sam could never eat his only companions.

By late summer 1967, Sam had withered from 190 pounds to barely 130. He could see the outlines of his bones against his skin. He had no energy and spent his days lying still, trying to conserve the few calories his body could digest from his diet of watery vegetable soup and occasional pieces of fat. The less he moved, however, the tighter depression and despair gripped him. Mental fatigue gained parity with hunger in his list of tormentors. He began slowly to lose his mind.

In August, a guard summoned him to quiz with Chihuahua. "You are in very great trouble, Sông," the little political officer said. "We are very angry with you. Your collaboration with Stockdale is going to make things very bad for you . . . Your attitude is very bad. You cannot afford to continue in this manner. You are already in very great trouble."

Chihuahua's charge utterly perplexed Sam. He thought to himself, "I'm sweating and starving to death in a tiny cell, completely cut off from everyone, and I'm in great trouble?" Sam remained stoic and nonchalant, but his mind strained to imagine what sins he'd apparently committed—or how the North Vietnamese could punish him any further. He lived in a sweltering, almost suffocating box, befriended only by spiders, preyed upon by insects. Guards had boarded his window. He slept on a bamboo mat laid on a dirty bunk. His broken shoulders and arm had healed slowly and poorly. Hunger constantly gnawed at him and weakened him more each day. The renewed vigilance of the Mint's guards had effectively ended communication between him and Howie Rutledge; he had no contact with other prisoners. Like every other POW, he had no idea if he'd ever leave. What trouble could he possibly cause, and how could it get worse?

"You are to be punished," Chihuahua pronounced. "You must be put in leg stocks. Probably you will be locked in them for the rest of your imprisonment."

With his best effort, Sam acted as if he didn't care. His reaction infuriated Chihuahua, who accompanied Sam and a guard detail back to the Mint. They pushed him into his cell and pulled him to a sitting position, with his legs stretched out in front of him. They set his ankles in the open stocks and swung the top closed. The bindings fit tightly around his ankles and pressed into his skin. Chihuahua surveyed the rig and warned the guards not to unlock the stocks, no matter what Sam might say. Then they left Sam alone.

He could either lie flat on his back or sit up with his legs straight in front of him. The tight stocks and chafing around his ankles made any significant movement challenging, although he forced himself to do straight-legged sit-ups on occasion until the discomfort in his ankles and his emaciated hips drove him to stop. Before the month ended, pus seeped from infected cuts around his ankles. Days stretched on without end, one after another. Sometimes, he lay still, neither feeling nor seeing. He didn't even swat at the mosquitoes and insects that played on his clammy skin. At other times, moments of claustrophobic panic seized him. He clawed at himself in a desperate yet futile rage. He never bathed; he disgusted himself. Days passed with slow indifference, one by one, until he had spent seventy-four days in the stocks. On the evening of that seventy-fourth day, he had nothing left: no spirit, no strength, no will, no hope. He fell asleep thinking, "It would be okay if I never woke up again."

That night a storm raced through Hanoi. Its winds ripped the boards off Sam's window. Fresh rain blew inside, and he began praying fervently, inspired by the tempest outside. Morning found a clear sky over Hỏa Lò Prison, and daylight spilled into his cell for the first time in more than two months. He felt peace. He recalled Lamentations 3:22–23, which he learned as a boy: "It is of the Lord's mercies that we are not consumed, because his compassions fail not. They are new every morning: great is thy faithfulness." The morning restored his hope, and Sam once again believed he would survive. Later that day, a guard entered the cell and unlocked the stocks. The metal bar swung up to reveal deep, bloodied indentations around his ankles. Sam reached to massage them. The guard hit him with a rifle.

"Get up," he ordered. "Dress up!"

Sam couldn't move. His muscles had atrophied, and two guards had to drag him out of the Mint. Sam's frail legs trailed across the Vegas courtyard as two North Vietnamese took him to the Riviera cellblock, where Jim Stockdale had spent the past weeks. Sam once again faced Chihuahua. The officer announced, "Stockdale has confessed."

"What are you talking about?" Sam answered, knowing that if Stockdale confessed to anything, the Camp Authority had tortured him.

"He has confessed to everything you and he have been doing in this camp to instigate revolt and disobedience."

"If he has confessed to anything it is because you forced him, you made him," Sam rejoined, watching Chihuahua's temper rise. "He didn't do anything voluntarily."

"That is not so. Here, see for yourself." He placed the signed document in front of Sam, who studied it. The typed words said that CAG and his collaborators aimed to overthrow the government of North Vietnam; that they ran a pervasive communication network contrary to the regulations of the Camp Authority. A nearly illegible signature followed the type. "Please, God, let him be all right," Sam thought. "Oh, God, help him." He knew CAG must have suffered mightily as interrogators extracted the statement.

"That may be his signature," Sam told Chihuahua, "but I can tell from the way it's written that it was forced from him."

"You must write your confession now," Chihuahua responded.

"You don't need anything from me if you've got Stockdale's," Sam said in his calm southern drawl. "I'm not going to write anything. If you want anything from me, you'll have to force me."

Sam watched Chihuahua's anger flare. He marched around the

desk and looked Sam in the face. "You are very obstinate," he said, then paused before continuing. "This camp has decided you are to be killed. Go back to your cell!" The guards began to return him to the Mint, but Chihuahua stopped them. "Before you die," he added, "the camp authorizes you to shower and shave."

Like a death row inmate about to eat his last meal, Sam stumbled into the Little Vegas bathhouse with his soap and razor. The flow of water over his filthy body made him forget about the death sentence, his second since arriving in North Vietnam. Even the tepid water felt divine as it washed away months of foulness. If the Camp Authority had fated him to die, at least he would meet his fate with some measure of cleanliness.

Once he returned to his cell, he debated his future. His thoughts alternated between peace with death and mistrust of Chihuahua. He'd wished for death just days earlier, and if it came now, he could accept it. In a way, it would bring relief, allowing him to escape the horror of his captivity. Shortly after his shootdown, he'd entrusted his life to God. Now, at what might be the end, his faith did not waver. Sam was prepared for death—but the Camp Authority did not plan to kill Sam Johnson. They had concocted something even worse.

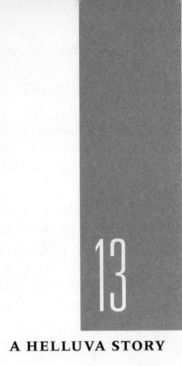

A HELLUVA STORY

With the prisoner population continuing to grow, the North Vietnamese built new facilities to house their captives. One location satisfied two needs: additional cells and strategic protection. In the summer of 1967, they moved more than thirty downed airmen into makeshift cells around the Yên Phú thermal power plant, which sprawled across five blocks not far from central Hanoi and had become a target for U.S. air strikes. Uncharacteristically, they let journalists and the public know exactly where they held these Americans so the information would trickle back to the U.S. military. The prisoners began their service as human shields.

They felt more like coal miners. When George McKnight arrived at the complex, he found himself in a small cellblock nicknamed Dirty Bird. Layers of coal dust rose from bins outside and blanketed the grounds, walls, floors, and often his own hair and skin. One inmate reported that the dust collected on his shoulders like black dandruff. George almost felt sorry for the Vietnamese families who'd previously made their homes in these rooms that the Camp Authority had converted to prison cells. At one time, Dirty Bird's eight rooms had had sizable windows, but they'd been sealed with bricks for the prisoners. Without ventilation, the rooms became oppressively hot.

After McKnight arrived in September, the guards occasionally pa-
roled him to a row of open-air enclosures across the corridor. These
cells—more like stable stalls—offered a slight reprieve during the
suffocating afternoons.

As he idled in a stall one day, locked in place with handcuffs, he
discovered a sliver of wire within his reach. He used it to pick the lock
on his cuffs. For several minutes, he just enjoyed the simple freedom.
Then he couldn't resist standing up and peeking cautiously down the
walkway outside. He found it deserted. Trusting providence and following his own sense of daring, he ventured out and walked quietly
along the corridor. He found an American slumbering away in another
stall. McKnight began shaking what appeared to be a young James
Cagney. Startled, twenty-four-year-old George Coker woke up and saw
6'2" McKnight looming before him. Coker, still groggy, thought he saw
an angel.

Soon, the two men began talking of escape. Dirty Bird presented a
unique situation. The guards wanted U.S. reconnaissance to report
POWs near the power plant, so they made Coker and McKnight carry
buckets or empty milk jugs on regular and very public excursions to
fetch water from a spigot several blocks away. To accomplish this, they
shouldered a long pole from which hung the buckets. They tapped the
pole gently as they walked, sending code to each other right under
their escorts' noses. Along the route, the POWs spotted the steel structure of a bridge not far from the prison. Coker had served as bombardier-
navigator and had spent hours studying the layout of Hanoi. He
remembered enough to know they were looking at the Long Biên
Bridge—formerly known as the Paul Doumer Bridge—which spanned
the Red River. The river, he recalled, flowed from China, through
Hanoi, and into the Gulf of Tonkin.

Typically, POWs never knew their location within Hanoi, but
now McKnight and Coker did. They knew how to reach the river,
which could provide a viable escape route. Further, since Coker and
McKnight were the sole inhabitants of their cellblock, the Camp Authority couldn't charge other POWs with conspiracy. Even with
those unique advantages, they had to consider any scheme to escape
from Hanoi a long shot—but the two companions had nothing to
lose.

George Coker, whose daring fifteen-mile escape attempt assured his sentence to Alcatraz.

"Look, this prison is a house of cards," Coker said to McKnight, trying to instigate the escape. "We could get out of here real easy."

Skeptically, McKnight replied, "Yeah, then what?"

"We go down there to the Doumer Bridge," Coker explained. "The river has to be running through there. We get to the river, swim down the Red River at night, get to the coast, steal a boat, and sail out there. I know where the carriers are and the flight patterns, and we'll go out there and get rescued."

To the older McKnight, the scheme sounded far-fetched. He couldn't foresee how they would ever make it out of Hanoi, let alone reach the Gulf of Tonkin. How would they make it to the river? Where would they find food? How would they avoid the peasants who traveled the river and fished its banks? How would they signal the fleet? McKnight pondered these questions during the coming days as the two debated the idea. A year as a POW had not affected Coker's determination, and he had a ready answer to each objection McKnight raised. Even so, he wasn't convincing McKnight. In fact, he never did.

McKnight never believed an escape attempt would work, but he knew that never trying would haunt him. He pictured himself returning home and having to confess, "I thought it couldn't be done, so we never tried." He considered himself better than that. Besides, escape ran in his family.

From the day in 1864 when George McKnight's great-grandfather Melvin Grigsby marched through the palisades of Georgia's Andersonville prison, he thought of little but daily survival and escape from the crowded plain that would claim more than 12,000 Union soldiers. Fortunately, when Confederate guards uncovered his first tunneling operation, they didn't catch Grigsby in the tunnel, and he avoided the progressive series of three punishments meted out by the guards: hanging by thumbs, languishing in leg and arm stocks, and finally joining the chain gang, where each weak and starving member had to drag a cannonball wherever he went. His next attempt came months later, after being transferred to Florence, South Carolina. As the Confederate guards assembled Andersonville arrivals at the Florence train station, Grigsby washed himself and donned white pants and a clean shirt he'd acquired. As the column of dirty Union captives marched toward the new camp just outside the city, Grigsby slyly fell out and simply became a local, blending in and sharing his views on the new Yankee prisoners. He surreptitiously faded into the background as the column moved on without him. Then he struck out for the coast. Along the way, his Virginia and Kentucky ancestry made him virtually indistinguishable from South Carolinians. His great-grandson would have much more difficulty blending into the local citizenry of Vietnam.

McKnight and Coker estimated the trip to the coast would take seven days. Both considered escape a long shot at best, suicidal at worst, but they were tired of being tortured and wasting away in filthy cells so far from home. As the war dragged on, escape seemed like the only way they might ever return. Above all, Article III of the Code of Conduct demanded that they make the attempt, even against long odds.

They'd need the cover of night, so they'd first have to unlock the cells where they slept. The simple locking mechanisms in Dirty Bird consisted of two iron pins, each a half inch in diameter with a loop at one end. The jailers had fastened one pin to the outside door frame so the iron loop at its head extended in front of the cell door, hovering over the loop of a perpendicular pin, which they had driven through the 2-inch thick door in place of a traditional handle. A simple metal hook or padlock would drop through the two loops, locking the pins together and trapping the prisoner in his cell. The jailers had driven the second pin through the cell door and pounded the protruding end into the back of the door with a hammer, effectively locking the pin in place. The would-be escapees scavenged sharp, pencil-sized pieces of metal that they employed as chisels and began digging into the wood around the ends of the pins. Eventually, they each freed the bent end so they could straighten the pins. Then they dug into the wood around the pins themselves. Once they sufficiently loosened the pins from the back, they could slide them out as they opened their doors inward. A padlock would still conjoin the heads of the two pins, but the second pin would no longer hold the door. The prisoners could simply walk out. On October 12, 1967—Columbus Day back in America—they decided to go.

After the guards finished one of their late-evening rounds, the escape began. The two conspirators placed trash they'd collected during the preceding days on their sleeping mats, then covered the rubbish with their blankets. In the dim light, a guard would think the prisoner still slumbered away on his mat. Coker and McKnight wanted to put as much distance as possible between themselves and Dirty Bird before the authorities discovered they were missing.

They both picked their handcuffs, and George Coker opened his cell door, gently pulling the door away from the lock, feeding the pin through the dug-out hole. The cell door silently pulled clear of the pin and left it dangling from its mate, now joined by a useless padlock. Coker stepped cautiously into the corridor and pulled the door closed, reinserting the pin and jamming it fast. As planned, he then knocked on McKnight's door, and the air force captain repeated the procedure. As McKnight knelt in the dark hallway and relocked his door from the outside, Coker's hand suddenly clenched his shoulder. Startled, he looked around and saw Coker, eyes wide and index finger pressed against his lips. He pointed to the hallway's end, where a guard had just walked into the latrine. They froze and watched him walk back into the guards' quarters. His eyes never shifted to the right or left. Had the guard proven more alert, the escape would have been short-lived. With the guard gone, Coker relaxed his grip and both men breathed again. They began creeping along the compound's interior walls, staying in the shadows until they climbed onto a roof.

Since the architects had originally designed Dirty Bird as part of a power plant, not a jail, its walls aimed to keep people out, not in.

Consequently, the pair made a relatively easy exit. Workers had piled crates and equipment alongside the buildings and walls, so climbing to the rooftop proved simple. After a short, soft-footed walk along the roof, they hopped onto another inner wall, climbed down a stack of boxes, and raced across a final stretch of ground to the outer wall. They scrambled up a mound of dirt and debris, swung over the wall, and dropped onto the street. From the time they'd arrived in Dirty Bird, it had taken Coker and McKnight less than three weeks to escape.

On the street, nothing stirred. They took a collective breath and began darting from cover to cover, navigating their way toward the river. They snuck along streets to the upper bank of the river and its floodplain. They slipped down a mud slope into the marshy bottom-land where they could hide in the shadows. As the two airmen crept through the paddies and marsh grass, scaling small dykes along the way, McKnight turned to Coker and said, "You know, George, someday you're going to have a helluva story to tell your grandkids."

"Right," Coker whispered back, "but first we gotta live long enough to have kids!"

About two hours after they escaped their cells, they arrived at the Long Biên Bridge. Hanoi's most prominent span practically glowed with floodlights and torches as crews repaired damage from the latest rounds of U.S. bombs. The light fell on the marsh at the river's edge, which the escapees would have to cross. Fortunately, the workers' attention never strayed from the bridge. Nobody heard the crackling of reeds or soft splashes below. Nobody noticed the two fugitives creeping through the grass, sneaking across the mudflat, and slipping into the river.

The escaped prisoners stripped down to their underwear and tied their wrists together with cords they'd taken from a clothesline. Thus conjoined, they eased themselves into the faster current and headed south down the Red River, toward the Pacific Ocean, the U.S. fleet, and sweet freedom. As they swam away from Hanoi center, the sounds of the city faded, as did the lights. George Coker forgot the chill of the river and gazed up at stars he had not seen since he stood on the deck of the USS *Constellation*, fourteen months earlier. For a moment, life became peaceful. The river carried little traffic at such a late hour, so the two men swam with cautious optimism for 15 miles. Six hours after they entered the water, dawn began to break. The sudden transformation of the sky reminded McKnight of Rudyard Kipling's poem "Mandalay."

On the road to Mandalay,
Where the flyin'-fishes play,
An' the dawn comes up like thunder outer China 'crost the Bay.

Dawn on the Red River indeed came up like thunder. One minute, night covered the river. The next, the sun raced into the sky. Activity along the banks increased. Skiffs began plying the currents; fishermen began casting lines and nets into the water to catch their morning meal. The conspicuous swimmers struck out for a deserted section of riverbank. They floated along the bank until they spied a washed-out hole where they could spend the day; they'd wait for nightfall to resume their journey. Exhausted, they pulled themselves from the river and slithered into their hiding place. They found it more cramped than the smallest cells in Little Vegas, but they could hear birds, smell the river, and see open sky above them. They forgot about their fatigue and hunger. For a moment, they had found freedom, of a sort.

Around nine o'clock, George Coker turned to his partner and calmly said, "Well, that's it."

"What do you mean, 'That's it?'" McKnight asked in a whisper.

Coker pointed upward. McKnight followed his friend's hand and saw an elderly Vietnamese man peering down at them, his eyes as wide and surprised as McKnight's own. The man hurried to tell others, and minutes later, locals had surrounded the skinny, wet Caucasians with farm tools and rifles. They put their hands on their heads; their great escape had ended. It was Friday the thirteenth, a date both escapees would forever consider particularly unlucky.

They quickly realized the peasants had absolutely no idea who they were. Nobody spoke the same language. They had nothing to identify them as airmen; villagers just saw two wet, scrawny Europeans in skivvies and T-shirts who'd washed up on the bank. The armed villagers led them to a nearby town, where an even-keeled English-speaking official began to question them. His eyes grew wide when his two captives confessed to escaping from Hanoi; they'd been caught, so neither saw any point in lying. The official listened patiently to their story, seeming more intrigued than angry. He produced a map and asked the Americans to trace their route. "Ah, that's quite a long way," he said. "Twenty-four kilometers!" The 15-mile adventure genuinely fascinated him.

Soon enough, a much less fascinated army officer arrived to escort the pair back to Hanoi, where they passed through the concrete archway of Hỏa Lò Prison, with its carved French appellation, Maison Centrale. Guards threw them into New Guy Village and locked their ankles in irons. Beyond that, however, they were not directly punished for their stunt. In separate interrogations, they told their agreed-upon story: how they unlocked their handcuffs, how they opened their cells, and how they crept through the streets to the river. They hoped that making it clear that they acted with no outside help would mean the Camp Authority would refrain from torturing them for names of collaborators.

When the interrogator asked him why he had tried to escape, George McKnight gave two answers. First, he explained that escape offered the only honorable option since he had surmised the North Vietnamese had aimed to kill him. Second, he argued, "Every soldier has a responsibility to escape capture by the enemy. Even you have that obligation, don't you?"

"This isn't about me," the officer responded defensively. "This is about you." McKnight had made his point.

Coker's interrogation progressed much the same. Like the local official who'd first interrogated them, the officers at the Hilton appeared almost in awe of the escape. They believed the story up to the 15-mile swim downriver. They could never fathom how Coker and McKnight—*Coc* and *Nich*—had swum so many miles. To produce a different, more plausible answer from Coker, they beat him. They cupped their hands as they cuffed his ears, and the resulting bursts of air ruptured both his eardrums. Still, he never changed his answer. The interrogators never would believe the scenario the Americans offered. Coker had spent a full year lying to his captors, and the one time he gave them a truthful answer, they didn't believe him. It didn't really matter; soon Coker and McKnight would no longer be able to cause problems. For the next twelve days, the partners served their time quietly in the Mint, which proved horrible in its confining isolation but much better than the punishment they had expected. Then, on October 25, 1967, the Camp Authority transferred them to a special facility nobody would escape.

14

THE BAD CAMP

Even after three weeks in leg stocks for spitting in the face of Pimples, Jim Mulligan and Jerry Denton could still laugh. One afternoon Jerry rolled over as best he could and said, "Jim, if this place gets any worse, it will be almost as bad as my plebe year at the academy!" Their laughter attracted a guard, who told them to be quiet. They just kept laughing, happy for the companionship that came as more new arrivals crowded into the Hilton, ending solitary confinement for many POWs.

In September, the Camp Authority resurrected the work-release program, and Bug asked the twosome—who had been freed from the stocks—if they wished to get fresh air by working in the city. Wanting to follow CAG's order not to work in town, they replied that they didn't dare leave the camp since they were terrified of the wrath of the Vietnamese people. Since Bug had so often threatened them with that very wrath, he had no response. Their time together in Stardust ended soon thereafter, on October 2. Guards hauled Jim Mulligan into a quiz room where an unknown officer sat behind the table. Three other American POWs crouched on stools before him. Jim looked around, wondering what new manner of harassment the Camp Authority had planned. "Today, I permit you to have roommates," the officer proclaimed. "Do you know each other?"

For the first time, Jim met fellow navy flyers Bob Shumaker and Harry Jenkins. He also met Major Lou Makowski, USAF. Trepidation became surprise, which quickly turned into elation. Jerry Denton, on the other hand, felt only depression as guards locked him inside a solitary cell in the Mint. Jim didn't yet know Jerry's fate, and he anticipated enjoying more companionship than he'd had since arriving in Hanoi. Shu, Harry, and Makowski, already roommates together, welcomed Jim to their Desert Inn cell, which he judged would pass any military inspection. The pair of bunk beds and personal effects were orderly, and the floors and walls were clear of Hỏa Lò's pervasive grime. Jim learned his roommates followed a rigid routine of exercise, conversation, and communication. The next morning, Makowski began doing exercises in front of the cell door, strategically blocking the guards' peephole. Thus shielded, Shu and Harry showed off their current project.

Before Jim Mulligan had arrived, the three roommates had discovered that an adjacent cell held a new arrival who didn't know tap code. To make contact, Shu and Harry used a 5-foot-long piece of copper wire, which they'd found and kept hidden in a small fissure along the wall of their cell. During the afternoon siesta, Shu would snake the wire through another crack and maneuver it across 4 feet of corridor. He threaded it between boxes of unknown materials left by the guards until it slipped through a drain hole that opened into the cell of Charlie Plumb, an F-4 Phantom pilot from the *Kitty Hawk* who had recently arrived in Hanoi. Shu scratched the wire against the metal drain and hoped Plumb noticed. Sure enough, Plumb began hearing what sounded like a cricket, except that it chirped far too regularly. He followed the sound and saw a wire moving rhythmically in the drain. Was it an American? Was it a trick? He debated what to do. Finally, he tugged on the wire.

Shu, holding the wire gingerly, felt the pull. He tugged back. When he received another tug from Plumb, he quickly recalled the wire. He affixed a sheet of toilet paper to its end. On the thin sheet he had copied the tap code's five-by-five grid. Above it, he'd written, "Learn this code then eat this note."

Shu threaded the wire across the corridor once more, and Plumb received the note with his first assignment. During each afternoon siesta, the two cells would communicate with tugs on the wire equating to taps on the wall. For example, two tugs followed by three tugs would indicate the letter *H*. The sensitivity of the wire tested their concentration, but the value of bringing Plumb online far outstripped the tedium and risks of communication. If they failed to bring a new POW into their circle of communication, Shu and Harry knew he would become vulnerable to despair and coercion. They wanted to lift their fellow aviator's spirits, but they also hoped to prevent Plumb from cooperating with the Camp Authority.

The three old roommates also sought to entertain their new cellmate. Harry Jenkins recited well-rehearsed verses of Robert W. Service's famous poem "The Cremation of Sam McGee," which he had committed to memory years ago and had recently practiced by tapping the poem's 888 words through the walls to fellow POWs. The familiar words brought Mulligan a feeling of warmth quite unlike the Arctic cold typically associated with the poem. He relaxed. United with his fellow Americans he could endure whatever the North Vietnamese had planned. His spirits rose day by day. Perhaps, he allowed himself to think, he had seen the worst.

In late October, keys rattled in the lock and the door opened. A guard sharply ordered Harry, Shu, and Jim to dress and gather their belongings, which they obediently rolled into their bamboo mats. The guards blindfolded and cuffed the three naval aviators and marched them toward the open gates of Hỏa Lò Prison. Outside the gates, the POWs heard vehicles idling on the street. Guards lifted Jim Mulligan, Bob Shumaker, and Howie Rutledge, who had been pulled from the Mint, into one truck. They hoisted Harry Jenkins into another. Harry heard another POW being stuffed into the truck bed and whispered his name, "Harry Jenkins."

"Sam Johnson," whispered the other prisoner.

"Shut mouth!" a guard barked.

The little convoy rumbled north through Hanoi, away from the colonial district and toward the Citadel of Thăng Long, the heart of the government sector and headquarters of the People's Army of Vietnam. The convoy turned onto Phố Lý Nam Đế and stopped just behind the Ministry of National Defense. From the sounds and distance traveled, the passengers deduced they had not arrived at the Briar Patch, the Zoo, Dirty Bird, or any other camp they knew existed. The trucks must have taken them to a new facility. A collective sense of foreboding grew among the blindfolded captives, and rightly so. They had arrived at Alcatraz.

Alcatraz (small white buildings at center), looking east.

The French constructed Hỏa Lò Prison to house Vietnamese captives of all types, with special cells for the more dangerous offenders. Yet the colonial administrators had found some political prisoners required more isolation than Hỏa Lò offered, so prior to 1954, they built a small facility a mile north of the main prison, on the grounds of the ancient Citadel. There, in windowless cells, they virtually entombed Vietnamese agitators, leaders, and diehards, keeping them isolated from their countrymen and the outside world. Here, they could neither incite revolution outside nor inspire fellow prisoners inside. With the exception of death, a prisoner could draw no worse fate than being sent to this isolated compound. Unending days and nights in these claustrophobic enclosures could sap the will to live from bold men used to leading others in resistance. The spot became arguably the most dismal prison in North Vietnam.

The North Vietnamese referred to the small compound by its

location—the Ministry of National Defense—or by its address, Number Four Phố Lý Nam Đế. After ousting the French in 1954, the North Vietnamese had closed this dungeon and allowed it to fall into disrepair. In the spring of 1967, they reopened its thirteen cells and began preparing them for American troublemakers. From across the detention system, the Camp Authority had identified the POWs they considered most dangerous, ungovernable, militant, intransigent, and, most importantly, influential with other prisoners. Then they banished these subversives to their darkest hole, where they could rot away, isolated from the men they'd once led and inspired. Essentially, they picked Jim Stockdale and his leadership team.

When the guards pulled Jim Mulligan from the truck, he felt like Jesus in the Garden of Gethsemane, aware that more horrors would soon come but resigned to his fate. He quietly walked through the prison yard's single gate, a heavy wooden door in a concrete wall. With one guard leading him and another following, Jim felt his way down four steps from the street level to the recessed yard. From the bottom edge of his blindfold, he watched his sandaled feet cross packed dirt, patched with weeds. The two guards turned him to the right, then suddenly stuffed him into a cell. Jim heard his cup, mosquito net, and bedroll land on the floor, and then the guards removed his blindfold and cuffs. They stepped back and closed the door. Jim heard the lock slide shut and looked around in horror.

A dim lightbulb revealed pale, plastered concrete walls that arched 9 or 10 feet overhead and surrounded him. The wooden door, braced with iron, had one of the prison system's standard peepholes. Above the door, Jim saw a barred transom covered with a metal plate perforated with holes for ventilation. A thin electrical wire snaked through one hole to fuel the dim bulb that he learned would burn all night. A second wire ran through another hole to a small speaker, which would relay the voice of Hanoi Hannah. Through the other holes came a steady flow of insects, led by mosquitoes, attracted by the light and the new human presence. The cell's width measured less than 4 feet. With his right shoulder against one wall, Jim could touch the other with his left hand. The cell ran 9 or 10 feet in length, with 6 feet occupied by a short bamboo bed frame on an elevated concrete slab. The solid walls had no windows. A rusty latrine bucket waited by the door.

Jim had just begun pondering his fate when he heard "shave and a haircut" tapped through his wall. He responded with "two bits" and learned that Jim Stockdale, CAG, occupied the adjacent cell. Earlier that day, CAG had been degraded, maimed, and entirely dispirited on the floor of Riviera One. He had been close to a complete breakdown. By moving him to this new camp, the Camp Authority had unknowingly missed their chance to subdue their nemesis permanently. Now reunited, the two senior officers could reach nobody else through the walls, and neither had much energy remaining, so they exchanged "GN GBU" taps and began their evening rituals. CAG lay back on his thin mat, and his mind started working on this new puzzle. He and Mulligan were together in an unknown jail, along with a small number of other prisoners he'd heard shuffling in throughout the evening. Tomorrow he hoped to learn the full lineup. Searching his mind for more clues, he recalled a threat Rabbit made five months prior, as he announced the Fink Release Program. Over the speakers in Little Vegas, Rabbit had warned that the Camp Authority was preparing a place for the worst American criminals—those diehards who refused to cooperate and who incited others. Had Rabbit made good on his threat? CAG found himself anxious to see what dawn would reveal.

For his part, Jim Mulligan rigged his mosquito net, said his prayers, and reflected on the day. He missed the camaraderie he had enjoyed the previous night in the Desert Inn. Now he had no friends to whom he could speak the simple phrase "Good night." He couldn't watch the slow breathing of other Americans at rest and feel the fleeting sense of normalcy provided by the rising and falling of their chests. He recalled how Rabbit had summoned him to quiz at the Zoo in June 1966 and promised small solitary cells to those who led the resistance. Like CAG, Mulligan wondered if he'd been referring to these very cells. The day had drained him; his mind needed rest to digest his new circumstances. For the third time that day, he made himself recite his memory bank of POWs, which now far exceeded 200 names. Then he fell into an emotionally exhausted sleep.

Suddenly, his ears detected keys rattling and a lock sliding—the most feared sounds in a prisoner's universe; they often meant that something bad would soon follow. From Jim's opened doorway, a voice yelled, "Get up!"

Jim turned to find Louie the Rat glaring at him. Called simply Rat by most Americans, the pointy-faced officer spoke English quite well. At

Rat's appearance, Jim hurried out from beneath his netting and bowed. The terror of what might happen next made him shiver, even in the warm air. His heartbeat quickened and he broke into a sweat. He waited.

"You are in the bad camp," Rat announced. "Tonight my guards will put you in the leg shackles as punishment for all your bad deeds."

Once Rat had made his pronouncement, a guard entered and placed Jim's ankles into 15-pound leg irons like those Nels Tanner had worn for 123 days. After the staff left, Jim lifted the irons around each foot as he slowly made his way back to his bed. He'd lift an iron, slide his foot forward, then repeat with the other foot. After making it across the small floor, he had to pull his weighted legs onto the bed and under the mosquito netting. In his weakened state, none of these maneuvers came easily. His body weight had plunged close to 100 pounds, and his formerly strong legs had withered to twigs. When he lay down, he realized the guard had fastened the irons backward. The straight bar rested heavily against his shins all night as he lay on his back—the only position the new rig permitted. The bar had rubbed his ankles raw by morning.

On that night of October 25, 1967, when the Camp Authority had come for the men who threatened them most, guards had walked Sam Johnson through the same gate Jim Stockdale and Mulligan had entered, but they had shoved the Texan into a different cellblock. When guards removed Sam's blindfold, he found himself in the dark, with only thin streams of light passing through the small holes in the metal plate above the door. He took a step forward and banged his shin into a solid object. Still handcuffed, he toppled facefirst onto the concrete sleeping platform where the guard had tossed his bedroll and other personal effects. The platform rose about 14 inches above the floor and stretched from wall to wall. Sam estimated that the platform covered 6 feet of the cell's entire length, which he pegged at around 10 feet. Like Jim Mulligan's cell, the width measured roughly 4 feet—although Sam's two arms were fairly useless as instruments of measure since his slowly healing shoulders still wouldn't allow him to lift either very well. (By year's end, however, he would be able to complete three push-ups.) Torture had crippled his right hand—which, reflecting the POWs' gallows humor, had earned him the nickname Claw—and he used it to trace the 2-inch-square peephole in the door. He prodded it but found it locked from outside. He noted a 4-inch gap between the door's bottom and the threshold. Surrounded by concrete, with little light and ventilation, assaulted by a dank odor, he felt as if he'd been sealed in a crypt. He sat quietly, wondering how long this new sentence would last.

Sam listened to the sounds of more captives arriving—shuffling footsteps, barked commands, the hollow echo of cell doors closing. He heard the clink of irons—leg irons—as guards progressed down the cellblock, clamping them on each prisoner. His door opened. A lightbulb flickered on, and a guard uncuffed him. The same man then locked irons around his ankles.

Their harsh experiences had conditioned the Americans not to communicate when guards were within earshot, so the walls stayed quiet. When the courtyard outside at last grew silent, the interior walls of the cellblock came alive as men began discreetly tapping to one another. First everyone fumed about the leg irons and windowless cells to which they'd been condemned. Then the captives tapped out their names to one another, cell to cell, and the lineup became clear. Commander Howie Rutledge occupied Cell One, closest to the compound's gate and the Ministry of National Defense. The Ichabod Crane of the group, jocular Commander Harry Jenkins, lived next door in Cell Two. The two commanders had lived within 30 feet of one another during almost all of their internment, which had allowed Harry to rib Howie often about being shot down while substituting for Howie on his birthday.

CAG's last cellmate, air force major and former Thunderbird solo pilot Sam Johnson, lived next to Harry in Cell Three. Hanoi's second American POW, mild-mannered and quietly subversive Lieutenant Commander Bob "Shu" Shumaker, would serve his time in Cell Four. Ever-stubborn air force Captain Ron Storz, who still refused to bow without threats or beatings, would serve in Cell Five, where his hatred of his tormentors would simmer dangerously. The celebrated author of the Clark Kent and Ben Casey fabrication, Lieutenant Commander Nels Tanner, took up residence next to Ron in Cell Six. Bachelors, escape artists, and attitude cases Lieutenant (Junior Grade) George Coker, USN, and Captain George McKnight, USAF, lived next to each other in Cells Seven and Eight, respectively. Cell Nine was left empty to further isolate Commander Jerry Denton in Cell Ten. The former senior officer at the Zoo would soon learn that he'd serve as executive officer to Jim Stockdale here in this smallest Hanoi outpost.

As each POW memorized the names of his new compatriots, a sense of pride filled his heart. Present among these nine were three of the five most senior active navy commanders in Hanoi; they'd soon learn the other two were just a few yards away. Rounding out the group were six younger men who'd frustrated, embarrassed, and challenged the Camp Authority more than any other prisoners.

These defiant patriots found themselves among kindred resistors. Cat and Rabbit had extorted information out of them only through significant torture. Even after submitting to the ropes, each of these fighters habitually bounced back, ready to make Pigeye go another round. Then they persisted in flouting the camp regulations and the camp staff themselves. While other POWs in and around Hanoi were also tough, daring, and dedicated, the Camp Authority considered these eleven men so disruptive, dangerous, and toxic that they opened another prison just for them. Now they would battle on, proud of their membership in this elite unit.

Along his back wall, George Coker tapped, "This place is like Alcatraz. What a lockdown." The others found the comparison to the infamous penitentiary fitting, and they passed his words through the cellblock. Jerry Denton, the ranking officer among the cellblock's nine POWs, soon agreed that they should call their new prison Alcatraz.

The next morning, across a 10-foot-wide entranceway from the cellblock holding the nine, Commander Jim Mulligan woke to a resounding gong and an unwelcome dose of Hanoi Hannah's propaganda from the speaker, but nobody appeared at his door for some time. The silence outside seemed eerie, very unlike the morning noises in bustling Hỏa Lò to which he had become accustomed. Daylight came underneath the door, helping the still-burning bulb light the cell. Finally a guard arrived to remove his leg irons and take him to empty his bucket. He stepped into a rectangular courtyard. Studying his new environment without his blindfold for the first time, he saw he occupied the middle cell of a small three-cell building with a roof of broken tile that abutted the yard's short east wall. Soon enough, guards would relocate him to the cell on his left, leaving an empty cell between him and Stockdale to hamper their communication.

Farther to his left, Mulligan saw a long, windowless concrete building of similar construction. His small cellblock was directly across from the first two cells in this longer building, although his door opened toward the courtyard's short west end, not south toward the second cellblock. He counted a total of nine doors to this cellblock as the guard walked him west across its length to the latrine. He could feel eyes straining through cracks or under doors to identify him. He wondered who languished behind each door. When he reached the building's end, he emptied his bucket into an elevated wooden latrine that had been fashioned above an old bomb shelter. He picked up a bamboo brush and methodically scrubbed out his bucket with deliberate strokes, sending his identifying signal, "JM." He gauged the compound's size as between 2,500 and 3,600 square feet, mostly of packed earth. In the northwest corner next to the latrine and catty-corner from the compound's entrance stood a pigsty, filled with swine that seemed better treated than the POWs. In the northeast corner, next to CAG's cell, he saw a bathing facility—really just a concrete cistern and wash sink. Several walls were just like those at Hỏa Lò, pale stone and concrete topped by shards of glass. He saw what he assumed were government buildings close by, rising above the walls.

After the guard had returned Jim Mulligan to his cell, he took CAG for the same walk. Through a crack in the mortar surrounding his cell door's upper hinge, Mulligan watched the air wing commander hobble into the yard. A month had passed since Mulligan had last seen him—a month CAG had spent in agony on the floor of Riviera One—but he looked as if he had aged twenty years. Grizzled and bowed, he still hobbled with a pronounced limp as he swung his crooked left leg outward with each step. Once he had scrubbed out his bucket and returned to his cell, CAG tapped to Mulligan, "I can see out. Let's see if we can find out who's in camp with us."

The two aviators watched the guards repeat the morning routine with the nine prisoners occupying the long cellblock to their left. Between them, they identified Howie Rutledge, Harry Jenkins, Sam Johnson, Bob Shumaker, and Jerry Denton. They could not identify four younger officers. They suspected they were agents in their network they had never encountered face-to-face. CAG knew he had command, with Jerry Denton his executive officer.

The North Vietnamese believed they had chopped off the head of the snake. They hoped that without these instigators and leaders, the entire POW population would become far more compliant. Jim Stockdale prayed that other senior POWs would assume command in Hỏa Lò and carry on the resistance, but for the moment, he had to focus on this new assignment, this new challenge. The hardened commander had no plans to change his attitude or methods. He could not care about what might transpire outside this postage stamp of a world, from which he would continue fighting for his country. Jim Stockdale was at war. With his ten soldiers, he commanded a willing and able force of brothers-in-arms.

The eleven subversives—the Alcatraz Eleven, as they would be known—were cut off from Hanoi's other detention camps, and at the moment, CAG's and Mulligan's cells were cut off from the other nine inmates. They could tap to each other easily enough, but how to reach across the courtyard to the other nine? As he surveyed the yard from the gap beneath his door, CAG noticed movement under the door of Nels Tanner's Cell Six. He realized that if he and Nels both crouched on their floors and looked out, they could see light reflected off the other's hand. Within forty-eight hours, CAG had caught Nels's attention. They began flashing their hands in front of the space beneath their doors, sending tap code visually. The angle between CAG and Nels proved optimal, and Nels soon sent to CAG the suggested name of his new command. "Alcatraz," Nels flashed. CAG approved.

The Eleven already knew they would not be able to wage battle across fields or skies, but they did think they'd be fighting in quiz rooms, brazenly facing off against their adversaries. The North Vietnamese had other plans, however. Instead of peppering their new inmates with questions at quiz, the camp administrators simply locked them in their cells and left them there. These diehards had no chance to resist. The Americans found themselves fighting inside concrete boxes, locked in desperate combat with an unrelenting enemy: boredom.

The hope and pride that had swelled upon first hearing the lineup of hard-liners began to ebb. Days passed indifferently as these warriors surrendered to routine and began to waste away in silence and misery.

Like all the POWs, George McKnight awoke well before 7:00 A.M. to a gong and Hanoi Hannah's voice. Until then, he could let himself believe he'd only experienced a nightmare; the new dawn would find him safely in his bed at home. Inevitably, each morning brought him back to Alcatraz. Yet another day locked inside a third-world jail, eight thousand miles from home. Taps from George Coker soon came through the wall, "How you doin' bud?"

"Another day in hell," McKnight often replied. Coker would encourage his friend as best he could; he was barely holding on himself.

Shortly after reveille, one of the camp's fifteen assigned staff unlocked Stockdale and Mulligan's cells to remove their leg irons. Then the guard would visit the other nine prisoners to do the same. Since the cells in the large block all had sizable gaps beneath the doors, the guard would often simply reach under the door to unlock the irons. A perfunctory kick from an inmate was common—as was a retaliatory twisting of the irons by the guard. Simply seeing another person or exchanging words—pleasant or not—had become food for these lonely souls starved for human contact. Guards added one more measure of inhumanity to the Alcatraz experience by denying them the sight of another human even as they unlocked their irons.

After unfastening all the irons, the guard would return to Jim Mulligan's cell. At the guard's direction, the aviator would stumble into the courtyard, blinking at the bright sunshine after passing the night in the dim twilight created by the cell's single bulb. His now-bony frame wore a flimsy, threadbare shirt that smelled of dirt and sweat six days out of seven. On the seventh day, Mulligan could wash his clothes.

The guard would escort him to the latrine, which swarmed with black flies. Then Jim would scrub out his bucket with the same filthy brush each day, sending the first message of the morning with his deliberate strokes. Jim Stockdale followed. Guards then worked their way down the nine-cell building. Since guards allotted prisoners only a short time to clean their buckets, the men of Alcatraz became more proficient than ever at using shorthand code. Each man adopted a one-letter name. Jim Mulligan claimed M, Jim Stockdale was S, George Coker was C, Jerry Denton was D, Harry Jenkins was J, and Sam Johnson was L since his seniors had claimed both S and J. George McKnight took G, and Howie Rutledge took H. The letter B represented Bob Shumaker, R stood for Ron Storz, and T identified Nels Tanner.

Often, the men used their morning speech to recognize important dates and lend moral support to an Alcatraz brother. For example, on November 13, someone would inevitably communicate, "Swish swish—swish swish swish (pause) swish—swish swish (pause) swish swish—swish swish swish." That translated to "HBH," which meant "Happy Birthday, Howie Rutledge." On that same day, the anniversary of Harry Jenkins's shootdown, another POW would brush out "HAJ."

The three letters meant "Happy Anniversary, Harry Jenkins." With each shootdown anniversary that passed, the men grew more confounded. *How had they been left here for so long? Would they ever go home?*

When the ten others had finished their business, Jerry ended the morning ritual by washing the entire latrine area, which gave him ample time to deliver the closing. Sometimes his messages provided information or instruction. To the irritation of some inmates, often-serious Jerry frequently used his platform to reinforce orders upon which he and CAG had already agreed. Other times, he offered inspiration. Once he brushed out "In Thy gentle hands, we are smiling our thanks." The men of Alcatraz found comfort in such messages. Their detestable conditions led them to despair, and they needed encouragement to thwart the Camp Authority's goals; they had to remember their blessings. For all the misery surrounding them, they had each escaped death at least once. Many pilots—many of their friends—had not survived their final flights.

One day, Jerry Denton gave a particularly lengthy oration as he swept and cleaned. He focused so hard on his work—communicating, not cleaning—that he failed to hear Rat approaching from behind him. When he sensed the commandant's presence, he turned and saw Rat grinning. "Denton," he said, "that is a very long message."

The administration seemed to know the men communicated with each other—and even seemed to know their methods—but instead of implementing the harsh punishments they had used at the Hilton and the Zoo, the North Vietnamese tacitly allowed some limited communication at Alcatraz as long as it wasn't too blatant. Rat and his guards seemed to refrain from enforcing the absolute degree of isolation on these caged souls. Quiet tapping became the men's primary sustenance; their meager daily rations—two bowls of sewer green soup and occasional pieces of animal fat—hardly qualified. The POWs eventually grew too bold, however, and began communicating too overtly. As a warning to follow the camp regulations, Rat, Alcatraz's commandant, clamped Harry Jenkins in irons for eighty-six days.

Once every week, a guard led each prisoner to the cistern and sink next to CAG's Cell Thirteen. There, the captive would strip and commence a washdown that nobody could equate with anything resembling a real bath. Each POW dipped a bowl into the cistern and poured water on himself. As fall progressed and temperatures dropped, the cold water could become breathtaking. Shivering, the prisoner would try to generate some lather from the stubborn brown soap issued once every six weeks, then use a wash rag to sponge himself as best as he could. After several weeks of the routine, George McKnight became concerned that a guard watched him too intently while he bathed. One day, he'd had enough and began shouting and shaking himself at the guard; guards deemed boxer shorts were appropriate for bathing from then on. While its hygienic value was debatable, the bath provided the men a priceless fifteen minutes outside their breezeless cells.

Weekly laundry provided the same opportunity. Prisoners slowly scrubbed a week's dirt and stink from their garments using dirty bath water and hung their clothes—essentially T-shirt, boxers, and pajamas—on a clothesline, savoring each extra second in the open air. Tasks complete, a guard would force them back into their sunless boxes for at least the next twenty-three hours and forty minutes. Occasionally they'd receive the opportunity to pick up their food at the table between Howie Rutledge's Cell One and the courtyard's gate, but more often, guards delivered the paltry meals to each cell.

The guards made sure the eleven Alcatraz inmates never set eyes upon each other. They only slipped once, inexplicably leaving Jim Stockdale's door unlocked on Christmas. CAG heard a guard march by, leading a prisoner to the bath trough next to his cell. He heard the prisoner stop, and his door suddenly flew open. There stood Harry Jenkins, who'd considered the unlocked door an invitation. Harry looked around bemusedly and grinned. "Gee, CAG," he quipped, "nice little place you've got here!" A flustered guard yanked Harry out of Cell Thirteen, his smile still beaming. The incident cheered CAG for weeks.

The men received their daily ration of three cigarettes before breakfast. Several of the inmates immediately smoked the first cigarette to stave off the hunger that had grown overnight and conspired with the unremitting lightbulbs to rob them of sleep. Later in the day, a guard would extend a torch through the peephole of each door so smokers could light their next cigarette; many indulged just to pass time, even though they often paid a price of one bow per light.

The men received their morning meals around 10:30 A.M. At the food table or cell door, they usually found a bowl of thin vegetable soup, perhaps with a piece of stale bread or chunk of fat, that left them no less hungry than they'd been before their meal. Tiny rocks in their soup often caused toothaches; the POWs never determined if the rocks were added intentionally. The eleven Americans received virtually nothing with protein. Their bodies grew thinner, and the pitiful rations often kept them too tired or light-headed for exercise; sometimes they'd need several minutes to gain their balance after standing up. Still, the POWs did their best to stay active, and over time they would pace the equivalent of many miles in their cells. The men picked up or received their second meals around 3:00 P.M. If guards needed dishes cleaned, they often chose Bob Shumaker for the chore.

Between four and five o'clock, guards distributed leg irons for the night, an indignity to which the prisoners eventually became accustomed. Once, the men nearly rioted when guards issued them the wrong irons. They each loudly demanded their own usual pair until the guards gave in; the men considered it a victory. Around six, Hanoi Hannah delivered a forty-five-minute report, which the speakers would replay the next morning. The broadcasts contained news about the war, ongoing diplomacy, and turmoil in the United States, presented with the expected bias. The POWs rarely found good news or reason to suspect a return home anytime soon. Occasionally, they heard propaganda statements made by peace activists, antiwar American politicians, or fellow POWs in other prisons; the latter variety disheartened the men in Alcatraz more than anything else.

After the evening's broadcast ended, each man began his bedtime ritual. Harry Jenkins would repeat the list of prisoner names he'd memorized, alphabetically and to a tune. Jim Mulligan did the same in his cell across the courtyard, and both men recited a scripture verse. Others prayed. Some lay still, thinking of home and being thankful they'd survived another day.

As the men bedded down for the night, they'd try to hold at bay their disheartening reality. The Eleven had no idea when their time in this wretched prison would end. They might suffer this routine for a year, a decade, or perhaps longer. They could only trust in God, hope their families knew they were still alive, and endure the next day.

Sunday's breakfast and worship service provided the only deviation from the daily repetition. As with Shu and Smitty Harris's piano concerts at the Zoo, the men found solace in imagined luxuries, and on alternating weekends Ron Storz and Bob Shumaker fixed elaborate Sunday breakfasts for each other. The chef would tap menus of eggs

Benedict, omelets, and pastries to his partner, who would extend appropriate compliments as the two men conjured the tastes of home. In Cells Seven and Eight, George Coker and McKnight did the same. After Sunday breakfast, taps went through the walls of the longer cellblock to start and end a half hour of meditation; Nels flashed the cue across the courtyard to CAG, who passed it to Jim Mulligan. All eleven men would quietly recite the Pledge of Allegiance and the Lord's Prayer in their respective cells. The eight navy men felt a brief connection to their carrier brethren at Yankee Station who were holding their own Sunday services aboard ship. They would reflect and pray, momentarily transporting themselves out of their cells, out of Hanoi. Eventually, each would have to return to the brutal reality of confinement at Alcatraz.

By January 1968, routine defined the corralled band of incorrigibles. Outdoor tasks occupied a minuscule fraction of the day, and quizzes rarely took place. In fact, the inmates sometimes hoped for a quiz just to break the monotony. They also hoped to glean new information to share with their neighbors. The rare interrogations they did have were routine, consisting of typical questions and what the prisoners considered Communist drivel. In their cells, the men communicated constantly although discreetly. They sent quiet taps from cell to cell, often relaying messages down the entire cellblock; Nels Tanner made sure to maintain communication with Stockdale and Mulligan in their shed across the yard.

Given the effort required to communicate by tapping, the men frequently tired of it or grew lazy. The two most senior officers, Jim Stockdale and Jerry Denton, engaged in extensive back-and-forth about policies and questions concerning their eventual repatriation. McKnight and Coker would pass communication from Jerry to Nels by tapping through their shared walls. Nels would then flash his hand beneath his door in code to relay the message across the courtyard. When Jerry began to suspect that McKnight abbreviated or skipped some of his messages, he rerouted his communication around McKnight directly to George Coker by banging tap code on the cellblock's back wall instead of the wall that separated him and McKnight. McKnight commed that the ruckus would get everyone in trouble, so Jerry ordered McKnight to transmit his messages two words at a time. Jerry would tap two words of a message and wait for McKnight to transmit the two words up the cellblock to Coker, who'd pass them to Nels. Then Jerry would send two more words. The practice made Mc-

Knight feel like a humiliated schoolboy, and Jerry certainly would have disciplined him like one if he'd seen McKnight rolling his eyes with each two-word transmission.

In fact, Jerry had misidentified his problem; it wasn't McKnight. Two weeks after Jerry began noticing discrepancies, George Coker tapped to McKnight and confessed that he'd grown tired of passing end-less policy communiqués between Jerry and CAG; he thought the two seniors were debating theoretical points and often repeating themselves anyway. As time had worn on, he began truncating the messages. Then he ceased passing them altogether. After an appropriate amount of time had passed, he'd just fabricate a response from CAG to Jerry. Even-tually, Coker had painted himself into a corner. Some answers required knowledge or experience beyond his twenty-four years, but if he posed the questions to Stockdale at this far-gone point, CAG would certainly notice Coker had been improvising. Coker asked Nels to arrange a pri-vate flashing session with CAG, which he did. Flashing code at an angle more difficult than Nels's, Coker confessed to Stockdale. Stockdale nearly laughed out loud. He was thankful Coker could not see his smirking face as he disciplined Alcatraz's youngest inmate, "[Don't] ever try to come between Denton and me," he flashed, doing his duty as CO. "We were in this outfit together before you were born!" In fact, they'd joined the Brigade of Midshipmen together the summer of Cok-er's birth. When Jerry himself discovered the subterfuge, the back wall of the nine-cell building barked with serious threats of a court-martial. The words frightened Coker, but he chose to ignore Jerry for the time being. He figured they'd discuss it when they got out—*if* they got out.

At present, Coker, Jerry, and the other inmates faced day after chilly day of overwhelming depression, alone in windowless cells, wearing leg irons for sixteen hours out of twenty-four. Minutes seemed to pass like hours. They focused on small gripes simply because there was nothing else to do. They'd lie on their mats, shivering under their thin blankets, wishing for spring, if not the beaches of California or Virginia. They had nothing to read, nothing to watch, and only Hanoi Hannah to hear. They would go days without using their voices.

Monotony settled upon the Alcatraz camp like a fog, seeping into each cell to compound the thirst, hunger, aches, and fears of its occu-pant. It ate at their minds, their souls, and their will to live. It plagued their every minute, and despite their efforts to occupy themselves, boredom never was far away. As they had learned in previous stints in solitary, each man consciously had to fight off gloom and despair. Losing that battle meant losing one's mind. Losing one's mind meant death or a lifetime sentence to North Vietnam; nobody thought the North Vietnamese would return a prisoner who'd gone insane.

The North Vietnamese did return some prisoners, however. In February 1968, Hanoi Hannah trumpeted the early release of three POWs; Cat had finally found volunteers for his Fink Release Program. He released them to two American peace activists on the sixteenth. When the speakers played farewell statements from the returnees, Jerry Denton wanted to cut their throats. At Alcatraz, morale plummeted and anger surged at the "slimies," as the Eleven quickly labeled the deserters. The POWs who remained in Hanoi would never forgive them. They believed the men had broken the BACK US rules—*we all go home together*—and walked out on their brother POWs. The men in Alcatraz wondered what had happened to the American resistance, so strong just months ago in Little Vegas.

At Alcatraz, weeks, days, hours, and minutes continued to drag by at a tortoise's pace. Surviving each interminable cell-bound minute eventually proved as challenging as enduring Pigeye's ropes. Each man developed methods of staving off insanity and keeping despondency at bay. Building houses became one widespread preoccupation, and the Alcatraz inmates would imagine constructing houses when they returned to America. They spent entire days—even weeks—meticulously designing floor plans and material lists for their new homes, calculating feet of lumber, number of bricks, square feet of tile, yards of piping, gallons of paint. Bob Shumaker badgered Sam Johnson and Ron Storz for specific building costs. George Coker built six houses. Wide verandas, screened against mosquitoes, surrounded a house in Key West where an air-conditioning system kept the tropical humidity at bay. He constructed a multilevel home on a sloping lot in Maine and built another house in Massachusetts with a deep cellar for wine and provisions for a long winter—were he not spending the season in Key West. The home in Maine took a particularly long time to finish; its rock chimney collapsed five times.

Aero-engineer Bob Shumaker revisited his knowledge of science and mathematics to keep his mind active. Shu learned that CAG played piano, and the two musicians spent several weeks calculating frequency ratios between notes on the musical scale. They flashed complex calculations under their doors and across the courtyard until they found their answer: the twelfth root of two.

Over time, Shu grew particularly interested in the concept of specific gravity—the ratio that compares the density of one substance to that of another. Shu scavenged various items for his experiments: a plastic button, an aluminum spoon, an iron nail. Then he rigged a balance by tying a string from his pajamas to the middle of a bamboo stick plucked from a broom. He tied a pebble to one end of the stick to act as the constant reference material and tied the test material to the other. He slid the test material toward the beam's fulcrum until the contraption balanced. He measured the balance point along the stick. Then he immersed the test object in his pot of water and measured its volume based on displacement. Using his measurements of weight and displacement, he'd calculate the specific gravity for each sample. Shu made his bleak cell into a working laboratory of discovery and distraction.

When he felt more sociable, Shu taught French to his neighbor, Sam Johnson, who proved an exceptional pupil. Almost every day, Shu tapped Sam five new words of French. When the Texan needed help with enunciation, Shu would tap out an English word that sounded like the French word under discussion. Sam absorbed every word, but after months of lessons, endless hours tapping a foreign language through the concrete wall, Shu reached the limits of his French vocabulary. Fortune interceded, and on a visit to the latrine, Shu found several pages ripped out of a French magazine; guards had used them as toilet paper. He collected the salvageable scraps, and their printed words became Sam's lessons for another six months.

Shu also gave more subversive lessons and taught Sam the classified code he'd learned in the United States, with which a small group of POWs had been encrypting their sporadic letters home. Very few men trained in the code were actually shot down, so once in Hanoi, Shu decided to share it with select other prisoners. As long as the POWs who did know the code were allowed to write, they'd secretly embed their letters home with prisoner names, the realities of their conditions, or whatever CAG ordered; occasionally they'd also receive letters from their wives that the government had encoded. CAG nicknamed the code Martini, and called Shu the "bartender" for the way he coordinated the efforts of several POWs to deliver hidden messages across multiple letters. When CAG or Shu was out of contact, Martini-trained POWs would send whatever they could.

Like Shu, all the other Alcatraz inmates became teachers, tapping lessons in their area of expertise to one another, enriching each other's minds even as their bodies wasted away. Neighbors became old friends, even closer than old friends. They shared secrets, hopes, fears. George McKnight could tell Jerry Denton or George Coker's mood simply by the sound of his knuckles—sadness, joy, trepidation all rang clearly through the wall. Knowing each other so intimately, McKnight and Denton would often speed through conversations, guessing the next word being sent and often double-rapping through entire phrases. They knew each other that well.

Perhaps because of these intimacies, siblinglike fights often erupted. McKnight and Coker scrapped like brothers through their shared wall, disagreeing on topics from sports to historical trivia to when they might go home. Heated academic arguments—truly unanswerable in a Hanoi jail cell—happened often, sometimes making the men of Alcatraz seem like a dysfunctional family at Thanksgiving dinner. The men often ended stalemates by placing bets—often wagering tacos—payable upon homecoming. Like a group of Las Vegas bookmakers, the men managed their accounts meticulously.

In his cell, Jim Mulligan focused on memories. He relived his time on *Enterprise,* and at NAS Jacksonville, family vacations, his wedding, college, school, and his childhood. Along the way, he regained friends he'd lost or long forgotten. He reached back to age two, when he recalled riding in a car with his grandparents down Route 110 to Salisbury Beach, Massachusetts. Seeing a stone planted in the ground, Jim asked, "Grandma, what's that?"

"That's an Indian cemetery."

"What's an Indian cemetery?" Jim asked.

He remembered her turning to his grandfather and saying, "Listen to him talk! He's not even two."

Similarly, Jerry Denton conjured images of squadron mates, scanning his memory as if it were a yearbook. He began by recalling the names and faces of his fellow aviators and then classmates at the Naval Academy and at McGill Institute. Eventually, he found himself remembering his schoolmates all the way back to his first-grade class. When Jerry told CAG about his memories of grade school, CAG replied that he had experienced the same phenomenon. "We are regressing," he flashed across the yard to Nels Tanner. "We're going back to our childhoods." Within months, Harry Jenkins could recollect the name and face of everyone with whom he'd ever shared a classroom. Nearly all the Alcatraz inmates discovered their long-term memory sharpening, even as other abilities dulled. They spent long days visualizing their entire lives.

If a prisoner found his cell neither too hot nor too cold—a maddeningly rare occurrence—and if he had become well enough accustomed to sleeping on concrete while wearing leg irons and being tormented by the interminable lightbulb, nighttime might offer him relief from mental acrobatics and the misery of his situation. Too often, though, the men had trouble sleeping, forcing them to survive even more minutes of conscious solitude. When Jerry found himself awake at night, he turned to the gecko lizards that congregated on the ceiling around the lightbulb. The colony, led by a large male Jerry named Bullmoose, fed on insects attracted by the light. Jerry observed intently as the big male courted mates and produced offspring who would join the competition for the insects. The larger lizards could leap from one wall to the other, catching a mosquito in the process. Those young who lost the competition for food would grow weak and fall to the floor of Cell Ten. Jerry cared for them as long as he could by swatting mosquitoes with his bamboo fan and feeding the wounded insects to the weakest lizards, but he could not save them all. The dying geckos offered one more distraction from his bleak reality.

Unfortunately for Jerry, the lizards showed little interest in the hundreds of flies that blanketed his walls and ceiling. Since the Camp Authority had placed him closest to the latrine, his cell hosted more flies than any other. The insects did at least present him with entertainment, and he occupied himself by killing flies when his interest in the geckos waned. Once, he counted 250 kills before he stopped.

In Cell Two, Harry Jenkins found himself developing an enhanced sense of smell and hearing. The smells of the food placed on the table outside his door, the steps of guards' sandals, the tiniest cough or softest tap from another American—none of these escaped Harry. He suspected his heightened sensory abilities connected him to other members of the animal kingdom, and he struck up a friendship with the mice of Alcatraz. He sacrificed crumbs from his own pitiful rations to buy the friendship of the only visitors he could host. The mice in his cell brightened many dark days.

Harry also used his gifts to lift the spirits of other POWs. During one walk to the latrine, he scavenged a loose nail, which he clasped between his toe and sandal until he'd returned to his cell. Once inside, he concealed the new treasure inside the hem of his boxer shorts so guards wouldn't discover it during a shakedown. That evening, Harry carefully laid his nail across the two exposed electrical wires that fed his bulb and speaker. Harry watched the nail spark, and his light went out—along with the other lights in Alcatraz. Harry had shorted the system. The guards replaced a fuse, and then Harry replaced the nail. Wires sparked, and Alcatraz went dark again. The eleven men enjoyed a relatively restful night in blissful darkness. The next day, the guards tested the system. With Harry's nail stored again in his skivvies, the wires worked just fine. From then on, whenever someone had a particularly rough day, Harry would tap, "Don't worry, I saw the phantom electrician in camp." That night, he would short out the lights and all would sleep well. The baffled guards never did solve the recurrent problem.

Each man in Alcatraz found his own way to fight, to pass time, to find purpose, to organize his day so he could maintain some modicum of control over his existence. On some afternoons, Jim Stockdale would hear the guard approaching with leg irons, realize 4:00 P.M. had arrived, and think, "I've been up since 6:00 A.M. doing these things and I haven't had a second to myself all day!" Yet no degree of mental discipline, no amount of creativity, no conversation—tapped, flashed, or brushed—could alter the fundamental reality of imprisonment at Alcatraz: at least twenty-three hours and forty minutes of each day locked inside foul cells, without seeing another American, often without speaking, week after week, month after month. They did not know when it would end. They all wondered, "How can this still be happening?"

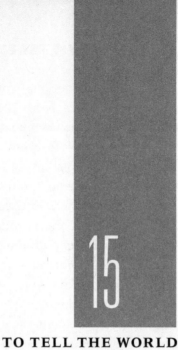

TO TELL THE WORLD

"Why do you want to fight against the just cause of Vietnam?" Hanoi Hannah asked American GIs on January 30, 1968; it was Tết, the Vietnamese New Year. "You can see you are losing. Lay down your arms! Refuse to fight! Demand to be taken home, now! Today! Do you want to die in a foreign land, eight thousand miles from your home?"

As the broadcasts droned on, the POWs at Alcatraz learned that North Vietnam and the Việtcộng had staged coordinated attacks throughout the South around Tết. In fact, North Vietnamese generals had planned much of their Tết Offensive at the Ministry of National Defense, just across the street from Alcatraz. According to Hannah, the People's Army and the People's Liberation Armed Forces (Việtcộng) had routed the Americans, the South Vietnamese army, and the puppet regime in Saigon. Reality differed somewhat. Indeed, seventy thousand Communist troops had violated the traditional three-day holiday truce between all parties and staged attacks across the countryside, in countless towns and, most startlingly, many of South Vietnam's major cities. A small unit breached the U.S. Embassy, rockets attacked the American base at Cam Ranh Bay, and General Westmoreland's own headquarters came under fire. In the United States, televisions broadcast scenes from across Vietnam: firefights, wounded soldiers, a faltering American mission. Ultimately, U.S. and South Vietnamese forces recovered from the surprise attack and effectively beat back the surge, but American casualties topped 20,000, with more than 5,000 killed from January through March of 1968. Insurgent losses were many times higher, yet the Communists accepted prices Americans would refuse to pay.

In the days immediately following Tết, the Camp Authority covered the walls of one Alcatraz quiz room with photographs from the offensive. A young sergeant walked the POWs along the walls, showing them images of victorious Communist forces, burned ruins in Saigon, and defeated Americans. Other photos showed images from the United States itself: peace marches, protests, and student rallies. Sam Johnson tried not to believe the pictures.

"What do you think?" asked the sergeant.

"I don't know," Sam answered.

"Look around you," he said, "You can see we are winning the war. How can you think the war will not be over soon? The United States will retreat and go home, and we will be the winners."

Rabbit visited during the same week and happily cast even more doubt into the minds of the Alcatraz Eleven. "Our just cause is winning," he gloated to Sam during a quiz. "Now you can see!"

"What do you mean?" Sam asked.

"You have seen proof!" Rabbit exclaimed. "Our photos, our radio! The United States has given up and will lose the war in Vietnam!"

"I cannot believe your photos or your radio."

"The bombing has stopped," Rabbit said. "Your country has deserted you. You will never go home. You have been left here to die."

"I can't believe that," Sam said. If he let himself believe that, he'd crack in a week—but months *had* passed since he'd last heard an American jet over Hanoi or wailing air raid sirens. Somewhere deep inside, he worried Rabbit might be telling the truth.

"You will see," Rabbit said with disturbing finality. "We are right." He sent Sam back to his concrete box, which now felt a little more like a tomb.

During the short walk back, Sam told himself that Rabbit and Hanoi Hannah were lying, as they had before. Without any information to the contrary, however, he wondered what had transpired in South Vietnam and what it meant for the men in Alcatraz. How many more years would they spend in their claustrophobic cells? Would the war ever end? Their government wouldn't abandon them, would it?

Locked inside Cell Three, Sam found the walls alive with discussion. Rabbit had lectured many of the POWs that day, and everyone had an opinion. "The U.S. will never give up on us," CAG flashed to Nels, who sent his message up and down the long cellblock.

"Never happen," agreed the optimist, Jerry Denton. "They won't leave us here."

Everyone desperately hoped their two leaders were correct.

No image defined Tết quite like a photograph taken on February 1, 1968. On assignment in South Vietnam, Associated Press photographer Eddie Adams noticed South Vietnam's national chief of police, Nguyễn Ngọc Loan, apprehending a suspected guerrilla on a Saigon street. Loan raised his pistol; Adams raised his camera. The police chief fired a bullet into the side of the suspect's head; Adams snapped a photograph. The handcuffed man slumped to the street, dead. The next day, the image appeared in newspapers across the United States. The savagery shocked the nation.

North Vietnam's real victory came in Tết's aftermath. Hanoi's strategists had bet that when the war's costs became too high, the American people would clamor for withdrawal; Tết proved them correct, precipitating a decided shift in America's opinion about U.S. involvement in Southeast Asia. President Johnson immediately declared the Communist campaign a "complete failure," and militarily, his statement had credence, as U.S. and South Vietnamese troops did recover and repulse the offensive, inflicting heavy casualties. However, America didn't buy Johnson's claims this time. By March 1968, 78 percent of the U.S. public believed the war would lead nowhere. Calls for withdrawal became more widespread. In Tết, the administration and the public saw a long-discounted insurgency stage a campaign across the whole of South Vietnam. The United States had nearly 500,000 troops deployed to Southeast Asia, and an endless cycle of aircraft carriers constantly came and went from Yankee Station, yet somehow America had still not won.

Newsman Walter Cronkite delivered a eulogy for the war in a February 1968 newscast. "To say that we are mired in stalemate seems the only realistic, yet unsatisfactory, conclusion. It is increasingly clear to this reporter that the only rational way out then will be to negotiate, not as victors, but as an honorable people who lived up to their pledge to defend democracy, and did the best they could." Indeed, America would spend the next five years trying to extricate itself.

On the long list of America's Tét casualties was twenty-three-year-old Ronald Thompson, Sondra Rutledge's first love. Vietnam might have already claimed her father, Howie—she hadn't yet learned if he'd survived—and now it had certainly claimed her fiancé, Ron. She was devastated by Ron's death but grew even more determined to advocate for the POWs still in Vietnam, one of whom she hoped was her father. That same year, Sondra's Madison High School political science teacher began a lesson on propaganda. He started by turning off the overhead lights and showing footage of North Vietnamese defenders downing an American airplane. For all Sondra knew, it was her own father's. That was just plain dumb and insensitive to do in a military community like San Diego, she thought. She and her good friend Joyce Kimball stood up; Joyce's father, a navy pilot, had died in a crash. They walked out of the room, and the entire class followed them; everyone knew Sondra's father was missing in action. Later that year, Sondra led a sit-in protest in the school courtyard after a journalism teacher encouraged students to speak out against the war. She and the other students took off their shoes and refused to budge, showing that students on all sides of the war issue could become activists. In the evenings, she still made local phone calls on behalf of the POWs.

On June 3, 1968, Sondra rallied a group to picket Democratic presidential candidate Robert F. Kennedy at San Diego's airport. She feared that Kennedy, if elected, might pull out of Vietnam without securing release of the POWs. Armed with placards reading DON'T FORGET POWS, Sondra's band of activists gathered at Lindbergh Field to meet the senator's airplane. Before Senator Kennedy disembarked, however, the San Diego police hustled the protesters into a paddy wagon. They took them to a nearby police station and kept them in the vehicle until Kennedy left the airport. The police made Sondra walk back to her car at the airport lot. Two days after Sondra was silenced, so was the young senator, assassinated just five years after his older brother.

In the aftermath of Tét and a narrow victory over primary challenger Eugene McCarthy in New Hampshire, President Johnson decided not to seek a second nomination as the Democratic candidate. Even as he prepared to pass the Vietnam conflict to yet another U.S. president, he reiterated his hope for peace while also restating his commitment to South Vietnam's struggle against Communist forces.

Speaking from the Oval Office, he said, "I shall not seek, and I will not accept, the nomination of my party for another term as your president. But let men everywhere know . . . America stands ready tonight to seek an honorable peace—and stands ready to defend an honored cause—whatever the price, whatever the burden, whatever the sacrifice that duty may require."

Johnson's speech affirmed his commitment to both a free and democratic South Vietnam and lasting peace in the region. He halted bombing in North Vietnam except areas near the DMZ, where troops and supplies still coursed into the South. He announced that Ambassador-at-Large Averell Harriman would meet his North Vietnamese counterparts anytime, anyplace, to negotiate. Seizing the diplomatic opportunity they hoped Tết might precipitate, North Vietnam chose Paris in May. Since North Vietnam and its southern ally, the National Liberation Front, refused to recognize the government in Saigon, and South Vietnam refused to recognize the NLF, neither South Vietnam nor the NLF would participate directly in the talks. Responsibility for peace thus fell to diplomats from Washington and Hanoi. At the outset, the North Vietnamese demanded a complete halt to the bombing before serious talks began. The United States, however, wanted to prevent Hanoi from using a halt to regroup, as they'd done during previous bombing pauses. Both the United States and South Vietnam balked at the North's insistence that the Communist NLF have a role in South Vietnam's political future. So while Johnson may have recognized the need to negotiate, he tried to do so as the victor. Further delaying peace, Hồ Chí Minh and Lê Duẩn, one of the North Vietnamese leaders most committed to military victory, still believed that the longer they waited, the stronger their negotiating position would become. They would not give up their goal of a unified Vietnam and had little interest in giving back territory their forces had taken. Consequently, the final year of President Johnson's term would yield little diplomatic progress while nearly 17,000 American soldiers died in Vietnam.

That spring of 1968 marked the Alcatraz Eleven's fifth month in exile. Jim Mulligan watched the overcast winter skies become clearer each day during his morning walks to the latrine. As the tropical spring unfurled, his cell ceased functioning as a refrigerator and instead became a furnace. The sun claimed more and more time each day to bake the ground, buildings, and inmates trapped at Alcatraz. In the early morning, it began heating Jim Mulligan's roof and his exposed wall. Then as it arched across the sky, it directed its rays on his cell door and its iron transom. Both quickly grew too hot to touch. From the roof tiles, door, metal plate, and walls, heat seeped into his cell and pressed upon him. It seared his lungs with each breath and began roasting him from the inside out. Like his comrades, Jim Mulligan spent his days lying on his mat, sweat soaking his body and drenching his thin boxer shorts, the only clothing he could bear wearing. Salty beads of sweat traced slowly down his face, and his two-quart ration of water—a guard filled his teapot twice each day—proved far from sufficient. As the cell grew hotter, he crouched by the narrow opening under the door to suck the slightly cooler air from outside.

On May 26, he lay on his sweaty back and prayed for aid. "Lord, you've got to help me," Jim pleaded. "I can't stand it any longer, Lord. Lord, you've got to do something." Seemingly in response, Jim heard the distant rumble of a thunderstorm. Inspired, he offered another plea, "Lord, make it rain, make it rain." Before the day ended, the rain arrived, cooling the tiles and walls surrounding him and dispelling the heat. Locked in his cell, he could neither see the raindrops nor feel the winds, but he offered his gratitude nonetheless.

"Thank you, Lord, thank you, Lord," he repeated. "When I get out and tell this story someone will say, 'It was just coincidence, the mere arrival of a fast-moving tropical cold front.' But you and I know it was more than that. In my direst need I begged for your help and you answered me. Thank you, Lord."

Whether divinity interceded or not, Jim believed it had, and that proved the most important thing. As days of captivity ticked by, the Lord became a crucial member of the Alcatraz brotherhood.

Unfortunately, the reprieve from the heat did not last. When June arrived, the summer of 1968 began in earnest. It proved no less brutal than the preceding one, which had plagued the residents of Little Vegas with so many boils. Enduring the heat in the Mint and the other Hỏa Lò cellblocks had proven difficult, but none of the POWs had experienced anything like the ovens of Alcatraz. The tile that covered Alcatraz's two buildings soaked up the season's heat and radiated it into the chambers below. The walls ensured none of the heat escaped.

By June, high temperatures averaged around 90 degrees Fahrenheit, with humidity levels to match. POWs estimated temperatures inside the cells at more than 110 degrees, even hotter than summer days they'd experienced on runways at NAS El Centro in the California desert. Sweat, body odor, honey bucket, and heat combined to make each breath nauseating. The men sat motionless in their cells as sweat trickled from under their matted hair, down their brows, ears, and necks. Streams meandered down their backs and chests. Long-term dehydration eroded the POWs' minds and bodies. Night brought only slight relief, as the walls radiated heat long after sundown. Worst of all, the inmates knew no relief would come until fall.

Jerry Denton realized the men in his cellblock needed relief sooner than that. If something didn't change, the POWs would have survived their ejections, years in Hỏa Lò's dismal cells, and countless torture sessions only to be broiled to death. He finally struck upon a plan. He and CAG placed the men on a gradual hunger strike; they each took slightly less food each day and claimed they'd become too hot to eat. Thus, they avoided a direct challenge to Rat. The next time Jerry saw a guard, he requested an audience with the camp commander. With Rat curious about the men's waning appetites, Jerry got his hearing.

A guard escorted him up the steps near Cell One and through the courtyard gate. He was turned left and guided along the narrow stucco quiz building behind the small cell block. The guard led him through one of its three doors to a small room with a concrete floor. A single lightbulb burned overhead, and green shutters covered a window that overlooked the rear of Jim Mulligan and CAG's cells.

Rat was seated behind a desk, waiting for him. When he'd taken his seat, Jerry said to Rat, "I want to congratulate you on carrying through on the excruciating treatment and putting us to a slow death by heat."

"No, Denton," Rat responded. "I did not know conditions were that bad. Our orders are to keep you isolated and in irons. We have no orders to kill you. We will study."

The appearance of Cat on June 19, 1968, hastened the Camp Authority's assessment. Cat still commanded the entire North Vietnamese prisoner detention program. When CAG saw him through his peephole, he frantically tapped to Jim Mulligan, "That's the Cat." As part of Cat's tour, Rat arranged an interview with Jim Mulligan, who, like the others, had taken to refusing food.

"Why do you not eat?" Rat asked when the interview began.

"I am not well," Jim replied. Rat translated for Cat, even though he understood English.

"Where are you sick?" Cat asked.

In answer, Jim stood up and took off his shirt. The officials gawked at his pasty, emaciated torso. All muscle had disappeared. Nearly every bone showed through his skin. "You are impolite," said Cat, switching to English. "Put on your clothes. I will punish you for your bad attitude."

"You can't punish me any more than you punish me now," Mulligan shot back. "I am more dead than alive. You keep me in the leg irons and you do not give me fresh air and I am dying here. I am lonesome for my family. I get no mail. I do not care what you do any more. I am sick and I am dying . . . It is too hot and I need fresh air."

The outburst surprised the officers, but Cat maintained his composure and leveled a soft question at Jim, asking about his family.

"I miss my wife and six sons," he answered. "On July 1 it is the birthday of my wife."

"If you eat your food the Camp Authority may have for you a letter on the birthday of your wife," Cat said. "Will you try to eat for me your meal today?"

Jim issued a halfhearted answer, and Rat ordered him back to the sauna of Cell Eleven. Jim bowed and shuffled off, purposely looking even more lethargic than he felt. Within the hour, Cat and Rat entered the courtyard with a chubby supply officer nicknamed Piggy in tow. Piggy opened Jim's door and winced at the wall of blistering air that hit him. He braced himself on the door and immediately jerked his hand away from the scalding iron and wood. Jim smiled and pointed to the iron-plated transom, which registered an even higher temperature. Piggy hustled off to talk with Cat and Rat. Later that day, work crews entered the courtyard and began covering the roofs with palm leaves and planting vines along the buildings, creating shade to combat the sun. Most importantly, the workers detached the metal plates covering the transoms above each cell door. Rusted screws slowed the work, but within two days, each cell had some protection from the rays above and an airway to vent the heat. The conditions remained oppressive, and the POWs would still suffer through a long summer, but at least they could now breathe.

Soon after workers pried the iron plate from Jim Mulligan's cell, a guard delivered a plate of rice, seaweed soup, and a banana. Jim ended his hunger strike, gulping down every scrap in the relative cool of his cell; he guessed the temperature had fallen nearer 100. On July 1, Cat kept his promise and gave him a letter from Louise.

As peace negotiations began in Paris that spring of 1968, Sybil Stockdale prepared for her annual migration to Sunset Beach in Connecticut. Before she departed Coronado, another military wife suggested she meet with Louise Mulligan. Mirroring military hierarchy, leadership roles on the homefront fell to the wives of senior officers. Thus Sybil led San Diego's League of Wives and Louise essentially led the less-formalized POW wives on the East Coast, although she would never have claimed that position. That summer, Sybil drove from Connecticut down to Virginia Beach for dinner with Louise, and the two POW wives sat down to what would be a momentous meal. Sybil shared ideas about mobilizing clergy and other public figures on behalf of the POWs, a tack that would give the wives more activist roles; no longer would they just provide each other with emotional support. They discussed the need to comply with the government's Keep Quiet policy, but the two headstrong women recognized that someone else had to take initiative considering Harriman and Johnson's lack of progress. Both women recognized the need for a national organization. By the dinner's end, it was agreed that Louise would formalize the POW movement on the East Coast and coordinate operations with the League of Wives on the West Coast. Together they would operate under the umbrella of the League of Families of American Prisoners of War and Missing. Sybil's League of Wives, Louise's network, and other small groups would begin using the common League of Families name, even as they retained their independence and, for the moment, remained primarily regional organizations.

Louise first needed to identify all the POW/MIA wives—from every branch of the military—living in the greater Norfolk area, but the navy, army, and air force refused to release any names. Not to be deterred, Louise and other local wives in her network soon learned that the Department of Defense had obtained foreign footage of POWs and was showing the reels at NAS Oceana; Defense had invited nearby army and air force wives and family members to help identify individual prisoners. Nobody had invited the navy wives, so they simply showed up. They met their air force and army counterparts and welcomed them to their sisterhood.

By the fall, Sybil had become fully convinced that government diplomats either could not or would not act to help the POWs. Her tolerance for the Keep Quiet policy had ended when Ambassador Harriman welcomed the early release of three more POWs in August. As Sybil and most members of the military community saw it, agreeing to selective early release violated the Code of Conduct. Their men had pledged—*sworn*—to accept no parole or special favors; their orders stated they should come home in order of shootdown. Future U.S. senator Lieutenant Commander John McCain—shot down in the same month that the Eleven arrived at Alcatraz—had resisted intense pressure from Cat to accept early release that very summer. Cat had hoped for a publicity victory by releasing the badly injured son of the newly installed commander of the U.S. Pacific Command, Admiral Jack McCain, but the young McCain flatly refused to accept Cat's offer. As punishment, guards beat him for four straight days and extracted a confession. Like McCain, other men had accepted punishment and deprivation rather than the favor of early release. The POW wives and their incarcerated husbands alike were galled by those who went home before their fellow prisoners.

In early September, Sybil read a *San Diego Union* article entitled "Red Brainwash Teams Work on U.S. Pilots," which described treatment of U.S. POWs. She immediately sent a pointed telegram to Ambassador-at-Large Averell Harriman, demanding to know how he would protect her husband and other POWs against these Geneva violations. In response, Harriman cabled, "Dear Mrs. Stockdale . . . North Vietnamese representatives here have indicated to me that the release last month of three pilots was a gesture of good will. I have urged them to give serious consideration to further releases, including those pilots that have been held the longest time, and those that have been injured. I am sure you realize that the welfare and early release of our men held prisoner continues to be upper-most in my mind. Sincerely, W. Averell Harriman."

"No, Ambassador Harriman," Sybil thought, "I'm *not* sure I do realize the welfare of the men is uppermost in your mind; nor do I think you, of all people in this world, should be advocating early releases, which are a violation of the Code of Conduct." Sybil wondered how the government could ignore a Code it had sworn its servicemen to uphold. Had she known of Jim's BACK US and "No early release" directives—and what men suffered for disseminating and following them—she would have found Harriman's suggestions even more offensive.

The ambassador's encouragement of more early releases left the POW wives aghast at the State Department's lack of military understanding—not to mention State's failure to make any substantive progress on properly freeing any prisoners or guaranteeing their Geneva rights. Sybil could hardly believe her country's POW policy revolved around arbitrary North Vietnamese benevolence. She wanted Lyndon Johnson to publicly shame Hanoi for its violation of the Geneva Convention—and she wanted him to bring her husband home. She felt he should either decide to win the war by employing America's full arsenal or withdraw after freeing the prisoners. More hesitation seemed only to assure more anguish for the POWs and their families, who all lived in limbo.

With dwindling confidence in her government's policies toward North Vietnam and its treatment of America's POW/MIA families, Sybil began to compose the article that would at long last break from the military's Keep Quiet policy; she started writing on the third anniversary of Jim's shootdown. She shared the idea with her confidant at the Pentagon, Commander Bob Boroughs, who expressed concern that the article could jeopardize the clandestine communication between Jim and Naval Intelligence. Still, Sybil adamantly believed the POW/MIA community needed someone to take the first step across the line that the government had, in her opinion, so senselessly drawn. She reasoned that once she broke the taboo, others would make the leap from passivity to advocacy. Commander Boroughs tabled his objections; he knew Sybil had made her decision, and privately he seemed to believe it was the right course.

She submitted her article to the Copley News Service, which owned *The San Diego Union.* They called several days later to ask if Sybil wanted to sell them the story. "Heavens no," she said. "I just want to tell the world the truth about what's happening to Jim." Copley assigned a reporter to write an article about her story. The October 27, 1968, *San Diego Union* carried the reporter's piece in section A, ending Sybil's three years of silence. The article described North Vietnam's Geneva violations, announced the role of the League of Families, and quoted Sybil as saying, "The North Vietnamese have shown me the only thing they respond to is world opinion. The world does not know of their negligences and they should know!" Sybil read over her words in bed that morning and wondered when the government would upbraid her for breaking their policy. When would her phone ring? As it turned out, she never heard a single word from the Pentagon, which was too preoccupied with military efforts to respond. With Johnson's term winding down and the antiwar movement growing, the State Department and the rest of the Administration also remained silent.

Louise Mulligan soon learned about the article. Like Sybil, she had lost faith in the government. Even though the Washington bureaucracy proved accessible—she could always speak with someone at the White House, Pentagon, or State Department—all their words and promises had done nothing for her Jim. In a meeting with Harriman, Louise shared her first letter from her husband, and the ambassador leaped to comments Jim made about receiving bananas, vitamins, oranges, meat, and vegetables—along with Piles Of Whole grain rice and Plenty Of Warm soup. Louise had figured out the hidden message and knew Jim received none of those things; Harriman missed the fiction. He did not think Jim playing "that famous game of solitaire" had any connection to solitary confinement; he thought Jim seemed fine. Louise rolled her eyes as her last bit of patience with the Johnson administration slipped away.

Back at home in Virginia Beach, Louise rallied the other East Coast POW wives, and together they composed a letter to the Department of Defense announcing their decision to bring their cause to the public, shedding the Keep Quiet burden. That members of the rule-bound military world would break ranks showed the depth of their disillusionment with the government. The Pentagon offered no resistance, and the women now accepted responsibility should their publicity bring harm to their husbands. Louise spoke with her six boys about how their lives might change, how people might begin asking questions. She also told them that someone had to fight for their father and his friends. She recalled the references to solitude in his first letter; thinking of his isolation steeled her courage. Louise called a reporter from the Norfolk-based *Virginian-Pilot,* and he arrived in short order to hear her story.

At Alcatraz, the summer of 1968 had passed hot and slow. An effeminate officer nicknamed Softsoap Fairy (alternately known as Slick) relieved Rat and ushered in a slightly more tolerable administration. Softsoap, as the POWs generally called him, wore fine clothes, had a solid command of English, and carried himself gracefully; he seemed to be an efficient administrator. Most important to the Alcatraz POWs, he instituted a ten-minute outdoor exercise period for each inmate; he also had guards erect a bamboo privacy screen around the bath area. The extra time outside their cells helped the prisoners—at least in some small measure—cope with the misery of the summer heat.

During those months, the eleven men grew ever-closer to one another. Both the Camp Authority and their fellow POWs would consider them the most defined clan of prisoners in North Vietnam. Part of their unity came from their stoic leader, so determined and respected. The nine men in the large cellblock organized a special message for their commanding officer on September 9, 1968, the third anniversary of his arrival in North Vietnam. As his men scraped out their morning greetings at the latrine, CAG noticed a chain message, started by Howie Rutledge and continued by the others. By the time Jerry Denton had finished his cleaning duties, Jim Stockdale had received the entire message: "Here's to CAG for three great years. We love you. We are with you to the end." Jim would forever maintain that he never received a medal that meant more to him than that message.

That fall, the hours of solitude spent locked inside Alcatraz's windowless cells continued to add up. The rare quizzes the men had were fairly innocuous, largely meant to worry them. Once, Rabbit visited the camp and summoned Bob Shumaker to an interrogation room, asking his second-longest-serving prisoner, "What is this American feminist movement I hear about?"

"That's the way a woman wiggles when she walks," Shu answered, managing to keep a straight face.

Perhaps as retribution for the joke, Rabbit taunted him with the prospect of Lorraine's infidelity; the Shumakers had now been separated for nearly four years. "Do you think your wife is remaining true to you?" Rabbit asked.

Shu calmly answered, "By now, she's probably run off and married the ice man."

Rabbit flipped through his translation dictionary, looking up the term "ice man." "My," he said, "you Americans have a strange sense of humor."

Short sessions like these aside, the North Vietnamese simply let these eleven stalwarts rot. In some moments, the POWs would have traded the temporary pain of the ropes for the isolation of their cells. Soon, they'd realize those wishes.

Hanoi Hannah added to their gloom by reporting news of the peace negotiations from Hanoi's perspective. She claimed that President Johnson realized his country could never defeat the people of Vietnam and now desperately sought peace. On November 1, 1968, she brought word that America had halted all bombing of North Vietnam. Johnson's move—a goodwill gesture, as he saw it—meant no new American captives would flow into the detention system, and thus neither would trustworthy news from the States; the Camp Authority still only sporadically distributed letters from home. The Alcatraz POWs recognized that even if they could interact with other prisoners, nobody would have any recent news. It was as if a dripping faucet had stopped. At the announcement, Sam Johnson's fears compounded. He saw his country checking its vast airpower, seemingly unwilling to win the war—and perhaps unwilling to free the POWs. In early November, Hannah announced that Richard Nixon had defeated Hubert Humphrey in the presidential election. Sam believed the president-elect would draw a tougher line. The Camp Authority anticipated the same and toughened its own stance.

With a new man in the White House and a new secretary of defense, many POW families saw an opportunity for change. They hoped this new administration would respond to the plight of U.S. prisoners in Vietnam and their families at home. Sybil Stockdale wrote California governor Ronald Reagan, hoping he'd serve as her emissary to the new administration, but Reagan's staff refused to schedule an appointment. Livid, Sybil dispatched a biting telegram to his office. The next week, Governor Reagan called her directly; she would never forget first hearing his resonant voice. When the two had finished their conversation, he had promised to pass Sybil's message to President-elect Nixon. For the first time since her long ordeal began, Sybil felt that a politician genuinely cared. The phone call renewed her spirits. She hoped 1969 would bring progress.

By early January, five other San Diego wives had written articles about the plight of POW/MIA families. Following the plans Sybil and Louise hatched that previous summer, the East and West Coast organizations continued transitioning from support groups to leagues of advocacy, from regional entities to one with national scope. The League of Families, or simply "the League," now also had member groups from across the country, including one organized in Texas by Sam Johnson's wife, Shirley. Leaders like Louise Mulligan spent entire days talking via telephone to activists throughout the country, sharing information, encouragement, and ideas. Together, these independent but coordinated groups pressured the military, government, and every other possible source for information and began educating Americans about the Geneva Convention. They flooded elected officials and news media with POW-related news and encouraged POW/MIA families to become activists and educators, telling their story to communities and press across the country.

In Virginia Beach, the local junior chamber of commerce contacted Jane Denton, requesting that she speak about the POWs at their monthly dinner. Not wanting to appear by herself, she immediately called Janie Tschudy, the wife of Jerry's bombardier-navigator. Together the two POW wives shared the information they'd kept to themselves for so long. They explained how the North Vietnamese had held and tortured their husbands for more than three years and how many families had received no word about whether their downed pilot had survived. Janie joked later that they'd ruined the members' evening; their stories were met with utterly shocked faces. Most audience members were unaware of U.S. POWs in Southeast Asia, and the stories of maltreatment startled them. Afterward, the members passed a hat for donations to help with the growing postage and telephone expenses the wives had been footing. Not one to solicit or accept money, Jane laughed and said, "If Jerry could see me now . . ." She knew he'd be proud.

The League organized a nationwide telegram-writing campaign in the days before the presidential inauguration, and on January 20, 1969, more than two thousand telegrams concerning the POW/MIA issue landed in the White House. President Nixon took office facing a community of families his administration could neither ignore nor silence. The new president responded to several families, informing them that he shared their concern and that "the subject of [prisoner] release and welfare will have an urgent priority in our talks in Paris." He would also share his concern with his new secretary of defense. Having proven they could mobilize America's military families and grab Washington's attention, the coalescing national network began distributing materials to the public, providing instructions for cabling the North Vietnamese delegation at the Paris Peace Talks to inquire about America's captive and missing servicemen. Members of the League courageously defied their government's Keep Quiet policy and raised their voices, hoping Washington and the world would listen.

Away from the national stage, the Alcatraz families weathered the storms of life, the misfortunes, large and small, that befall most families in one way or another; these families just faced them without a husband or father. A family of seven had to weather more storms than most, and the close of the decade saw Jane Denton struggle with her oldest boys—four headstrong young men cut from their father's cloth. They were aged twelve to eighteen at the time of their father's shootdown in 1965. The youngest, Madeleine, Michael, and Mary—who called themselves the "M Society"—ranged from one to eight.

With her husband already in Hanoi, Jane had no interest in seeing another Denton deployed to Vietnam, but her eldest son, Jerry, had joined the army and earned his pilot's wings; his best friend, Billy McFarland, became a helicopter crew chief. Jane loved both dearly and wanted neither to go. Since Jerry already had a relative in theater, army policy kept him stateside. Billy went, however, and the news of his death in South Vietnam struck Jane and her son hard. Two months later, in June 1969, Jerry sat his mother down on the couch at Watergate Lane. "Mom," he said, "I need to go; it's my duty. I'm requesting deployment to Vietnam." Jane didn't want him to go, but she understood. The next month, she saw her oldest son off to war just as she'd watched her husband leave three years before. She prayed both would return.

To her further distress, at 2:00 A.M. one morning later that same year, Jane received a phone call from her third-born, Jimmy. Earlier that night, he had borrowed his roommate's motorcycle and promptly wrecked it on a wooded stretch of road near Elon College in North Carolina. Paramedics found him and sped him to the hospital, where two doctors struggled to remove the smashed helmet from his head. Three days later, the navy had him transported to the Portsmouth Naval Hospital, where he spent five weeks in a body cast. Her son's crash offered Jane one more reminder of her boys' mortality. Jane needed her husband at home, as did her children. Perhaps, they hoped, the coming year would see his return.

On the far coast, Phyllis Rutledge had taken her family to Mission Bay, just north of San Diego, to celebrate Independence Day the previous year. The family was sitting at a picnic table talking about the night's coming fireworks when they heard somebody scream, "Get him out!"

They charged down to the shoreline where a boy had just laid fifteen-year-old Johnny Rutledge on the shore; he'd been injured diving into the bay. He was conscious but limp. Phyllis saw blood running from his head. Paramedics arrived shortly, and Phyllis and her three daughters tailed the ambulance to the hospital. As nurses shaved Johnny's head, his sister Sondra held his hand. He looked down and said, "I can't feel your hand."

Hours later, doctors explained that he'd broken his neck and probably crushed his spinal cord. Phyllis had to decide then and there whether doctors should perform surgery, which extended the hope of healing but carried a real possibility of death. She'd once relied on Howie to make such heavy decisions, but two and a half years of being on her own had taught her self-reliance. She decided to operate. Fortunately, Johnny survived the surgery, but he never regained feeling; he'd be paralyzed for life. In the coming weeks, his nine- and ten-year-old sisters did their nightly homework at the hospital; his mother hardly left his side. Johnny feared that his father wouldn't be able to look at him again. Phyllis just hoped Howie would return; how could she bear any more of this alone?

16

WE WILL BREAK YOU NOW

After the U.S. presidential election, Mickey Mouse, the hard-nosed former commander of Hỏa Lò who'd prepped Jerry Denton for his 1966
television interview, replaced Softsoap as commandant of Alcatraz, although Softsoap remained on the camp's staff. Mickey Mouse's arrival
heralded a bitter winter.

Early on a mid-December morning. George McKnight woke up
and began the ritual he had kept for fourteen months. First, he accepted
that Hanoi, Hỏa Lò, the Briar Patch, and Alcatraz had not all been part
of some nightmare. Then he tapped to his neighbors. Jerry had scarcely
tapped back when they heard a victorious hoot erupt from the empty
cell between them. A guard sprang out, shouting, "You communicate,
you communicate!"

A chill shot through Jerry's body. The game had suddenly changed.
For months, the Camp Authority had tacitly allowed communication
inside Alcatraz. Now, under Mickey Mouse, they'd assigned more guards
to the courtyard and had apparently revived the edict prohibiting communication, which previously the North Vietnamese used as a favorite
pretense to torture prisoners for propaganda statements. Jerry and
George sensed higher authorities had handed down new orders to the
administrators at Alcatraz: The government wanted more propaganda,
and their little camp would be forced to produce it.

The guards came first for George McKnight. After a severe beating in one of the camp's quiz rooms, George spent thirty-six hours hunched forward with his elbows tied to his knees, receiving intermittent beatings. He finally agreed to write an apology for communicating. After he composed the apology, the guards administered the treatment twice more, yielding two verbal statements, which the interrogators tape recorded. After more than a hundred hours of duress and deprivation, guards hauled him, nearly incapacitated, back to his cell. The others heard George collapse heavily. After several moments of silence, he slowly tapped, "Purge. I say no comm." His brothers could hear the pain in his taps and realized the Camp Authority had instituted another crackdown.

Jerry Denton tapped back to McKnight, "Keep the volume up and if you get caught, you tell them that I *ordered* you to do it."

From across the yard, Stockdale flashed, "It looks like we're going to take it on the chin, one by one. So let's go in and take it on the chin."

Jerry took it next. "You have been caught communicating," Mickey Mouse said when Jerry had been dragged into the interrogation room. "You must apologize. You must write letter to President Hồ Chí Minh and apologize for your crimes."

Jerry refused, incredulous that after four years they wanted even more statements. Mickey Mouse ordered him to be taken to another room, where a guard positioned him against a wall and forced his arms above his head. If Jerry lowered them, the guard pushed them up again. If he needed additional incentive, the guard would prick his palm with a sharp nail. The drill lasted for two solid days. When Mickey Mouse returned on the third day, Jerry still refused to apologize. The guards locked irons around his ankles, then pulled his arms behind his back and cuffed his wrists. When a day of hauling his bound body across concrete floors proved ineffective, the staff employed a new method—one Jerry had never encountered before.

A guard laced Jerry's wrists and forearms together, then bent his torso forward, spreading his elbows so they squeezed over his bent knees. The insides of his arms pressed against the outsides of his calves and thighs, just below and above his knee joints; his knees nearly touched his cheeks. His thighs pressed on his chest, making his lungs strain to accommodate each breath. Pain coursed along his viciously bent spine, the tip of which now bore most of his weight as his feet were kept 12 inches off the ground on an overturned stool. Then the guards inserted the pole. This was new to him, but he soon realized it served as the linchpin for the torture rig. They snaked the bamboo shaft through the gaps between his elbows and knees, where it began cutting off circulation in his arms and legs. When his condition became unbearable, Jerry began to pass out. When he tipped over onto his side, however, the floor would knock the pole out of the rig. Pressure eased and circulation resumed. The restored circulation—the allodynia that Pigeye had used to such great effect—electrified his arms and legs, snapping him back to consciousness. He would return to blinding agony as pins and needles became daggers and knives. As Jerry grappled with the rig, Mickey Mouse flippantly said, "Denton, we will break you now."

Jerry soon passed out again, and six guards descended upon him, helping to revive him with kicks and punches. The guard nicknamed Jack Armstrong swung at Jerry as he lay hogtied and helpless on the ground. Jerry spat at him and lunged forward pathetically, attempting to head-butt him. Jerry saw tears of compassion in Jack Armstrong's eyes, and he stared at the guard in wonderment as Jack left the room.

Jerry battled the remaining guards and the rig for nearly eight hours. Maybe he could, just perhaps, outlast Mickey Mouse. He would endure; he would not apologize, but he could not win. After three excruciating cycles of passing out and then jolting back to consciousness, his arms had turned black. His spine wanted to crack. His lungs still struggled for each breath. He couldn't help but scream. He would do anything to make it stop, even write an apology. He had reached his breaking point.

The next day, he wrote a letter to Hồ Chí Minh. He apologized for bombing North Vietnam. He asked for forgiveness. Then guards hauled him—beaten, sore, feverish, and nearly unconscious—back to Cell Ten, where he collapsed onto his bamboo mat and did not move. It was December 23, 1968. The next day, the guards pulled Jerry from his cell, blindfolded him, and marched him to the Plantation. He wished he had been able to enjoy the walk. At the Plantation, a guard untied Jerry's blindfold and led him into a banquet room, complete with champagne, a table of food, and Cat. The commandant of the North Vietnamese prison system beamed at Jerry.

"Ah, Denton," he said, "good to see you again. How are you?"

Jerry couldn't believe the question. He told Cat he'd been tortured. Cat ignored him and continued pleasantly, asking, "How are conditions?"

"Terrible," Jerry replied. "Can't eat because of the torture."

Plowing ahead, Cat asked, "Is there anything I can do for you?"

"Only if you do it for everyone."

Cat grew angrier. "All right, Denton, eat that banana," he said. He pointed to a nearby table's spread.

Jerry declined.

"It will be good for you," Cat insisted.

"If everyone gets a banana, I will take it."

That did it. Cat screamed, "Shut mouth! You eat banana! That is an order!"

Jerry didn't flinch. Cat ordered him back to Alcatraz.

On Christmas morning 1968, Mickey Mouse called Jim Mulligan to quiz and presented him with three letters: one from Louise, one from his brother, and one from his parents. In three years, he had received only three letters from his wife, and he scurried back to his cell to feast on the words from home. As he read his letters again and again, he felt sorry for Harry Jenkins and Howie Rutledge. To the POWs' knowledge, the North Vietnamese had yet to acknowledge that these two aviators remained alive. Consequently, the Camp Authority did not allow them to send mail, nor did Mickey Mouse let them read any letters sent by their families, who still hoped Harry and Howie were prisoners, not casualties.

For four Christmases now, a pall had hung over the Rutledge and Jenkins families as they each gathered in their respective homes to mark another year of uncertainty and tried to find some cause for celebration. Like the Stockdales, Harry's family had read an unconfirmed report in a Soviet *Pravda* article that he'd survived. The article described a particularly tall aviator arriving in Hanoi; Harry measured 6'5". Yet they'd received no confirmation from North Vietnam or the U.S. intelligence agencies. Howie's family had likewise heard nothing, but this Christmas, as every Christmas, the best presents under the Rutledge tree had tags reading "Love, Daddy."

When brought in for a Christmas quiz, Howie brazenly asked for coffee and a ticket to Saigon. Mickey Mouse's generosity did not extend that far. However, Nels Tanner, who was shot down in October 1966, finally received his first letter from home that Christmas. Bob Shumaker was permitted to spend much of the holiday playing chess with Sam Johnson. They'd fashioned boards out of mosquito nets, which had a distinct grid pattern in their weave. Using the makeshift boards and shreds of toilet paper or trash as game pieces, Shu and Sam spent hours tapping moves through the wall. Others soon made their own boards, and silence would settle over Alcatraz during matches, broken only by muffled shouts of surprise, anger, or "Checkmate!" Arguments sometimes erupted during the heated games, and once George McKnight pointedly tapped to Jerry Denton that he'd been a boxer; Jerry backed off. Perhaps in the holiday spirit, the guards didn't crack down.

That Christmas night, peace fell over the courtyard of Alcatraz. Inside the cells, solitary lightbulbs burned on indifferently. Sometime after Jim Mulligan had fallen asleep, Mickey Mouse ordered him up. The Camp Authority seemed to respect Jim's faith, and he hoped Mickey Mouse might take him to a church service, as he had the previous Christmas. It would surely be another propaganda stunt, but the excursion might provide a chance to contact POWs in other camps. Whatever his destination or circumstances, he simply treasured any time outside his cell.

Jim donned the red-and-pink-striped suit, and Mickey Mouse ushered his blindfolded prisoner into a waiting vehicle. Using the Vietnamese name the Camp Authority had assigned to Jim, Mickey Mouse said, "Mun, I take you to your Christmas celebration in the big Hanoi church of the Catholics."

For months, Jim had seen nothing beautiful, nothing inspirational. In his cell, he looked at dim, bare walls for at least twenty-three hours and forty minutes each day, often more. In quiz rooms, he saw stark walls, save occasional portraits of Hồ Chí Minh. When the guards removed Jim's blindfold, he found himself inside what he'd later learn was St. Joseph's Cathedral, staring at a painting of St. Francis kneeling at the cross. Above the cathedral's altar rose gold arches and stained-glass panels, emitting a magnificent glow. He'd seen few sights so beautiful.

Jim spied Cat escorting another POW to the nativity scene at the front of the church, near the main altar rail. The American locked eyes with Jim, then put his arm behind Cat's back. The friendly gesture appalled Jim until he noticed the POW's finger had begun to move in

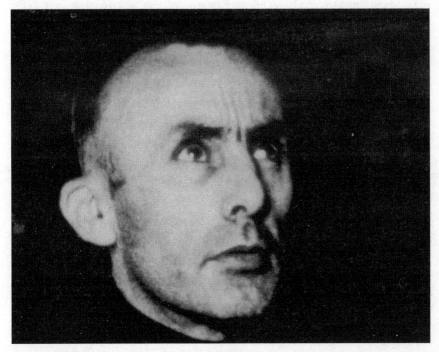

Jim Mulligan at St. Joseph's Cathedral in Hanoi, Christmas 1968.

code, "Dick Stratton." Jim watched Stratton, a pilot from the USS *Ticonderoga*, walk to the crèche and kneel. With his prisoner occupied at the crib, Cat walked over to Jim Mulligan.

"How are you?" he asked.

"I am well, thank you," Jim answered. "May I kneel at the crib before Mass starts?"

"Of course you may go there now," Cat said, and Jim hustled toward the altar before Stratton left. Cameramen near the altar captured the scene of the North Vietnamese offering lenient treatment to American prisoners on their Christian holiday.

Jim knelt beside his fellow aviator just as Stratton finished his prayer and began to rise. Jim grabbed the leg of his pants to stop him. Bowing his head and speaking as if he were deep in prayer, Jim told Stratton, "Eleven of us are one block north of the Plantation, in solitary and in irons. I'm Jim Mulligan. Rutledge, Jenkins, Johnson, Shumaker, Storz, Tanner, Coker, McKnight, Denton, and Stockdale are with me. We are okay."

Stratton quietly listened to Jim's message, then left reverently. Likewise, Jim crossed himself and stood. When he turned around, he found Mickey Mouse glaring at him.

"You communicate, you communicate," Mickey Mouse accused, keeping his voice low enough to avoid attention.

"Oh, no," Jim replied defensively. "I only pray to the Father on this Christmas celebration at the beautiful manger scene you have provided for me. Ask the men of your cameras that were filming as I prayed. They must know that I do not communicate. Ask them, they will tell you this is so."

Mickey Mouse either believed Jim or elected not to make a scene. Jim walked back toward the pews and observed several other Americans sitting by themselves or in pairs. After he'd taken his place, he heard someone enter the pew two aisles to his rear. He turned around and saw Jerry Coffee. When Jim had attended Mass the previous Christmas, he'd made brief contact with Coffee. At the time, he'd tried to send him a message about the eleven men in Alcatraz, but he was not certain what Coffee understood. He now had another chance, so Jim appealed to Mickey Mouse; he wanted to visit with his old friend. As Mickey Mouse wavered, Jim begged him to grant this harmless Christmas favor. He consented.

Jim turned around and said, "Jerry Coffee, Merry Christmas. I'm Jim Mulligan. How's your wife, Bea, and the children? I got a letter from Louise and my six sons. Did you get a letter? I am in the same state as last year. We are all okay. The eleven of us! Are you okay?"

"Merry Christmas, Jim," Coffee replied. "I'm fine. I got a letter, too. I got it okay." Coffee winked, which Jim took to mean he understood the message about Alcatraz.

"Enough, enough," Mickey Mouse broke in. "You speak too much to your friend."

That ended Jim Mulligan's Christmastime communication at the cathedral. He settled into his pew and focused on the service. He listened to the priest's sermon, translated by Rabbit, who stood near the front. Jim struggled to hear the reverent words coming from the lips of the young officer responsible for so much ungodly suffering. At least, he thought, he could receive communion. He gave thanks.

When Mass concluded, Mickey Mouse herded Jim into a waiting vehicle and drove him away from the beauty of the cathedral and back to the ugliness of Alcatraz. At the door of Cell Eleven, an angry Mickey Mouse turned on Jim and said, "Mun, tonight you have played the fool with me. You are a bad man. You violate the regulation of the camp. You communicate to your compatriots. You will be punished."

Jim really didn't care. Dick Stratton now knew the identities and location of the Alcatraz prisoners, and Jim trusted Stratton would spread the word through the prison system. Besides, he had been able to worship on Christmas Day. Jim had always been a devout Catholic, and a year had passed since his last communion. He felt peace even as Mickey Mouse stormed off and a guard clamped Jim in irons for the night. The door slammed shut and he heard the lock engage. With that, Christmas 1968 at Alcatraz ended, and the worst was still to come.

As the year 1969 began, the eleven prisoners speculated about their homecoming. Everyone placed bets on their date of release from Hanoi. The winner would choose the location for the Alcatraz reunions. The losers would pay in tacos when, God willing, they got home. Optimistic Jim Mulligan picked June 1969. Other near-term predictions went tapping through cell walls and flashing across the courtyard. When Mulligan heard CAG's estimate, he thought his commanding officer had lost his mind. He chose February 1973.

"After the next [presidential] election," CAG had tapped. "Then we'll be going home and not before then."

On January 8, 1969, Jerry Denton finally received his punishment for the banana confrontation at the Plantation. In one of the quiz rooms outside the Alcatraz courtyard, Mickey Mouse inquired about Jerry's Christmas Eve encounter with Cat. Jerry responded that he had simply abided by the Code of Conduct, which prohibited him from accepting special favors. Then the officer gave Jerry a new order: Read the North Vietnamese news to the camp. Jerry stubbornly refused, and Mickey Mouse put him back into the torture rig he'd faced before Christmas. Mickey Mouse also opened the room's green shutters so other POWs could hear Jerry's screams. For two awful days, they did. At last bested by the pole and ropes, Jerry submitted. When the guards untied the bindings, he convulsed grotesquely on the floor long enough and severely enough for the guards to summon a doctor. When the spasms subsided, Jerry read a North Vietnamese script into a tape recorder. The two days of agony had taken such a toll on him that his first tape bordered on incoherence. The next day, Softsoap had Jerry do additional takes until he judged one passable. Soon, the daily news came blaring over the speakers. Jerry's deliberate mispronunciations drew laughs from his ten fellow inmates. The North Vietnamese turned off the recording and sent Jerry back to his cell.

"They want us to write letters asking Hồ Chí Minh for amnesty," Jerry tapped, referring to what he'd been told in his session. "If they're working on some kind of release, they can't just turn us loose without losing face. They have to have some kind of justification, some kind of admission of guilt. Then Uncle Hồ can forgive us. Don't make it easy for them. Hold out as long as you can."

Mickey Mouse seemed momentarily to retreat from his goal of obtaining apologies and instead just had Softsoap try to convince Jim Mulligan to read the news, noting how his friend Jerry had already complied. The crusty Irish Catholic fired back, "Bullshit. You tortured him badly, and if you want me to read, you'll have to torture me the same way." Apparently, Softsoap and Mickey Mouse decided the difficulty of making these diehards cooperate was not worth any gain from broadcasting their words. Thus ended the short-lived reading campaign of 1969.

Quiet reigned over Alcatraz for the next three weeks. Then, late on the night of January 24, 1969, the intestinal worms breeding inside Harry Jenkins began causing severe cramping in his abdomen. He asked guards for morphine. They refused, so he asked them to shoot him. They refused again. The pain grew and Harry began shouting, *"Bào cào, bào cào!"* Sad Sack, the lone guard on duty, callously told him, "No *bào cào*," and ordered him to sleep. The command incensed Harry. His raised voice—and the expletives he began employing—caught the attention of the other inmates. His neighbor, Sam Johnson, heard a guard enter Harry's cell. Then he heard a rifle collide with flesh and bone.

"They're beating him," Sam thought with horror. "He's sick and asking for a doctor and they're beating him!"

He put his mouth to the crack in his door and shouted, *"Bào cào! Bào cào!"*

Rousted from sleep, the other prisoners waddled to their doors wearing their leg irons. They stood there, each in his separate cell, banging against his windowless door while shouting, *"Bào cào!"* A riot had erupted in Alcatraz.

Sad Sack rushed to Jim Mulligan's cell, which was just yards away from Harry's. Jim's peephole flew open and the guard's face appeared. "No *bào cào*!" he screamed. *"No bào cào!"*

Enraged and defiant, Jim callously screamed back, *"Bào cào*! Get a doctor! There's a sick guy over there."

"No *bào cào*!"

"Yeah, *bào cào*," Jim bellowed. *"Bào cào*! Get a doctor you lazy son of a . . ."

Sad Sack pounded on Jim's door with his rifle, sending a loud echo pulsing into the cell, but Jim just kept yelling. Before long the prisoners heard more guards arrive in the courtyard, and they received assurances that Harry would see a doctor, which he soon did.

Many of the Alcatraz men later considered this their finest hour. They had united as one against the Camp Authority and risen up on behalf of a fellow POW, and they had won. They remained locked in their cells, hungry, skinny, clad in threadbare pajamas, tortured, and injured, but they had still been victorious.

Despite this victory, Alcatraz's commanding American officer had seen enough. CAG had long since lost his tolerance for the North Vietnamese keeping his men in leg irons, in solitary, on a starvation diet, and without adequate clothing in the middle of winter when so many were already unhealthy or sick. The next morning, as soon as the sun lit the compound, Jim flashed under his door to Nels Tanner, ordering a hunger strike. "Everybody goes to the food pot when we are taken out to get our rations," he sent. "But nobody takes any food for three days."

The prisoners of Alcatraz first defied the Camp Authority at their morning meal. With a furious staff watching, they defied them again that afternoon. One by one, they walked to the table but refused to take food. Their termerity reminded CAG of a line from Joseph Conrad's *Lord Jim*, "A certain readiness to perish is not so very rare, but it is seldom that you meet men whose souls, steeled in the impenetrable armour of resolution, are ready to fight a losing battle to the last."

Before daybreak on the following morning, a guard violently opened Jim Stockdale's door. A detail waited outside as Jim followed orders to gather up his belongings. One man grabbed his roll while another bound his wrists with wire. Someone tightened a blindfold around his eyes and pushed him out of the cell. From beneath doors and through peepholes, ten pairs of American eyes watched the aging fighter pilot hobble across the yard, swinging his stiff leg. Mickey Mouse seemed to consider Jim Stockdale dangerous even in this state; he had assigned five men to guard him.

Before the POWs even began their morning routine, the North Vietnamese were driving their leader through the streets of Hanoi, away from Alcatraz, away from the men he had led in resistance, away from the men who had followed him with absolute devotion. His soldiers would not learn his fate for nearly an entire year.

Shortly after the noon siesta began that late January day, a guard came to Jim Mulligan's cell; the time for punishment had arrived. Jim put on every stitch of clothing he had: socks, shorts, short-sleeved shirt, and sweater. Then he pulled on the dark shirt and pants he wore for quizzes. He wore the layers not as protection against the January chill but as padding against the punishing sticks, fists, and ropes he might soon face. The more clothes the better, POWs had learned. The guard pushed Jim out of his cell and to the left, toward the gate that led to the alley behind the Ministry of National Defense. As he shuffled along, he used a new version of tap code the Alcatraz prisoners had pioneered. Coughs or snorts represented ones or twos in the matrix, a throat clear was three, a hawk signified four, and spitting or sneezing meant five. Jim coughed and snorted "M MVG," for "Jim Mulligan moving."

In response, he heard "Cough, cough—cough, cough (pause) cough—snort, snort (pause) hawk—spit,": GBU (God bless you).

Jim turned the corner to his left, walked several paces, then entered one of the camp's quiz rooms. Softsoap was waiting. After Jim had bowed, Softsoap explained that the previous day's commotion had embarrassed the Camp Authority and violated the camp rules. He fingered Jim as a prime instigator and demanded an apology. Jim declined. Softsoap put him against the wall with his arms raised. Eight hours later, Softsoap returned. "You must write an apology to the camp commander and all this will be over with," he said.

"All right," muttered Jim. "I'll write." Softsoap provided pen and paper.

"I apologize to the camp commander for my actions in support of the sick American who needed medical attention," Jim wrote. "This event would not have happened if your guard on duty had done his job and reported to the authorities the American 'Bào cào.' (signed) J. A. Mulligan, CDR, USN."

Softsoap read the statement. "This will never do," he said. "You must repent. You must give yourself over to me and do what I tell you."

"That's it," Jim said, pointing to his statement. "That's all I'll write."

"Then I must turn you over to my guards," he declared. "They will persuade you to see the error of your ways. You cannot stand up against them, you cannot last!"

"Maybe I can't, but I'll sure die trying," Jim shot back.

"You fool," exclaimed Softsoap. "You fool! Do as I say before you are injured. No one cares about you. Your people won't care about this. Write! Give yourself to me and do as I say. Things will go much better for you here. This is the bad camp. We have a good camp where you can go. There are Americans happy there. Make it easy on yourself and cooperate."

"No," Jim yelled. "No! I won't write. The others here won't write. I don't care if no one else cares what I do. I care and that's all that counts." He pointed in the direction of the Alcatraz courtyard. "And they care, too! What you do to one of us, you must do to all of us here."

"Then I leave you with my guards," Softsoap said. He left, and Jim's night began.

Sad Sack and four other guards entered the room and clamped three sets of irons on Jim's legs, then bound his hands and arms behind his back with ropes, immediately cutting off circulation. They pulled the ropes, yanking his arms nearly over his head and forcing his face into his crotch. Laughing, the guards turned Jim into a ball of agony. The numbness crept up his arms, starting in his fingertips, then progressing through his hands and wrists to his forearms and shoulders. His body shook uncontrollably. His head reeled from punches; his ribs ached from kicks. It went on and on. He finally said, *"Bào cào."*

"No *bào cào*," mocked Sad Sack. Jim guessed that the riot he'd helped to cause had landed Sad Sack in trouble with his superiors. The guard saw his time with Jim as vengeance. He seemed to relish his grim business, ignoring the pleas coming from his victim. Jim wanted desperately to deny Sad Sack the satisfaction of hearing him scream—of knowing he had won. Yet he succumbed. When his scream drifted through the Alcatraz courtyard, his brothers suffered with him. They knew nobody could withstand torture; they had all reached the same point before. Perhaps worse, each POW knew that his own screams would soon follow. The North Vietnamese had launched another purge, another effort to force statements. Soon each Alcatraz inmate would find himself in that same torture room, facing the guards and their ropes, destined to break.

When Sad Sack finally stopped, Mickey Mouse visited the convulsing remains of Jim Mulligan. "Will you write for me?" he asked, taking over the interrogation from Softsoap.

"Yes, I'll write," Jim whispered. Days before, he had basked in the glory of a battle won, fought together with his brothers in Alcatraz. Now, defeated and alone, Jim sat at the table with what the POWs called a blue book—a blue-covered notebook—and copied a letter of apology that Softsoap had originally drafted.

The administrators collected Jim's completed letter, as well as his quiz suit, sweater, and socks. He stayed in the room for six days, always in irons, always cold, always hungry, always fearing the next click of the lock. During his stay in the quiz room, the camp commander made him write to President Nixon, the *Enterprise*, his squadron, and bases back home. Each time Mickey Mouse would ask for a letter, Jim would refuse. Then Sad Sack or another guard would rope him, beat him, or otherwise torture him until he submitted.

When Jim returned to his cell, he found himself the sole occupant of the small three-room shed; the North Vietnamese had not brought back Jim Stockdale. Mulligan immediately began flashing under the door to Nels and Ron. They told him that two POWs from the nine-cell building had been pulled into quiz rooms. The Camp Authority had added renewed fervor to the Blue Book Purge of 1969.

After working over Jim Mulligan, Mickey Mouse deliberately made his way through his prisoners by rank. When Bob Shumaker's turn arrived, he refused to write a letter of apology to Hồ Chí Minh for bombing North Vietnam. Guards forced him to kneel on the concrete floor of a quiz room for twelve days wearing irons around his ankles and cuffs around his wrists. Regular beatings were also administered. By the time he agreed to write, Shu could see the bones of his kneecaps. In an alley outside the walls of Alcatraz, guards beat Nels Tanner with a fan belt to coerce his statement, administering his punishment over seventeen grueling days. Yet all the victims kept their wits even as they submitted and wrote letters or taped insincere statements. They tainted confessions with as many tip-off phrases as they could manage. One confession noted, "Such famous men as the great Latin American humanitarian S.P. de Gonzales were against the war." Spoken aloud, the name became "Speedy Gonzales." The humor hardly balanced out the suffering, however.

On his way to the quiz room, Major Sam Johnson tried to forget the screams he'd heard during the past weeks. Each cry had felt like a dagger. He'd prayed hard for his friends. Now he could feel their prayers for him.

"The United States is going to leave you here, you know," Softsoap began as Sam took his seat; Softsoap and Mickey Mouse had become joint leaders of Alcatraz quizzes. "The Vietnamese people love you, Sông. You do not understand that. They want to let you go home. But we cannot unless you write a letter of apology for your crimes."

"I can't do that," Sam answered.

"You will think about it," Softsoap ordered. Then he rose and walked out the door. Sam spent five days in the room, sleeping on the concrete floor in between daily lectures from Softsoap. On the fifth day, Sam sensed Softsoap's patience waning. When he left, he gave Sam pen and paper to write a letter; instead Sam mentally practiced his French. He was thoughtfully conjugating verbs when Softsoap returned. "You have not written your letter," he observed. "You will be punished."

Softsoap walked out, and a guard entered. He tied Sam to a stool. Then four large, uniformed female soldiers entered the room. One shouted, and they descended upon him, hammering him with fists and rifles. With his hands tied behind his back, Sam could not defend himself against the blows. The women paid special attention to his temples and badly healed shoulders. When his stool toppled, they went after his ribs with their boots. The women's shrieks filled the room as Sam prayed,

"Oh, God, let me black out!" Then, with genuine trepidation, he began to think, "Maybe they won't stop until I'm dead." He tasted blood in his mouth; bile crawled up his throat. Finally, a guard ended the melee. Softsoap entered the room to accept the inevitable statement.

"You sit there," he said, referring to a small table. "Now you write."

"I can't write," Sam said truthfully. He still had little use of his arms or right hand, so Softsoap had him sign a typed statement.

"What have I done?" Sam asked himself afterward, as he cried from pain, shame, and defeat. "I gave in too easily, I should have held out longer . . . In the end, we all give them something, just to hang on to sanity, to life . . . but it will be nothing of any real value. Anyone who knows me will recognize that letter is garbage."

As he tried to reassure himself, Sam heard a whisper and recognized the voice of Jerry Denton, whom Softsoap had secured in an adjacent torture room. "Sam," Jerry whispered from his window, "Sam, it's okay, buddy."

"I made them write it, Jerry," the Texan whispered back, "but I had to sign it."

"It's okay, Sam," Jerry said. "You're okay. Hang on. You did good."

When guards returned Sam to his cell, he prayed for forgiveness. Then he sent a message to Bob Shumaker. "I'm sorry," he tapped to his neighbor. "Pass it down to the others." Sam desperately needed absolution. Of course he had it already; everyone had been there.

With Stockdale still absent, the ten inmates at Alcatraz endured the very worst the Camp Authority could mete out—fists, whips, belts, ropes, stools, and ever-cruel isolation. They began to notice that one of them, Ron Storz, had increasing difficulty handling solitary. Ron had always been tough, even high-spirited; nobody questioned his optimism and courage, but four years of harsh imprisonment had taken its toll on the thirty-four-year-old father of two. At Hỏa Lò, he'd taken to hunger strikes, and he decided to revive the practice at Alcatraz. By refusing to eat, he could retain control of one part of his life; Softsoap and Mickey Mouse controlled the rest.

Some of his fellow Alcatraz inmates thought Ron believed release was imminent and wanted to go home gaunt, a walking testament to the cruelty of the North Vietnamese. Others believed that solitary confinement was gradually killing him—days upon weeks without real personal contact were wearing away his will to live. Above all other things, Ron loved watching the sunrise, and some thought that four years without seeing the sun's bright rays spill over the eastern horizon simply broke his heart.

Ron Storz with son, Mark, and infant, Monica, just weeks before he deployed to Vietnam.

Whatever the ultimate reason for his decline, Ron's 6'2" frame withered to 100 pounds. He was even skinnier than Jim Mulligan. His mental state declined as well. Through the wall with Shu, he told his fellow inmate that he worried he was getting fat. His statements left Shu dumbfounded; he had watched Ron's formerly toned physique wither away. Bouts of irrationality seemed to plague Ron, perhaps partially attributable to a case of beriberi, a disease of the nervous system that Ron might have contracted due to deficiency in thiamine, or vitamin B-1, found in whole grains and fresh meats, vegetables, and fruits. With no fresh food, the POWs already had precious few nutrients in their diet; Ron's reluctance to eat made him even more susceptible to such an illness. "If something doesn't happen to me soon, I don't think I'll be able to make it through the summer," he flashed across the courtyard to Jim Mulligan one day.

Nels spent hours tapping on their shared wall, trying to lift Ron's spirits, but Nels could do nothing to counteract the demoralizing abuse guards and interrogators could deliver in a quiz room.

Eventually—and despite his condition—the Blue Book Purge reached Ron Storz. Mickey Mouse had him hauled into one of the quiz rooms outside the courtyard and broke him as he'd broken everyone else. Ron submitted and signed a statement admitting "crimes against humanity." His weakness and failure—as he perceived it—left him feeling despondent. After securing his confession, the North Vietnamese permitted him to shave. They provided him with a razor and left him alone in the quiz room.

That day, the Alcatraz prisoners heard a commotion coming from the vicinity of the interrogation rooms. Guards rushed out of the cellblock area, panicked. From Cell One, Howie Rutledge saw guards and doctors rushing along the alleyway. "What happened?" he yelled at a passing guard. "Storz dying!" the guard called back. Ron had used the razor to cut his wrists.

For several days, the remaining nine prisoners learned nothing about their friend. Then a guard finally responded to Jerry Denton's persistent questions. "That guard," he replied, pointing to another North Vietnamese soldier. "He gave Storz blood." A transfusion had saved Ron's life.

When Ron returned to Cell Five, his friends encouraged him to eat. Jerry repeatedly *ordered* him to do so. Ron seemed to appreciate the concern but ignored the orders. He appeared far more interested in flashing across the courtyard to Jim Mulligan. Ron knew that Stockdale's departure had left Mulligan isolated in the small three-cell shed, and he took it upon himself to keep Jim connected with the others. As they flashed code to each other beneath their doors, they developed a special friendship.

Jim prayed for his family in Virginia Beach at reveille and taps; otherwise he locked away his memories of them so he could focus on surviving each day. Conversely, Ron flashed about his family constantly. He mused about his five-year-old daughter, Monica, just an infant when he'd been sent to Vietnam. He bragged to Jim about his son, Mark. Jim suspected their memories haunted Ron during his every waking hour. Jim began detecting the severe harm each day alone inflicted upon Ron's ever more fragile mind. The Camp Authority only worsened his state by constantly threatening him, telling him, "You will die here."

One day in the early summer of 1969, Jim hunkered down on his floor to peek under the door and check for guards. He heard a thud come from the long cellblock and saw Ron's scrawny arm emerge from the 4-inch gap beneath his door. His arm didn't move. Jim called, *"Bào cào,"* to get the attention of the guards. This time, thankfully, they listened.

Using a wire he scavenged from the bath area, Jim had drilled a multitude of tiny peepholes through the wall of his corner cell, giving him views of the prison yard. He removed the lint-and-soap plugs that concealed the holes, then watched what happened. Guards rushed to Cell Five, and when they opened the door, Ron's unconscious body rolled out. Officers and medics arrived. Ron had passed out. Jim watched the guards carry his friend's limp body outside the gate, where they put him in a room beyond the courtyard.

The men saw Ron each day as the guards escorted him to the latrine. His skeletal frame and hunched walk terrified his friends. Always the pragmatist, Jerry Denton used Ron's trips to the latrine to exchange information and orders as Ron scrubbed out his bucket, just yards away from Jerry's cell. The guards had started to treat Ron differently from the others, often turning a blind eye as their increasingly erratic prisoner-patient conversed with his ranking officer. Jerry quickly learned that while Softsoap helped Ron recover by giving him a Bible, he also tempted him with offers of repatriation. Ron asked Jerry questions about amnesty and parole. Jerry explained conditions of early release to Ron, noting that POWs would not be violating the Code of Conduct if they accepted early release because their lives were in danger. Jerry hoped the information would convince his dying friend to leave. He hoped that Ron might accept an offer of freedom and save himself before it was too late.

As the summer progressed, however, Ron's condition continued to decline. On one of his visits to the latrine, when Ron didn't hear Jerry's response to one of his questions, Ron angrily shouted, "Well, I know who my *real* friends are!" His condition worried and saddened Jerry and the others, who had known Ron as a caring ally and resilient fighter. Torture, solitary, illness, and deprivation had taken their toll.

The year 1969 saw the most brutal of times at Alcatraz, and not just for Ron Storz. The inmates were brought back to the quiz rooms, and their visits there grew progressively longer. The men accepted the challenge each time, knowing they'd lose, and wondering to themselves if they would ever leave Alcatraz. Hanoi Hannah and Mickey Mouse provided little encouragement. The inmates discounted everything they heard from the Camp Authority, but with no outside source of information, they wondered whether the reports of upheaval at home and the stalemate in Vietnam might be true.

When Sam Johnson and Mickey Mouse squared off at a quiz in May 1969, the commandant asked the Texan how he could support Nixon's new bombing campaign in Cambodia. "Your country is the aggressor," Mickey Mouse said. "How can you support what they are doing?"

Sam knew little of the campaign but said he hoped America would take all of Vietnam, to which Mickey Mouse replied, "The American people are against you. *They* will cause us to win this war."

Trying to ignore the North Vietnamese propaganda, the POWs debated their homecoming inside their cellblock. "The North has got to be scared that Nixon is going to destroy all their supply routes," Sam commed to Shu.

"Calm down, Sam," Jerry responded from Cell Ten. "This thing isn't over yet."

"Maybe not, but Nixon is getting ready to close it down."

"It's going to be a long war," Harry Jenkins added. "[The Cambodia bombing] is just one more effort—one more move without the support of ground troops." Even Harry, who considered everything a good sign, realized the U.S. military couldn't quell the insurgency from the air.

"One year," Sam predicted.

"Probably more like two," Jerry answered, uncharacteristically pessimistic.

One night a few weeks later, Mickey Mouse walked into a quiz room where Jerry had managed to fall asleep despite being in rear cuffs. When Mickey Mouse woke him, Jerry thought that the North Vietnamese officer seemed unusually excited. "Denton, I have something to tell you," he said. "I know you usually don't believe me, but time will prove I am telling the truth. I have just come from a meeting at headquarters. I have receive information to make provision for *two* more years." He held up two fingers and clarified, "I must provide for *two* more Christmas. The war will go on!" In fact, the Camp Authority would eventually need to make provisions for *four* more Christmases.

17

BLACKMAIL

That January morning in 1969, ten pairs of eyes had watched through cracks and peepholes as five guards herded Jim Stockdale out of the Alcatraz courtyard, the commander hobbling along as best he could. The gate had closed behind him, and the sound of his awkward stride had faded. The men heard an engine start and a truck rumble down the street, carrying him to an unknown fate. The truck had, in fact, driven Jim straight to Hỏa Lò Prison. When he heard the gates open and smelled the musty air, he knew exactly where they had taken him.

He could never forget the prison's distinct smell, and even with the blindfold tightened around his eyes, he could have made the walk to Room Eighteen without escort. He knew the steps from the sidewalk through the gates. He recognized the echoes in the tunnel that led toward the Heartbreak courtyard. He hobbled across a familiar sidewalk and into Room Eighteen, the site of so much agony. The guards removed his blindfold, pushed him inside, and left.

He looked through a crack in the French doors and saw Rabbit and Pigeye walking toward him. He knew they would make his return to the Hanoi Hilton particularly unpleasant. Just as he shuffled away from the peephole, the doors burst open and in walked his old adversaries.

"It is you who has caused me to be brought back here from my new office," Rabbit began. "I don't like it. We'll get you this time, you son of a bitch."

Referring to the Alcatraz riot and hunger strike, Rabbit continued, "I don't want to talk about what happened at the camp you just left. I want to know only one thing: Will you be my slave or not?"

Jim answered, "No."

In seconds Pigeye manhandled him into leg irons and nylon straps. Then he plied the trade that had made him so feared and despised among the POWs. He jerked Jim's arms behind his back and bound his forearms together from wrist to elbow. Then he tightened the straps, one pull at a time, watching Jim begin to shake involuntarily. Eventually, Pigeye could cinch the forearms no tighter. That cued him to begin ratcheting Jim's arms higher and higher behind his back, forcing his haggard face closer to his outstretched knees. With his head stuffed between his thighs and his windpipe and lungs nearly crushed, he could scarcely breathe. Rabbit just watched placidly. By midmorning, Jim had uttered, "I submit."

Victorious, Rabbit had him write a statement that said, "I understand that I am a criminal who has bombed churches, schools, and pagodas of the Democratic Republic of Vietnam. I have opposed the Camp Authority and incited others to oppose the Camp Authority. I know the nature of my sins, and I now submit to you to do whatever you tell me to write, say, or tape." Rabbit left, smug, his morning's job complete.

Jim suspected Rabbit and Cat had more concessions in mind, and when he looked through his peephole that afternoon, he saw Rabbit and Pigeye on their way back to Room Eighteen, presumably for the next round. Rabbit assigned Jim a spot on the floor, and once the American had seated himself at his feet, he said, "You have never submitted a complete report of your military activities in the months preceding your capture. We need to know the number of people and the names of everybody in your units. Take this paper and sit in that chair and list the titles of your units, the number of people normally assigned, and their names."

If Jim could have rolled his eyes without reprisal, he would have. The North Vietnamese had run him and countless other POWs through this exercise, which revealed virtually no useful military information—especially now, considering nearly four years had passed since the

POWs last saw their units. Requests for these biographical statements generally preceded demands for propaganda statements, and Jim would not go easily. Despite the consequences that he knew would come, Jim shouted, "No!" The day's second session began.

"Đán, do not scream," Pigeye whispered into Jim's ear after he'd roped him up and begun forcing his head toward his feet. "Do not scream, Đán." Screams required breath, and at the moment Jim had none; he was suffocating. Only submission could save his life.

Pleased with Jim's second surrender of the day, Rabbit directed him to write his biography. "Put at the top of the paper: 'Secret Personnel Report,'" he said. "Now, how many men were on your ship?"

"I once read in a newspaper that there were over three thousand people on a carrier of that size," Jim said.

"Okay, put that down," Rabbit said. "Now write down the names of all the officers and enlisted men who were assigned."

The drill lasted for an hour, Rabbit asking useless questions, Jim supplying useless answers. Jim did notice that Rabbit seemed embarrassed by some questions. It became clear that his superiors had asked him for certain specifics that Rabbit considered inconsequential, but his duty bound him to go through the motions. Finally done for the day, Rabbit rose to leave. Then he looked down at Jim and said, "You are to get no food until you learn your lesson. The guard will bring you water."

Before Jim had left Alcatraz, he had placed his men on a hunger strike to protest the treatment shown to the ailing Harry Jenkins. In Alcatraz, the men went hungry together on their own terms, but in Room Eighteen, Rabbit had control.

The next day, Rabbit began the drill anew. His prisoner reluctantly completed "My Secret Report on the Defenses of My Ship," "My Secret Report on Aircraft Tactics over the Target," and "My Secret Report on All the Targets I've Struck."

When Jim again grew stubborn and refused to comply, Rabbit produced a photograph of eighteen-year-old Jimmy Stockdale, doubtlessly taken from one of the many letters that Sybil sent but Jim had never received. "If you ever want to see this boy again, you must change your attitude," Rabbit said. The photograph proved insufficient motivation. Pigeye soon put Jim back into the ropes.

As Pigeye worked on him, Jim's mind transported him away, just as his survival instructors had taught him. *Get your head out of the box,* they'd repeated as he was, in fact, stuffed inside a small box during SERE training. Room Eighteen soon became distant and Jim's mind retreated to Alcatraz, where he could draw strength from the ten men who served alongside him, who understood what he endured. He imagined himself ambling along the cellblocks behind the Ministry of National Defense and eventually arriving at the door of Jim Mulligan's cell. He remembered the words to "When Irish Eyes Are Smiling," the self-assigned emergency tune Mulligan would whistle should he find himself in great distress; each of the Eleven had selected a tune shortly after arriving at Alcatraz. Next, Jim strolled pleasantly across the quiet walkway to Cell One and remembered Howie Rutledge's emergency song, "Oklahoma." He walked to Cells Two and Three, reciting "Maryland, My Maryland" for Harry Jenkins and "The Eyes of Texas" for Sam Johnson. He had finished singing "The Pennsylvania Polka" for Bob Shumaker and had begun "The Sidewalks of New York" for Ron Storz when he suddenly became aware of Rabbit shrieking at him, there in Room Eighteen, demanding he submit.

So the week continued, Rabbit—now often joined by Chihuahua—pressing Jim for information, Jim giving nothing true or valuable, Pigeye facilitating the process as necessary. Jim knew they were building a thick file of information they thought he was not allowed to divulge. Even though his information was more than three years old, Jim was sure they'd try to use it as leverage against him. He accused Rabbit of blackmail. Rabbit did not recognize the word initially, but the next day, he told Jim, "I looked that word up in my dictionary and you are right—this is blackmail."

Rabbit extracted a statement, which read, "To the General Staff Officer, Dear Sir: Here is a summary of the military information that you requested. I would like to present this and would be willing to do so at your office if you so desire. This material should be of value to you, and it is the first installment of more to follow up on your request. James Bond Stockdale."

Upon signing the letter, Jim received his blanket roll, a mosquito net, bread, and soup. He happily used the first two gifts. The blackmail admission had infuriated him even further, however, and in protest, he refused to touch the food.

Six days after beginning the interrogation, Rabbit walked into Room

Eighteen and told him, "I have come from the general staff officer. He thanks you very much for your secret information and says it will be very helpful. He realizes that according to your Code of Conduct, you can be put in prison in America for giving him that valuable information. He

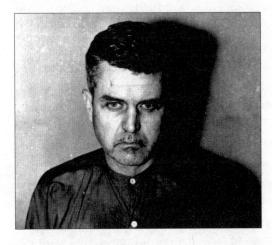

Jim Stockdale ("CAG"), the highest-ranking naval officer in Hanoi.

says, however, that your being the source of it will be kept in strict confidence as long as you are coopera- tive." So this was how the Camp Authority intended to blackmail him.

Rabbit added, "[The general staff officer] suggested that you be permitted to take a bath and become more comfortable." Pigeye appeared with soap and a razor. To Jim, a razor heralded a publicity stunt; they wanted him clean-shaven for the cameras. Pigeye escorted his prisoner across the Heartbreak courtyard and into Heartbreak Hotel, the cellblock Jim had first inhabited upon his arrival at Hỏa Lò three and a half years ago. Pigeye pushed him into Cell Eight, the bath facility, and left. Jim's mind raced. How could he foil Cat? How could he keep himself from being a pawn?

He turned on the faucet, which issued forth its familiar weak stream of marginally clean water. How he wished the wall's graffiti— *Smile, you're on Candid Camera*—were true. He stripped and positioned his backside between the shower and the door. Then he stuck his head under the water and lathered his matted hair, which had gone unwashed for more than a week. He wet the razor and placed it near the back of his neck. Then he began working the razor forward, shaving down the center of his head. As he tugged the dull razor through wiry hair and weak lather, it ripped a path of bare skin, marked by long cuts and bleeding nicks from the blade. Blood spilled onto his hands and the floor; it trickled down his head and onto his shoulders.

He heard the peephole open behind him. Pigeye screamed, "Đán!" The door burst open, and Pigeye disarmed his prisoner. He dragged him outside, stark naked, soapy, and bloody. He returned him to Room Eighteen much earlier than Rabbit and Chihuahua had planned. Both were still busy fastening what was intended to be a hidden tape recorder under the quiz table; they'd planned to secretly record Jim reading his letter aloud. At the sight of their prisoner, they couldn't hide their shock.

Expecting the ropes, CAG sat down and stretched out his legs. Nobody issued any orders for torture. In fact, Rabbit indignantly yelled, "No! You are not entitled to the ropes!" The two officers frantically discussed the situation, and Jim learned that sure enough, Cat had planned a public appearance and interview that night. The secret tape would have substituted had Jim refused to deliver the rehearsed statement—empty platitudes, admissions of American imperialism, and an apology—when the show began.

On orders from Rabbit and Chihuahua, Pigeye commandeered clippers and attempted to bring the rest of Jim's head into line with the shaved streak. Jim's hack job foiled any attempt at repair, however, and the three officials went to find a hat to cover his unsightly head. They left their captive by himself.

At once, Jim surveyed the room for tools and ideas. How could he counter the hat? His eyes fell upon the mahogany quiz stool. He picked it up and started butting it against his cheekbones. Again and again he hit himself with the wooden seat, bludgeoning one side of his face, then the other. His cheeks began to swell, forcing his eyes to squint. Blood ran onto his shirt from cuts opened by the beating. He grunted with each blow. He heard civilians who worked in the prison offices gathering outside, trying to peer through the window to see what was causing the disturbance. Then he heard Rabbit yelling, cutting through the crowd toward the door, followed by Chihuahua.

Standing over his bruised and bloodied prisoner, a furious Chihuahua asked, "What are we to do? You tell me what we are going to tell the general staff officer about the trip downtown after the way you have behaved."

Emphasizing his superior rank, Jim replied, "You tell the major that the *commander* decided not to go."

That night, Jim crawled across the floor of Room Eighteen, dragging his leg irons behind him, and pulled himself onto his blanket to rest. He thought of the photograph of Jimmy that Rabbit had waved in front of him earlier that week; he hoped his performance would make his son proud. He thought about how he had resisted his interrogators, making them torture him for every bit of information. He took pride in his hunger strike, despite the physical harm it caused him. He found satisfaction in foiling Cat's plan to parade him before the world. He hurt all over, and he knew he would hurt again, but for the moment, he felt victorious. He remembered his classic literature and recalled Fyodor Dostoyevsky's *Notes from Underground*. He now understood what the story's narrator—the famous "Underground Man"—knew: "What man wants is simply *independent* choice, whatever that independence may cost and wherever it may lead."

Anytime CAG and his fellow hard-liners managed some small victory, the Camp Authority inevitably beat them back down the next day. So it didn't surprise him when Rabbit reappeared the following morning. Stockdale had gulped down a ball of laundry detergent that brought about dry heaving to make himself seem sick. Rabbit didn't buy it and waited for the performance to end, then asked CAG to write to Sybil and explain that he'd fallen ill.

He grabbed the tablet and wrote, "Dear Sybil, I'm sick. Your friend, Jim."

"No, you don't get it," Rabbit said. "You have black malaria. You might die at any time, and she must know that. Now I want you to know that I'm through with you. I hate you. All we have been doing is just furnishing you a stage on which to perform. You are the world's greatest actor. And you love it! I have been granted permission by the general staff officer to leave this case. This is the final document I intend to get from you. Shall I call the guard?"

Jim realized that should the Camp Authority kill him in the coming months, should he die in Pigeye's ropes or on the floor of Room Eighteen, this undated letter would allow them to claim that he died of malaria. By the time the U.S. government recovered his remains—*if* it ever recovered his remains—no evidence would exist one way or the other. Jim decided to skip a final bout of torture under Rabbit's supervision. His fifth draft read, "Dear Sybil, sorry to inform you that I'm very ill. I'm told I have malaria. It's a very serious illness and I'm weak. I want you to know I send you my best regards, Jim." Rabbit taped him reading the letter, then walked out.

Several weeks later, in mid-March, Pigeye escorted Jim from Room Eighteen to a room across the Heartbreak courtyard. The number "5" marked its door. As Jim put his belongings inside, Pigeye opened a tool chest and indicated that Jim should help him take the room's door off its hinges. There in the open courtyard, these two longtime opponents converted a typical door into a cell door, sawing and hammering, reinforcing panels, and installing a peephole for guards. They communicated with gestures and grunts more than words, with Pigeye always calling Jim "Đán." When Pigeye was distracted, Jim drove a nail through the door and then clawed it out, creating his own peephole, which he disguised with lint. Once they'd rehung the door, he ironically felt pride in fashioning such a bulwark for himself. Pigeye likewise seemed genuinely satisfied. The guard made a motion that resembled a salute and left Jim alone in his new room, locked behind their refurbished door. Pigeye would never again lay a hand on Jim Stockdale.

While the Camp Authority had Jim agonizing in Room Eighteen or confined to Room Five during that winter of 1969, the new administration in Washington grappled with its unwelcome inheritance. "I'm not going to end up like LBJ holed up in the White House afraid to show my face on the street," President Richard Nixon promised an aide. "I'm going to stop that war. Fast." Nixon's new national security adviser assumed a more prescient tone. "We will not make the same old mistakes," Henry Kissinger said. "We will make our own."

Indeed they would, but they did carry out their promise to begin extricating the U.S. military from the war. In his first year, Nixon reduced the U.S. troop presence from 536,000 to 475,000, gradually shifting responsibility for the war to South Vietnam. By the end of 1970, troop levels would fall to 335,000, and a year later, to 157,000. Yet Vietnam still would claim more than 20,000 American lives during Nixon's first term. As he had promised in his campaign, Nixon pursued "peace with honor," an exit he designed to leave America's international prestige, a non-Communist South Vietnam, and his own presidency all intact.

*   *   *

By the time newly appointed Secretary of Defense Mel Laird took office in January 1969, he had seen nothing positive come from Johnson and Harriman's previous years of silence and diplomacy toward Hanoi. Personally encouraged by the budding activism of the POW/MIA community, Laird quickly reassessed the Pentagon's approach, tapping Deputy Assistant Secretary Richard G. Capen as the point man for the prisoner issue. Living in San Diego's navy community, Capen knew the grief, confusion, and frustration felt by the families of America's missing and captive servicemen, and he dove into his new role. In March, Capen, State Department representative Frank Sieverts, and former Korean War POW John Thornton flew to San Diego to visit with local members of the League of Families. The navy and air force assisted Capen by assembling the families at the NAS Miramar Officers' Club. Among the audience at the March 26, 1969, event were Lorraine Shumaker, Phyllis Rutledge, and Sybil Stockdale. Reflecting the skepticism created by four years of frustration, the wives had already nicknamed the three delegates the "Washington Road Show," and they planned to let the new administration know exactly what they thought.

Capen knew he'd receive four years' worth of pent-up anger that evening, and after dinner he listened to the wives vent about the previous administration's policies and actions—*inaction*, really—regarding their missing or captured husbands. One wife smashed a framed painting she said represented the air force's commitment to taking care of its own. She gave the delegates the remnants, asking them to pass the pieces along to the Pentagon. When her turn came, Sybil explained that most families had received no mail in more than five months. They thought the government's Keep Quiet policy had likely worsened the POWs' situation. The wives believed that North Vietnamese officials felt no pressure and had no incentive to comply with the Geneva Convention. The assembled women let the new administration know they wanted a new policy. Dick Capen left determined to give them one.

In Washington, Capen's team collected intelligence about conditions in Hanoi from several agencies, including the Defense Intelligence Agency, the Office of Naval Intelligence, the National Security Agency, and the CIA, and began to grasp the unimaginable misery North Vietnam inflicted upon American POWs. They found encoded messages and carbon letters from POWs, like those sent by Bob Shumaker and

Jim Stockdale. The agencies had decided not to disclose any of the intelligence for fear of compromising sources or causing the North Vietnamese to halt the flow of mail. Since the State Department was trying to negotiate an end to the conflict, they had discouraged releasing any facts that might offend North Vietnam and disrupt the peace talks, which were approaching the end of their first year having accomplished nothing. Capen's team noted the lack of progress the State Department had made in negotiations and that prisoner mail—the families' only mode of contact with prisoners—had virtually stopped even without revelation of the intelligence secrets concealed in letters.

At a weekend retreat with Defense leadership, Secretary Laird reviewed Capen's findings and agreed to publicize the information about prisoner mistreatment. New secretary of state William Rogers and National Security Adviser Henry Kissinger both objected; Averell Harriman visited Laird personally to plead that Defense not release the information. They all worried that the North Vietnamese might walk away from negotiations or kill those prisoners whose conditions would corroborate the accusations. In the press package detailing North Vietnam's Geneva Convention violations was a photograph of injured navy Lieutenant Commander John McCain, son of Admiral Jack McCain, Commander, Pacific Command. Capen met with McCain to explain the potential risks to his son; he would withhold the photograph at the admiral's request. Admiral McCain replied, "You do what you have to do."

The Joint Chiefs of Staff, including Chief of Naval Operations Tom Moorer and General Earle Wheeler, the chairman, pushed for disclosure, overruling the State Department's wishes. Still, the call ultimately fell to Laird, who was determined to help his captured servicemen and give their families hope. He decided the Pentagon would "Go Public," as the campaign became known, with its findings and bring worldwide pressure to North Vietnam. The United States would no longer let Hanoi's claims of lenient treatment go unchallenged. If Laird couldn't bring his men home, he could at least inform the world of their struggle.

On May 19, Sybil Stockdale received a call from two members of the Washington delegation—Frank Sieverts from State and Dick Capen from Defense. "Before you leave [to take your children to school] this morning," Capen said, "we wanted you to know that here in Washington, in just a few minutes, the secretary of defense is going to do the thing you've been wanting him to do for so long. He's going to publicly denounce the North Vietnamese for their treatment of our American prisoners and for their violation of the Geneva Convention. We know you've been working long and hard for this day, and we wanted you to be the first to know."

After nearly five years, the government abandoned its Keep Quiet policy. Sybil smiled, satisfied that the pressure brought by the wives had led to the policy change. She was particularly happy that the secretary happened to choose Hồ Chí Minh's birthday for his announcement.

That day, in a Pentagon briefing room, Secretary Laird called on North Vietnam to release U.S. POWs and to abide by the Geneva Convention. He left no question about his reasons or their offenses. "The North Vietnamese have claimed that they are treating our men humanely," he said. "I am distressed by the fact that there is clear evidence that this is not the case. The United States Government has urged that the enemy respect the requirements of the Geneva Convention. This they have refused to do." He turned the meeting over to Capen and questions erupted from the nearly one hundred members of the press in attendance.

Laird's bold declaration dealt a blow to Hanoi's strategy of gaining sympathy by advertising their supposed humane treatment of POWs. Moreover, it reversed the diplomatic path the previous administration had so unsuccessfully pursued. The course correction earned the secretary a blistering phone call from Henry Kissinger, who still feared that the revelations would hinder his peace talks, but Laird and Capen believed their policy change would help the Americans in Hanoi. Nixon chose not to intervene.

Capen became his department's face for the POW/MIA families and would meet with more than five thousand family members during the coming years. He and Laird saw the community growing in influence, and within two years Laird would advise Nixon, "If the families should turn against the administration on the POW/MIA issue, we believe that general public support would also." In the administration's view, the wives were an asset, albeit a volatile one. In the wives' view, the Department of Defense had at last begun to find its backbone. Less than one month after Laird's salvo against Hanoi, Sybil received her first letter from Jim since January 1967. She'd spent sixteen months wondering whether her encrypted letters had condemned him, wondering if he were still alive. Now she knew he at least had survived.

Within months, though she wouldn't know it, prison conditions in Hanoi would begin improving.

The month after Laird's announcement, Sybil and another POW wife, Karen Butler, flew to Los Angeles to meet with *Look* magazine. The Pentagon's May announcement had shed light on the general prisoner-of-war issue, but League of Families members believed the home-front angle still needed more attention. Unfortunately, *Look*'s West Coast editor seemed less than receptive to a story about POW/MIA families. Sybil's morale, so high in May, began to slide. "I'm crazy to try to tell the world the truth about all this," she thought. "These people don't care, and I'm never going to be able to get through to them."

As they stood up to leave, the two women told the editor to contact the League secretary in San Diego should he change his mind. "You have an organization?" he asked, suddenly more interested. They told him about the League, and he decided the group's campaign would in fact make a good story. Reinvigorated, Sybil called Louise Mulligan in Virginia Beach to discuss ideas about expanding the League's national presence; the two had no way of knowing their husbands had spent the entirety of 1968 living just 5 feet from each other. Bob Boroughs at the Pentagon also weighed in, suggesting to Sybil Stockdale that a national organization could garner more attention than a disparate network of groups or individuals. By the fall of 1969, the groups comprising the League of Families were beginning to call themselves the *National* League; they would formally change to that name the next year. The organization had twenty-four regional coordinators and 350 members on its mailing list. Sybil Stockdale served as national coordinator. Led by Sybil, Louise, and members like Jane Denton, Evelyn Grubb, Maureen Dunn, and Phyllis Galanti, the organization aimed to pressure the military for more information about POWs and MIAs, to make everyone in America aware of the POW/MIA issue, and to encourage fellow wives and family members to become advocates for their husbands and sons.

The American press joined the battle as well. When the lead North Vietnamese delegate at the stalled Paris Peace Talks stated that Hanoi would not release a list of prisoners until the United States withdrew from Vietnam, *The Washington Post* called his stance "retrograde." *The New York Times* covered the efforts of these women on behalf of their husbands, running a photograph of Sybil sitting on the Capitol steps after a day of lobbying Congress; the wives were at last beginning to garner the attention of the country's politicians. *CBS Morning News* interviewed Sybil in early August, and *Good Housekeeping* planned a fall feature on the National League. Sybil spoke with the *Today* show's producers, and they seemed intrigued by the idea of POW/MIA families confronting the North Vietnamese in Paris. She began plotting. By the end of summer 1969, the National League had begun to win over Washington and America. Paris was next.

THE CAPTAIN OF MY SOUL

Toward the end of that same summer, Jim Stockdale's long exile in Room Five, behind the door he and Pigeye had fashioned in March, came to an end. The sound of Jim's distinct gait echoed across the Little Vegas courtyard once again as he hobbled between his new cell in the Mint and the washrooms of the Sands. When some long-serving POWs heard his stiff-legged step, they knew CAG had returned from God-knows-where, having overcome God-knows-what. During one of his walks to the latrine, the camp speakers played the "Bob and Ed Show," as POWs had taken to calling the broadcasts made by two senior POWs. They both had decided to oppose the war and regularly delivered antiwar propaganda over the camp network. The broadcasts infuriated Jim; they violated his BACK US edict, which prohibited statements on the air without taking torture—and the broadcasts were terrible for morale. As he walked he rattled his bucket: "BS." He heard someone coughing a response in one of the Vegas cell blocks. He registered four coughs, then two: "R" for "Roger." The POWs agreed with Jim's assessment.

Removing the infectious Alcatraz Eleven from the general prison population in October of 1967 had, to an extent, achieved the Camp Authority's goals. They capitalized on the leadership purge by isolating the remaining seniors, which caused some junior officers to begin accepting the special favors that accompanied compliance. Strict crackdowns on communication and a constant shuffling of prisoners in and out of the Hilton also hindered the regeneration of an organized opposition.

One POW who arrived shortly after the Eleven's exile reported he didn't hear an American voice in Thunderbird for five weeks. The Camp Authority had cracked down, and many POWs were afraid to gamble—and the usual players weren't there to cast the dice; they were locked in Alcatraz.

When Jim Stockdale arrived in Bath Six one August day, he looked at the protruding end of a wire that attached a ceiling tile to the rafters. The wire bent northward, indicating a new note awaited him from POW Dave Hatcher, one of his only correspondents. Jim's heart leapt, but he kept calm and casually checked behind him to ensure a guard wasn't watching. Clear, he reached under the sink and parted the cobwebs that concealed an empty toothpaste tube. He pulled a piece of rough toilet paper from the tube and tucked it away in his pajama pants.

Jim's guard Hawk dutifully frisked him for notes and other contraband before and after his baths, since that time presented his one opportunity to communicate with other prisoners, but Jim had learned to circumvent this measure. He observed that Hawk possessed a country boy's modesty and would not watch Jim bathe naked, nor would he frisk Jim's crotch. That gave Jim all the cover he needed.

After the guard returned him to his cell in the Mint, he took out the note and unfolded it gingerly. He settled down on his honey bucket as he did so. If a guard should open the door or the peephole, he would have to drop the paper into the bucket's mess. With one eye on the peephole and an ear listening for approaching footsteps, he began reading. Dave Hatcher and his Stardust roommate, Jerry Coffee, had penned four lines of poetry with pencil lead stolen from a quiz room. Jim instantly recognized the words as the closing stanza of the poem "Invictus:"

> *It matters not how strait the gate,*
> *How charged with punishments the scroll,*
> *I am the master of my fate:*
> *I am the captain of my soul.*

Inspired by these lines, Jim recalled the poem's preceding three stanzas, drawing strength from their words. The English poet William

Ernest Henley had written "Invictus" in 1875 as he recovered from surgery, but now the poem seemed intended solely for the Americans in Hanoi, the men in Alcatraz, and their bloodied leader.

In late August 1969, he received another note from Hatcher. Hatcher knew the Camp Authority had disconnected the speakers in the Mint, so he sent CAG a long note summarizing farewell statements read over the prison radio by two of the three POWs who'd accepted early release that month, the third grouping of three prisoners to participate in the Fink Release Program. Only one of these most recent three, young Doug Hegdahl, had left with the blessing of the acting POW leaders at his camp.

In 1967, at age nineteen, Seaman Hegdahl had fallen overboard the cruiser USS *Canberra* and been captured in the Gulf of Tonkin by North Vietnamese fishermen. When he arrived at the Plantation, he convincingly played the fool with his interrogators. His youth, enlisted rank, and apparently dim wit made him a candidate for early release; the Camp Authority viewed Hegdahl as a potential patsy and an opportunity to demonstrate their leniency. Senior POWs sensed that possibility and commissioned the sailor to memorize the names of all known American POWs. They ordered him to accept early release, if offered. By August 1969, Hegdahl had learned 256 names and had been offered his freedom. When the North Vietnamese released him into the hands of a peace delegation that month, he carried those names home to America and publicly confirmed the allegations of POW mistreatment made by the Pentagon in May. His revelation of flagrant Geneva violations outraged the public and added to the international pressure on Hanoi to improve conditions. Once he gave his initial testimony, Hegdahl visited numerous families and bases, including NAS Miramar in San Diego. There, young Sondra Rutledge approached him and asked, "Do you know the name Rutledge?"

Hegdahl looked at her and said, "Howie." Her hope swelled even as the government remained silent. Hegdahl's names also gave comfort, but not confirmation, to the Johnson, Storz, and Jenkins households; they still had heard nothing from their loved ones directly.

Back in the Mint, Jim finished reading Hatcher's note, which he'd signed "McKinley Nolan." The actual Nolan, an army private, had either defected or been taken captive in South Vietnam in 1967; he often recorded propaganda that the North Vietnamese broadcast to their POWs. Jim shredded the note and placed the remnants into his bucket. He usually replied to Hatcher using strings from his pajamas, into which he would laboriously tie small knots that corresponded with tap code; he considered it his version of Braille. Responding to this most recent note, however, Jim decided to use toothpaste, a broken sliver of plastic, and brown toilet paper. He dipped the plastic into the toothpaste and began to write, "Dear McKinley . . ." He ranted about the Fink Release Program, which in his isolation, he'd been less able to combat; he thanked Hatcher for serving as his bridge to the camp. He carefully completed his reply and began to sign it "Chester," the alias he'd begun using for prison correspondence; the name was inspired by *Gunsmoke* sidekick Chester Goode, who, like Jim, had a stiff leg. All of a sudden, from behind him, a Vietnamese voice calmly inquired, "What are you doing?"

Jim's hand froze. He turned around to see a guard nicknamed the Kid peering through the door's peephole. Jim maintained his composure, although he silently berated himself for not hearing the guard's approach. He answered, "Just looking at these old letters from my wife the Camp Authority lets me keep in my cell." He had spread old letters across his bunk to help disguise his task.

"No," said the Kid. "I mean what are you writing? I was watching your arm move."

The Kid ordered him to the wall, and Jim complied, even as he repeated his original answer. The Kid then called for the turnkey, Hawk. When he looked away, Jim tossed the toothpaste tube into the corner. Then he returned to the bed to straighten the papers before Hawk arrived with the key. As he shifted about the piles, he slyly palmed his note and hid it in his crotch. By the time Hawk and the Kid entered the cell, Jim had raised his arms above his head, while fervently hoping the note stayed put. Hawk frisked Jim, then ordered him out of the cell so he could begin a search. Jim stood against the corridor wall; the note began slipping down the inside of his thigh. When Hawk had upturned the room and found no contraband, he frisked Jim again. Then Jim stepped back toward his cell, attempting to keep his bony thighs pressed together against the note. He noticed an expression on Hawk's face that registered both amusement and pity. Then it turned to surprise as the note fluttered out from Jim's pajama leg and landed on the floor. Hawk snatched the note and ran out of the Mint; the Kid followed after locking Jim's cell behind him. Helpless, Jim waited for the hammer to fall.

Hawk came for him that evening. The guard blindfolded Jim and led him through Little Vegas and into the kitchen, where Jim smelled cooks preparing another pitiful meal. His escort led him behind the kitchen, then up two steps. A door opened. Hawk untied the blindfold and pushed Jim into an apparently unused closet infested with cobwebs. He sat down in several inches of dust, and Hawk secured a set of leg irons. Then Hawk locked the door and left Jim feeling like the Camp Authority had sealed him in yet another tomb. He became the first American to experience this makeshift cell, which he nicknamed Calcutta, after the Black Hole of Calcutta, the Indian dungeon that allegedly suffocated more than 120 British prisoners of war in a single night.

Inside the 3-by-6 closet, he contemplated his situation. They had the note. Its very existence could prove devastating. The Camp Authority had taken extraordinary measures to keep him quarantined, and they seemed to believe they had succeeded. The note would prove that he still plied the streams of communication that ran through the prison. Further, it would prove others collaborated. He thought back to the 1967 summer purge—the Stockdale Purge, as POWs still called it—that visited so much suffering upon so many, whether or not they had participated in the underground he ran from his Thunderbird cell. Remorse pressed on him heavily. Now this new note—a note that he had failed to hide—would unleash another round of terror.

The prisoners at Alcatraz remained unaware of CAG's trials or whereabouts, but Hanoi Hannah brought other news from outside their insular colony. "The very best medical care is being given to our beloved leader," Hannah announced to the inmates in late August, as Hồ Chí Minh's heart began failing. "All Vietnam's medical expertise is available to him. We are confident of his recovery."

"Yeah right," Sam Johnson tapped with his one usable hand to Bob Shumaker, who still had an untreated fractured back. "We know what North Vietnam's best medical care is all about."

"He's a dead man," Shu responded.

Shu and Sam considered themselves fortunate still to be among the living. The Blue Book Purge had progressed at full throttle throughout the spring and summer of 1969, with guards brutalizing the Alcatraz POWs for more and more statements. Even Ron Storz had taken his share of beatings. Since they typically interrogated the prisoners in order of descending rank, by late August only Lieutenant (Junior Grade) George Coker—who often referred to himself as "the ensign," the navy's lowest rank—still remained untouched. For months, George had listened as higher-ranking officers were led out of their cells for long stints in torture rooms. When they returned, George would tremble as they tapped out their grim stories. He felt as if someone had tied him to a railroad trestle and made him watch a freight train approach. When the train hit Captain George McKnight, Coker knew he'd be next.

He began withdrawing into himself, no longer tapping to others, searching for some last reservoir of internal strength to combat what was to come. Then, on August 25, the train arrived. A guard opened Coker's cell and motioned him out. Terrified, he walked as bravely as he could out of the courtyard and into one of the stark quiz rooms in the alley. A team of guards awaited him. They worked on him for seven days, during which Coker got little sleep as they forced him to sit on a stool or concrete floor with his arms manacled behind his back. They also forced him to stand against the wall with his arms raised, which sparked hard memories of his two-month ordeal at the Zoo in 1966.

On the eighth day, guards unbound his hands and left him in the quiz room. George looked about for ways to avoid cooperating. His spied a wooden desk. He pulled open the top drawer and shoved his right hand inside, then started slamming the drawer again and again. If he couldn't write, he couldn't sign a confession. When Mickey Mouse returned, he calmly assessed the damage and decided to bring in a tape recorder. "You bring that in here and I will destroy it!" George thundered. "You will have to kill me." George surprised even himself with the outburst. He usually could control his temper around interrogators. He knew that acting out his frustration would just cause even more trouble.

Mickey Mouse eventually made George use his uninjured left hand to write. George filled his statements with tip-off phrases and the outright lies he'd so often told to interrogators. When the officers deemed his writing unacceptable, guards stripped him naked and lashed him fifty times with a fan belt.

George refused to break, but he knew he'd reached his limit. "I can only take one more day," he admitted to himself. "I can't last any longer."

"We have our belts and ropes," Mickey Mouse emphasized to his prisoner, seeming to perceive George's impending collapse. "You are going to do this. You think about this very seriously because tomorrow we whip you again.

"And tomorrow," he added, "you get one hundred."

George vowed to last as long as he could that next day but realized he would break by the afternoon. Once he'd again sat down before Mickey Mouse, ready for the day's promised hundred lashes, his adversary pronounced, "You have a very, very bad attitude, and we will determine what we're going to do with you." Then nothing happened; Mickey Mouse returned George to his cell, where he tapped the news to his neighbors. The response baffled everyone. Something had changed.

As he reflected on his strange salvation, George was filled with gratitude and respect for his fellow prisoners. If any one of them had broken just one day earlier, Mickey Mouse would have begun George's interrogation one day sooner, and he, too, would have broken. He fully understood another reason each American endeavored to hold out as long as possible—to protect his fellow prisoners.

That night, the Alcatraz inmates listened to sounds of mourning come through their speakers. They began to understand the abrupt end of George Coker's session, as funeral music and eulogies played on the radio. Hồ Chí Minh had died. It was September 2, 1969. Just seven days later, Jim Stockdale would complete his fourth full year as a prisoner in North Vietnam.

The seventy-nine-year-old revolutionary's death had spared George Coker, but it only gave a short reprieve to Jim Stockdale, who had been waiting anxiously in Calcutta as the Camp Authority debated his fate, his punishment for exchanging notes with Dave Hatcher. They had left him bound in Calcutta for several days, a treatment that seemed odd to Jim. After catching him red-handed, the Camp Authority typically would have sought its retribution quickly; something must have delayed his arraignment. Then, from guards' comments and the camp speakers, he had deduced Hồ Chí Minh had died. In the darkness of Calcutta, he'd wondered what he'd have said to the Communist leader had he seen him on his deathbed. "Good-bye, you old bastard," he thought.

The morning of September 3, guards ended CAG's brief stay in Calcutta and escorted him to Room Eighteen, so familiar to him after his three years and 359 days as a POW. He found Bug waiting, along with Hawk and another guard. Bug had apparently advanced in position since the POWs had met him upon their 1967 arrival in Little Vegas; his temperament had not improved. Bug charged CAG with several crimes, then ordered him to his knees.

"I only have one knee," Jim responded. "I'll do the best I can." With his stiff leg out to the side, he settled onto his right knee.

"Who is McKinley?" Bug asked, Jim's note in front of him. "We have no McKinley in this place."

"That's a joke," Jim explained. "I was writing about McKinley Nolan, the American soldier who deserted . . . and sends those tapes to the 'Voice of Vietnam' all the time. Don't you know who I mean? Don't you laugh at those tapes like we do?"

The response didn't satisfy Bug in the least. More questions came, and Jim evaded or bluntly refused to answer them. Bug beat him about the face with a 2-foot-long strip of rubber taken from a tire but went no further. Jim felt like he had faced the junior varsity squad; Rabbit and Pigeye would have had their answers in fifteen minutes. Instead, he and Bug debated the meanings of specific words in the confiscated note. Bug continued trying to learn the real identity of McKinley Nolan, and Jim grew weary from the endless questions. By the afternoon, his knee ached miserably and his face bore cuts and bruises, but he had given up nothing of value. As the session wore on, Bug took occasional breaks and left the room. During those interludes, Hawk and the second guard would look the other way as Jim rolled onto his side to relieve his right knee. When they heard Bug returning, they would push Jim back into position and resume their stern demeanor. The long day ended with Bug having learned nothing. Jim had protected the note-drop procedure and Dave Hatcher's identity.

That night, a guard brought his bedroll to Room Eighteen. He loosely bound Jim with ropes, then watched the prisoner crawl onto the mat like an exhausted castaway climbing onto a life raft. Then Bug returned. The sight of Jim prostrate on the mat sent him into a rage. He yelled, "Đán! Đán! Get on your feet. You are not to rest! You will sit in that chair all night. You will contemplate your crimes against the Vietnamese people. These are bad days for us. Our beloved president is dead. You have seen nothing yet. Tomorrow you will give me details. You will see. Tomorrow is when we start; you will be brought down!"

Jim pulled himself onto the chair, and Bug left, locking the French doors behind him. Jim speculated about the next day. "Tomorrow is the day," he thought. "Another purge . . . My fault again. I don't have a hint about what happened at Alcatraz after I left. How many of them died in the ropes trying to protect me? Why is it I who cause all the trouble . . . I've got to go on the offensive; I can't just wait for the axe to fall and then be sorry about it. I'm right where I was last winter when Rabbit and Chihuahua went for the hat [to cover his partially shaved head]; I've got to *do* something. I have to stop that interrogation; I have to stop the *flow*. If it costs, it costs."

He looked around the room. He saw neither razor blades nor a stool—the implements he used to foil his interrogators during his last visit to Room Eighteen, more than five months earlier. His gaze fell upon the glass windows in the room's doors. He stood up and turned off the light. He heard no sounds coming from the courtyard outside; he guessed most of the prison staff were still mourning Hồ Chí Minh. He dragged his leg irons to the French doors and shattered a pane of glass with the heel of his hand. Nobody seemed to hear. He picked a long shard of glass and carried it back to his chair. He found an artery in his left wrist and began hacking at it. Blood spurted forth. It ran down his hand and pooled on the floor as he stabbed again and again. Then he put the shard into his bloody left hand and hacked at his right wrist. As the blood poured out he wondered, "Is this the right thing?" He kept hacking. He wouldn't let down his men. He was resolved to bleed out his life there in Room Eighteen—or at least show Cat how far he'd go. At all costs, he would avoid the inevitable confession after the next day's torture. He knew the ropes could make him divulge the names of his correspondents and the secrets of their network. When he did, those men would bend and bleed, perhaps die. He would place the entire system in jeopardy. No, he would not talk. With this final act he would protect his men. Soon, Jim fainted, collapsing onto the cold, blood-splattered floor.

Later that evening, he became aware of movement, voices. He slowly opened his eyes. As they refocused, he found guards and officers filling Room Eighteen. A doctor had bandaged his arms. Guards were stripping off his clothes and mopping the floor with them. Others poured water onto the floor and over the bloody American. Someone put a pair of clean shorts on Jim's naked body. Then Bug began yelling at him, "How dare you do this? *Why* did you do this?" Jim did not answer. The room darkened, voices faded, and he passed out again.

The next day, a considerably more composed Bug entered the room with two cups of hot tea. He offered one to his convalescent adversary. They sat across a table from one another, sipping from their cups. Bug asked, "What made you do that terrible thing?"

CAG opened up. "I'm tired of being treated like an animal, being followed, questioned, hounded," he boomed. "I'm a prisoner of war and I'm tired of being nagged to death."

Bug repeated his government's unchanging position: Jim was a war criminal, not a POW. Then he changed subjects. That was the last time he ever mentioned the note or the American communication network.

At Alcatraz, the ten inmates wondered what changes—for better or worse—North Vietnam's next leader would bring. They'd learned enough through interrogators and Hanoi Hannah to know the names of several party leaders, and they staged a contest to predict Hồ Chí Minh's successor. Sam Johnson and Jerry Denton correctly picked Lê Duẩn, the general secretary of the Communist Party, who had effectively ruled alongside Hồ Chí Minh as secretary since 1960. As Hồ's health declined, Lê Duẩn's sway had increased even more, and his ascension dashed Nixon's hopes for easier negotiations. Ever tenacious, Lê Duẩn would lead the party until his death in 1986.

As North Vietnam's new leader, Lê Duẩn presided over a sweeping change in prisoner treatment. That fall, the Politburo issued a policy stating, "Although we do not consider the enemy pilots to be prisoners of war (POW), bound by the 1949 Geneva Convention on the treatment of POWs, we still apply the principles of this convention in our humanitarian policy."

The resolution showed, for the first time, concern for prisoners' health, living conditions, and ability to worship together. It stipulated that prisoners could send one postcard per month and receive one package every two months. It also stated, "From now until 1970, [we

will] gradually allow the American enemy pilots that we are holding in
secret to contact their families via postcards." In time, that would
mean the world for the Jenkins, Johnson, and Rutledge families. The
directive even noted the Ministry of Foreign Affairs was considering
allowing Red Cross visits.

It appeared that America's POW/MIA families had achieved a major
goal, less than twelve months after Sybil Stockdale first broke the Keep
Quiet policy that had silenced families for more than three years. The
fast-growing National League of Families had wanted to bring worldwide pressure to Hanoi, and they'd succeeded. When the Department of
Defense also went public with intelligence, the pressure increased, and
North Vietnam at last seemed to respond, perhaps using the change in
leaders as the pretense for a more internationally acceptable detention
program. The battered men in Alcatraz desperately needed the new
policies; they'd begun to doubt how much longer they could hold on.

In the first harbinger of change, Softsoap again traded posts with
Mickey Mouse, something all inmates saw as positive, and he began in-
stituting the gentler regime. When a guard caught Jerry Denton communicating the following month, Jerry earned an audience with the
returned commandant. "Denton, you have been caught communicating," Softsoap declared. "You know what has happened before."

"Yes," Jerry answered.

"I am going to surprise," Softsoap said happily. "This time you will
not be punish. We still have regulation and you have broken it, and I
will criticize you for it. But as long as I am in authority, there will be no
more punishment for communicating."

Jerry nearly cried. Back in the cellblock, the POWs speculated
about the change; as usual, Harry Jenkins thought it a good sign. Still,
nobody wanted to test the guards. The next day, however, one caught
Jerry communicating again. When Softsoap simply lectured him in response, the men of Alcatraz began to believe. Softsoap asked Jerry how
he could improve conditions, and while he didn't grant the navy commander's request for a Ping-Pong table, he did institute a third meal
each day. Later that week, when guards made their morning rounds,
they brought with them hot loaves of bread. Sam Johnson said a prayer
of thanks as that first warm loaf filled his shrunken stomach. Throughout much of their imprisonment—and all their time at Alcatraz—the
prisoners had only received two meals each day; neither had ever filled

their bellies. Accompanying the bread was a daily teapot of hot water. When a guard also gave Jerry a woven basket, Jerry made a confused expression. The guard said, "Tea," then hugged himself to convey that the basket would insulate the tea. In addition, the cobra baskets, as Americans called them, proved excellent hiding places for all manner of contraband.

In another positive move, guards received permission to have prisoners help with yard upkeep. With a bamboo broom, prisoners—often Bob Shumaker—would spend hours thoroughly sweeping the dirt courtyard. Shu became the anchorman for Alcatraz, sweeping efficiently in code, broadcasting news or opinions to his fellow inmates.

Even more change was afoot. One morning a guard came to Sam Johnson's cell. "You may walk outside today," he said as he unlocked Sam's leg irons. Sam stretched and then cautiously ventured outside. The guard motioned toward the center of the courtyard. Swinging his arms, Sam stepped forward and spent the next minutes striding freely around the warm yard. For the first time since he had arrived in Hanoi, he could take steps without a gun barrel or a jailer's hands pressed upon him. He looked at the buildings of Hanoi visible above the wall; he listened to the noises and traffic outside. Then he looked at their primitive camp with its pigsty. It seemed to him that time in Alcatraz had stopped ages ago and never started again.

A few weeks later, the prison took a leap forward when guards built a fire in the courtyard to heat water in a large cauldron. That day, each man received hot water for his bath. When the warm water poured over his body, Sam Johnson felt pure joy for the first time in many years. His last warm shower had been at Ubon Royal Thai Air Force Base in April of 1966, more than three years earlier.

The relationship between opposing commanding officers also changed. Jerry and Softsoap began to engage in more broad-ranging discussions during quizzes. During one particular session, the two discussed the politics and history of North Vietnam. Jerry acknowledged that by siding with French colonialism, Western powers had pushed Hồ Chí Minh toward Russia and China. "But," Jerry said, "what I can't understand is the Communist suppression of political, religious, and press freedoms."

"Denton, you have seen more and read more, and you know more than I do," Softsoap responded. "You can make argument that I cannot answer. But you must understand we never have security. We always fight. We have no unity. Under French there was no security, no law for Vietnamese. If Vietnamese woman raped, or peasant murdered by French, there would be nothing that could happen to those that did it. We had nothing but corruption . . . Now for the first time we have security. We do not have other things, but for the first time we have precious security." Jerry noted tears in Softsoap's eyes as the officer grasped his forearm and implored, "Do you understand that?"

Softsoap's statement touched Jerry and he felt genuine pity for his counterpart. Jerry believed most of his captors would have traded Hồ Chí Minh's system for a new life in America if given the chance. However, while the end of torture helped those sympathies emerge, the North Vietnamese still confined the POWs to concrete cages, so the glimmers of compassion proved fleeting.

The POWs speculated endlessly about what the changes meant. "They're trying to change our treatment without actually endorsing the Geneva Convention," guessed Sam Johnson.

"Maybe," said Jerry Denton. "I'm not sure what to think just yet."

"I think they are getting ready to move us all together," said another inmate. "Maybe we are going to go back with the others at Hỏa Lò."

Jerry said, "I think we can do anything we want and get away with it now."

Confident that torture had at long last ceased, the men took advantage of their new freedoms. They couldn't help but think the war's end might be near and their banishment to this abominable place almost over. The return of Ron Storz only stoked those hopes. Shortly after Thanksgiving 1969, guards had transferred Ron to Jim Stockdale's old Alcatraz cell, ending his three months' convalescence in a quiz room outside the courtyard. He and Jim Mulligan, who now shared the small cellblock, tapped throughout each day, just as Ron had resolved to comm frequently with him from across the courtyard after CAG was taken away in January. That same week Ron returned, Jim had received a Thanksgiving package from Louise. It contained Life Savers and wool L.L.Bean slipper socks with leather bottoms, which he donned immediately. Jim had never received a more treasured present and told his friends of this small good fortune.

"I'm freezing," Ron tapped to Jim several days later. "I need the socks."

"I'll leave them on the line," Jim tapped back without hesitation. "Pick them up when you get your clothes."

After Ron had worn the socks, he tapped that *he'd* never received a better present. Jim just wished they'd help his mind as much as his feet.

The prisoners wished they could restore their brother's spirit and replenish his will to live, but Sam Johnson realized Ron had a long road to travel. From beneath his door Sam observed him walking to the cistern; he looked emaciated, and his face displayed a haunted gauntness. Ron still ignored Jerry Denton's orders to gain weight. While he had told his compatriots he had resumed eating, they soon learned differently. Ron became too ill to empty his own latrine bucket, so guards assigned the duty to Jim Mulligan. When Jim dumped Ron's bucket into the latrine, he poured out the previous day's food rations, undisturbed as far as he could tell. Some still believed that Ron clung to his plan to go home emaciated, a testament to North Vietnam's Geneva violations. He also told Sam Johnson that he feared the North Vietnamese would put him into the ropes again if he regained his strength. Maybe he suffered the compounding mental effects of solitary, depression, disease, and malnutrition that prevented him from thinking straight. Or perhaps he had other reasons he never shared. Whatever the causes may have been, his condition continued to deteriorate even as the camp environment improved. He seemed beyond help.

GBU

On September 28, 1969, just weeks after her husband nearly bled out his life in Room Eighteen, Sybil met five other National League members at New York's John F. Kennedy International Airport. Together, the five wives and one father represented the U.S. Air Force, Army, Navy, and Marine Corps. The independent delegation of worried family members—they kept government involvement to a minimum—held a small press conference, then boarded a TWA flight to Paris using tickets donated by *Reader's Digest*, one of the nation's largest-circulation magazines at the time. Once in Paris, Sybil checked into the Intercontinental Hotel and dialed the Embassy of North Vietnam. She spoke with Xuân Oánh, temporary head of the North Vietnamese delegation.

"Yes, Mrs. Stockdale," he said. "We've heard about you and the government man with you."

Sybil truthfully assured him the man was simply the father of a marine POW, nothing more. Oánh said the embassy would call her if they decided to grant her request for a meeting. She repeated the hotel telephone number three times, and the line went dead. Each afternoon, Sybil stayed in her room, waiting for the phone to ring; others took morning and evening shifts. Every other day, she phoned Oánh, just to remind him. Finally, on Saturday, October 4, at 10:00 A.M., he called.

He invited the delegation to four o'clock tea at the embassy that after-noon. Sybil spent the day rehearsing in the mirror and dry-heaving her nerves in the bathroom. As the meeting grew closer, she composed herself and donned the eighty-nine-dollar pink wool suit on which she'd splurged for the 1965 ceremony during which Jim had assumed command of Air Wing 16 aboard *Oriskany*.

At 4:00 P.M., the six Americans arrived at the North Vietnamese Embassy and were seated at a low table across from four dark-haired North Vietnamese officials. Tension gripped the group; Sybil tried to break it by borrowing Xuân Oánh's reading glasses. One by one, the family members each read aloud their requests for information about their husband or son. The North Vietnamese panel listened passively. Toward the end of the meeting, Sybil asked if every POW/MIA wife and mother needed to come to Paris seeking information. Giving their only direct response during the meeting, the North Vietnamese em-phatically answered, "No." They wanted no more attention called to this blemish on their reputation. The prisoner issue had suddenly be-come significantly more troublesome.

Before his visitors departed, Oánh pulled a July 31 *New York Times* clipping from his pocket. It showed the picture of Sybil resting on the steps of the U.S. Capitol. He waved it and said, "We know all about you, Mrs. Stockdale. We know you are the founder of this movement in your country, and we want to tell you we think you should direct your questions to your own government."

Sybil rattled off the long list of contacts she'd made in the U.S. gov-ernment, then handed the North Vietnamese letters from other mili-tary families; Oánh issued a notably vague promise to answer them by mail. Not wasting her opportunity, Sybil made a particularly personal and pointed inquiry. She asked for evidence that her husband no lon-ger languished in solitary confinement. Oánh answered with stone-faced silence, and the meeting ended abruptly. Staffers showed the Americans a propaganda film, then served them tea and candy. Sybil wondered if the North Vietnamese served her the same candy Jim had written about in one of his early letters. As they exited the embassy, they met the international press, who carried their story to the world. The delegation explained that North Vietnam had promised—loosely— to study the problem and notify them of their findings. Until then,

however, the families would exist in an anguishing and uncertain purgatory.

Later that fall, the Alcatraz squawk boxes carried more unsettling
news. Hanoi Hannah reported 200,000 demonstrators had marched on
Washington in October 1969 to protest the war. The following month,
she reported that more than 250,000 had come to the American capital—
the largest antiwar protest in U.S. history at that time. The prisoners in
Alcatraz had no means of confirming or countering the news force-fed
to them by the Camp Authority. To them, much of it sounded preposterous, yet the recordings played by interrogators and broadcast over
the radio sounded so real. What was happening outside their cells?
What was happening to their country? They had no means of knowing
for sure, but learning about the lack of diplomatic or military progress
would not have heartened them.

At home, public support of the war declined further. Americans
held vigils and demonstrations, often called "moratoriums," in cities
across the country. John Lennon's song "Give Peace a Chance" ranked
among the most popular of the year. Nixon realized the war's dimin-
ishing domestic backing further eroded his negotiating position. "The
more divided we are at home, the less likely the enemy is to negotiate
at Paris," he explained to his constituents. However, as Lyndon Johnson had once said—only partly in jest—North Vietnam never had much
incentive to negotiate. Now, unfortunately for Nixon, much of his war-
weary nation just wanted to bring home its soldiers and forget about
Vietnam. Pursuing his pledge of "peace with honor," Nixon had coined
the tongue-twister "Vietnamization" for his gradual transfer of military responsibility to the South Vietnamese army and the government
in Saigon. In 1952, a young Richard Nixon had charged then-President
Truman with losing China to Communism, as Truman had failed to
stop the overthrow of Chiang Kai-shek's pro-Western government by
Mao Zedong's Red Army. Now, President Nixon did not want to lose
Vietnam in the same manner. He hoped to extricate U.S. forces while a
non-Communist government still held power in Saigon. He banked
that a U.S.-trained and U.S.-subsidized South Vietnamese army could
repel the NLF and the North Vietnamese long enough for him to claim
an honorable exit. Nixon did not want to be blamed if South Vietnam

fell. Meanwhile, Americans wondered how many years this gradual withdrawal would take. More troops would die, but for what? And what would become of the prisoners?

Several months after Sybil returned from Paris, the North Vietnamese began requiring that all future prisoner correspondence be sent on small, standardized, six-line forms via the Committee of Liaison with Families of Servicemen Detained in North Vietnam (COLIAFAM), an independent group led by American antiwar activist Cora Weiss. In return, Hanoi would give prisoner mail to COLIAFAM for distribution to families in the United States. The prisoners would use the same six-line, postcard-sized forms. Some speculated that the North Vietnamese had deduced prisoners were using long multipage letters to send home encoded information, names of prisoners in particular.

When she heard about the change, Sybil immediately called Bob Boroughs, who'd continued at the Pentagon after the change in administration. "Why doesn't the State Department insist on a more proper channel?" she asked, rather indignant that she'd have to rely on an antiwar activist who kept such close relations with the people holding her husband in leg irons for sixteen hours per day.

"I'm not sure someone over there at State didn't suggest this idea you object to," Boroughs said. "As much as I hate it, though, you've got to send your letters through them. It may improve chances of getting our stuff through to your husband."

Indeed, the volume of mail received by families would nearly triple in 1970.

Despite the Go Public campaign launched by Secretary of Defense Melvin Laird and his deputy, Dick Capen, the wives still questioned the White House's commitment to the prisoners. If Nixon's Vietnamization transferred ownership of the war to South Vietnam and America withdrew before forcing a treaty with the North, would Hanoi ever release them? Shortly before Thanksgiving, Sybil arranged an interview with Channel 6, the ABC affiliate in San Diego, and decided to use the opportunity to get a firm, supportive statement from the president, who still had not personally engaged the POW/MIA issue. In preparation, she called the White House and asked to speak with three presidential advisers whose names she'd picked up in magazines. The operator reported each one as out of the office. Sybil left messages, but none called back. Shortly before her interview, she dialed the White House and again asked for Deputy Assistant to the President Alexander Butterfield. The operator reported he was still unavailable.

"For crying out loud," Sybil shouted. "What are you doing around there, having a fire drill? I have to go on ABC-TV in thirty minutes, and I want some assurance the White House is even aware of the POW issue."

A new voice suddenly came on the line. "This is Alex Butterfield, Mrs. Stockdale," it said. "I can assure you the president is very concerned about the prisoner issue."

"Well, how close are you to him so you know that?" Sybil asked.

"I sit fifteen feet from his desk," Butterfield said, "and I give you my word he is doing everything he can about the situation."

"Well, he needs to do something publicly," Sybil fired right back. "We aren't going to wait forever. I have to go now or I'll be late for the program. You tell him what I said."

On December 8, just seven days after the government held its first military draft lottery, Frank Sieverts at the State Department invited Sybil to the White House for a reception and press conference with the president. Louise Mulligan received a similar invitation, and the two allies met in Washington for the event. On the morning of December 12, Louise fastened a miniature pair of gold naval aviator's wings to her lapel—the same wings Jim had given her when he proposed. In a neighboring room, Sybil again donned the pink wool suit she'd worn in Paris. These two leaders, along with twenty-three other POW/MIA family members, rode a bus to meet President and Mrs. Nixon. After the initial reception, Louise, Sybil, and three other wives joined the president in the Oval Office before the formal press conference began. In their private moments, Sybil handed the president a letter expressing the wives' concern with his Vietnamization policy. "Many of us are concerned that the gradual de-escalation of the war in Vietnam may leave the future of our prisoners in limbo simply because there may be no specific end to the war," the letter read. "We must ensure that the prisoner situation is carefully considered at each step in your program for the withdrawal of American forces from Vietnam." The wives believed that the Vietnamization policy benefited Nixon politically but that North Vietnam would never free their husbands without signing a treaty that ended the war or at least linked a U.S. withdrawal to prisoner release.

When time came for the press conference, Louise, Sybil, and the others lined up beside President Nixon in the Roosevelt Room. "Ladies and gentlemen," the president began. "I have the very great honor to present in this room today five of the most courageous women I have had the privilege to meet in my life." These wives stood by the president as he told their story, and the public saw their fear, felt their painful uncertainty, and—regardless of the listener's position on the war itself—realized how North Vietnam was upturning these innocent lives. During 1969, Nixon had noticed the nation's growing support for these women, and while he did seem genuinely concerned about their plight, he also recognized the political advantage in the POW issue. From that day forward, with the encouragement of Secretary Laird, Nixon calculated the reactions of America's POW/MIA families in his plans for Vietnam.

The president concluded his statement and left the room while the wives fielded questions from reporters and shared their stories. Their personal trials had become America's battle, as the nation was reminded about the heart-wrenching situation these families confronted. The public learned more about the Geneva Convention and renewed their calls for the enemy to honor it. At long last, these brave women had convinced the president to stop allowing North Vietnam to flout the rules of war.

When the wives had answered the last question, they filed toward the door. Sybil stopped short and turned around. "Merry Christmas!" she said to the press corps. Then the women walked out of the Roosevelt Room, confident but feeling a twinge of sadness. Sybil and Louise both faced a fifth Christmas without their husbands.

As Louise and Sybil were preparing for their meeting at the White House, Frenchy, the notoriously volatile commandant of the Briar Patch, assumed command of Alcatraz. The Camp Authority had placed him back in charge of some of the POWs who'd experienced his most brutal methods, like Ron Storz and George McKnight, whom he'd sentenced to slit trenches for so many hours during the summer of 1966.

He never had time to implement his brutal tactics at Alcatraz, however. It seemed a move was afoot.

National League of Families White House press conference with President Richard Nixon, December 1969. Louise Mulligan and Sybil Stockdale are second and third from the left.

"You're all moving out of here," Ron Storz loudly told Jerry one early December day on his way to the latrine; by this time, Ron no longer even bothered to communicate surreptitiously. "The guards told me they are sending you out. But I'm not going."

"Of course you're coming with us," Jerry Denton said. "We're not letting you stay here by yourself."

"It will only be worse if I leave," he replied. "Besides, it's all a bluff. It's a trick to try and get me to eat, but I'm onto them. If they do move us, they will never let me be with you. They'll separate us."

"That won't happen, Ron," Sam Johnson chimed in through his transom. "Things have changed some. Can't you feel that it's different now? We'll all be together."

When Jerry met Softsoap at quiz, he demanded, "If we are going to move, you must make Storz go with us."

"You are not going to move," Softsoap answered. "No need to worry about it."

Several days later, Jerry revisited the subject and got a different response. "You may move," Softsoap said. "It is not certain. But your Storz may do as he likes." The Camp Authority had given Ron the unprecedented choice of choosing his future. Sadly, Ron seemed determined to remain at Alcatraz even if his nine compatriots relocated.

On December 9, a guard thrust open the door to George Coker's cell and told him to roll up his belongings into his sleeping mat. Along the cellblock, other prisoners were ordered to do the same. The long-awaited move had come. Frenchy personally delivered the order to Ron, who recoiled at seeing his bitter adversary and refused to roll up anything. Instead, he began yelling at Frenchy. Nobody could clearly hear the exchange, but one could imagine Ron's reaction to seeing the man who inflicted so much abuse upon him during the Make Your Choice campaign. Ultimately, Ron's refusal to choose the cooperative path had led him to Alcatraz. Now, Frenchy stepped back from Ron's avalanche of angry words and simply locked Ron back inside Cell Thirteen.

Ron rapped to his neighbor Jim Mulligan, "Don't believe him, don't believe him; we are not going to move."

Resigned to his friend's delusion, Jim told Ron to eat and to request a cellmate when the time came, hoping that perhaps some other American might care for him. In turn, Ron asked Jim to see his wife, Sandra, if and when he returned to the United States. Although he thought Ron would likely die in North Vietnam, Jim asked Ron to visit Louise should he return home first.

Like so many other prisoners throughout history, Jim had carved a record of his stay into the wall of Cell Eleven. "Jim Mulligan," he had etched. "20 March 1966, CDR. USN here 25 Oct. 1967–."

Now he could add an ending, "9 Dec. 1969."

With guards waiting outside his door to begin his transfer, Jim hurriedly tapped the last message Ron Storz would ever receive from a fellow American, "GBU CU LATR . . ." Jim added the three periods for emphasis.

Ron tapped back, "GBU."

That evening, the rest of the POWs began vacating Alcatraz, having each spent twenty-five months—more than 750 days—in those cells.

They wondered how they had survived and thanked the Lord that the Camp Authority decided to let them out. They hadn't met their worst fear: dying old and forgotten in this small corner of the world.

Softsoap had returned to help Frenchy manage the transfer, and as guards put Jerry in the waiting truck, the former commandant stopped him. "Ah, Denton, this time you will not ride in handcuffs," Softsoap said. "We will blindfold, but you will not be uncomfortable. And Denton, do not forget tea basket."

With a wink, Softsoap handed Jerry his tea basket; he likely knew Jerry had converted the basket into a treasure chest of contraband. Jerry didn't know how to react to such a gesture from a man who had treated him like an animal for so long. Before he could decide how to respond, another guard tied on his blindfold and pushed him into the truck with the others.

A few of the men thought this next journey would end at Gia Lâm airport, at the doors of a waiting U.S. Air Force transport. Jim Mulligan, Howie Rutledge, and Jerry Denton let themselves think of waking up with their families on Christmas morning, far away from Alcatraz, far away from Hỏa Lò, far away from Pigeye's ropes. McKnight and Coker prepared themselves for the possibility of something even worse; false hopes had burned them too many times. Each mulled his own thoughts as they rode in silence through the chilly streets of Hanoi, never to see Alcatraz again.

They did not drive to the airport. Instead, the convoy rumbled south through the city, eventually slowing as the trucks eased over a curb. The POWs heard gates swing open. A familiar smell of squalor, fear, and sixty years of misery filled each man's nostrils. They had returned to the Hanoi Hilton. Tears began streaming down Jim Mulligan's face as guards put him in a one-man Stardust cell. He had allowed himself to entertain the possibility of repatriation, and the bleak reality of even more harsh confinement initially dispirited him, then stoked his anger. "You bastards!" he ranted. "You can't do this to me! I'm supposed to be going home!"

When Howie Rutledge saw how little had changed inside the Hilton, he wondered if the interrogation practices remained the same as well. He had thought the North Vietnamese had ended torture when Hồ Chí Minh died; he'd become used to the gentler regime at Alcatraz. When he looked at the small cells, heard the scurrying bugs and vermin, and sensed the unchanged wretchedness surrounding him, he wondered if the concessions had only applied to Alcatraz. He thought he'd survived the worst, but had Hỏa Lò now become even more austere than Alcatraz? He hoped the Eleven would at least be together. He reported in from his one-man cell at the end of the Stardust hallway and learned Harry was across the hall.

"Johnson?" someone else whispered.

"Down here," Sam called loudly.

"Mulligan over here," Jim said; Jerry Denton called out as well.

"Shumaker and Tanner over here," Shu reported.

A voice asked, "Where are Coker and McKnight?"

"They rode over with us from Alcatraz, so they must be here somewhere."

"What about Ron?" someone asked. Jim Mulligan had not had time to tell the others about his final exchange with their ailing friend.

"Ron!" the returnees began shouting. They heard no answer. Then a guard stormed into Stardust yelling, "Shut up! Shut mouth! No talk!"

The seven men in Stardust brazenly talked on, unafraid of the Camp Authority. Sam Johnson felt a relative sense of relief as he lay down for his first night without leg irons in more than twenty-five months. They all had rejoined the rest of the American POWs after exile to Alcatraz, but Sam couldn't stop thinking about Ron Storz. He, along with the rest of the returnees, also wondered if CAG was now close by. They'd learned nothing of his fate or whereabouts since he'd been taken from Alcatraz ten months before.

By month's end, the group had learned that George Coker and George McKnight, now famous throughout the POW population for their 1967 escape from Dirty Bird, occupied adjacent cells in the Mint, where they had spent their last days before transferring to Alcatraz. They found it no less miserable than they remembered. The nine men returning from Alcatraz had all endured two years of purgatory only to find themselves in the exact place they left in 1967, prospects for homecoming no brighter.

When Jerry Denton could locate no higher-ranking officer available and able to lead, he formally took command of the approximately eighty POWs in Hỏa Lò and the roughly 280 other prisoners scattered throughout camps in and near Hanoi. Hỏa Lò held six officers senior to Jerry, but for various reasons, they could not take command. The Camp

Authority had sealed Robbie Risner inside New Guy Village and had also sequestered several air force colonels who had virtually no contact with the POW population. During one of Sam Johnson's trips to the bathhouse, another POW whispered that Cat had Jim Stockdale confined to a cell in Thunderbird with an air force lieutenant colonel who threatened to report him if he communicated. In fact, the man feared Jim's tactics would land him in trouble, and Jim considered him a psychopath. When Cat returned Jim to his old cell in the Mint later in 1970, isolated as he was, he actually felt relieved to escape his cellmate. Whatever the circumstances surrounding other leaders, some POWs felt nobody but Jerry Denton had the guts to take over.

On his first morning back in the Little Vegas section of the Hanoi Hilton, Jerry encountered Cat. The two seniors passed each other in the courtyard. One wore ragged shorts and carried a towel, soap, and honey bucket; the other led a cadre of attendant soldiers and wore a well-pressed uniform with recently shined shoes.

"Ah, Denton, I believe," Cat said with his hand extended.

"Yes, Denton," Jerry confirmed, coming to attention but chafing at Cat's intentional slight. Cat knew exactly who Denton was; the pretense infuriated him.

"Long time since I see you, Denton," said Cat.

"Yes, not since the banana and the torture," Jerry growled, the memory of Christmas 1968 still in his mind. As always, Cat took meticulous care of his appearance, but Jerry noticed something had changed. The commandant of the prison system had lost his swagger. Unbeknown to Jerry, he had also lost his position. Once commandant of the entire prison system, Cat now commanded only Hỏa Lò, a significant demotion. Cat, it seemed, had become a scapegoat when the government had changed its policy on torture.

Although he could never explicitly acknowledge it, Cat likely knew that Denton would serve as the prison's ranking American officer, and the next morning, he called Jerry into his office. "I have some very important announcements, Denton," he said bluntly. "I, other officers, and many of the guards had in our rage allowed ourselves to vent our anger on the prisoners and were responsible for deviations from our Vietnamese tradition of humane treatment. I have been required to make public self-criticism for my mistakes, and from now on you will be allowed to follow the Code of Conduct."

The statement floored Jerry; Cat had actually admitted he had tortured Americans. He'd almost apologized.

"I will prove by my deeds that my words are true," Cat continued, "and I want ideas from you on how we can apply humane treatment, including games and movies. We shall have many discussions in the future. Here are French-Vietnamese and English-French dictionaries for consultation to make sure we understand each other. Maybe you would like to explain to the *girls* in the kitchen about menus."

The married father of seven declined Cat's insinuated offer, saying, "No, we can't accept that."

With a suit-yourself gesture, Cat said, "Just follow reasonable orders and don't insult guards."

This cordial meeting differed in almost every way from the pair's last encounter, during Christmas 1968 when Jerry and Cat feuded over the banana. After the two men parted, Cat kept his promise. No American ever faced the ropes again.

The Alcatraz Eleven, as they'd become widely known to other POWs, had been removed from the Hilton on October 25, 1967. In the approximately two years since then, Jerry found that the Camp Authority had made life easier for its other prisoners, introducing new amenities such as a community pool table. Nine prisoners had accepted early release, and while some stalwarts who remained behind had done their best to lead, the past two years had in general seen the organization built by Stockdale and Denton wither. For a variety of reasons and in several cellblocks, the collective will to resist the North Vietnamese had waned.

Upon his return, Jerry found a group of POWs in the Desert Inn who were not toeing the line, as he saw it. Some did not know tap code, and many read antiwar statements on the camp radio. Some also wrote articles for *New Outlook*, a camp propaganda magazine. Jerry heard these prisoners received better food, enjoyed exercise outside, and voluntarily decorated the prison's utility room for Christmas and Tét. Rumors emerged that cooperative parties even got beer, and to bored prisoners, rumor quickly became fact. The Alcatraz veterans set about rectifying the situation.

They let Little Vegas know that torture had ceased in September of 1969; POWs could refuse to comply without fear of the ropes. Jerry's first order called for everyone to abide by Jim Stockdale's old BACK US policies. He also issued a simple corollary. "No write, no read, and no talk on the radio." The Alcatraz men began sending out the orders by tapping, whispering over shower stalls, and flashing across courtyards. The phantom electrician of Alcatraz even commandeered the camp speaker network to spread them. Using the wiring in his cell's speaker to buzz code through the public address system, Harry created a camp-wide telegraph system that baffled the prison staff. He broadcast Jerry's directives across Little Vegas using the Camp Authority's own propaganda system.

From the Stardust cell he shared with Bob Shumaker, Nels Tanner began observing the routine of four isolated air force seniors. Every day a guard walked them from their cells in New Guy Village to the Little Vegas bathhouse. "Try writing a note," Shu suggested to Nels. "Just hold it up in the window when they walk by. Maybe we can get them to write one back."

The next day the officers passed the open window. Nels whispered, "Pssst! Psst!" One prisoner looked up, and Shu recognized Robbie Risner, his face alight with excitement. Risner's eyes flashed to the message scrawled on brown toilet paper, "Write note."

The next day, Shu and Nels had a new message ready, "Pool room under right table leg," referring to the pool table the Camp Authority had placed in Riviera, which they'd seen Risner visit. On their next trip to the pool room, Shu and Nels found a note from Risner and left one of their own in its place. Shu also stashed other notes in the communal room. Several weeks later, one fluttered down from a light fixture while Mulligan and Denton were playing pool; Denton quickly palmed it before a guard noticed. Jim marveled at Shu's craftsmanship; every nook in Little Vegas seemed to hold one of his tightly rolled notes. Comm between Stardust and the Desert Inn often relied upon Shu hiding and receiving notes in a designated bathhouse stall; he'd use pajama string and small balls of soap to affix notes behind the pipes that supplied the sinks. Thus the Alcatraz Eleven—the Alcatraz Gang, as some had taken to calling them since Ron Storz had yet to turn up—continued bringing American POWs back into the resistance network.

Some prisoners had no interest in listening to the hard-liners from Alcatraz, and many of their whispers and notes went unanswered. In particular, three senior officers in the Desert Inn refused to stop reciting statements over the radio and writing antiwar articles, not wanting to forfeit the better food and outdoor privileges they received. With no prospects of release anytime soon—based on reports from Hanoi Hannah, it seemed the war might last indefinitely—they had little interest in revisiting the days of subhuman treatment, even though they'd been told torture had ended. In contrast, other prisoners began testing the Camp Authority, finding it had fewer teeth. Most Americans stopped giving up propaganda and ceased reading statements over the camp radio, which immediately raised morale. Undeterred by their exile to Alcatraz, the seven members of the Eleven in Stardust restored the system of resistance and subversion they'd run so effectively during their last stay in the Hilton.

Just before Christmas 1969, on December 23, Jim Mulligan moved into Stardust Six with Jerry Denton. Since his capture in July 1965, Jerry had lived in solitary confinement with the exception of the less than four months living with Jim during the summer of 1967. After nearly 1,500 days locked up without a friend, Jerry's isolation had at last ended. The two men pounded each other's backs in a tight embrace. When they stepped back to look at each other, each thought the other looked like hell. Jim thought Jerry had aged ten years. "My God," he said to himself. "What are they trying to do with us?" As the two Catholics offered prayers of thanksgiving that night, they also remembered Ron Storz and others still in solitary. "God, it's hard to live alone," Jim thought.

Two days later, on December 25, Hawk, the guard who'd confiscated Jim Stockdale's note in the Mint the previous summer, led Jerry and Jim Mulligan to a room decorated with a Christmas tree and a nativity scene. They found Bug waiting for them with an uncharacteristically friendly attitude. He directed them toward a wall covered with photographs and typed pages. Upon inspection, Jim and Jerry found images of visiting U.S. antiwar delegations and peace demonstrations. One picture showed the aging Vietnamese priest who had officiated Jim's Christmas Mass leading a parade through the streets of Hanoi; Jim assumed he cooperated with the government in exchange for their tolerance of his ministry. The posted literature contained all manner of antiwar propaganda and Communist dogma. Whatever Bug's intention, the displays just hardened the Americans' attitudes toward their captors.

The two forgot the propaganda when Hawk appeared with hot coffee laced with sugar. Jerry and Jim relished every sip. To their surprise,

Hawk poured refills. Jim—so deflated upon his return to Stardust—began to believe he had, in fact, endured the worst. What followed cemented that impression. As the two POWs drank their second cup, Cat entered the room in his khaki uniform. He took two heaping plates from a shelf of food and personally offered them to Jim and Jerry. "Feast yourselves," he said. Jim thought his one slice of turkey was more meat than he'd seen altogether since his capture. Cat left and returned with large bowls of noodles in meat broth. Grinning broadly, he said, "Eat, Denton. Eat, Mulligan." The recipients bowed politely and said, "Thank you, Commander."

Jim said grace and asked the Lord to care for their families at home. Then the two men cleaned their plates of turkey, carrots, potatoes, and greens; they drained their soup bowls. Having digested more food at once than he had in nearly three years, Jim issued a loud burp. Hawk heard it and smiled. That evening, Bug called the roommates to quiz and distributed mail and staples from home. Louise and Jane had sent freeze-dried coffee, toothpaste, vitamins, Life Savers, protein pills, and soap. The men went to bed reading short six-line COLIAFAM letters from their wives and feeling truly optimistic.

MAYDAY!

Two months into 1970, guards escorted Harry Jenkins into the cell occupied by Howie Rutledge. For most of their days in Hanoi, the two men had been within 30 feet of one another; they'd lived through twenty-five months at Alcatraz in adjacent cells. Since November of 1965, Harry had never relented in his insistence that he'd gotten bagged because he'd volunteered to cover Howie's birthday flight. The story had formed the basis for a close friendship.

The reunion of these two proved particularly fortuitous since a flu epidemic swept through the cellblocks, plaguing a number of POWs, including Howie. After more than four years without dental care, Howie's crowns had taken to falling off as well. POWs forever fretted about dental problems, since a broken crown or cavity could lead to tremendous pain or serious infection. While desperately ill with the flu, Howie accidentally swallowed a crown as he chewed the bits of cabbage in his soup. Nearly immobile on his bunk, he still managed to panic. Harry assured him it would come out in the end. The next day, Harry searched through the fresh slop in Howie's honey bucket and fished out the crown. Ever after, Howie maintained that no man ever demonstrated truer friendship. After the incident, Harry began collecting gum and anything sticky he could scrounge. He'd stash the material inside the curved handle of his drinking cup until Howie needed fresh

adhesive to anchor his crown. His bonding agent of choice soon became Wrigley's chewing gum, which often appeared in the intermittent care packages that the Camp Authority allowed through as 1970
progressed.

Soon George Coker and George McKnight were transferred from
their separate cells in the Mint to a room together in Stardust. Except
for Jim Stockdale and Ron Storz, the Alcatraz Eleven had reassembled.
By the end of February 1970, only one still lived alone: Sam Johnson.
In Alcatraz, the eleven men had endured solitary confinement knowing they did so together. Now, Sam knew each of his friends in Stardust
had a cellmate. He heard them whisper of playing pool together in
Riviera. They took meals together, as if sharing a table in the mess halls
and wardrooms they'd known before being shot down. Sam knew they
talked quietly inside their cells and thus had less need to risk communicating with others; the North Vietnamese still forbade communication
between cells, and unlike Softsoap at Alcatraz, the authorities in Little
Vegas still punished offenders. Leg irons were a popular penalty for in-
fractions, but the staff could no longer employ torture. Other inmates
couldn't risk causing trouble for themselves or for Sam, should he be
caught. Gradually, the traffic of taps to Sam's Stardust cell subsided.
With nobody to monitor the hallway for guards while he tapped or
whispered, his isolation grew. He sat dejectedly on his bunk, seeing no
other souls but the guards who delivered his food or escorted him to
the latrine. While other POWs visited the pool table with their cellmates, Sam shot pool by himself, never allowed a competitor and facing the difficulty of practicing with his injured arms and stiff right
hand. Four years after dislocating one shoulder and breaking the other,
they still didn't have the strength to lift him above shower stalls or to the
high windows in Stardust so he could see another American. He longed
just to lay eyes upon a fellow prisoner. The chill of winter, the poor rations, and the stinking honey bucket all became secondary concerns. He
tried to pray. Often, he could not even find words. In their stead came
tears. Loneliness started to crush Sam Johnson.

With the gang increasingly concerned about Sam's isolation, Jerry
Denton brought the problem to Cat's attention. "Ah, Denton," Cat said,
"I am your good uncle. I have good nephews and bad nephews. Johnson is a bad nephew. He will never have roommate." Two years in Alcatraz had apparently not lessened the grudge the Camp Authority held

against Sam Johnson; Sam could never figure out why they considered him so deserving of special punishment. When Jerry passed the latest news to Sam, he tapped, "Don't worry, Sam. We'll think of something." Truthfully, though, Sam's fellow POWs could do little.

The big, affable Texan had never experienced despondency like that which visited him during the winter and spring of 1970. Only his misery in the Mint, locked in stocks during the summer of 1967, could compare. He had no energy left, and his will to survive began to wane. The thirty-nine-year-old noticed he now walked with an old man's shuffle. Even trips to the shower left him drained. Sometimes, he would stand and stare at his cell wall until he fell exhausted onto his hard bunk. Still, he could barely sleep. With each passing day, he had to struggle harder to endure the next hour.

"It's too much," he thought. "I can't go on any longer." He wondered why Cat persecuted him so persistently. "They hate me," he told himself. "They want to break me." The reason didn't matter; Cat was succeeding. Sam had not felt such fear since he stood before the village firing squad shortly after his capture and impromptu trial en route to Hanoi. Now he felt that dreadful emotion creeping into his mind once again. Without hope of relief, he turned to God.

In his cell and without any other recourse, he dropped to his knees and asked the Lord for help. He implored him to take away all his fear, loneliness, and depression. Sam gave himself over to the God he hoped still retained control over his plight. He spent the next days in prayer. His cell became a church, and he found the assurance that God still watched over him. He gained a holy strength with which to fight.

Like Ron Storz, Sam chose to use the only weapon he had: his own body. Since they'd left Alcatraz and treatment had improved for most, Sam suspected release was imminent; optimists Jerry Denton and Jim Mulligan were convinced of it. Surely, Cat would not release Sam looking horribly malnourished. Fasting seemed like his last option. He began eating only a portion of each meal. When the guards brought him larger servings, he ate only the same small amounts. Solitary confinement had driven Sam and Ron to the same dangerous conclusion.

Once he became aware of Sam's decision, Jerry Denton discussed the problem with the men in Stardust. Concerned with Sam's survival, they agreed to initiate a broader hunger strike on their friend's behalf. Like Sam, Jerry did not believe the Camp Authority would send their prisoners home looking like victims of Andersonville; nor did he believe they could afford killing the prisoners the outside world knew they held. Perhaps in this new era of relative humanity, a hunger strike would work. Jerry issued the order, and the fast began on April 30, lasting for three days. To Jerry and Jim's knowledge, most POWs in Little Vegas participated. Cat and Bug were furious. After three days of no food, the POWs took half rations until May 11, when the fast ceased; most men were not strong enough to continue any longer. As a result, Cat did begin allowing some prisoners to visit other cellblocks, but he did nothing for Sam.

The Alcatraz clan tried their best to help their friend, but for the most part, they could only tap or whisper encouragement during the short periods when guards left them in peace. If other opportunities arose, they took them. One day in the bathhouse, Sam heard a "psst" over the trickle of the bathwater. He looked up to see George McKnight's broad smile appear over the stall's partition. A guard saw it, too, and stormed in, screaming, "No! No!" before he herded George back to his cell. Still, just the sight of his friend had lifted Sam's spirits.

McKnight kept trying to help his fellow air force officer, and several days later, he found Sam in the bathhouse again. He began singing, "Ohhhh, there are no fighter pilots down in hell. Oh, there are no fighter pilots down in hell . . ." Sam joined him, singing the classic lyrics that countless overserved pilots have sung in bars around the world.

"Oh, there are no fighter pilots up in Wing," the air force men sang, launching into another verse. "Oh, there are no fighter pilots up in Wing. The place is full of brass, sitting 'round on their fat ass. Oh there are no fighter pilots up in Wing . . ."

Before they could sing increasingly profane stanzas, the guard heard them and dragged a wet, naked, and grinning George McKnight back to his cell. The song lingered in Sam's head for days, and it brought tears each time he sang the chorus to his audience of dingy walls.

The moments with George alone could not rescue him, however. Sam continued his hunger strike, growing ever weaker. On May 15, he collapsed in the game room during one of his solitary sojourns to the pool table. After two guards returned him to Stardust, he received a message from Jerry Denton. "Sam," Jerry tapped, "I'm giving you a direct order. Stop the fast. Don't hurt yourself." Sam obeyed, trusting God would provide another way out.

During that trying spring of 1970, Cat did extend his bad nephew the privilege of writing his first letters home since his 1966 shootdown. Before penning any letters, Sam had to learn to write again. His right hand had still not recovered from his ejection and the torture sessions with Pigeye. He could not grasp a pen or pencil. Time and again, his paralyzed hand would drop the pen as he tried to write. Frustrated, he'd pick it up from the floor and try again.

Eventually, he taught himself to write left-handed. He spent hours practicing the alphabet so Shirley could read his letters without realizing the extent of his injuries, which he knew would worry her, and he began mentally composing letters encrypted with the Martini code Bob Shumaker had taught him in Alcatraz. When guards arrived with the official six-lined COLIAFAM forms, Sam laboriously wrote out his memorized words as the guards watched impatiently. Under their very eyes, he secretly folded covert information concerning POW names and other strategic information into his sentences. When the letters were approved, Sam felt victorious. Those small triumphs gave him the strength to survive one more day.

In June, Cat finally ended his unexplained persecution of Sam Johnson. One day, a guard opened Sam's Stardust cell and said, "Dress up. You're going to visit your friend Denton."

Shaking all over, Sam pulled his pajamas over his boxers. He walked out of his cell, turned down the dim corridor, and walked to the next cell. The guard opened the door, and Sam Johnson faced Jerry Denton and Jim Mulligan. Sam had not seen either man face-to-face since 1967. With tears welling in his eyes, Sam pulled himself to attention and raised his crippled right hand to his brow. He held a rigid salute and said, "Major Sam Johnson reporting, sir."

Jerry returned the salute. Then the two seniors grabbed Sam and pulled him into the cell. The friends embraced and slapped one another on the back, each trying not to think about the appearance of the others. The haggard gauntness of Jim and Jerry had surprised Sam, as had Jerry's graying hair. Even though they knew of his condition, the two cellmates had been shocked upon seeing Sam's deteriorated appearance. His 6'2" frame weighed less than 125 pounds; gray had crept into his hair as well. Hard living in Hanoi took its toll on them all.

Jim felt tremendous sadness seeing Sam and knowing the solitary hell he had endured these past three years, and the past five months in particular, but his joy at seeing his air force friend overpowered the sadness. Jim and Jerry shared the periodic gifts from home that the Camp Authority had allowed them, and the three captives spent the day together playing cards and simply being in each other's company. Late that afternoon, a guard arrived to take Sam back down the hallway into solitary confinement. The three men stood, emotions overwhelming them. Sam could not even muster the words "good night."

Several days later, Sam got roommates: Nels Tanner and his French instructor at Alcatraz, Bob Shumaker. The three men had lived within 20 feet of each other for three years yet had never seen each other face-to-face. They remained in Stardust Three together until late July, when a guard opened the door, looked at Sam, and said, "Roll up!" Fear shot through Sam's entire body. "Back to solitary," he thought. "I can't do that again. Please, Lord, I did forty-two months solo . . . please, no more." He slowly gathered his belongings. Fearing the worst for their friend, Nels and Shu embraced Sam, careful not to hurt his shoulders. Sam walked into the hallway. The guard prodded him forward, then thrust Sam inside Stardust Four, which had only a single bunk. The door slammed, and Sam slid his back down the wall until he rested on the floor, depression sweeping over him like a fast-moving Texas thunderstorm. Then the door opened again, and the guard dragged Sam across the hallway and into Stardust Five. Inside, he found Jim Stockdale.

Shirley Johnson spent four years waiting for a letter from Sam. She and her family had never surrendered their ardent belief that he remained alive, even though they received no indication of his survival until released POW Doug Hegdahl carried his name out of Hanoi in August of 1969. Shirley had prayed and spent sleepless hours wishing to find an envelope postmarked Hanoi in her mailbox. Then, one day in the spring of 1970, it appeared. Six lines of text filled the small CO-LIAFAM card, but it wasn't Sam's handwriting. Yet from the words, it seemed as if Sam had written it. Shirley was baffled. She sent the letter to the Department of Defense in Washington, where analysts studied it and then telephoned Shirley. The young man on the phone surmised that Sam had written the letter with his left hand. Shirley refused to believe it. "That can't be," she said. "He's right-handed."

"We're quite sure," the officer confirmed. "The analysis of his handwriting indicates he has been through a lot, but he has come through with strength. He's okay."

Still, Shirley couldn't believe her husband had been injured so badly. "I don't believe it," she thought. "That would mean he's lost the use of his right hand. No, I won't believe it. It's got to be something else. He's probably using a concrete surface to write on—that's why the writing is so shaky and uneven." At least Sam was still alive. At home, more voices had begun demanding the North Vietnamese treat him and the other POWs better and return them safely.

Nobody had been shouting louder than Louise Mulligan. Despite his professed support for the POWs, Nixon had also talked about separating the prisoner issue from the issue of the war, but Louise would not have it. On a nationally syndicated talk show after her December 1969 White House visit, she discarded the polite deference she'd extended to the president in person. Furious that he had begun withdrawing U.S. troops without any assurances related to POWs, she charged, "This president is the first president to label our troops expendable." Her volley mortified Bob Boroughs at the Pentagon, but he'd learned that Louise and Sybil were not his to control. Though the POWs did not yet know it, they had no better advocates than the women they loved.

Louise shouted again as she opened the May 1, 1970, National League of Families conference in Washington, D.C., calling, "Mayday!" from the podium in Constitution Hall. She echoed the same international distress call so many pilots had uttered as their planes fell toward North Vietnam. National League members had come to Washington for this inaugural national conference to show their solidarity and determination. U.S. Senator Bob Dole, a World War II veteran, had personally taken up their banner, standing virtually alone at first. Dole had promised to fill Constitution Hall for them, and he delivered an audience of more than three thousand. While Louise and other wives remained unsatisfied with the government's efforts—their husbands were still imprisoned—politicians from both parties began following the president's lead and rallied to these women's cause, which had finally captured the hearts of the nation. Senate doves Edmund Muskie and Michael Mansfield agreed to cosponsor the event along with hawks Barry Goldwater and John Stennis. Sybil Stockdale and Ross Perot served as cochairs; both had testified at a House National Security Subcommittee

hearing on the prisoner-of-war issue two days earlier, along with Jane
Denton. The Air National Guard flew seven hundred POW/MIA relatives to Washington for the event; the families drew strength from the
assemblage of officials and military brass. Senators Dole and Goldwater, Vice President Spiro Agnew, and Secretary of Defense Laird all

Louise Mulligan, delivering
her "Mayday" address,
May 1, 1970.

delivered speeches. *Apollo
13* commander Jim Lovell
gave the keynote. Four of
the five Joint Chiefs of
Staff attended, and rank
insignia twinkled like stars
among the audience.

Despite the star power
in the hall, perhaps Louise
Mulligan's stirring invoca-
tion affected the audience
members   most   deeply.
Upon   hearing   Louise's
shout, one MIA wife felt as
if a large door had swung
open, ending her solitary anguish. Louise couldn't stay for the acco-
lades, however. Immediately after her speech, she rushed out the rear
door and returned home to Virginia Beach for her youngest son's First
Communion. Five of six Mulligan children still lived under her roof,
and they needed their mother's attention. Sybil Stockdale's children,
however, attended college or boarding schools, giving her more time to
tend to official League business. She led the next day's session, which
incorporated the National League of Families of American Prisoners
and Missing in Southeast Asia, the new official name for the organization. Sybil became chairman of the board.

The formally coalesced organization would continue its mission to
educate the world about provisions for prisoner treatment as estab-

lished by the Geneva Convention—and North Vietnam's willful disregard thereof. Sybil and the National League aimed to supplement the government's work and create a groundswell of indignation that would force North Vietnam to change its practices if it wished to be respected in the international community.

She implored members to share their plight with the nation, and indeed the public rallied to the POW/MIA cause. For a brief moment, America focused on these women and their work, but only hours after Louise's speech moved so many National League members, news broke about the U.S. invasion of Cambodia. Protests erupted throughout the country as citizens objected to Nixon's expansion of America's involvement in the region. On May 4, Ohio National Guardsmen killed four student protesters at Kent State University, plunging America deeper into unrest and leading to even more demonstrations. Nearly 100,000 marchers converged on Washington, D.C., on May 9. Yet still, in the midst of this division, the National League's activists gave patriots of all persuasions a common cause: military families and captured and missing servicemen in Vietnam. Women like Sybil and Louise reminded their countrymen that whatever their opinion of the war, they should support the men called to fight it and the families that bore their sacrifice at home.

On the West Coast, students at San Fernando Valley State College—today renamed Cal State, Northridge—also mobilized to support America's POWs and created what would become one of the defining symbols of the POW movement in the United States. It began with a chance visit by air force veteran and future congressman Bob Dornan to the campus offices of Voices in Vital America (VIVA), a conservative, student-run campus organization. Dornan had recently returned from South Vietnam, where he'd met a villager of the American-allied Montagnard tribe who kept a sliver of aluminum from a wrecked U.S. aircraft and wore it as a bracelet. The mountain tribesman gave Dornan one to wear himself so that he would not forget his allies in Vietnam; the tribe believed the bracelet established a special connection with their new friend. When he visited San Fernando Valley State, Dornan wore the bracelet as he introduced VIVA student volunteers to several POW wives. The families' tragic stories moved the students, and after Dornan related the tale of the Montagnards, someone exclaimed, "We need to put one of those bracelets around every wrist in America!"

VIVA had found a new calling, a way to remind America of the hardships faced by its POWs and MIAs.

Under the leadership of student Carol Bates, VIVA decided to distribute similar bracelets to the public. They selected a company in Santa Monica for the job, and the firm minted five hundred the first week. In darkened engraved letters, bracelets bore the name, rank, and date of loss for a serviceman known, thought, or hoped to be held captive in Vietnam. Production eventually rose to forty thousand per week as the public rallied to VIVA's cause and clamored for the bracelets. The company hired more than a hundred college students and veterans who manufactured more than five million bracelets, which VIVA sold at $2.50 apiece for nickel-plated bracelets or $3 for copper. Such unlikely pairs as Richard Nixon and George McGovern wore bracelets, as did John Wayne and Dennis Hopper, Bob Hope and Cher. Shirley Johnson made sure every Dallas Cowboys player had one. The bracelets became uniquely American jewelry, binding citizens of all politics to the servicemen fighting the war, even as more Americans turned against the conflict itself. At least one member of almost every family that knew a POW or MIA serviceman wore a bracelet, hoping to return it to the POW when he returned. Millions of bracelets were worn by people who never knew a single captured or missing serviceman.

VIVA used proceeds from sales to support the National League of Families, help POW/MIA families in need, and produce bumper stickers and a variety of products that called attention to the POW/MIA issue. Many of those products carried the simple black-and-white image that the National League of Families had recently adopted; that image would become the enduring symbol of the POW/MIA movement for years to come.

In January 1970, when navy Lieutenant Commander Michael Hoff's A-7 Corsair went down over Laos, his wife, Mary Helen, joined the National League, wondering if she still had a husband. The young national organization lacked a recognizable symbol, and as she became more involved, Mary Helen began developing a vision for a new banner. She approached the country's oldest flag manufacturer, Annin Flagmakers, with the idea of creating a flag for the National League. The family-owned company, founded in 1847, agreed to help. Mary Helen, who recalled a photograph of POWs wearing black-and-white pajamas, explained to Annin, "I don't want a lot of colors. We need a stark, black-and-white flag." The company contacted Newt Heisley, a World War II U.S. Army Air Corps pilot turned graphic designer. When he received the assignment, his son, a veteran, had recently battled hepatitis, which had left him emaciated and weak. His gaunt features reminded his father of what a POW might look like, and he used his son as a model for the silhouette of a prisoner's bowed head, which he imposed on a large circle of white. He drew a guard tower and barbed wire in the background. Above the white circle were the letters POW and MIA, a white star separating the acronyms. A length of chain fence ran below the flag's main image. Designing the flag stirred Heisley's memories of his long wartime flights in C-46 transports. The vast South Pacific had claimed many fellow pilots, and he recollected gazing over the waters, considering the horror of being captured, then forgotten. With those thoughts in mind, he added the words YOU ARE NOT FORGOTTEN along the bottom of the banner.

In 1971, the National League approved the flag but decided against filing any trademarks; they wanted anyone—*everyone*, in fact—to use the image. Soon it appeared on banners, bumper stickers, T-shirts, motorcycle jackets, items of every sort. The flag came to remind America of this nascent yet powerful movement and its simple plea, Don't forget our men.

The Alcatraz Gang had not laid eyes on Jim Stockdale since he'd been escorted out of their compound in January 1969. Now, nineteen months later, on a July day in 1970, he stood in Stardust Four, terribly frail and wearing baggy pajamas, facing Sam Johnson.

Like long-parted brothers, the two men embraced and held on to each other as they both cried tears of joy and relief. Sam and Jim had not been together since they ran the communication network from their Thunderbird cell three years prior. That had also been the last time Cat allowed Sam a cellmate and the last time Jim embraced another American. Both had spent nearly three years without a friendly human touch. Once the guard left, the men sat down. Sam looked at their band's battle-scarred leader and saw the toll his resistance had taken. Sam knew that even before arriving at Alcatraz, Jim had likely suffered worse treatment than perhaps any other prisoner who remained alive. Now he learned about Stockdale's days after his banishment from

Alcatraz, his sessions with Rabbit and Pigeye, his stays in Calcutta and the Mint, and his experience of nearly bleeding out his life in Room Eighteen the previous September. Sam marveled at the endurance and will of this battered aviator. As he related his nightmare, Jim spoke hesitantly and often allowed his thoughts to trail off unfinished. His battles with the Camp Authority and the responsibility of leading so many men had aged him far beyond his forty-six years. Sam thought Jim's eyes looked nearly dead, no longer filled with intensity and authority. When Sam told him Ron Storz had remained behind at Alcatraz, he slumped to the floor and cried.

As Sam sized up Jim Stockdale during their first hours together, he heard taps coming from Jerry Denton in the adjacent cell. "Does Stockdale want to take command?" Jerry asked.

Sam asked Jim, who hung his head and answered quietly, "No, I'm not on my feet yet."

He replied to Jerry on Jim's behalf, "Remain in command for a while yet."

As they spent their days together, Sam felt Jim's fear and sadness become a physical presence in the small cell; those emotions had somehow replaced the self-assurance Jim had once exuded. Even Jim Stockdale had limits, and with plenty of time, unrestrained power, and no qualms of conscience, Cat and Rabbit had found them. His conversation continued to come with difficulty. After so many years of speaking only to Cat and other North Vietnamese officers—and then only begrudgingly or abrasively—he had trouble finding the words to express himself. Endless torture and solitary confinement had dulled his brilliant mind. His condition terrified Sam. "He'll get better," Sam told himself. "All he needs is a little time. I'll help him understand that the horrors of the old days are behind us. He'll get over this . . . Oh, Lord Jesus, please let him get better!"

"Jim," Sam said gently, "since Hồ Chí Minh's death, things have changed. You don't have to worry about torture anymore. The Vietnamese are under new orders now. They can't pressure you into relenting if you refuse to cooperate with them. We can resist without being punished."

Jim hesitated to believe Sam—understandable given the trauma he'd experienced and the unchanged physical conditions there in Little Vegas; rats and roaches still ran unchecked through the cellblocks, and filth was as pervasive as ever. Later that same day, Cat presented Sam with an opportunity to show Jim the new regime. Cat called the two former cellmates to a joint quiz. "Ah, Sông, you and Stockdale together again," he said from behind the table. "But you must be good. You will obey the rules. If you don't, you will not be allowed visits. If you continue in disobedience, we will punish you." He slid a script across the tabletop. "If you are truly repentant, you will write this. You will agree to obey all the camp rules."

"No," Sam said, clutching Jim's scarred wrist to reassure him, "we're not going to write that." Cat directed a question at Jim. Sam heard him inhale sharply, and sensed the conditioned reflex of fear emanating from the commander. "I'll speak for Stockdale," Sam said.

Cat flew into a rage and yelled at the reunited and still-insubordinate duo. He sent them back to Stardust under a deluge of threats. Yet several hours later, when a guard brought them a deck of playing cards, they knew Cat's threats had been empty. Cat never revisited the incident, and Jim's fear at long last began to dissipate.

The next time Jim Stockdale saw Cat, the commandant requested that he meet a visiting professor from the Massachusetts Institute of Technology; Jim envisioned an entire antiwar delegation. "I assure you there will be no propaganda," Cat almost pleaded. "The old days are gone; no longer do we dictate. All I want you to do is see him."

"No," Jim said. "You know I won't do that."

"You and I are the same age," Cat said, almost as if talking with an old friend who'd disappointed him. "We have some college, and I just hoped you would do this. You know I have obligations to meet, and I have pressures on me, just as any military man does." Jim thought Cat might actually put his arm around him.

Still Jim refused. Instead of erupting, Cat summoned a guard and walked out of the room alongside his American counterpart. "How long has it been?" he mused.

"It's been four and a half years," Jim answered.

Cat thought for a moment, then said, "I am afraid it's going to be a while longer."

Cat was indeed feeling pressure from his own higher-ups. That year, Jerry Denton, who had more interaction with Cat than most, noticed the camp commander's emotional state had slipped with his apparent position in the military hierarchy. He developed a facial tic; his hands shook; he lost weight. Then, sometime in mid-1970, he disappeared from the camp. Neither Jerry Denton, Jim Stockdale, nor any other POW ever saw him again.

During Jim Stockdale and Sam Johnson's first weeks together, Jim would sit idly by as Sam tapped to the other nine Alkies—as some had taken to calling themselves—during the guards' midday siesta. After several weeks of recuperating in Stardust, surrounded by his gang, however, the old CAG began to reemerge. Sam noticed his shoulders squaring, his still-hobbled gait reclaiming its purposeful stride. His skill with tap code resurfaced, and his knuckles once again rapped the wall like a woodpecker's beak. He deciphered taps almost as fast as the gifted Bob Shumaker. In their cell, he and Sam engaged in conversations about flying, philosophy, and the vast range of subjects that intrigued his academic mind. It became apparent that the North Vietnamese had never completely extinguished the fire in this warrior. His soul still harbored its embers, and now fellowship with his Alcatraz brethren had rekindled them. By Thanksgiving, Jim Stockdale had relieved Jerry Denton, reclaiming his post as the ranking naval officer in Hanoi and the POWs' leader. To the Alkies, all seemed right in their world. Stockdale had returned, and they felt unified. They had once again mobilized most of the POWs against the Camp Authority and resolved to go on waging war from their outpost in the enemy's capital.

In the fall of 1970, the women of the National League of Families continued mobilizing America, enlisting every conceivable ally in their mission. The American Red Cross and *Reader's Digest* escalated letter-writing campaigns they'd begun in late 1969. The organizations had flooded Hanoi and the offices of the North Vietnamese delegates in Paris with mail protesting their country's violation of the Geneva Convention and pleading for information about missing U.S. servicemen. The Red Cross named the campaign "Write Hanoi." So many people participated that the two organizations began another coordinated campaign in early 1971 that inundated the Hanoi post office with 679,000 postcards. The Red Cross also distributed 6.5 million brochures in the U.S. entitled "5 Minutes and 25 Cents," which suggested that five minutes of writing and a postage stamp could save a POW's life. The brochures appeared on seats at football bowl games, in telephone billing statements, and everywhere volunteers could place them. From a donated trailer in Virginia Beach, Louise Mulligan and other local National League members distributed stickers, sent out Christmas cards, and convinced companies to donate billboard space—anything to remind the public about the POWs.

On December 1, 1970, David Bruce, a former ambassador and a current envoy at the Paris Peace Talks, publically accused North Vietnam of violating specific Geneva Convention articles. At a press conference in Paris, he criticized the North Vietnamese government for parading POWs in the streets, torture, solitary confinement, malnourishment, inadequate medical care, failure to allow religious services, failure to allow POWs to write home as often as required, failure to deliver mail and packages from the United States, failure to release wounded POWs, not issuing a complete list of prisoners held, not informing the United States of prisoner deaths, and not allowing camp inspections by third parties. Several weeks later, President Nixon wrote to the families of America's POWs and MIAs, reinforcing Bruce's message with his personal commitment to improve prisoner treatment and bring the men home. The nation and world remained divided about the U.S. role in Vietnam, but they could agree on the importance of the Geneva Convention.

That last month of 1970, North Vietnam released the names of 368 U.S. prisoners to representatives of Senators William Fulbright and Edward Kennedy, who would carry the names home. Families finally learned the fate of their loved ones, and North Vietnam allowed every prisoner to write home in time for Christmas. The Rutledge and Jenkins families heard from Howie and Harry after five years. Every day during that period, Phyllis Rutledge had walked to her mailbox on Mount la Platta Court, just outside San Diego, hoping for this letter. Every day its absence had whittled away at her hope that Howie remained alive. Then, as another lonely year came to a close, the letter arrived. Howie's distinctively elegant handwriting spelled out her name and their address. Inside, she found the first words he'd been able to write to her since he flew his last mission in November 1965—half a decade before. "I am living testimony to the power of your prayers, your love, and faith," he wrote. "I know, in my heart, that you and ours are equally well, and for the same reasons. Keep faith, for we will have our reunion, whether in this world or the next."

Phyllis turned and ran into the house, screaming to her children, "He's alive! Your daddy is alive!"

Just days before Christmas, a similar scene took place at the Jenkins household. Marj found the letter in the day's mail and waited until her three children had returned home from school to open it. Together, they read the first letter from Harry since November 1965. It lifted the cloud of uncertainty that had hung over their household for so long.

Among the names North Vietnam disclosed were twenty U.S. servicemen who, according to the North Vietnamese, had died from wounds sustained at shootdown or from disease. So a member of Senator Kennedy's staff dialed Sandra Storz with a heavy heart. The list the senator had received from North Vietnam confirmed that her husband, Ron, had died in captivity. The news devastated Sandra and ten-year-old Mark; six-year-old Monica had never really known her father. The photo of Ron they'd received in July of 1967 had given them hope, but after three years without further word, their expectations had begun to wane. Now they bore the heavy, final weight of his death. Ron would not return.

O SAY CAN YOU SEE?

At 1:00 A.M. on November 21, 1970, the aircraft carriers *Oriskany* and *Ranger* initiated one of the largest nighttime flight operations of the long war. From their positions in the South China Sea, they launched more than fifty aircraft into North Vietnam, all to stage a massive diversion. As North Vietnamese air defenses concentrated on the navy's incursions, a covert flight of air force helicopters and combat planes raced across Thailand and Laos, then dropped low over the dark countryside of western North Vietnam, beginning Operation Ivory Coast. Roughly 250 men had volunteered to serve under World War II legend Colonel Arthur "Bull" Simons on what he advertised as a "moderately hazardous" mission that had no guarantee of success. The fifty-six Green Berets Simons chose sat inside the helicopters, ready to liberate American servicemen held prisoner in North Vietnam.

The flight roared over the Hanoi suburb of Sơn Tây shortly after 2:00 A.M. and descended on the nearby prison camp, which POWs had nicknamed Hope. Two helicopters landed inside the camp and unloaded their well-practiced Green Berets, who engaged more than a hundred North Vietnamese defenders. Armed with bolt cutters, the special operations force stormed through the prison compound to free the seventy to eighty POWs they expected. When they reached the cellblocks, however, they found the cells empty. Over the bark of Kalashnikovs and shouts in Vietnamese, the team reported "negative items" over the radio. Twenty-seven minutes after the engagement began, helicopters returned to Thailand without any POWs. Although the Sơn Tây raiders did not free any prisoners, the U.S. government had publicly demonstrated to Hanoi and to an increasingly skeptical public that America had not forgotten her captured servicemen.

Ten miles away, fifty-two U.S. POWs formerly held at Hope caught glimpses of artillery flashes in the nighttime sky. They listened to the pulse of helicopters, the noise of supporting attack aircraft, and the boom of artillery. From afar, these captives witnessed the raid meant to rescue them. U.S. intelligence had not learned that in July 1970, the well at Sơn Tây had run dry and the North Vietnamese relocated the prisoners to Camp Faith, a new facility closer to Hanoi. Four days after the November 21 raid, armed North Vietnamese guards moved them again, sweeping into Faith and loading the fifty-two former Sơn Tây prisoners into trucks bound for Hỏa Lò Prison. Once the POWs were inside the Hilton's thick walls, the guards herded them into the western section of the garrison, which no Americans had previously inhabited.

The Sơn Tây raid had an effect almost as important as any rescue. The North Vietnamese had spent the past five years dispersing their prisoners throughout the region, but the U.S. incursion convinced the Camp Authority to concentrate most of its American prisoners in the heart of Hanoi, where no helicopters could reach them. They began holding them inside large rooms in the western area of Hỏa Lò, which until the late fall of 1970 had held six hundred to eight hundred Vietnamese civilian convicts and POWs from the South Vietnamese army. After the raid by the Green Berets, the Camp Authority had relocated the Vietnamese prisoners to accommodate the American population. Given the number of U.S. captives who began arriving at the Hilton from Camp Faith, the Zoo, and other nearby facilities, the Camp Authority had no choice but to end isolation and begin group detention for most prisoners.

The change began taking effect in December and finally reached Little Vegas around Christmastime. On the night of the twenty-sixth, Jerry Denton heard large numbers of camp personnel enter the Little Vegas courtyard. He pulled himself up to the barred window and looked out. "It must be some sort of move, Jim," he called to his roommate, Jim Mulligan. "I can see the water girls and cooks moving dishes from the main area and taking them out to the main entrance towards Heartbreak Hotel."

The Alcatraz veterans heard guards enter their Stardust cellblock. The North Vietnamese threw open cell doors and issued the order, "Roll up!" The ten prisoners complied, each rolling his paltry belongings into his bamboo sleeping mat. The group trudged in single file toward the Heartbreak courtyard. Guards lined the path, but they showed no malice toward the captives. In fact, they seemed cheerful. When Jim Mulligan stumbled, a guard nicknamed Parrot reached out to steady him. "Go easy, Mun," he said.

They passed through the corridor adjacent to Heartbreak Hotel—those eight cells that held so many awful memories of their early days as POWs when they thought they'd return home by the following Christmas. Then they emerged into an unfamiliar section of Hỏa Lò: a ring of three long buildings that surrounded a sizable dusty courtyard spotted with thin trees.

After a thorough shakedown in one of the smaller two buildings, the Alcatraz Gang walked through a barred gate and into Room Seven in the largest building, which bordered the courtyard on three sides. Much like the building's other six rooms, Seven was a large open cell roughly 50 feet long by 20 feet wide and filled with more than forty grinning Americans. The Gang saw faces they hadn't seen since past deployments or since training at Pensacola, Nellis, Kingsville, or Colorado Springs. They found their fellow longtime POWs, some of whom they'd only known as a knuckle on a shared wall or a fleeting glance in a previous cellblock. Howie Rutledge had spent the better part of five years all by himself. Only taps, flashes, and his faith had sustained him. Now he watched forty-six Americans smiling, embracing, laughing, and talking. He marveled at this turn of events—how once he had risked so much to send taps through a wall, perhaps just a sentence per day. He believed the Lord had seen him through the wilderness. Bombardier-navigator George Coker reunited with his pilot, Jack Fellowes, who apologized for losing their A-6 Intruder and condemning them to so many years in Hanoi. "No sweat," George replied. When Fellowes had apologized before, just after their shootdown, Coker had told him they'd make it, and they had. Coker turned away from Fellowes, and Jim Stockdale and Jerry Denton embraced him. The two seniors had only seen Coker—Cagney, as Stockdale still called him—through the cracks of their Alcatraz cells, never in person. By this time, Jerry had forgiven George for fabricating orders to and from CAG while they were in Alcatraz. Bob Shumaker looked about and noticed that nobody could stop smiling, himself included. For the first time, the Alcatraz Gang could look upon each other, together, face-to-face.

The Americans called their new home Camp Unity, in honor of Stockdale's "Unity over Self" edict. As the initial euphoria of this grand reunion subsided, the Alcatraz survivors began asking about the one friend the North Vietnamese had forced them to leave behind. Nobody had any news about Ron Storz. Nobody had seen him. The Gang had let themselves hope that Ron might have survived, but in their hearts, they knew he probably had not. He did not appear in Camp Unity, and nobody else had seen him. They felt a wave of sadness as they realized their friend had almost certainly never left their secluded prison behind the Ministry of National Defense.

That night, the reunited POWs could not think about sleep. Jerry Denton proposed a different way to spend the evening. "Hey, it's still practically Christmas," he said. "Why don't we have a church service? Rutledge, help me out here."

With Howie thus conscripted, Robbie Risner volunteered himself and George Coker to quote scripture. "And Sam will sing, won't you, Sam?" Jerry asked.

Sam Johnson resisted, protesting, "Shirley won't even let me sing in church when there are other voices to cover me up!"

"It doesn't matter," Jerry said. "Just sing a Christmas carol."

In a gentle Texas tenor, Sam sang "Silent Night." His voice choked with emotion—both the happiness of being together with these fellow survivors and the sadness of missing yet another Christmas at home. He wondered if he could make it past the first stanza. Mercifully, the residents of Room Seven came to his aid and joined their voices with his.

For the first time since they entered captivity, the Americans sang together and worshipped the God to whom so many had turned so often. George Coker, Robbie Risner, and Howie Rutledge were leading the final "amens" of the service when the room's main door suddenly swung open. "No authorize!" yelled several guards as they stormed into the room. "No authorize! Be quiet!"

The squad pushed Coker, Risner, and Rutledge back into the crowd. "Not allowed!" admonished an officer, reminding them of the camp policy restricting worship and assembly. Once the officer and the guards left, the POWs laid out their bamboo mats on the cold concrete, head to head, shoulder to shoulder. They fell asleep in Room Seven, thankful they were at long last together and wholly undeterred by the Camp Authority's attempt at discipline.

If the Alcatraz veterans were a football team's starting offense, the men of Room Seven rounded out the Super Bowl roster. Intentionally or by coincidence, the Camp Authority had assembled many of its worst troublemakers in this room. Locked up along with the rogues of Alcatraz were Bud Day and John Dramesi, who'd both attempted daring escapes; John McCain, the admiral's son who had refused offers of early release; venerable Korean War ace Robbie Risner; Billy Lawrence, who had led resistors at the Hilton in the absence of Stockdale and Denton; and a host of other long-serving reprobates who had waged their own personal wars against the Camp Authority. Room Seven's senior ranking officer, Lieutenant Colonel Vern Ligon, USAF, was serving his second tour as a prisoner of war; he had already survived thirteen months in Nazi Stalag Luft 1 during World War II. Ligon had entered captivity in late 1967, and although he'd had less experience than the early arrivals at battling the Camp Authority, his rank gave him command of the more than 350 men in Camp Unity. Robbie Risner, Jim Stockdale, and Jerry Denton formed his senior leadership team. Collectively, the POWs called them the Four Wise Men.

Life improved markedly for the men in Unity as group imprisonment replaced solitary confinement. The men finally had open space inside where they could move around freely. Breezes wafted through large barred windows; bricks and boards no longer blocked the sunlight. A large raised sleeping platform covered much of the floor in the rooms; each night, men crowded onto it. The close quarters sometimes led to short tempers, but nobody missed the small cells of past years.

For the first time since they arrived in Hanoi nearly six years ago, the men no longer had to use their cursed honey buckets. Instead, they had a pair of concrete latrines, which unfortunately gave off an equally vicious odor. In the summer, a man could as easily breathe in flies as air. Still, the new facilities far outclassed the buckets. Prisoners were also allowed to take baths more frequently. Most importantly, the men could see, touch, and converse with fellow Americans. During their first days together, many men scarcely slept as years of pent-up conversations continued through the night.

In Room Seven, veteran POWs began readjusting to having daily contact with other people. Clinical psychologists could not have designed a more effective reacclimation process for men who'd endured long stints alone; they learned how to coexist again. In solitary, these men had rarely needed to consider anyone else. The "G2," as Room Seven's residents called former boxer George McKnight and former wrestler George Coker, had particular trouble sharing their new space. One day, when a POW told Coker to put his cup elsewhere, the two nearly came to blows. On another occasion, McKnight set his bowl down on the floor and a fellow POW advised him, "You can't put that here." McKnight checked his fists but confronted a situation his mind could barely grasp. The G2 and the other POWs gradually adjusted to sharing space with others.

Perhaps predictably, it took this roomful of hard-liners less than two months to begin pushing their newfound privileges. Tapped as chaplain by Robbie Risner, George Coker began assembling Room Seven for church services on Sundays, defying the Camp Authority's rule against assembly. A guard promptly reported the first gathering to Bug, who reminded the POWs that the Camp Authority forbade meetings of any kind. "How would you like to go back to the 1967 treatment?" he threatened. The officer had, in effect, challenged the practice of religion. These military men, many of whom had relied so heavily on faith to survive the preceding years, considered religious freedom a right, not a privilege. In Jim Stockdale's mind, the North Vietnamese had thrown down a gauntlet.

The leadership in Camp Unity decided to stage a showdown on Sunday, February 7, 1971. Anticipating the morning worship, Bug led a detachment of guards into the courtyard. The squad assembled by the gate of Room Seven as the POW choir, Bob Shumaker among them, began the service. The room's youngest occupant, twenty-seven-year-old George Coker, recited scripture and delivered the homily. When George finished, Howie Rutledge stepped to the forefront and began reciting the 101st Psalm, "I will sing of your love and justice; to you, O Lord, I will sing praise." By this time, three guards had stepped into the room. George Coker saw the explosive combination of fear and anger in their eyes as they glared at the three leaders while nervously watching the crowd of worshippers that surrounded them. "No talk! Be quiet! No authorize!" the guards shouted as they brandished their bayoneted rifles. The congregants ignored them. When Howie finished his psalm, Robbie Risner delivered the benediction with Hawk standing before him, shouting at him to stop.

After Risner dismissed the assembly, three guards came for George, Howie, and him. They grabbed the lay leaders roughly and hustled them out the gate at bayonet point. As they passed Bug, he sneered and told them, "Now you will see that my hands are not tied!"

The guards lined the three offenders up along the sidewalk outside the room, 10 feet apart, their backs to the building, their faces toward the guards. Then from inside, they heard singing. Air Force Major Bud Day had begun an unmistakable song, "O say can you see, by the dawn's early light . . ."

Prisoners had not heard "The Star-Spangled Banner" sung aloud since their captivity began. Tears came to many eyes as every voice in Room Seven rose with Day's. The men grasped the bars on the high windows and pulled themselves up so their voices would carry across the courtyard. POWs in other rooms began singing along. The chorus swelled even as guards rushed into the rooms, crying, "No authorize! No authorize! Quiet! No singing! Down! Get down! No window!"

The prisoners just kept singing.

Like the flag that had flown over Fort McHenry in Baltimore Harbor during the War of 1812, they, too, had survived a fierce siege. They carried scars from savage interrogations during which they'd hoped for death. Hunger, rats, mosquitoes, brutal beatings, broken bones, dysentery, fanatical guards, thirst, heat, cold, torture, and isolation had all failed to break them permanently. After battling through the pain, they had proven their resilience time and again in the Zoo, the Briar Patch, the Plantation, the streets of Hanoi, Room Eighteen, and Little Vegas. Ten of them had lived through the hell of Alcatraz. On this day, with this song, they told each other and all of North Vietnam that they had endured the worst; they would survive the rest. On that Sunday morning, the words of America's national anthem carried over the walls of Hỏa Lò Prison and spilled into the North Vietnamese capital for all to hear. The men who sang it would never forget the triumph of that moment.

The men for whom they sang it—Robbie Risner, Howie Rutledge, and George Coker—would never forget it either. Bug led the three in-stigators out of Camp Unity and back to Heartbreak Hotel, where their long sentences had first begun. With a chorus of three hundred voices singing the anthem for them, Robbie Risner felt 9 feet tall. George Coker, on the other hand, felt 9 *inches* tall. He feared his return to Heartbreak signaled a return to the old times—the beatings, the isolation. He read-ied himself for another hard stint alone. Indeed, the easy days had ended for the three celebrants. They found the conditions in Heartbreak's Cell Four unimproved since the mid-1960s. Guards clamped two men to the narrow bunks, and the third got the floor, which proved as filthy as ever. They weren't beaten, although they would have accepted blows for the satisfaction of leading the day's service. Once settled, they heard more noise coming through the wall that separated their cell from Room Seven in Camp Unity.

The POWs had begun to sing again, moving on to "God Bless Amer-ica," "Battle Hymn of the Republic," "America the Beautiful," "Califor-nia, Here I Come," and "The Eyes of Texas." George, Howie, and Robbie could hear what the guards and the people of Hanoi heard: a stockade full of Americans singing together as loudly as they could in trium-phant protest. The North Vietnamese turned on the courtyard loud-speaker, hoping to drown out the singing with music of their own. The prisoners just sang louder.

When the men tired of singing, a chant began. In collegiate tradi-tion, the men of Room Seven shouted, "This is Building Number Seven, Number Seven, Number Seven. This is Building Number Seven, where the hell is Six?" Building Six picked up the chant and challenged Build-ing Five, which in turn challenged Building Four. The chant circled the courtyard, making its way through all the Big Rooms, as the Camp Unity cellblocks were often called, until it ended at Building One. The walls reverberated with the noise. Jerry Denton smiled as he listened to his men releasing the frustration of a long and brutal incarceration. Their captors had locked them behind bars, walls, and doors, but still the North Vietnamese had lost control. For a time, the guards stood by, yelling and banging on gates to no avail, not knowing how to quell the Church Riot of 1971.

Soon, however, troops with tear gas and bayonets arrived to put the celebration to rest. Prison guards opened the barred gates of each large room, and the soldiers charged in, fully dressed in combat gear. They backed the POWs against the wall, pressing their bayonets against men's stomachs. The camp finally went silent.

The following day, Sam Johnson heard rumors that the Camp Authority planned to punish Room Seven for instigating the riot. Sure enough, a Vietnamese voice came over the camp speakers to announce, "No wash." No bathing for one day.

"Big deal," Sam said with a laugh. Considering the infrequency of baths in the preceding years, they could certainly hack one day's restriction. For the most part, the Camp Authority had lost its teeth. Bug did reserve some harsher sanctions for Jim Stockdale, Jerry Denton, and Vern Ligon, whom he deemed jointly responsible for the Sunday rebellion. His detail rounded them up and marched them into Building Zero, a separate cellblock that was subdivided into smaller two- and three-person cells. Guards tossed the three leaders into a two-bunk cell and locked Jim's left leg and Vern's right leg together in a single pair of leg stocks, forcing them to share a bunk. Jerry received his own bunk and his own pair of stocks. "Well, I guess we just can't stand prosperity," Jim Stockdale remarked. The threesome would be locked in stocks for thirty-eight days.

Perhaps most dishearteningly, their honey buckets returned. The trio spent the next five weeks flat on their backs, legs locked in place, using the bucket when they needed it. The men's primary entertainment came as Jim and Vern, who shared a bunk, engaged in comical exchanges as they answered nature's call in close quarters.

"Excuse me," one would say to the other.

"Certainly," the other would reply in exaggerated fashion.

"Sorry about that," the offender would repeat.

"Don't give it another thought."

At one point, Jim Stockdale realized they were actually having fun. Even as they were locked in stocks, they could at least laugh. The present situation in Hỏa Lò differed in almost every way from the early years. The Camp Authority had ceased torture, restrained vicious guards, and—at times—even improved rations. In this new environment, the Alcatraz men found a stint in stocks bearable, even easy by comparison. Camp Unity marked a new chapter in their imprisonment, and that winter of 1971, the prisoners found themselves in the

communal detention camp many had imagined when they first arrived in Hanoi years ago. Instead, they had spent up to five years in
conditions worse than they ever could have imagined.

The Church Riot soon brought new freedoms. After Bug had locked up
the ringleaders, the Camp Authority gave the POWs the right of limited
assembly. "Camp authorize church service on Sunday for fifteen minutes," a North Vietnamese officer announced over the loudspeaker.
"Can have choir and sing, but for fifteen minutes—no more!"

The Camp Authority had backed down. In this triumph, Sam
Johnson saw God's hand and gave thanks. "We're prisoners in a hostile
land, raising a ruckus and pushing for our demands—they could take
us all out and shoot us if they wanted to," he prayed, "but you've inter-
vened again. Thank you, Lord."

Not all celebrations involved prayer, although many POWs offered
their own. The fresh victory inspired the senior officers remaining in
Room Seven to organize a secular celebration to mark the sixth anniversary of Bob Shumaker's capture, February 11. In all of American
military history, only naval aviator Ev Alvarez (taken in August 1964)
and Green Beret Jim Thompson (captured by the Việtcộng in March
1964)—both of whom were being held elsewhere in Hanoi—had served
longer sentences as prisoners of war. Fellow naval officers led Shu's celebration and roasted him with a mix of true and utterly fabricated stories
from his past. As a memento, the men presented Shu with an oversized
medal of tin and toilet paper. Room Seven grew as raucous as the Cubi
Point Officers' Club on a Saturday night in the Philippines. Like many
good parties, Shu's anniversary came with a hangover. The next day,
new Room Seven leaders Jim Mulligan and Harry Jenkins found themselves forced to join Jim Stockdale, Jerry Denton, and Vern Ligon in
Building Zero. Orson Swindle, a leader in Room Six, quipped about
Room Seven, "Damn, you'd have to get in line to get in trouble in that
crowd!"

At home, families also began pushing boundaries. After six years
of waiting, they were plain fed up with their government, even with its
Go Public efforts. For all his compassion, President Nixon hadn't properly returned any POWs or extracted any real promises from North
Vietnam. The leaders of the National League of Families demanded a
meeting with both the president and Henry Kissinger. They'd last met

with Nixon in 1969 and now had been promised a meeting with Kissinger on Saturday, January 23, 1971, shortly before the Church Riot
erupted in Camp Unity. Louise, Sybil, and several other board members
traveled all the way to Washington, D.C., only to learn that Kissinger
couldn't attend. He sent Deputy National Security Adviser General Alexander Haig in his place. Haig walked into a firestorm.

Standing before a large White House conference table, he apologized for Kissinger's absence, then recited rote lines the wives had heard
many times from a host of White House, Pentagon, and State Department subordinates. They wanted real answers from Kissinger himself.
Louise Mulligan interrupted Haig and told him as much. Before he
could respond, another POW wife said her piece. Then another stood
up, stamped her foot, and leveled her finger at the general, furious that
she couldn't see Kissinger after flying cross-country for the meeting.
Haig fielded hard volleys from all sides of the table.

He offered a rescheduled meeting in two months. Indignant, Sybil
said, "We don't want to wait two months to see Dr. Kissinger, General
Haig. We want to see him in two days. We'll still be here on Monday."

Within twenty-four hours, they were scheduled for Monday. When
the wives returned to the White House, Kissinger asked them, "What
did you do to my general?"

Then he joked to the table that General Haig had fled when he
heard the National League was returning. The levity ended there, however. The National Security Adviser and lead U.S. negotiator in Paris
promised and delivered straight answers. Unfortunately, Kissinger offered no hope for any near-term resolution. The women left the meeting feeling crestfallen. "At least Jim doesn't know," Sybil thought to
herself.

Both Sybil and Louise's husbands remained unsure of the future and
instead were more concerned about surviving their current stints in
stocks. As fallout from Shu's anniversary celebration, guards had sent
new Room Seven leaders Jim Mulligan and Harry Jenkins to Building
Zero; now most of the Alcatraz seniors were together. Upon entering
the cellblock, Jim coughed an "M" and Harry coughed and sneezed "J,"
their old Alcatraz identifiers. They heard a "D" coughed and hawked in
response by Jerry Denton. Jim and Harry lay down in a 7-by-7, two-
bunk cell while the guard fastened their ankles in separate stocks.

They would spend the night—and the coming thirty-seven days—flat on their backs. Once each day, one lucky man could leave to empty their buckets. With rear ends chafing from their fixed positions, the seniors christened Building Zero "Rawhide."

In their shared cell, Harry Jenkins kept Jim Mulligan crying with laughter by telling him the plot of a movie almost every night. Using his long arms and unfailing sense of humor, Harry would entertain his cellmate with one-man renditions of Hollywood films. His lone audience member found his monologues uproariously funny; Jim marveled at his wit and memory. Of course, with the exception of the movie titles Harry had made up nearly every word. They tried singing as well. With iron bars firmly immobilizing their ankles, they put new words to Gene Autry's cowboy tune "Back in the Saddle Again," singing, "Whoopi-ty-aye-oh, Rockin' to and fro, we're back in the irons again . . ." Nobody ever lacked for laughter while in the company of Harry Jenkins.

Howie Rutledge and Robbie Risner spent two days in Heartbreak for their role in the Church Riot before guards transferred them to Rawhide, leaving behind George Coker. He would be Heartbreak's lone resident for six weeks, linked to Camp Unity only by tapping through the wall to Room Seven—and few men in Seven could translate tap code fast enough to understand George, who'd practiced so intensely in Alcatraz.

In Rawhide, Howie was reunited with his Alcatraz neighbor Harry Jenkins, and the communicative pair quickly discovered a group of recently transferred officers known as "the Bulls," a nickname for full colonels. Since mid-1965, the mantle of POW leadership had passed primarily between Robbie Risner, Jim Stockdale, Jerry Denton, and, recently, Vern Ligon, but they were not always the most senior officers. The Bulls outranked them, but the Camp Authority had kept these colonels in nearly absolute isolation since their arrivals. They did not know tap code, nor did they know much about the experiences of their fellow POWs. While the Alcatraz seniors had heard of the Bulls, they had never managed to contact them until now.

Harry and Howie immediately began teaching the Bulls tap code and sending them notes by various means. They invented at least one new courier system, crushing toothpaste tubes into marble-sized balls and shooting them under doors between the guard's regular rounds.

The little balls would zing across hallways, trailing long strings with notes attached. When a note-toting marble became marooned in the corridor, Harry passed word along the cellblock. One cell sent several straws of bamboo through the small holes that the men had drilled between their cells. Harry and Howie tied the straws together with strings pulled from their pajamas. They slid their improvised bamboo pole beneath the door, hooked the stray marble, and recovered it just before the guard returned. They had narrowly avoided stocks or irons for communicating; Harry considered their luck yet another good sign.

With all the seniors now communicating, the ranking officer, Colonel John Flynn, USAF, one of the Bulls, assumed command and the 4th Allied POW Wing entered service. The leaders chose "4th" because they were fighting America's fourth war of the century. They used "Allied" since a South Vietnamese pilot and three friendly Thai prisoners also lived in Rawhide and had quickly become important assets, as they translated guards' dialogue and helped pass communications. As flyers, they chose "wing" as their unit designation. The leadership divided the POWs into squadrons according to rooms—Room Seven would be one squadron, Room Six another. The leaders issued policies and created a staff administration led by the senior officers. For their motto, the Wing selected "Return with Honor" because they aspired to do just that.

In March of 1971, Howie Rutledge, Jim Stockdale, Harry Jenkins, and Jerry Denton were all moved into one of Rawhide's 7-by-7 cells, where they shared two small bunks. From tight quarters in Rawhide, the senior officers ran the 4th Allied POW Wing like the active-duty unit it was.

With POWs no longer concerned about day-to-day survival, the command system focused on regulations concerning bedtime, latrine duty, and hygiene—all of which seemed trivial compared to the bold BACK US directives that had united the men against the oppressive regime of the early years. George Coker particularly chafed under rules regarding the direction POWs could walk or run inside their rooms. This wasn't high school track, he'd fume to anyone who would listen.

To complicate the leadership structure, the seniors in each room lived with the men they commanded, unable to benefit from the usual distance the military placed between ranking officers and their subordinates. With so much time spent in the same space, coping with boredom, eating together, and sleeping head-to-head, men grew plain tired of one another. Personality differences overlooked during times of danger became sources of bickering and occasional fights. Depression and other emotions long suppressed by the challenge of daily survival surfaced. Men finally had the time to contemplate all that might have transpired in America since their outside lives effectively ended in the mid-1960s. Arguments about every imaginable issue sprouted like weeds; of course, many proved entirely irresolvable in the captives' present imprisonment. Jerry Denton, one of the Four Wise Men, felt like Moses leading the ever more quarrelsome Israelites as they neared the Promised Land after decades of wandering.

The five most senior members of the Alcatraz Gang ensured orders reached the entire Wing by finding new ways to communicate across the courtyard from their quarters in Rawhide and, after September 1971, from their new quarters in the adjacent Building Eight, generally known as Blue. Blue had three small rooms with three beds each, a dining room with a table and nine chairs, and a wooden fence that hid its small courtyard from the rest of Unity. The five Alkies shared the space with four air force colonels. Once in Blue, Harry Jenkins in particular wasted no opportunity to fashion new communication methods. When a rat knocked a rusted pocket knife off a roof and into the 12-by-12 common area, Harry snatched it up. That evening, he worked the blade open using grease from their most recent meal. He honed the knife and soon cut hiding nooks into every piece of wooden furniture he could find—and he also used the knife to fashion a long stick. Blue shared a back alley with Rawhide, and using a shard of mirrored glass affixed to the end of his new stick, Harry constructed a periscope that allowed him to look for guards in the alley. After he saw it was clear, a second conspirator—usually Howie Rutledge—could whisper safely with Robbie Risner and other leaders in Rawhide. The men in Blue would then pass information to Bob Shumaker or Sam Johnson across the courtyard in Room Seven.

During the guards' noontime siesta, Howie would sit on the shoulders of Harry Jenkins, the tallest POW in residence, and raise and lower Harry's stick in and out of a pipe in their roof. Shu would also sit on someone's shoulders and look through the high barred windows of Room Seven to decipher the code. One day, Shu saw a guard sneaking along the roofline of Rawhide and Blue, stalking the bobbing stick. Helpless, Shu watched him get closer and closer until he grabbed the stick and caught Howie. Howie received several days' punishment for what he swore had been his first attempt.

In the eyes of the Camp Authority, passing information still ranked among the gravest sins a prisoner could commit. Yet despite their efforts to stop them, flashes, notes, and taps still sent orders sailing around the courtyard to the Wing's more than 350 members. The Thai prisoners who served as custodians helped the Americans by literally sweeping notes back and forth across the grounds. The POW network chugged along defiantly, as it had for more than six years, everywhere from New Guy Village to the Zoo to Little Vegas.

A small number of men chose not to participate in the Wing, however. When American POWs were first sent to Camp Unity, the Camp Authority placed seven prisoners by themselves in Blue, where they spent much of 1971. For the previous three years, these first residents of Blue had willingly given propaganda statements to the North Vietnamese. Two of the three senior officers in the group had hosted the "Bob and Ed Show" that had so irked Jim Stockdale in Little Vegas; they still made frequent broadcasts. Under the direction of the three seniors, the four junior officers among them cooperated in giving propaganda.

By sequestering them in Blue, the Camp Authority hoped to shield these officers from the influence of other cellblocks. Consequently, these collaborators, as many considered them, became known as the "Outer Seven." The Four Wise Men found their statements highly inappropriate and told them as much. From Rawhide, Jim Stockdale managed to get a message to the Outer Seven, despite their isolation in Blue. "Write nothing for the V," he sent. "Meet no delegations. Make no tapes. No early releases. Are you with us?" While the POW leadership certainly allowed men their private thoughts—and many had differing opinions about the war—the leaders believed it unacceptable for a senior officer especially to contradict Wing policy by helping the North Vietnamese or making anti-American statements.

"We actively oppose this war," two of the seniors responded to Jim. The third senior agreed with Stockdale, and eventually he and the four junior officers began adhering to the policies set by the 4th Allied POW Wing. The Wing leadership stripped the two heretical seniors of military rank and authority. Jim planned a court-martial once they returned home. As guards and interrogators sensed the mounting animosity directed at the collaborators, the Camp Authority sent the Outer Seven to the Zoo and moved nine of the senior POW leaders into Blue. At the Zoo, in the suburbs of Hanoi, five of the Outer Seven continued to abide by the rules set by the POW leadership. The holdouts became known as the "Damned Two." Many prisoners still resented the "Repentant Five" who'd returned to the fold, but Stockdale reminded the Wing, "It is neither American nor Christian to nag a repentant sinner to the grave." By 1972, the one repentant senior had been transferred from the Zoo back to Camp Unity, where he assumed command of Room Seven. Even upon their eventual return to the United States, most POWs would never forgive the Damned Two.

To make the most of their idle time, and to put to use the variety of talent and knowledge within the Wing, the POWs created a veritable university in Camp Unity. Bob Shumaker found a broad audience for his math and science lessons. Since engineers abounded among the aviators, Shu's students would spend hours working like high schoolers to solve complicated equations. They eventually calculated trigonometric tables—sine, tangent, cosine—for every angle between zero and 90 degrees. The teams completed all their calculations without the aid of paper or pencil. As they worked, the time passed less painfully and their minds grew sharper.

While most POWs parachuted into North Vietnam wearing wristwatches, almost none arrived at Hỏa Lò with one still in his possession. So to substitute, Bob Shumaker and others in Room Seven engineered a pendulum with a two-second period. They calculated that they'd need a piece of string 39 inches long. Since they had no ruler, they used the remembered height of several POWs as a baseline to gauge the proper length. They tied a piece of soap to the precisely measured string, started it swinging back and forth, and began counting off the time in increments of two seconds. They used their jury-rigged clock to time speeches given by the Room Seven public speaking club.

Sam Johnson taught aerobatics, drawing upon his time as an air force Thunderbird pilot; even the navy flyers listened intently as he described four-point rolls, Immelmanns, and Cuban Eights. In the tradition of his tinkering father, who had a reputation for fixing anything, Nels Tanner taught car repair. Tough George McKnight taught the Charleston, a popular class for which the men in his room cleared the floors. Flyboys would kick up their heels to George's counts and instructions, swinging their legs and imagining the American music and women they missed. The men found instructors for just about every subject that could help pass the time. Self-made textbooks and translation dictionaries abounded, written on sheets of brown toilet paper. For ink, they mixed combinations of ashes, ground-up pills, water, and other materials. They found sugar useful as an adhesive agent. The Camp Authority considered all POW writings contraband and often confiscated their laboriously manufactured textbooks. The POWs had plenty of time to make new ones. The men in Unity wanted to return home better men; their improvised university helped them along that path.

In pursuit of entertainment more than enlightenment, George McKnight and Bob Shumaker learned to juggle and stand on their heads. The POWs in Room Seven also designated Sunday, Wednesday, and Saturday as movie nights. Volunteer "movie-tellers" would spend hours recounting and reenacting motion pictures they recalled from home. Once, Harry Jenkins delivered a particularly fine rendition of the Cary Grant classic *North by Northwest* to his audience in Blue. As he had in Rawhide, locked in irons next to Jim Mulligan, Harry made up most of the story. Years later, he would receive good-natured telephone calls from repatriated POWs who called his bluff after seeing the genuine movie.

As 1971 progressed, the authorities began distributing mail from home more often. Letters usually brought joy, but some brought sadness—death, divorce, hardships at home. Some POWs found that their wives chose not to wait for their return; others learned parents had died. In Bob Shumaker's case, Rabbit gave him a heavily redacted letter informing him that his mother had died suddenly. The news added to the depression Shu constantly battled; when he later discovered the Camp Authority had withheld the letter for more than a year, he was furious. He also received letters with photographs of a growing son and a vibrant twenty-eight-year-old wife, without a husband, without a father, without him. Shu hadn't seen them in more than six years now. He did his best to combat the sadness of that irreplaceable lost time, but ultimately retreated into himself and into science as the depression came on.

Harry Jenkins flipped through a magazine, one of the luxuries that had begun trickling into camp, and was surprised to find a Green Bay Packer stuffing his long hair inside his helmet. Marj sent Harry a photo of his own sons, their hair not too long, seated with arms out straight to their knees. Between them sat their sister, her arms crossed. Harry saw the four straight arms and realized they corresponded to bars on uniform shoulder boards; Harry had made captain.

In addition to letters, packages from home became more frequent and bountiful, although POWs suspected the staff pilfered from them. They grew suspicious when they observed guards casually munching on Planters peanuts.

Not all goods were innocuous or humanitarian, however. In San Diego, Phyllis Rutledge followed government orders and hid military-supplied notes inside care packages. Sometimes, she'd pack toothpaste tubes inside which the government had stashed all manner of contraband. In Virginia Beach, Louise Mulligan did the same. Given the items wives smuggled in—and the encoded letters Alcatraz prisoners sent home—the North Vietnamese did have some legitimate grounds for their accusations that the United States used humanitarian channels illicitly.

One day, the guards gave Jim Mulligan and Jerry Denton packages from Louise and Jane. Jerry got protein powder, while Jim found instant coffee in plastic baby bottles along with a bag of shriveled prunes. "Prunes and baby bottles?" he remarked. "What the hell is she trying to tell me?" He couldn't imagine why Louise had sent him prunes. Then he bit into one. He heard a crunch and pulled a small capsule from his mouth. He pried it open and found microfilm. The forty-five-year-old had an officer with younger eyes read it; the government had sent a list of known POWs for confirmation. In his next postcard home, Jim sent an encoded reply. Sam Johnson made a similar discovery in the summer of 1971 when he sucked on a piece of candy and something wedged itself behind his teeth. He picked out a small brown sliver and began rubbing it. It unfolded into a piece of microfilm roughly 16 millimeters wide. "Shu," he whispered. "Look at this!"

Bob Shumaker rushed over to take a look. He whistled softly. "Hold on," he said. "Get somebody on the window to watch for the guard!" Lookouts posted, Room Seven huddled around Sam, who slowly massaged and smoothed the film. He squinted at the tiny print. Five years in prison had eroded his fighter pilot's vision, but he could make out one line, *"The New York Times."* Sam passed the film to young George Coker to read aloud. George started with the date, "Saturday, November 21, 1970," the previous fall. He read every word of the front page. Most notably, he read that Green Berets had raided the prisoner-of-war camp at Sơn Tây. The men finally understood why the North Vietnamese had hurriedly consolidated their prisoners in downtown Hanoi. News from home and reports about the rescue attempt were spiritual food for starving men. America had not forgotten them.

PEACE IS AT HAND

On December 18, 1971, more American prisoners began flowing into the Hanoi Hilton as the navy and air force resumed the air operations over North Vietnam that President Johnson had halted in 1968. The new POWs experienced a registration process that differed markedly from that suffered by men like Harry Jenkins and Howie Rutledge; torture had ended.

For the longtime prisoners, the new arrivals became a resource. The POWs appreciated anything that advanced their knowledge of the world events that had taken place since their shootdowns. More than six years had passed since the North Vietnamese ushered the first Americans into the Hilton. So much had changed at home, yet the POWs only knew fragments—details passed in code from new prisoners, comments in the sporadic letters, or suspect news in the propaganda still dispensed daily by Hanoi Hannah. Many prisoners had yet to accept the reports of widespread domestic protests against the war. Bob Shumaker stuck with the view of the war he'd held when he'd deployed in 1964, despite anything new captives might say. Like most early shootdowns, he would not change his mind inside a Hanoi jail, and he intentionally ignored every word Hannah said.

By 1972, captivity and the seemingly never-ending war had disheartened a substantial number of the nearly four hundred U.S. POWs in North Vietnam. Most men hadn't turned against the United States, but many had simply grown weary of the war. Some POWs sided with the protesters back home, although their sentiments did not drive them to collaborate with their captors. In a conflict that seemed destined never to end, more than a few POWs believed escape was their only hope for ever returning home. Accordingly, the POW leadership formed an escape committee that included veteran escapee George McKnight. Bob Shumaker served as communications liaison and coordinated the mailing of multiple letters laced with Martini code so that the escape committee could notify the U.S. military of their plan. The more Shu considered options for escape, however, the more he became convinced that nobody could safely escape the prison or, for that matter, the teeming city of Hanoi. He also thought an escape would bring the kinds of violent repercussions felt by POWs at the Zoo after John Dramesi and Ed Atterberry had attempted an escape in 1969. The two had been caught, Atterberry died during a subsequent torture session, and the Camp Authority took vengeance upon other prisoners. Shu envisioned a similarly bad outcome and quit the committee in protest.

U.S. intelligence had already received his coded messages, however, and on May 2 and 4, 1972, two SR-71 Blackbird reconnaissance planes streaked over Hanoi to create two sonic booms, the agreed-upon signal that an extraction force would be waiting to recover fugitive POWs at the mouth of the Red River. Considering the low odds of success and the certain fallout for the POWs who stayed behind, the Wing's senior ranking officer, Colonel John Flynn, vetoed the operation, and no prisoner ever made an attempt. With escape not a realistic option, the men put their hope in their government. Surely their president wouldn't strand them in Hanoi.

Hanoi Hannah gave them no encouragement. That spring, she reported that columns of tanks had led 120,000 North Vietnamese troops into South Vietnam, beginning the Easter Offensive. General Võ Nguyên Giáp planned to wallop the South Vietnamese army, secure more territory for the NLF, and improve North Vietnam's bargaining position in Paris. As America's slow withdrawal neared its completion—only 6,000 U.S. combat troops were still in Vietnam—the North realized that new territory seized would likely become territory kept when they finally signed a settlement with Nixon and Kissinger after more than three years of negotiation. General Giáp also aimed to prove that Nixon's

Vietnamization strategy had failed, that South Vietnam couldn't support itself, even with American B-52s helping from above. North Vietnamese prime minister Phạm Văn Đồng similarly planned to demonstrate the North's undiminished will and warfighting ability, which he hoped would convince the American president that he could either exit Vietnam now or remain ensnared in a costly losing gambit that his electorate would not support.

The Americans had expected the Easter Offensive in March but had not anticipated its scale. Northern troops pushed into the South, occupying cities and former U.S. outposts. It became clear to Nixon—if it hadn't been already—that South Vietnam lacked the ability to defend itself in the long run against the Vietnamese Communists. However, conscious of America's need for leverage in Paris and to demonstrate his commitment to South Vietnam, Nixon ordered the mining of Haiphong Harbor, strangling Hanoi's seaborne supply line. Then he unleashed his B-52s and ominously promised, "The bastards have never been bombed like they're going to be bombed this time." June saw Operation Linebacker drop 120,000 tons of bombs on troops and supply lines fueling North Vietnam's operations below the DMZ, with the massive bombers taking off on missions around the clock at the rate of three per hour; Hannah and the Camp Authority avoided mentioning that news to the POWs. When North Vietnam's Easter Offensive and the United States' retaliatory Operation Linebacker ended in October, the North had improved its position in the South and in Paris at the cost of an estimated 100,000 primarily Vietnamese battlefield casualties. Henry Kissinger and Hanoi's lead negotiator, Lê Đức Thọ, resumed talks in August, eight full years after the Gulf of Tonkin incident and three years after President Nixon began withdrawing U.S. troops. As before, representatives from neither the National Liberation Front nor the South Vietnamese government directly participated in the negotiations. North Vietnam and the United States would dictate the future of South Vietnam.

Hanoi had set the 1972 American presidential election as its diplomats' deadline for resolution, a goal the U.S. negotiators shared, although neither party publicly disclosed it. As their mutual deadline loomed, both sides began to position themselves for an agreement. For years, the United States had demanded North Vietnam recall its troops from the South, but Kissinger realized that neither South Vietnam nor the United States had the leverage or firepower to make the People's Army move anywhere. On this point, Kissinger conceded. In return, his counterpart Lê Đức Thọ dropped his insistence upon the dissolution of South Vietnamese president Nguyễn Văn Thiệu's government. Two major roadblocks to peace disappeared. Thọ proposed a cease-fire, a prisoner exchange, and an American withdrawal. North Vietnamese troops would hold their positions below the DMZ, and a coalition "council of national reconciliation" would organize elections in South Vietnam. The two sides reached an accord on October 21, 1972, but work still remained for Kissinger. Now he had to obtain Thiệu's signature on a document that all but assured the end of his reign in South Vietnam. Enraged by the conditions Kissinger had negotiated, Thiệu immediately denounced the proposed treaty. Kissinger and Nixon leaned hard on their beneficiary, but Thiệu only issued a list of new stipulations that Kissinger considered "preposterous" and North Vietnam found, not surprisingly, unacceptable. Still, despite these setbacks, as the 1972 U.S. presidential election approached, Kissinger held a press conference and proclaimed, "Peace is at hand."

In Camp Unity, Sam Johnson heard Hanoi Hannah report, "United States and North Vietnam have reached agreement."

"This is it," Sam proclaimed out loud. "It's going to happen this time. It's almost over." He felt his heart pounding in his chest.

In reality, however, the end of the war had not come. Nixon and Kissinger had both overestimated their ability to intimidate their adversary and dictate their ally. Days after trumpeting the purported agreement, Hannah reported, "United States refuses to sign peace proposal." Sam's spirits immediately fell.

Unwilling to alter the original terms of the agreement to meet the South Vietnamese president's new demands, Thọ returned to Hanoi on December 13. The next day, a furious President Nixon issued a seventy-two-hour ultimatum to North Vietnam and leaned even harder on Saigon. The threats failed to revive discussions.

On the night of December 18, 1972, Jim Mulligan, Harry Jenkins, and U.S. Air Force Lieutenant Colonel Joe Kittinger set a piece of bread under a large wash bucket on the floor of their room in Blue. Then they propped up the bucket with a stick. Joe tied a string to the stick, and the three senior officers retreated to their bunks, where they began a silent vigil, Joe holding the end of the string, the three men all intently watching the bread. Soon, one of Hỏa Lò's rats emerged from a hole in the wall. It slunk toward the bucket and tried to take the bait. Kittinger yanked the string and the bucket crashed down over the sizable rodent, capping their evening's entertainment.

Happy with their night's prize, the three POWs lay down beneath their mosquito nets for Jim Mulligan's 2,467th consecutive night in Hanoi and Harry's 2,590th. Suddenly, air raid sirens began wailing across the city. The lights in Camp Unity went out. Jim heard three surface-to-air missiles launch nearby. He leapt to the window and saw rockets streaking across the night sky. Exhaust trails crisscrossed the heavens while muzzle flashes from antiaircraft artillery turned the sky momentarily white. Then he heard distant rumblings that sounded like long burps from the deepest, loudest Gatling gun he had ever heard. The ground began to shake, and the ceiling showered them with plaster. In fact, Jim was hearing and feeling strings of eighty-four 500-pound bombs hitting the ground milliseconds apart: carpet bombing. He knew enough to recognize what was transpiring. "It's a B-52 raid, Harry," he said to his fellow Alcatraz survivor. "Pack your bags. We're going home."

For the next six nights, the bombers came. In wave after wave, explosions rolled across Hanoi to the cheers of the POWs. The bombs also worried Jim Mulligan, though. He pulled aside Parrot, one of the guards he considered a good soldier, one of the men just doing his job. Jim said, "Parrot, I don't want to see you get hurt. Take my advice and do not go out of the camp. It's the safest place in Hanoi. Tell Hawk and Ichabod also. You stay here in camp with us, and you will be safe from the bombs." Pointing skyward, Jim added, "They know we are here."

Each night the POWs scurried about their cells, vying for the best observation points. Many POWs napped during the day so they could stay up and cheer for the coming night's aerial show. Hundreds of sorties flew over North Vietnam and its capital city during those initial days. To the American POWs, it appeared that the United States had finally decided to win the war. Then, on Christmas, no bombs fell. No aircraft disturbed the peaceful celebrations observed in Camp Unity. In each building and room, POWs sang hymns, recited the Pledge of Allegiance, and listened to a homily. For Jim Mulligan, it was the first hopeful Christmas in Hanoi. The next day, the onslaught resumed, dropping yet more explosives on North Vietnam until the skies again emptied on December 30. By the time the last bomb of Operation Line-backer II had fallen, the United States had dropped more than six million tons of ordnance on the small country in eight years. The "Christmas Bombing" campaign destroyed many of Hanoi and Haiphong's indus-trial and military facilities and claimed 1,623 civilian lives, according to the North Vietnamese government's reports—a terrible number, but one relatively small considering the intensity of the bombing. Ame-rican pilots and planners had attempted to avoid civilian areas, and the North Vietnamese government had long ago evacuated nearly 75 per-cent of its urban population to the countryside, removing them from harm's way. North Vietnam inflicted its own damage as well. The air force lost ten B-52s and sixty-one men over North Vietnam. Thirty-three survivors were sent to Hỏa Lò Prison; twenty-eight airmen lost their lives. Sixteen other B-52s went down over water or neighboring countries due to battle damage or operational failures.

After weathering eight days of relentless pounding, North Viet-nam finally responded to an American diplomatic overture. Both par-ties wanted a treaty. North Vietnam had lost more than one million troops during the war. More than two million Vietnamese civilians on both sides of the DMZ had also perished. Leaders in Hanoi knew that the sooner America left, the sooner the regime in Saigon would crum-ble, and the sooner they'd realize their longtime goal of unification. As for the Americans, wounded numbered well over 150,000, and expenses tallied more than $111 billion, nearly $686 billion in modern dollars. Little patience or support for the war remained among the U.S. elector-ate. Even Nixon just wanted it to go away. As the United States prepared to resume negotiations in Paris, the president cabled Thiệu in Saigon, demanding, "You must decide now whether you desire to continue our alliance or whether you want me to seek a settlement with the enemy which serves U.S. interests alone." Thiệu had no choice but to consent.

In Camp Unity, the POWs had learned of the Paris negotiations from newly captured B-52 crews, and they wondered how soon the end would come. The Camp Authority told them nothing, but in Janu-ary 1973, they noticed promising signs. From their courtyard, the POWs could see a 200-foot-tall radio tower to the northwest. The North Viet-namese had kept the tower darkened at night to deny attacking aircraft a landmark. The men reasoned that when hostilities ceased, the tower's lights would shine through the evening. In late January, the tower's lights burned long after nightfall. No more air raids assailed Hanoi; no more sirens blared in the night. An unmistakable change had come to the city and its central prison. Although the Camp Authority still denied them concrete information, the POWs began to suspect that the war had, at long last, ended. They just hoped their president had remembered them in the negotiations.

In Paris on January 23, 1973, Henry Kissinger and Lê Đức Thọ initialed an agreement that their countries' heads of state would soon formalize. In Virginia Beach the next day, Louise Mulligan and Jane Denton heard President Nixon announce the news to his war-weary nation, including families like theirs, whose loved ones had spent nearly eight years in prison camps while America struggled to untangle itself from Vietnam. They realized, of course, that many families had lost their beloveds forever.

"To all of you who are listening, the American people," Nixon said, "your steadfastness in supporting our insistence on peace with honor has made peace with honor possible . . . Let us be proud that America did not settle for a peace that would have betrayed our allies [or] that would have abandoned our prisoners of war." Louise greeted the news in guarded fashion. Only when she knew Jim was on an American airplane home would she truly believe the war had ended.

Four days after North and South Vietnam, the NLF, and the United States all signed the treaty, the Camp Authority assembled Unity's 4th Allied POW Wing for the first time. The men would wear no shackles, and their own officers would lead them. Bob Shumaker walked out of Room Seven and into the courtyard, where nearly 350 Americans began gathering. Shu fell in with his roommates and stood at attention. He looked around warily and saw the war's most ragtag unit form around him. Some men went shirtless; others wore their red-and-pink-striped pajamas; yet others wore only T-shirts and boxers. Press from North Vietnam and foreign countries crowded into the courtyard to witness the Wing's reaction to the forthcoming announcement. The commandant of Hỏa Lò Prison walked before his assembled prisoners and stood on a small box. Speaking through an interpreter, he announced the war's end. He listed the conditions of the treaty, eventually arriving at the one the POWs most wanted to hear. He announced that their release would come in increments of approximately 120 men at two-week intervals, beginning February 12. They would leave in order of shootdown, first to last.

The Americans heard the word "departure." They were going home.

George McKnight had pictured this moment many times over seven years, but he had envisioned it filled with wild cheering from the prisoners, a cathartic release of long-held frustration. When the commandant made the announcement, however, George surprised himself. He didn't rejoice. He looked around calmly, trying to digest the news, not entirely believing it. He saw many other likewise stone-faced expressions. Some simply wanted to deny the North Vietnamese and the gathered press the satisfaction of seeing them celebrate. Others, like George Coker, would not trust the enemy. Even as preparations for release began, he still expected North Vietnam to renege.

Standing stiffly in his pajamas and rubber sandals in the camp courtyard, Lieutenant Colonel Robbie Risner executed an about-face, turning toward the Wing. "Fourth Allied POW Wing, atten-hut!" he commanded. The Americans came to attention, some 350 sandals stamping on the dirt courtyard of Camp Unity, sounding like a small thunderclap. Risner saluted the ranks of POWs facing him. Each squadron commander—the leader of each building or room—snapped a salute in return. Pride shone on the faces of the fighting men assembled in Hỏa Lò Prison, this unexpected mission almost complete. Each of the nine squadron commanders then turned to his men, and together they barked, "Squadron, dis . . . missed!"

The POWs returned to their rooms, and some began to celebrate away from the eyes of the Camp Authority. Later that afternoon, the Wing's leaders signaled an official statement from Blue across the yard to Room Seven. "No celebrations, no fraternization or friendliness, and no unnecessary confrontation with the prison guards," they ordered. "All conduct will be dignified, professional, and on the guarded assumption that release is imminent. We will operate from a position of cautious optimism."

In the coming days, the Camp Authority began to reorganize the prisoners according to their dates of capture. Rooms Four, Six, and Seven filled with 116 flyers downed before July 1966—the first batch of POWs scheduled for release. From the Alcatraz Gang, only George Coker and Nels Tanner were held in a different room.

The Camp Authority could never erase the scars these captives bore as evidence of their mistreatment, but they could at least present them to the world well fed. The North Vietnamese supplied their prisoners with an extra half loaf of fresh bread with each meal. As they counted the days until their release dates, the POWs cooked for themselves in the courtyard and feasted on vegetables as well as canned meat and fish. Some men gained 10 pounds or more during their last month in Hanoi. Ingenious as always, Bob Shumaker worked with others to track prisoners' weights by submerging them in the courtyard's water tank. They'd measure the volume of water displaced and then, knowing that a cubic foot of water weighs approximately 62.4 pounds, calculate the man's body mass. North Vietnam also wanted to send the POWs home well dressed, wearing bright sweaters or suits, but the POWs preferred to wear their prison pajamas. After some wrangling, the two parties decided that their homecoming uniform would be black shoes, a long-sleeved oxford, dark blue trousers, and a khaki windbreaker.

The Camp Authority held final quizzes for Jim Stockdale and Jerry Denton—two long-serving POW leaders who'd caused them more difficulty than they'd ever imagined possible. Chihuahua presided over Jim's debriefing, bringing up the blackmail fodder that Rabbit had elicited during those 1969 torture sessions in Room Eighteen. "The former general staff officer has asked me to warn you against saying anything bad about the camp authorities or about the Vietnamese people when you get home," Chihuahua said. "He reminds you that in the course of your stay here he has had you write many documents that he can acquire."

Using Cat's real name, Jim fired back indignantly, "That sounds to me like more of Major Bài's blackmail bullshit."

Chihuahua corrected him. "Major Bài no longer speaks for the Vietnamese government." For Jim, that statement confirmed Cat's fall from power. The guards then herded the commander back to his room without further discussion. When Jerry's turn came, Mickey Mouse, who had overseen so many interrogations in Alcatraz and the Hilton, asked how he would describe his experience when he returned to America.

"I haven't answered your questions this long," Jerry replied. "Why should I answer you now? Why do you care what I say anyhow? There are hundreds of men who will speak when they get home."

"You have credibility, Denton," Mickey Mouse said.

"What do you expect? Don't you know I'll tell about the torture?"

"Yes, we expect that."

"Why do you want me to tell you what I will say?"

"We afraid when you get home and make speech, Mr. Nixon will not give us aid he promised," Mickey Mouse explained. "Public would not allow."

"I will say that through 1969 you treated me and the others worse than animals," Jerry answered.

"Yes, but is that all?"

"No," he said. "That is not all. Late in 1969 you came off the torture. After that, to my knowledge, you did not resort to extreme punishment. You then acted within your conscience, such as it is."

"That's the truth, but other may not tell the truth."

"If there is any exaggeration, the senior officers will take care of that," Jerry concluded. Then, as Jerry rose to leave, the North Vietnamese officer who'd been his hated adversary stood with him and said earnestly, "Denton, you're a good man."

The remark left Jerry speechless.

On the night of February 11, 1973—the eve of their scheduled departure—Jim Mulligan stayed up late reading newly distributed letters from home. As he read, he recalled that in early 1969, the Alcatraz Eleven had bet on their release date. The optimists chose homecoming dates in 1969 or 1970. The realist, Jim Stockdale, chose February 1973.

23

GOD BLESS AMERICA

A guard awoke Sam Johnson well before dawn on February 12, 1973. The Camp Authority had delivered piles of shirts, jackets, pants, and shoes to Room Seven, and Sam found items that fit him, then discarded his prison rags forever. Like other POWs, he received a black bag that contained a toothbrush and toothpaste and room for what other items he chose to take. He watched some men stow their pajamas; others took mementos of different kinds. Sam packed only the dented metal drinking cup he'd kept for seven long years. Everything else he just wanted to forget.

The Camp Authority provided a breakfast of warm milk, bread, bananas, and coffee. Then they ordered the Americans to assemble in double columns. By 8:00 A.M., the men idled in formation under overcast skies. POWs scheduled for release in the coming weeks crowded the windows of the surrounding buildings and flashed thumbs-up signs to their homeward-bound friends. George Coker, Nels Tanner, and the others did their best to mask their envy; that day more than three hundred POWs would remain behind in Camp Unity, the Plantation, and the Zoo, scheduled for repatriation in the following weeks.

Bob Shumaker, the second aviator taken prisoner, stood at the column's head beside Ev Alvarez, the first. After eight grueling years of captivity, Shu's face still retained the boyish charm that had captured Lorraine Shaw's heart ten years prior. They had married just eleven months before he left, and he prayed he could win her heart all over again. Behind Shu, the POWs lined up in order of shootdown: 116 men downed between August 1964 and July 1966. The columns waited in place for more than an hour; men became anxious, then suspicious. Finally Jerry Denton, the senior officer in the first subgroup of the day, received word that departure time had arrived. He called to Ev Alvarez, "Ev, we're going to march out in formation. You count cadence." Jerry wanted his men to exit the Hanoi Hilton like soldiers. His voice rang out in the courtyard. "Right face! Cut 'er off, Ev!"

Ev and Shu led the exodus out of Camp Unity, past Heartbreak Hotel, and through a damp Heartbreak courtyard. Jerry Denton marched five rows behind Shu; had Ron Storz survived, he would have walked between them. They passed the empty cells of Little Vegas to their left and the rooms of New Guy Village to their right. Soon the columns approached the archway of the prison's main entrance, through which each American had first entered Hỏa Lò, injured, blindfolded, bloody, and bound. As he marched through the tunnel toward the open gates, Bob Shumaker thought of his first night in Room Nineteen, just yards to his right. Twelve men behind Shu, Jim Stockdale remembered almost dying on the floor of Room Eighteen. He recalled the rainy day in 1965 when he'd arrived at this horrible place to begin this 2,714-day trial that only now neared its end. As he stepped toward the prison gates, he thought of Ecclesiastes 9:12, "For man also knoweth not his time: as the fishes that are taken in an evil net, and as the birds that are caught in the snare; so are the sons of men snared in an evil time, when it falleth suddenly upon them."

George McKnight, Harry Jenkins, and Howie Rutledge followed, each having arrived in Hanoi during November of 1965. Jim Mulligan and Sam Johnson were toward the twin columns' end with other early-1966 shootdowns.

Shu emerged from the tunnel, exited the gates, and marched onto Phố Hỏa Lò, his first time on Hanoi's streets without blindfold or handcuffs. The columns turned and marched toward six waiting buses, passing crowds of curious civilians, soldiers, and children along the way. The capital city had not seen so many Americans together since the march of July 6, 1966. These prisoners had lived within earshot of so many citizens, yet most in Hanoi had never seen the men locked inside the old prison at the heart of their city.

The Americans boarded the waiting buses, and their drivers started off to Gia Lâm airport on the east bank of the Red River, just across from downtown Hanoi. Since the sidewalks couldn't contain the crowds of onlookers, children and adults had spilled into the street, blocking the buses. Policemen and soldiers cleared a path through the masses. As the buses inched forward, children waved and smiled. Adults who had borne the cost of war stood by, reserved. Some wore military pith helmets, just as Pigeye always had. Others wore traditional straw *nón lá*, one last reminder of the differences between these two warring countries. As the buses broke through the crowd and gained speed, small groups of boys chased after them.

While a light rain fell, the convoy rumbled through North Vietnam's capital. Some Americans smiled; most simply sat on the worn bench seats, looking out the windows without expression. At least one would casually hold out his arm, middle finger extended to Hanoi in farewell. Despite the hell he'd endured, Jerry Denton came to tears as he thought about the hardships the North Vietnamese people would face while living under a Communist regime. He could leave; they had to stay. From his seat, Sam Johnson recalled the poignant words he'd seen just before he filed out of Hỏa Lò Prison. An American airman had scratched a final message into a plaster wall: "Freedom has a taste to those who fight and almost die that the protected will never know." Sam would always remember the phrase, and he would recall it with tears of understanding. The buses rolled northeast through the city and approached the Long Biên Bridge. George McKnight remembered slipping into the Red River, now just below, when he and George Coker made their 1967 bid for freedom. That attempt had likely assured their sentence to Alcatraz and their membership in its special fraternity.

The buses stopped a mile short of the airport at a small building, where Jerry Denton saw Rat waiting to receive them. He remembered Alcatraz's first commandant sarcastically asking, "How do you like your new home?" as he locked Jerry into Cell Ten five and a half years ago. Now, as the POWs walked off the bus, Rat issued them sandwiches, fudge, and beer—their first suds in years. "We would like this to be a pleasant memory," he said matter-of-factly.

The anxious Americans milled about the holding area, awaiting the order that would send them to the airfield and the promised transports. When the North Vietnamese announced a delay, the skeptics thought the worst, but an hour later, the men spied a white cargo plane breaking through the gray clouds. Even on the overcast day, the four-engine C-141 Starlifter seemed to shine. It had the white-and-gray paint scheme of the 63rd Military Airlift Wing, and its prominent tail bore a red cross. Most important of all, the men saw the black letters that spelled out U.S. AIR FORCE painted along the plane's side.

Two buses brought the first load of forty POWs from the holding area to the airfield. The men again formed two columns and advanced through a small ocean of North Vietnamese soldiers, civilians, and media. Shu headed the left column and halted just short of a flapping green canvas tarp that shaded a cleared area of the tarmac, bordered on three sides by spectators, most of whom were North Vietnamese. To his left, he saw four government representatives from North Vietnam and three American officers, who had arrived on a transport plane two hours earlier, verifying transfer papers at a table covered with white linen. In the center of the open processing space stood an air force colonel, smartly dressed in a blue uniform.

As he continued to scan his surroundings, Shu spied Rabbit. The officer who had caused so much suffering stood serenely by a simple podium. In his hands, he held a roll of names. He and the air force colonel, Al Lynn, met the column, and Rabbit, list in hand, motioned Shu toward the colonel. Shu shook the hand of the American officer and stepped into freedom. For Bob Shumaker, the first member of the Alcatraz Eleven to receive his liberty, exactly eight years and one day had passed since he had ejected from his F-8 Crusader.

An air force escort met him at the far side of the processing area and walked him toward the waiting C-141. They walked beneath the plane's right wing and the two jet engines hanging beneath it. They negotiated a pack of foreign press at the rear of the plane and proceeded up the ramp through the open doors. Air force flight attendants welcomed him aboard. Shu would never forget catching his first scent of perfume after smelling nothing fresh for so long. Jerry Denton walked up the ramp minutes later. Tears or smiles—and often both—marked every face as the first freed prisoners gathered in the plane. Hidden from their captors, they could finally show their emotions.

Within ten minutes, thirty-seven POWs had come aboard, and medics had loaded three stretchers bearing recently injured B-52 crewmen. Thirty-eight-year-old mission commander Major Jim Marrott, USAF, closed the gate of aircraft 660177—the Freedom Bird or Hanoi Taxi, as it would become known—and started his plane's four turbofans. He noted a second C-141 behind him, taxiing toward the flight line to accept the next load of POWs. Marrott steered his plane toward the runway, and his navigator flipped a thumbs-up to the Americans still on the ground. The plane taxied to the runway's end, fired its engines, and rumbled down the strip. The POWs inside grew quiet. As the 340,000-pound behemoth gained lift, Marrott pulled back on the yoke. At 1:36 P.M. local time, the plane rose into the sky. The POWs celebrated so wildly that Bob Shumaker thought they might stomp the bottom right out of the aircraft. They were going home.

As the transport banked toward the South China Sea, a crew member announced that the Miami Dolphins had won Super Bowl VII one month earlier. "What's the Super Bowl?" one POW responded; professional football's first-ever championship game followed the 1966 season, after many POWs had already been imprisoned in Hanoi.

Thirty minutes later, the second C-141 gave chase, carrying Jim Stockdale, Harry Jenkins, Howie Rutledge, George McKnight, and thirty-six other free men. Then the last two buses left the holding area and arrived at Gia Lâm's tarmac. When the third C-141 came into his view, U.S. Navy Lieutenant Commander Jerry Coffee turned to U.S. Air Force Major Sam Johnson. "Damn, Sam," he said. "I never thought I'd call an air force plane beautiful, but that one surely is." The prisoners put aside any interservice rivalry; on this day they all considered themselves air force men. As the last two buses unloaded and the men formed columns, Jim Mulligan spied Hawk, one of the few guards for whom he ever had any respect, standing nearby. In Jim's estimation, Hawk had always performed his job efficiently and fairly. When their eyes met, Hawk pulled himself to attention and offered a salute. Jim Mulligan returned it.

Mulligan turned back to the POWs and barked, "Left face, forward march!" and the men began their final march on North Vietnamese soil. He called, "Platoon halt," when they arrived at the processing area. He saw Mickey Mouse, Bug, and Softsoap in the gathered crowd; only Cat appeared to be absent. Jim repressed the urge to bolt from the line and strangle his former tormentors. For him, forgiveness would not come easily. He had hated every one of his 2,522 days in North Vietnam, except for this one.

Jim Mulligan stepping into freedom at Gia Lâm airport, February 12, 1973. Sam Johnson is five men back, head bowed.

Sam, Jim, and the others listened to Rabbit's voice one last time. If they heard it again, it would only be in nightmares. One by one, Rabbit called their names and each man stepped forward, saluted Colonel Lynn, and walked to freedom.

Once inside the third C-141, hard-liner Jim Mulligan sat down and cried. A nurse came to comfort him, "It's okay, Captain Mulligan," she said. "It's all over with, and we are going to take you home." Then he noticed the bracelet around her delicate wrist. He read the engraving: CAPT. JAMES A. MULLIGAN JR. 3-20-66. Jim, like many other POWs, had received a promotion during his years in prison, although he hadn't found out until that moment. Along with Jim, Howie, Jerry, Harry, and CAG had also attained captain; the air force had awarded Sam Johnson the equivalent rank of colonel. On the plane, Sam took a seat several rows behind Captain Mulligan, and his thoughts turned to the friend they'd left behind. As the other men boarded, a State Department representative sat down next to him to verify a list of prisoner names, comparing his list against those Sam had memorized. Sam interrupted him; he needed to know about Ron.

"Do you show Ron Storz on your list?" he asked. Sam still held on to the faint yet earnest hope that Ron had survived. After all, nobody had ever confirmed his death.

The official showed Sam his list. One line read, "Ron Storz, U.S.A.F, died in captivity." Ron had died on April 23, 1970, alone at Alcatraz. The Camp Authority had buried his body outside Hanoi in a simple grave, marked R.E.S. 23.4.70. Now Sam knew for sure. Ron's wife, son, and daughter would not rush into the arms of their husband and father at a homecoming ceremony. They would only have memories of him as a young, vibrant pilot, promising to return.

"Why, Ron, why?" Sam wondered silently. "Why couldn't you hold on just a little bit longer?" He would, of course, never find an answer. He just hoped that Ron's spirit knew that the rest of the Alcatraz Eleven had made it.

Soon this third aircraft began its takeoff run. It gathered speed, then rose into the sky, propelled by forty cheering men.

Early on the morning of February 12, 1973, in Virginia Beach, the Mulligans and Dentons—Louise, Jane, and thirteen children—watched their televisions intently; countless other households around the world joined them. Young Jerry, who had returned safely from his tour in South Vietnam, was among them. At her grandmother's house in New Hampshire, eight-year-old Monica Storz sat alone in a guest bedroom, clutching a picture of her father, Ron. She watched the same images as the other families, still hoping to see her father walk off the plane with the others. Despite having been told of his death, she still hoped he'd somehow come home.

At 3:20 A.M. on the East Coast, all those anxious viewers saw the first C-141 touch its wheels to the runway at Clark Air Base in the Philippines. The families watched breathlessly as the Hanoi Taxi rumbled to a halt before a waiting crowd. People waved homemade banners: WELCOME HOME. YOU HAVE KEPT THE FAITH. WE LOVE YOU. Televisions showed two air force men hurriedly roll out a red carpet. Cameras panned over thick crowds of well-wishers, capturing one of the few happy scenes in this long and unpopular war.

The plane's rear passenger door opened. The light applause that had pattered like a steady rain since the aircraft landed suddenly became a thunderous torrent. Screams, whoops, and shouts joined the applause. Banners waved, people cried, and the noise grew louder still. Into this jubilant atmosphere emerged Operation Homecoming's first returnee: Jerry Denton, now forty-eight years old and the senior officer aboard the first plane. He walked down the yellow ladder and onto the tarmac, trying to absorb and understand the crowd's exuberance, which few POWs had anticipated. Planeside, he greeted Admiral Noel Gayler, Commander, Pacific Command. Then the freed prisoner turned to the crowd, nearly eight years of imprisonment behind him. He stepped toward the twin microphones that would carry the two simple sentences he'd composed during his flight from Hanoi—the first official statement given by the returning American POWs. Blinking back tears, Jerry Denton spoke to the world.

"We are honored to have had the opportunity to serve our country under difficult circumstances," he said. "We are profoundly grateful to our commander in chief and to our nation for this day."

He paused briefly; he felt unsatisfied with his prepared remarks. The POWs needed to say something more; *he* needed to say something more. The words began to well up from his heart. His voice breaking with emotion, he added, "God bless America."

Tears came quickly and happily at the Denton home on Watergate Lane. The Pentagon had notified the families whose loved ones were slated for release on February 12, but nobody had told the Dentons that Jerry would be first off the plane. Suddenly, he had walked down the steps and they saw him for the first time since his May 1966 television interview, where he'd blinked out "T-O-R-T-U-R-E." The children—several of whom were young men now—listened to their father's words and saw his strength renewed, his purpose evident, his spirit unbroken.

Admiral Gayler echoed Jerry's "God bless America" as he reached for Jerry's hand. Jerry received the handshake, then walked toward the color guard standing near the plane's tail. He pulled himself to attention and saluted the American flag. Then he walked down the red carpet to the waiting blue hospital buses. One hundred and fifteen POWs would follow him down the carpet. They walked proudly. Many powered along with limps from injuries left untreated for years. Others walked awkwardly, unaccustomed to shoes after years of wearing none. Almost every man beamed as he savored his first steps outside North Vietnam. A fleet of buses shuttled the returned POWs past the airport's throngs and down roads lined with people cheering and waving flags; the entire base had mobilized to welcome them home.

For years, George McKnight had given himself sponge baths with dirty, tepid water that nobody dared drink. So when he arrived at Clark's hospital, he headed straight for the showers. En route, he took a detour to experience something else he'd been without: flushing toilets. In the shower stalls, he found genuine soap and clean, fast-running water streaming from shiny nozzles. He had no doubt his body still had dirt on it from 1965, and he scrubbed himself from head to foot over and over. "Hey, McKnight," a POW in line called. "Get out of there! There're other people here." McKnight lingered a bit longer, letting the warm steam and hot water wash away seven years of grime, dirt, and painful memories. Unlike McKnight and many of his compatriots, Bob Shumaker spent just minutes in the shower. Now unfamiliar with such quantities of water, he worried the endless stream would drown him.

As the afternoon became evening, the POWs grew restless; they wanted food. First, though, each POW had instructions to visit a doctor. After Sam Johnson's examination, his doctor delivered the worst news possible. "We'll have to restrict your diet," the doctor said and began to issue the Texan a card requiring him to receive a bland diet, fearing his digestive system couldn't handle rich American food. Numerous other POWs received the same cards, which became instantly and universally despised.

Sam Johnson especially would not have it. "Let me eat," he howled. If he had survived the food served in Hỏa Lò, he felt sure his stomach could hack anything coming from the base kitchen. The doctor asked what he wanted.

"I want steak and ice cream," Sam declared.

"That's too rich for you right now," the doctor said.

"That's what I want."

"I can't let you have that yet."

"I'm telling you, I can eat anything!" roared Sam; he had antici-pated this first meal for years. His doctor—like most other base physi-cians that evening—relented. Sam felt as if he'd just beaten up the school bully. With the doctor's permission slip in hand, he strode down the hall toward the meal of which he'd dreamed for so long.

In the mess hall, Sam found ravenous POWs descending upon food stations and piling absurd amounts of food on their plates; most devoured every last scrap. Sam walked straight to the dessert station. A young steward asked what Sam would like. "A banana split," he answered, and got one with all the trimmings. Instead of sitting down to finish it, Sam jumped directly into the line for dinner. As he ravenously devoured the bananas, ice cream, syrup, and whipped cream, he ordered a T-bone steak, medium rare. Perhaps given the late hour—it was well past dinnertime—the chef suggested eggs instead. Sam decided to order both.

After their first real dinner in American territory, some POWs went to bed; some visited with one another. Others lost themselves in newspa-pers and magazines, trying to recapture missed years and learning about the new world they had so suddenly been thrust back into. The men also began making their first telephone calls home, reconnecting with loved ones who, in some ways, were now strangers. Originally limited to ten minutes, the calls averaged forty. In the span of seven or more years, much change—and often sadness—had come to many American fami-lies. Howie Rutledge would return a grandfather, but he'd also learn of the swimming accident that had paralyzed his son Johnny in 1968. When his wife delivered the news, Howie paused before asking, "Phyl-lis, do you blame yourself for Johnny's accident?" Through tears, she responded that she'd harbored guilt since the accident—*if only they hadn't gone to the bay to celebrate the Fourth of July.*

"Phyllis, I trust you in all things," Howie said. "I don't blame you for anything that's happened and I know you did your very best. That's all anyone can ask. We can do all things through Christ who strengthens us." Hearing those words, she knew her husband had returned a different man, a man with renewed faith. Composing herself, she stressed that Johnny had not lost his passion for life and couldn't wait to see his father.

In his first phone call, Jim Stockdale explained to Sybil, "I have a stiff leg, but I think it gives my walk a little style." Sam Johnson told

Shirley of his injured arms and right hand; Shirley asked if his hair had grayed, as hers had. Lorraine Shumaker—just twenty-two years old when her husband left—heard Bob's voice and felt her protective emotional wall crumble. She'd spent eight years steeling herself for what this first conversation might bring; during all those years, she'd only received eight letters. Yet when they first spoke to one another, neither Lorraine nor Shu felt as if a single day had passed since they'd parted.

Jim Mulligan felt only a boundless joy as he listened to an operator connect him with his family in Virginia Beach. "Is Mrs. Mulligan there?" Jim heard the operator ask one of his sons. "She has a call from Captain Mulligan in the Philippines."

"Mom, it's Dad!" the boy screamed. Jim listened happily from afar as his whole family began to celebrate. "Jim?" Louise's voice asked. "Jim, is it you?"

"I love you, Louise," he said, and he heard her cry with relief. Jim talked with his wife and then his sons, whose voices he could no longer recognize. When the conversation ended, handsets on both sides of the Pacific were wet with tears.

Every POW had been assigned an aide, and Jim looked at his and said, "Let's get moving. I've got to get out of this place and get home."

When this first day of freedom ended, George McKnight retired to his room at the base hospital and pulled back clean blankets to reveal crisp sheets covering a soft mattress. For once, he had a pillow. He lay down for his first secure night's sleep in years. The next morning, he would learn that several men, so used to sleeping on hard concrete, had trouble falling asleep; George had not. The next day, he woke early simply to enjoy his freedom. Tailors arrived to take his measurements. Not long thereafter, he buttoned up the blue jacket of an air force uniform, his eyes moist like many others.

By April 1, 1973, 456 American servicemen held in North Vietnam would pass through Clark Air Base; 27 had died in captivity. Others would come to Clark from South Vietnam, Cambodia, Laos, and China. In total, Operation Homecoming would see the return of 566 military personnel—164 from the navy and Marine Corps, 325 from the air force, and 77 from the army.

On February 13, Jim Mulligan pressed his aide to speed his processing. As the military physicians and psychologists weren't sure what physical or emotional injuries the POWs had sustained, they planned a stringent four-day quarantine to observe the men's health and state of mind. Captains Mulligan and Denton wouldn't have it. When Jim Mulligan completed his final physical, he made his doctor call the officers coordinating flights home. "This is Captain Mulligan," he said. "Now hold on." He passed the phone to his doctor and said, "Tell 'em, Doc."

"Captain Mulligan is released," the doctor said with resignation.

Mulligan phoned Jerry Denton's aide and ordered, "Lookit, I'm released. You get Denton ready and get him on that first plane with me!"

Headstrong until the last, these two officers would catch the first ride home. Others followed soon after as once-skeptical doctors conceded that these men had survived years of imprisonment with their minds intact.

In the coming days, the men departed Clark for the United States on transports that each carried twenty POWs, twenty escorts, a medical crew, and a public affairs officer. They first flew across the Pacific to Hickam Air Force Base (AFB) adjacent to Pearl Harbor on Oahu. After an arrival ceremony, an hour-long layover, and a press briefing, they left in another C-141, bound for one of four air force bases on the U.S. mainland, where they would transfer to smaller C-9 Nightingales for the last segment of their trip.

Although most were on separate flights, Bob Shumaker, Jim Stockdale, George McKnight, Howie Rutledge, and Harry Jenkins all flew to San Francisco's Travis AFB in the coming days. McKnight disembarked there; the others flew on to San Diego. Sam Johnson returned to Kelly AFB in San Antonio, then hopped to Wichita Falls. Jerry Denton and Jim Mulligan landed at Scott AFB, just east of St. Louis, then traveled on to Norfolk. Several weeks later, in early March, Nels Tanner and George Coker would land at NAS Memphis and JFK International in New York. At every landing, news crews swarmed the family reunions, broadcasting them to national audiences who clamored for updates on the POW story.

As Jim flew eastward across the Pacific from the Philippines to Hawaii, Louise received a phone call from President Nixon. The president thanked her for her service and officially informed her that Jim had begun his long journey to Virginia Beach. Feisty until the last, Louise pointedly replied, "There are some of us who didn't agree with your policies, Mr. President. The war went on far too long."

"Yes, I understand that," he replied, "but we can be glad they're coming home."

When Louise had said good-bye and hung up the phone, she closed that chapter in her life forever. Other families received similar phone calls, not from the president himself but from Pentagon contacts, informing them that their long wait was at last nearing its end; their husbands were coming home.

In the early morning hours of February 15, 1973, the airplane bearing Jim Mulligan and Jerry Denton winged over the port community of Norfolk, Virginia. The returnees saw the dark expanse of the Chesapeake Bay, outlined by the lights of the surrounding cities. On these very waters, only sixty-two years earlier, aviation pioneer Eugene Ely first flew an aircraft off a ship, beginning the proud tradition that Jim, Jerry, and so many other POWs had carried forward. In the shadows of Hỏa Lò Prison and in the solitude of Alcatraz, naval aviation had tallied some of its greatest victories.

Jerry and Jane Denton, February 15, 1973.

As the airliner descended toward the runway, the two new captains looked over the warships moored at Naval Station Norfolk. Jim saw Pier Twelve, where he'd kissed Louise good-bye on October 24, 1965. That was the first time she had cried when he left for sea. As he boarded the *Enterprise* that day, he had wondered if her tears were a bad omen. In the end, perhaps they portended good. Jim had come home after all.

When the turbines of the C-9 had spun down, Jerry Denton and

Jim Mulligan emerged from the doorway. They looked out over a crowd that seemed comprised of every navy family in the area. They saw friends from Naval Station Norfolk, NAS Oceana, and Naval Amphibious Base Little Creek. Representatives from Fort Eustis and Langley Air Force Base added army and air force uniforms to the picture. Floodlights gleamed on the ramp, still wet from an evening rainfall. A band played. A line of police cars stood ready to escort the returning heroes; Jerry had never seen so many flashing lights. The two friends walked down the floodlit stairs from the cabin. Shortly after 2:35 A.M., they each stepped onto Virginia soil, delivered a brief speech, then faced a small mob of family. The seven Denton children, followed by Jane, bolted across the tarmac to meet their father. Louise and the six Mulligan boys rushed to embrace Jim. The two captains could scarcely recognize some of their children. A joyous reunion took place in the chill of that wet February night. Minutes later, in their private car, separated from the noise of the crowd, Jerry and Jane wrapped themselves in each other's arms, scarcely believing they were together again. They did not want to let go.

Looking out over the Hill Country, Sam Johnson savored his return to Texas airspace. He gazed out across a blanket of fresh snow—something he hadn't seen for seven years. He produced a cigarette, a habit he picked up in Hanoi. He lit it, stared at it thoughtfully, and decided not to smoke it. He would never light another. As the plane neared its next destination, an air force officer approached Sam and said, "Colonel Johnson, we'd like you to say something to the press."

"It ought to be Robbie Risner," Sam said. "He's the senior officer [on board]."

"We'd like it to be a Texan, sir," replied the officer, who knew Risner would not disembark until he reached Oklahoma. Minutes later, the plane's wheels squeaked onto the landing strip at Sheppard Air Force Base and rolled to a stop before a gathered crowd of friends, strangers, press, and family. Wearing his air force blue, with a colonel's silver eagles on his shoulders and cap, Sam stepped out of the plane to cheers. At the stairway's bottom, he faced a swarm of cameras and microphones. "It's the greatest feeling in the world to be back on Texas soil," Sam said, eyes brimming. More microphones and cameras closed in; reporters peppered him with questions. Sam tried to look past them, just wanting to see his family. He swatted at a microphone, and a public affairs officer announced, "I think we have had enough of this for now."

Sam pushed through the crowd of media. Suddenly, his son, Bob, appeared and embraced him. Seconds later, his daughters, Gini and Beverly, reached him, too. Then he saw Shirley, the woman he married twenty-two years ago. The family embraced each other tightly, as if Sam might be taken away again at any point. A long reunion had begun; Sam would get to know his family once again. His children— fifteen, twelve, and nine when he left—were now twenty-one, eighteen, and fifteen. He'd missed so many memories, so many firsts, but by God, he'd come home. As he started his life anew, he did what he could not at his base in Thailand, in the Hanoi Hilton, or at Clark Air Base in the Philippines: Sam Johnson ate Tex-Mex for five days straight.

In December of 1964, twenty-two-year-old Lorraine Shumaker had waved good-bye to her husband and returned home with their newborn infant. She never dreamed she'd spend eight years raising Grant by herself. She'd expected to watch her husband fly over NAS Miramar as his squadron returned eight months after deployment. Now, eight *years* later, Lorraine found herself preparing an eight-year-old boy to meet his father for the first time. That morning, as she applied her makeup in the bathroom, her son walked in and looked up at his mother—the only parent he had ever known. She sensed concern in her shy child and worried that he wouldn't hug the man who would arrive in several hours' time. Lorraine turned to Grant and asked, "What are you going to do when you see your daddy?"

Grant didn't comment; he just shrugged his shoulders. "Well, I'm going to run up and give him a big kiss," Lorraine said. Then she added a challenge, "And I'll beat you to him."

Hours later, on the tarmac of NAS Miramar, Lorraine and Grant watched a U.S. Air Force jet bank over the California hills and glide toward the airstrip. When it had arrived at the ramp and powered down its engines, an air crew rolled a set of stairs to its passenger door. Wearing a khaki uniform with three gold commander's stripes on each black shoulder board, Bob Shumaker stepped into the warm California sunshine. He jogged down the steps and met two naval officers, who then escorted him toward a podium and the waiting color guard—but he would never deliver the speech he had planned.

From the edge of the crowd, Lorraine Shumaker pointed to her husband and said to her son, "There's your daddy." Grant had been less than two months old the last time he saw his father; now he saw a complete stranger walking toward him. That didn't matter. Grant bolted across the tarmac, racing to the man people had told him about since he could remember, the one they told him to be proud of, but the one he did not know at all. He reached his father at a sprint. Shu scooped up his eight-year-old son and held him tightly as Grant fastened his arms around his father. Grant's POW bracelet—which bore Shu's name and shootdown date, February 11, 1965—shone in the morning light.

Bob Shumaker reunited with his family after 2,923 days in captivity.

Holding his son, Shu walked to meet Lorraine. Then he held them both—his wife in his right arm and his son in his left—and kissed his wife. His son beamed at the thousands who'd gathered to welcome his father home—his father, Bob Shumaker, the second American aviator taken captive and the longest-serving member of the Alcatraz Eleven.

That same runway also welcomed home Jim Stockdale, CAG, the indomitable warrior who confounded, defied, and subverted Cat, Rabbit, and the North Vietnamese Camp Authority perhaps more than any other prisoner. Certainly, few paid such a high personal price or set such an example. His stiff leg would always remind him of the cruelty he experienced in the Mint, Riviera, and Alcatraz, but memories of Hanoi receded into the past as he flew from San Francisco to NAS Miramar. The crew gave him the copilot's seat, and he watched California pass beneath him: Stanford, Palo Alto, Los Altos Hills; the sprawl of Los Angeles; then finally San Diego County. The C-9 settled over the dry hills ringing the city and entered the Miramar break, the familiar landing pattern Jim had flown countless times as he prepared for war. Tactical runs around Miramar had readied him for those days in August 1964 over the Gulf of Tonkin that led his country deeper into the war in Southeast Asia, but drills at Miramar had not sustained him during his seven years in Hanoi. Rather, his mind, the faith shared among prisoners, and the love of his family, who now awaited his imminent return, had kept him alive during that horrid term of imprisonment.

On the previous afternoon, February 14, a dozen Valentine's Day roses had arrived at 547 A Avenue for Sybil Stockdale. The accompanying card read, "God Bless You, Syb. All my love, Jim." In the coming days, he'd learn just how much Sybil had done for him and his men. The next morning, Jimmy, Stanford, and Taylor nailed a gigantic WEL-COME HOME banner across the front porch; Sid would arrive home from boarding school in time for dinner. Then a navy car pulled up to the neatly mowed yard, and the Stockdales climbed inside for the ride to Miramar, across San Diego Bay from their home in Coronado. From the Miramar tarmac, they watched a distant silver flash in the sky become an airplane that stopped yards from where they stood.

Jim pulled and pushed himself out of the cockpit and dragged his leg toward the boarding door. Then the time came for him to exit. "Stand up straight, now," he told himself, thinking of Sybil. "You've got to make her proud." He emerged from the plane, forty-nine years old, unable to raise his left arm, scarcely able to bend his left leg. His hair had turned nearly white. Yet nobody could have borne himself with more pride than Jim Stockdale. He stepped down the stairs and strode to a microphone to address the crowd. Sybil watched him from several yards away, noting the four new captain's stripes on his shoulder boards and disapproving of his uniform's stiff new khaki hat. She knew that her husband had always preferred the well-worn hat of a fighter pilot.

"For the past seven or eight years," Jim's voice rang out, "I doubt that there was a prisoner of war in Hanoi who did not occasionally hum that old refrain, 'California, Here We Come.' Well, California, we have come."

With sunlight warming the concrete tarmac beneath him, he closed his brief speech with a nod to the philosophers whose lessons had seen him through the gauntlets of Hanoi. Addressing the crowd of anxious families, he said, "As that Athenian warrior and poet Sophocles wrote over 2,400 years ago, 'Nothing is so sweet as to return from the sea and listen to the raindrops on the rooftops of home.' We're home. America, America, God shed His grace on thee." When Sybil heard her husband quoting Greek texts, she knew Jim—the same man she had always loved—had truly returned.

Jim Stockdale had served the proudest command of his career, leading the incorrigibles of Alcatraz against a determined foe. When those words fell from his lips, he had completed the final task of the longest deployment and toughest assignment he would ever have. His duty faithfully discharged, he turned to his family and stepped toward them. Husband and wife held each other in an embrace that they had imagined for nearly eight years. Then Jim felt the arms of his sons encircling him, welcoming him home.

CAG returns.

•   •   •

By early March, the ten survivors of Alcatraz had all arrived on U.S. soil. On tarmacs from San Diego to Norfolk, they met their families in joyous planeside reunions followed intently on television and in print by an enthralled public. The plight of the prisoners and their families had, in many ways, become America's plight, and both had endured. For a time, the POWs' return consumed the country. A decade of war abroad and unrest at home had torn at the very seams of the republic. In February of 1973, the haggard yet resilient men who walked off those C-141s at Clark Air Base brought the nation together again, however briefly. In a war that had no clear ending, no moment of ultimate triumph, their return brought sorely needed closure. America briefly forgot about her divisions, as citizens of all stripes paused to honor the POWs returning from Vietnam. For many in the United States, their homecoming marked the end of a long and painful era.

In numerous ways, the Alcatraz Eleven were unlucky. Shot down, they endured years of solitary confinement and brutal torture, the likes of which they'd never even contemplated. Yet the ten survivors fulfilled the sincere promise they'd made when they departed home so many years ago: they would return. Vietnam had claimed more than 58,000 American lives—young men who would never walk off a plane to public fanfare. Many of their families would not experience the same outpouring of compassion that their POW/MIA counterparts received. More than 300,000 soldiers returned wounded, some disabled for life. Others returned physically intact but emotionally shattered. Many never received a welcome of any sort. The *New York Times* framed the public fervor surrounding Operation Homecoming by comparing Vietnam to Korea: "[The Korean war] was not so divisive as the Vietnam war. That war had heroes and a somewhat sympathetic press. The Vietnam war has had neither until now."

By the time they began their journey home from the Philippines, the Alcatraz Gang all knew Ron Storz had died in the desolate prison that had tested them for more than two years. They had all suffered, lost weight, staved off depression, and occasionally wished for death. They had all come close to sharing their friend's tragic fate. They would never forget him. Those tiny cells had welded them together, creating an eternal bond.

These surviving ten left Alcatraz and Hanoi believing that because of one another and for some higher purpose, they had survived.
Yet they had not struggled in the torture rooms of Hỏa Lò or in the
cells of Alcatraz simply to get home. They had fought valiantly—often
desperately—in order to uphold their nation's Code, which had become
their own. Through all their trials, they remained devoted to their
brotherhood of fierce Americans, bound together by unparalleled ad-
versity and unequaled sacrifice. In the winter of 1973, after long years
of battle, the survivors of Alcatraz emerged victorious and proud, bodies
scarred but consciences unblemished. With their fellow veterans at
their side, they once again set foot in their beloved country and faced a
grateful nation with heads unbowed. They returned precisely as they'd
hoped: They returned with honor.

EPILOGUE

It was a bright March day at Arlington National Cemetery. The sun had chased away the winter clouds, and its rays fell on the Old Post Chapel, where George McKnight delivered a eulogy over a flag-draped casket that held the repatriated remains of Ron Storz. George spoke about his friend, the one who did not return. Sadly, he couldn't say—nor would he ever fully know—exactly what happened to the ardent patriot who suffered inside Cell Five at Alcatraz.

On that warm day in 1974, surviving members of the Alcatraz Eleven and other returned POWs had gathered at Arlington to bury their brother-in-arms. After the service in the chapel, the mourners followed a horse-drawn caisson to an open grave in Section Eleven; all agreed the section's number was particularly fitting. In their dress uniforms, veterans saluted the casket that carried their friend. A rifle detail's volleys echoed against the hillside; jets thundered overhead. A bugler played "Taps." An officer presented Sandra Storz an American flag and expressed the nation's gratitude. Amid the beautiful yet heartbreaking ceremony, Sandra and her two children drew comfort from the presence of Ron's fellow officers and his brothers from Alcatraz. His family at long last found closure as his remains were committed to American soil.

After the service, George McKnight penned a heartfelt letter to Ron's children, hoping to help them understand their father and the sacrifices he made for his country and fellow POWs. Ron's partner from the Hanoi March, Wes Schierman, spent several days with the Storz family, sharing stories of the courage and loyalty that distinguished Ron during his years in prison. Schierman and Orson Swindle would become father figures to Mark and Monica, doing their best to pass along Ron's strong values and abiding patriotism. Mark received the silver cross and chain his father had worn during his incarceration, which were returned with his remains. Monica had already inherited his brilliantly blue eyes. At a reunion years after Operation Homecoming, former POW Ed Davis, who'd once tapped "agony" to Jerry Denton as he'd expressed the pain of torture, began crying when he first saw her. "I know exactly who you are," he said through tears. "You have your father's eyes." Ron's memory would live on.

Finally home, these heroes quietly returned to work, to life, putting their days in Hanoi behind them. Within three months, all received new commands and returned to active duty; Sam Johnson, George McKnight, and George Coker received new flying assignments. Each tried to reprioritize his life around the values they had contemplated and relied upon during their years of solitude. While such trials would have likely proven impossible for many to survive, the American POWs had faced them like any other mission and had endured them like elite soldiers. Their actions and unity not only ruined the Camp Authority's plans but also enabled these men to keep their wits and self-confidence and to recover quickly upon their return. They gracefully blended into their families and neighborhoods, neither requesting nor expecting any special favor for their unique sacrifice.

In the whirlwind of homecoming and their quick returns to duty, the men began to move past the bitterness of imprisonment and isolation; the faces and voices of the men who tormented them started to fade. They received grateful letters from strangers; churches, schools, and civic clubs invited them to speak. From across America, hundreds of people happily sent their POW bracelets back to the men whose names they'd worn and not forgotten. For years, at many of their speaking engagements, Alcatraz POWs would be approached and handed a well-worn bracelet bearing their name. The survivors and their children still have many of the bracelets; they occasionally find yet another one waiting in the mailbox.

While they all moved on, nobody who suffered through the tribulations of imprisonment in Hanoi would ever truly forget the guards, the pain, or the cells and prisons that siphoned away years of their prime. Nor could they forget the men with whom they served. Of the Alcatraz survivors, only Sam Johnson and Jim Stockdale ever returned to Vietnam. The others simply had no interest in revisiting that country or Hỏa Lò Prison, which today stands as a museum. The forlorn buildings and courtyard formerly at Number Four Phố Lý Nam Đế—the place that they knew as Alcatraz—are gone forever. While none of the Alcatraz POWs would be called upon to fight another war, the surviving members of the Eleven know that they ran the gauntlet once; they could do so again for their country, for their families, for each other.

"I wouldn't trade it," says Jim Mulligan of his experience. "Now, I wouldn't volunteer to go through it again, but if I was on the cat [catapult] and knew I had to go through it again, I could handle that."

As for Jim Stockdale, he would always maintain, "That was where I was supposed to be." His wife, who had undergone such an ordeal at home, didn't necessarily agree.

Mulligan, Stockdale, and the other Alcatraz veterans view their days in captivity differently, but none feel the regret one would expect. With no way to recover those years, the men choose to view them as a growth experience; they had time to reflect on their lives and priorities in ways their stateside peers never did. After enduring years of unspeakable trials neither they nor their countrymen could have anticipated, these POWs left Hanoi with their heads held high, their loyalty tested and proven, and their faith strengthened—something that would guide them for the rest of their lives. All the POWs suffered greatly; most survived and fought heroically. No one group endured any more than the eleven brothers of Alcatraz. No other band of prisoners underwent such a defining shared experience—certainly not one so horrendous and so long. Consequently, more than any other group of POWs, the survivors remained close, bound by their collective time in the cells behind the Ministry of National Defense and their dedication to helping each other survive. Yet these ten survivors never saw themselves as different from other hard-fighting captives; they knew that all POWs had made deep sacrifices. In the tradition of America's great heroes, the men of Alcatraz are humble, they are gracious, and they count their blessings.

None of these veterans could have endured their ordeal without their families, the hope of returning to those they loved. In many ways, those they loved ultimately brought them home. The organization founded by the Alcatraz wives and other POW/MIA family members had, in fact, helped bring the POWs home alive. In an era when society, particularly the military, largely expected women to follow the rules, the wives and mothers of America's captured and missing servicemen crossed barriers and founded one of history's great women's movements, although male family members were also involved. The National League and its resolute members made the world focus its attention on Hanoi's behavior, and the Camp Authority's policies quickly changed in response, sparing men who'd neared the end of their strength. The League would not let the U.S. government or its citizens forget our prisoners of war. The POW wives stepped aside after their husbands' 1973 repatriations, and MIA family members began leading the organization, committed to accounting for every missing man, working alongside the Defense Prisoner of War/Missing Personnel Office, which remains active today.

Like VIVA's POW/MIA bracelets, America's first cause-related wristbands, the National League's black-and-white flag came to symbolize the Vietnam War and the men who fought it, long after the conflict's end. In 1979, on the first national POW/MIA Recognition Day, theirs became the first flag other than the American flag to fly above the White House. By 1998, federal law had decreed that it fly each year on Armed Forces Day, Flag Day, Independence Day, Memorial Day, National POW/MIA Recognition Day, and Veterans Day. On those days, the flag waves above major military installations, national cemeteries, national war memorials, the White House, U.S. Postal Service offices, and offices of the secretaries of defense, state, and veterans affairs. Many state governments follow suit. The black-and-white flags also line the halls of Capitol Hill's office buildings, where one welcomes visitors to the office of Congressman Sam Johnson.

Most days, Sam and the other survivors don't even think back to their years spent across the Pacific. They have forgiven their captors, or at least chosen not to dwell on them. They have moved on from being soldiers; they are now citizens and neighbors first. Most people who live on their streets have little idea what the gray-haired couple next door endured during Vietnam. Scarcely anyone ever mentions the Alcatraz Eleven outside the circle of returned Vietnam POWs, and rarely within it. Typically, the memories and stories only resurface when they're together, and while visits have become less frequent as they've aged, the surviving members of the Eleven still visit each other as often as they can. Yet even when they're together, their wives prefer to let the war remain in the past, a closed chapter of their lives.

Against the odds, these couples' marriages endured not only the long separation of Vietnam but also Hanoi's lingering demons and the POWs' returns to regular life. Perhaps more than other spouses, the Alcatraz wives all steadfastly protect their husbands and display the loyalty and understanding only such an arduous mutual ordeal could engender. Alcatraz's two bachelors, George Coker and George McKnight, both found wonderfully devoted wives to whom they're still married today.

Coker, the youngest inmate at Alcatraz, arrived at JFK International Airport in early March 1973. He spent some time with Nels and Sara Ann Tanner in Covington, Tennessee, before returning to active duty as a flight instructor at NAS Oceana, Virginia. He later transferred to NAS North Island in Coronado to serve as flag aide to Rear Admiral Jim Stockdale. While in San Diego, George smartly surrendered his bachelor status to Pam Easton; they married in April 1975 and had three children. George retired from the U.S. Navy in 1986 as a commander after a long career that concluded at the Atlantic Fleet Command Center. He became a scoutmaster and watched his own son achieve the rank of Eagle Scout, just as he had decades before. Today, George and Pam reside in Virginia Beach, not far from the Oceana break, as naval aviators call the air traffic pattern. From his shaded back porch, George can spend long afternoons listening to the sweet noise of navy jets.

When McKnight returned to the United States, he visited his high school and the priest he'd tried so hard to make proud in North Vietnam. As he told the priest about his experiences, the toughened air force flyer started crying. The man's inspiration had helped George survive.

After McKnight came home from Vietnam, he entered the War

College to update himself on military tactics, which had changed so much over seven years. There, he met and married Captain Suzanne Sexton, an air force nurse. After his wedding, he qualified on the F-4 Phantom and then embarked on an international adventure. He spent a year with the 463rd Tactical Fighter Squadron at Royal Air Force Station Lakenheath, northeast of London. His next assignments took him to Camp New Amsterdam in the Netherlands and to the Democratic Republic of the Congo as defense air attaché. He declined a desk job and spent much of his time piloting a twin-prop King Air across Africa, landing on airstrips of concrete, grass, and dirt alike. It proved a fine assignment for a true pilot. His final posting took him and Suzanne to Ottawa, Canada, for nearly four years. Colonel McKnight retired in 1986, the same year as his partner at Dirty Bird, George Coker, and the McKnights now live along the South Carolina coast. George McKnight had joined the air force so he could travel, and of his thirty years in the service, he had spent twenty-six outside the United States; seven were in Hanoi.

Nels Tanner stayed in his native Tennessee, reuniting with his two children and his wife. He retired as a captain after thirty-two years of naval service and began flying for Federal Express. Later, Nels survived a hard fight against cancer. He would have discovered the disease much too late had a particular nurse—George McKnight's wife, Suzanne—not become concerned about his coughing during an Alcatraz reunion. Thankfully, Nels sought treatment. He and Sara Ann found a magnificent lot outside Covington on which to build a house Nels had partially designed in his mind while in Hanoi. The Tanners still live there, offering exceptional Tennessee hospitality and home cooking to family, friends, and visiting authors.

On Harry Jenkins's first full day in San Diego, Howie Rutledge settled the bets they'd made in Hanoi; a tray of tacos and a banana split promptly arrived in Harry's room at Balboa Naval Hospital, where the POWs spent several days under observation. Howie also sent Harry a Hershey bar. In July 1974, Captain Jenkins assumed command of the USS *Denver*, an amphibious transport deployed to the South China Sea. The *Denver* assisted South Vietnamese refugees as helicopters ferried some 7,500 civilians onto her flight deck. With no space or alternative fields to land all the empty helicopters, the *Denver*'s crew pushed several aircraft overboard. Harry did find enough room on his flight deck to keep two helicopters and had them painted navy blue and emblazoned with *Denver One* and *Denver Two*. Every captain needed his own birds, Harry reasoned. For their first mission, Harry sent them to a nearby aircraft carrier for ice cream. When an admiral ordered *Denver* to disband its air force, Harry cabled back, "What if we paint them black and only fly them at night?" The admiral did not respond.

After he retired from the navy, Harry built an airplane in the garage of his Coronado home, and he loved nothing more than flying through the skies of Southern California. Sadly, a crash ended his life in 1995. Nobody would ever forget Harry's humor and optimism, which had helped so many POWs make it to the next day.

When Captain Howie Rutledge returned to San Diego, he met his wife, Phyllis, on the tarmac at NAS Miramar. They drove to Balboa Naval Hospital, where his four children waited. He walked into his room and found his three daughters circled around his paralyzed son. Johnny feared his father wouldn't look at him, but Howie unhesitatingly embraced them all, instead ashamed of his own scarred body. Several days passed before Howie would take his shirt off. Before his stint in prison, the fighter pilot's fighter pilot had often prioritized navy over family. After returning, he found a second chance to be a better father to his two youngest children—and he became a doting grandfather to eldest daughter Sondra's son, Stan.

After getting resettled, he placed one of his first phone calls to the U.S. Navy, demanding to know why they'd never told his family he was a prisoner of war. He knew of Stockdale's encoded information and other intelligence the government had gathered but had not passed on to Phyllis. He never did receive a satisfactory answer.

Howie continued his naval service and took command of NAS Cubi Point in the Philippines. He served his final tour as commanding officer of the NROTC program at the University of Oklahoma. Too soon after retiring, he faced cancer, which proved a tougher adversary than even Pigeye. He succumbed in 1984.

Captain Jim Mulligan retired after more than thirty-one years of uniformed service and then ran a successful family business until his civilian retirement. Louise returned her full attention to raising their six sons. Despite the gusto and leadership she provided for America's POW and MIA families, those years pained her greatly, and once Jim returned, she put that era behind her for good. The Mulligans, who have known each other for seventy years, never left the navy community of Virginia Beach, where they still reside, just five blocks from the home Louise bought in 1966, anticipating Jim's eventual return. The couple spends many afternoons poolside with George and Pam Coker, who live nearby, and are supremely gracious hosts to all. The Mulligans have seventeen grandchildren and nine great-grandchildren, who all received Louise's smarts and Jim's drive. They share six of their grandchildren with Sam and Shirley Johnson; Jim Mulligan III and Gini Johnson married in 1981. Their offspring are collectively known as "the POW grandchildren."

After returning to his beloved Texas, Colonel Sam Johnson took command of the 31st Tactical Fighter Wing at Homestead Air Force Base, Florida; seven years in Hanoi had not diminished his love of flying even the slightest bit. In 1979, he retired after a twenty-nine-year military career. He was elected to the Texas House of Representatives in 1984 and has represented the Third Congressional District of Texas in the U.S. House of Representatives since 1991. His right hand never fully healed from the traumas of his ejection and Pigeye; he still writes with his left. Yet this senior congressman's left-handed handshake remains strong, and his rich laugh carries a warmth that betrays none of the suffering he endured for his country all those years ago.

Sam Johnson's French instructor, Bob Shumaker, earned his PhD in electrical engineering in 1977. He served as superintendent of the Naval Postgraduate School and on the staff of the Chief of Naval Operations at the Pentagon before retiring from the navy as a rear admiral in 1988. Like Harry Jenkins, he built his own airplane, which he still flies regularly out of Warrenton, Virginia. As this author can attest, Shu hasn't lost his touch in the cockpit—he still executes a flawless aileron roll. His son, Grant, inherited his father's passion for flight and for academic detail—he became a private pilot and a neurosurgeon. Shu and Lorraine live together in the notably airy home he designed while in the confines of Alcatraz Cell Four. From their back porch, they watch sunsets over their pasture, just as he dreamed during those long days locked inside the windowless world of Alcatraz.

Like Bob Shumaker, Jerry Denton also reached the rank of rear admiral, one of several Class of 1947 Naval Academy graduates to do so. That exceptional class produced a U.S. president, two Medal of Honor recipients, a billionaire investor, a CIA director, and a chairman of the Joint Chiefs of Staff. To that, Jerry added his own extraordinary record as a U.S. senator, representing Alabama on Capitol Hill from 1981 until 1987. He retired to his hometown of Mobile, Alabama, where he ran a foundation to support the federal government's Denton Program, which he created as a senator to enable military aircraft and commercial ships with available space to transport humanitarian supplies to foreign countries. Jane Denton passed away in 2007, shortly after the couple returned to Virginia. In 2010, the navy named the new SERE School at Portsmouth Naval Shipyard in Senator Denton's honor. Jerry has sixteen grandchildren and six great-grandchildren. He lives with his wonderfully kind second wife outside Williamsburg, Virginia, close to family, friends, and—of equal import to Jerry—a golf course.

In a 1976 White House ceremony, President Gerald R. Ford presented Vice Admiral Jim Stockdale with the Medal of Honor, the country's highest award for valor. With the medal hanging from his neck and seven rows of bright ribbons on his chest, Jim became one of America's most-decorated naval officers. Sybil Stockdale became the first active-duty wife to receive the Navy's Distinguished Public Service Award. In 1981, Jim began a twelve-year tenure at Stanford University's Hoover Institution, where he taught philosophy and focused on Epictetus and others who helped him endure his time in Hanoi. In the 1992 presidential election, Jim served as Ross Perot's running mate. America watched this seasoned warrior navigate a candidacy he intended only as temporary, a simple favor, until Perot chose a permanent running mate. National office had never interested Jim Stockdale. Unfortunately, many Americans missed an opportunity to understand this remarkable leader and reluctant candidate. The Stockdales eventually retired to Coronado, California, and enjoyed their days together—sitting on the same porch where Sybil had waited so anxiously for letters from Hanoi. Jim passed away in 2005. His funeral was held in the Naval Academy Chapel, below the image of Christ on the sea, an image that had appeared so vividly to him in the Zoo in January 1967. In 2009, the Alcatraz Gang gathered once again to commission the guided missile destroyer USS *Stockdale* (DDG-106). Her motto is "Return with Honor."

Today, a bronze statue of Jim Stockdale looks over the grounds of the U.S. Naval Academy at Annapolis, Maryland. It stands outside Luce Hall, which houses the Stockdale Center for Ethical Leadership. The sculpture does not depict Jim with a vice admiral's three stars or in the dark uniform of an officer. Instead, the figure carries a pilot's helmet, wears the boots and flight suit of an aviator, and has the stance and certitude of a combat-tempered leader. The statue depicts CAG as what he always was at heart: a fighter pilot.

Each of these eleven men—these Alcatraz Eleven—had come to Vietnam with a uniquely strong constitution; the married among them had wives with equal mettle. Their shared trials only fortified their devotion to one another, their nation, and their mutual cause. Together, they overcame more intense hardship over more years than any other group of servicemen and families in American history.

We should not forget.

ACKNOWLEDGMENTS

In December 2011, I visited a united Vietnam and had tea with the grandson of General Võ Nguyên Giáp, the Vietnamese general who defeated a colonial French regime, then led the war against South Vietnam and the United States. His grandson and I met at the general's beautiful Hanoi residence, amid relics of our shared history. From glossy black-and-white photographs, the specters of Vietnam's past watched us. As sons and grandsons of the generation that fought the war, we each spoke of our respective country's future, neither of us recalling battles that raged before our birth. Today, new generations of Vietnamese and Americans endeavor to honor our past and all those who served under difficult circumstances. We try to understand what was, while creating what will be. Amid the progress of modernity, only monuments, memories, and ghosts remain at places like Hỏa Lò Prison. Once, those ghosts were very real.

By the time I walked through the gate of the Hanoi Hilton, four decades had passed since my countrymen filled its cells. Just several blocks away, at the modern Hilton Hanoi hotel, former POW and ambassador to Vietnam Pete Peterson began helping me understand this foreign country and what transpired during our long war. Through the former ambassador and friends like Vice Admiral Tom Kilcline, I began meeting a cast of participants, observers, and students who taught me about those difficult years.

Men like Bob Destatte and Paul Mather shared the knowledge of lives spent working on the POW/MIA issue. Former POWs like Ev Alvarez, Jerry Coffee, Lee Ellis, Paul Galanti, Dan Glenn, Porter Halyburton, Dave Hatcher, Ron Mastin, Red McDaniel, Charlie Plumb, Wes Schierman, Orson Swindle, and Ross Terry helped me understand the bad—and the good—that came with captivity in Hanoi; many were kind enough to review the manuscript. A special thanks goes to artist and historian Mike McGrath for his untiring help and expert drawings. Members of the navy community including Heidi Lenzini and Michael McDaniel at the Naval History and Heritage Command, Rear Admiral Peter Booth in Pensacola, and professors Hite Spencer and Rick Ruth at the U.S. Naval Academy also helped in countless ways. The work of Fred Kiley, Stuart Rochester, John Hubbell, Vernon Davis, Craig Howes, George Herring, Stanley Karnow, Lien-Hang T. Nguyen, Bùi Tín, and numerous other authors proved immeasurably helpful, and I appreciate their efforts to capture aspects of this important story. Thanks also to Hill Goodspeed and Richard Latture at the National Museum of Naval Aviation and the U.S. Naval Institute. For helping me understand the medical aspects of the prisoner experience, I'd like to thank Lieutenant Colonel Randy Rizor, MD. President Jimmy Carter (USNA '47) and the extraordinary Louie Zamperini provided help and inspiration.

Special thanks to Andrea Alvord, Philip and Charlotte Blackburn, Pete and Carolyn Booth, Charles and Lee Hight, John and Kathy Landon, Pat Palma, Matt and Mary Sawhill, Buey Tut, Mary Ellen Wiggins, and the fabulous residents of Garfield Street, who kindly took care of me in their respective homes and cities. I'm particularly grateful to George and Paula Foot for a creekside retreat in the Rockies and to John and Mimi Rogers for the spot on the coast. Additional thanks go to all those who reviewed the manuscript and helped ensure I correctly recorded myriad facts and countless intricate details.

Speaking of those facts, no single book could completely record the experiences of eleven POWs and their families over eight years. I have done my best to weave together diverse accounts to create a story that accurately represents the experiences of the Alcatraz Eleven, and I hope readers and other POWs will understand I could never tell every story from every perspective. The history of Vietnam and our involvement therein inevitably sparks controversy. Dedicated historians have produced entire volumes that still leave some details unexplained. I have endeavored to present the conflict's history succinctly but realistically so that readers might understand how American pilots came to spend eight years in Hanoi.

The literary agent who first believed in me, Jack Scovil, passed away before I finished the manuscript, but I'll always owe him a special debt. Sincere thanks to his business partner Russ Galen, a true advocate who took up the flag and carried us through the homestretch. At Thomas Dunne Books, Peter Joseph championed this project and helped me frame and recount this epic story. Melanie Fried lent her boundless editorial talent to the manuscript as well. I'm also grateful for the continuing support of the Madison Park team that has included Peter and Melanie as well as Margaret Brown, Joe Rinaldi, Pete Wolverton, and Tom Dunne.

My friends and family have been wonderfully supportive as always. Will, Emma, and Holly Gibby always relieved the pressure of writing, and Suzanne Foote was ever patient and understanding, unfailing in her support, keen insights, and belief in this project and in me. I'm especially glad that Trevor Ulbrick found time between world-saving jobs to join me for the round-the-world adventure that brought us to Southeast Asia. I'm forever indebted to a special friend in Hanoi for showing me the very best of Vietnam and helping me understand its people and its past—and letting me glimpse its future as well.

More than 770 known Americans were captured during the Vietnam War, and they valiantly upheld those high standards we expect of our servicemen and they, in turn, expect of themselves; 113 POWs did not survive. Every man has a valuable story and his own unique perspective. Far more than eleven individuals disrupted the Camp Authority's plans, caused Cat and Rabbit fits, and resisted with their every fiber. Far more than eleven men served as leaders and aspired to—and did—return with honor. To me, they are all heroes, although no more so than the men who fought the war in other places, under different sets of difficult circumstances. To a one, our Vietnam veterans will tell you that the real heroes are the men who did not return. Likewise, all the families who underwent this ordeal and who refused to forsake our

POWs certainly deserve our admiration. Their stories remind us of the sacrifices made not just by those who wear the uniform but by those on the home front.

Above all, the men, wives, and families of Alcatraz have opened their lives and given me a gift of understanding and inspiration that I never expected. They have patiently revisited very difficult phases of their lives and still had the good spirits to enjoy dinner with me afterward. I am grateful for their friendship; I am lucky to know them. With each new story I heard, I grew more convinced that America has never assembled a finer band of men and women. I will always remain in awe of what they endured and accomplished. I hope I've told their story well. I hope it inspires America like it continues to inspire me.

Finally, to all our POWs and Vietnam veterans: GBU.

NOTES

Much of the preceding narrative stems from extensive interviews with surviving members of the Alcatraz Eleven, Alcatraz family members, other POWs who served in Vietnam, and other POW family members. Multiple first-person sources contributed to and/or confirmed many anecdotes and quotes in this manuscript. Unless otherwise noted, dialogue and description of specific events comes from materials provided by and first-person interviews conducted by the author with the following POWs and family members. Often quotes are cited from books written by or about Alcatraz POWs; since those quotes were recalled at dates closer to actual events than more recent interviews, the author considered those specific recollections most reliable.

Captain Gerald Coffee, Commander George Coker, Mrs. Pam Coker, Mr. James Denton, Rear Admiral Jeremiah Denton Jr., Mr. Jeremiah Denton III, Mr. Michael Denton, Colonel Lee Ellis, Commander Paul Galanti, Mrs. Phyllis Galanti, Commander Danny Glenn, Mrs. Sondra Rutledge Hamelin, Lieutenant Colonel David Hatcher, Mr. Brian Jenkins, Mr. Christopher Jenkins, Mr. Kirk Jenkins, Colonel Sam Johnson, Mrs. Monica Storz Lovell, Lieutenant Colonel Ronald Mastin, Mrs. Dorothy McDaniel, Captain Eugene "Red" McDaniel, Commander Michael McDaniel, Captain Michael McGrath, Colonel George McKnight, Mrs. Suzanne McKnight, Mrs. Cyndi Tanner Mincy, Mrs. Gini

Johnson Mulligan, Captain James Mulligan Jr., Mrs. Louise Mulligan, Mrs. Sandra Storz Pelton, Mrs. Phyllis Rutledge, Colonel Pete Peterson, Major Wesley Schierman, Mrs. Lorraine Shumaker, Rear Admiral Robert Shumaker, Mr. James Stockdale Jr., Mr. Mark Storz, Lieutenant Colonel Orson Swindle, Captain Nels Tanner, Mrs. Sara Ann Tanner, Captain Ross Terry, Mrs. Janie Tschudy, Commander William Tschudy.

Unless otherwise noted, detailed figures and statistics about POWs are taken from data compiled by Captain J. Michael McGrath, NAMPOW historian.

Permission for quotations from *In Love and War,* by Jim and Sybil Stockdale, granted by U.S. Naval Institute Press, Annapolis, Maryland.

1. BLACK SEA AND AMERICAN FIREPOWER

7   "In 1956 . . . 535 lives." Robert Rubel, "The U.S. Navy's Transition to Jets," *Naval War College Review,* Spring 2010, 49–59.

7   "Another offered . . . unforgiving airstream." Tom Wolfe, *The Right Stuff* (New York: Farrar, Straus, and Giroux, 1979), 22.

8   "Just as he . . . ready to go." Jim and Sybil Stockdale, *In Love and War* (New York: Bantam Books, 1984), 12.

8   "Un-strap . . . getting in!" Ibid., 13.

8   "Behind the . . . of sound." *Chance Vought/LTV History, University of Dallas Special Collections,* http://www.utdallas.edu/library/unique coll/speccoll/hac/vought/LTVhistory.html (accessed May 17, 2012).

9   "Jim's father . . . Class of 1947." Jim Stockdale and Jerry Denton belonged to the U.S. Naval Academy's Class of 1947, but due to the Second World War, the class graduated in 1946.

10   "Once below cloud . . . reported none." As with many incidents that evening of August 4, recollections differ on the wording of the alert. The phrases "torpedo in water," "hydrophone effect," and "noise spoke" were all attributed to the sonar team. It's useful to note that as policy, sonar operators tended to overreport (versus underreport) the severity of a threat, since not identifying a torpedo could result in losing the ship.

10   "Around 9:30 . . . no results." Anthony Austin, *The President's War* (New York: J. B. Lippincott, 1971), 279.

10   "By the time . . . into the night." Edwin E. Moise, *Tonkin Gulf and the Escalation of the Vietnam War* (Chapel Hill: University of North Carolina Press, 1996).

10   "Perhaps unbeknown . . . the confusion." Eugene G. Winchy, *Tonkin Gulf* (Garden City, NY: Doubleday, 1971), 190.

10–11   "He walked . . . torpedo wakes." Stockdale 1984, 21.

11   "Review of action . . . further actions." John Galloway, *The Gulf of Tonkin Resolution* (Cranbury, NJ: Associated University Presses, 1970), 62.

11   "[America's] reply . . . hostile operations." Lyndon Johnson, "President Johnson's Television Report Following Renewed Aggression in the Gulf of Tonkin," August 4, 1964, *University of Texas, School of Information*, http://solstice.ischool.utexas.edu/projects/index.php/LBJ_Gulf_of_Tonkin_Speech (accessed June 5, 2012).

12   "In a move . . . Tonkin incidents." Sven Kraemer and Marshall Wright, *Presidential Decisions: The Gulf of Tonkin Attacks of August 1964* (Washington, DC: Vietnam Information Group/Department of Defense, 1968). http://www.nsa.gov/public_info/_files/gulf_of_tonkin/chrono/rel2_wright_kraemer.pdf (accessed July 28, 2012).

2. WELCOME TO THE HANOI HILTON

15   "President Johnson . . . for themselves." "LBJ." *University of Houston, Digital History Collection*, http://www.digitalhistory.uh.edu/disp_textbook.cfm?smtID=2&psid=3461 (ID 3461).

15   "Yet by . . . not combat." Robert S. McNamara, *In Retrospect* (New York: Random House, 1995), 169.

18   "In 1896 . . . Hỏa Lò Prison." Nguyễn Thi Hiên, *Hoa Lo Prison Historic Vestige* (Hanoi: Sun Advertising & Trading Co., 2010), 3–5.

19   "In 1913 . . . cramped cells." Ibid.

20   "In this new conflict . . . Communist dogma." Central Intelligence Agency, *Vietcong Policy Toward and Exploitation of U.S. Prisoners of War* (Declassified, Saigon: CIA, 1967).

20–21   "The Ministry . . . for the Americans." George J. Veith, *Code-Name Bright Light* (New York: Dell, 1998), 17–19.

20–21   "The Ministry . . . obtain it." Garnett Bell and George J. Veith, *POWs and Politics: How Much Does Hanoi Really Know*, Center for the Study of the Vietnam Conflict Symposium, Lubbock, TX, Texas Tech University, 1996. Stephen Young, "How Hanoi Won the War," *Wall Street Journal*, August 3, 1995.

22   "The treaty . . . humane treatment." International Committe of the Red Cross, *International Humanitarian Law—State Parties/Signatories*,

http://www.icrc.org/ihl.nsf/WebSign?ReadForm&id=375&ps=P (accessed March 12, 2013).

23–24   "Article I . . . States of America." Stuart I. Rochester, *The Battle Behind Bars: Navy and Marine POWs in the Vietnam War* (Washington, DC: Department of the Navy, 2010), 22.

24   "The Eisenhower administration . . . Indochina War." Stanley Karnow, *Vietnam: A History* (New York: Penguin, 1983), 148.

24   "One U.S. . . . in Indochina." George C. Herring, *America's Longest War* (Boston: McGraw-Hill, 2002), 36.

25   "As his failed . . . against the war." Bùi Tín, *From Enemy to Friend: A North Vietnamese Perspective on the War* (Annapolis, MD: U.S. Naval Institute, 2002).

25–26   "To withdraw from . . . be defeated." Lyndon Johnson, "Speech at Johns Hopkins University: Peace without Conquest (April 7, 1965)," *Lyndon B. Johnson Presidential Library*, http://lbjlib.utexas.edu/johnson/ archives.hom/speeches.hom/650407.asp (accessed May 25, 2013).

26   "I don't think . . . I ever saw." U.S. Department of State, *Foreign Relations of the United States, 1964–68, Volume XXVII, Document 53*, https://www.mtholyoke.edu/acad/intrel/vietnam/lbjbundy.htm (accessed May 9, 2012).

26   "When they asked . . . any longer." Interrogators seemed interested in this subject and also asked POW Rod Knutson and other prisoners if their fathers were farmers.

28   "The next day . . . the latrine." Craig Howes, *Voices of the Vietnam POWs* (New York: Oxford University Press, 1993), 86. While Craig Howes attributes the event to June 1, author John Hubbell says May 15, which seems more likely, given the date of Ron's arrival and the week of preparation Shu undertook before executing the note drop.

28   "He found . . . Storz, USAF." John G. Hubbell, *P.O.W.: A Definitive History of the American Prisoner-of-War Experience in Vietnam, 1964–1973* (New York: Reader's Digest Press, 1976), 43.

30   "After four months . . . cheeks hurt." Howes 1993, 86.

3. DEAD OR ALIVE?

32   "As the new POW . . . his next drop." Jeremiah A. Denton Jr. *When Hell Was in Session* (Los Angeles, CA: WND Books, 1998), 41.

33 "One day, his . . . Bancroft Hall." Anne Chancey Dalton, *Jeremiah A. Denton, Jr.: Vietnam War Hero* (Birmingham, AL: Seacoast, 2012), 42.

33–34 "Just two days . . . ship's waist." Naval Historical Center, *A-6 Intruder,* http://www.history.navy.mil/planes/a6.htm (accessed July 17, 2012).

34 "A dark-suited civilian emerged . . . successful mission." Associated Press, "Hanoi Claims Photo Shows Downed Fliers," July 23, 1965.

34 "Once they arrived . . . into North Vietnam." Jeremiah A. Denton Jr. *When Hell Was in Session* (Los Angeles: WND Books, 1998), 6.

34–35 "Upon Jerry's . . . frame in place." Hubbell 1976, 64–65.

35–36 "As he worked . . . without harassment." Larry Guarino, *A P.O.W.'s Story: 2801 Days in Hanoi* (New York: Ivy Books, 1990), 35–36.

36 "He called to . . . figure it out." Ibid., 37. Hubbell 1976, 64.

37 "Thus POWs . . . Bless America." Guarino 1990, 59.

42 "What are you . . . stammered away." Stockdale 1984, 117.

43–44 "The next morning . . . in her arms." Ibid., 116–19.

44 "On the last . . . navy personnel." Ibid. 119.

45 "Trouble stirred . . . forged ahead." McNamara 1995, 214–24.

45 "Each week . . . U.S. aviators." National Archives, *Statistical Information About Fatal Casualties of the Vietnam War,* http://www.archives.gov/research/military/vietnam-war/casualty-statistics.html#year (accessed August 17, 2012).

4. I SUBMIT

47 "Across from him . . . midforties." Hubbell 1976, 52.

47–48 "The man seemed . . . camouflage netting." Stockdale 1984, 156.

48–49 "Under Pigeye's direction . . . he passed out." Hubbell 1976, 128–29.

50 "When time . . . somewhere else?" James A. Mulligan, et al., "Harry T. Jenkins," *The Brown Shoes*, http://thebrownshoes.org/AcrobatPDF/JENKINS,%20HARRY%20T.%20JR.%20%20%201-47.pdf (accessed June 3, 2012).

50–51 "As he parachuted . . . definitely had." Barbara Powers Watt, ed., *We Came Home* (Toluca Lake, CA: POW Publications, 1977).

51 "On the second . . . father's occupation." "Farmer" was written in English, an odd departure from the Vietnamese language and characters typically used for other entries.

53   "The criminals . . . turn in violators." Howes 1993, 118.

53   "Syb, you . . . dirty body." Stockdale 1984, 153.

53   "On the wall . . . Candid Camera." Gerald Coffee, *Beyond Survival* (New York: Berkley, 1990), 131.

54   "The next morning . . . Jim Stockdale!" Hubbell 1976, 130–31.

54   "Oh, hi . . . brought it back." James B. Stockdale, "Captain Harry Tarleton Jenkins Jr. USN (ret.) Dies in Plane Crash in Arizona," *Coronado Eagle*, August 15, 1995, 1.

54   "The Enemy Proselytizing . . . obtain them." Bùi Tín, e-mail, September 27, 2012.

55   "When Howie . . . first day." Rochester 2010, 23.

55   "Howie balked . . . severely punished." Howard and Phyllis Rutledge, *In the Presence of Mine Enemies* (Old Tappan, New Jersey: Spire Books, 1973), 27.

56   "By evening . . . as broken." Ibid., 26–31.

56   "Shortly after . . . are you from." Ibid., 34.

58   "You have no right . . . problems are resolved." Stockdale 1984, 157.

58   "When do you . . . this spring." Ibid., 159.

59   "Nguyễn Văn Bài." Due to lack of access to Vietnamese documents, the name of the commandant of the North Vietnamese detention system cannot be verified, but based on information and interviews obtained from U.S. military debriefers, DPMO, and returned POWs, it seems the commissar's name was likely Nguyễn Văn Bài, often misattributed as "Bui." Rabbit's name, while known, remains unidentified in the text as he has spent much of his life since the war working to help children and citizens in Vietnam who still suffer from the conflict's lingering effects.

59   "Stockdale . . . end this war." Stockdale 1984, 160.

60–61 Back in the cell . . . to do now." Ibid., 171.

5. T-O-R-T-U-R-E

63–64 "They left him . . . of his fate." Hubbell 1976, 115–16.

64–65 "Frustrated, Ron . . . bound to lose." Robinson Risner, *The Passing of the Night: My Seven Years as a Prisoner of the North Vietnamese* (Old Saybrook, CT: Konecky & Konecky, 1973), 72–73.

66   "So it happened . . . contraband notes." Frederick Kiley and Stuart

I. Rochester, *Honor Bound: American Prisoners of War in Southeast Asia* (Annapolis, MD: Naval Institute Press, 1999), 135–36.

66–67 "They searched . . . God bless you." Risner 1973, 75–76.

66–67 Before anyone . . . most of all." Hubbell 1976, 111.

67 "GBU had become . . . for you." *Return with Honor*, directed by Freida Lee Mock and Terry Sanders, 2004.

67–68 "While the code . . . POW ranks." Howes 1993, 26, 92. Hubbell 1976, 153.

68 "Well, Denton . . . eat shit." Denton 1998, 58.

68–69 "His morale sank . . . five minutes more." Ibid., 59–60.

73 "The built-up . . . needles sensation." Randy F. Rizor, MD, interview by Alvin Townley, September 15, 2012.

73 "Okay . . . Okay." Hubbell 1976, 176.

73–74 "Jerry eventually . . . pass out." *Prisoners of Hope*, directed by Bernie Hargis, 2001.

74 "Now, Denton . . . tape recorder." Denton 1998, 87–89.

74 "He described . . . defeated and despondent." "Hanoi's Pavlovicms," *Time*, April 14, 1967, 43.

74 "Then he praised . . . government and people." Cuban broadcasters who aired the confession reported the voice as that of Jeremiah Denton, but no definitive confirmation was issued.

74–75 "Then Jerry went . . . said Jerry." Denton 1998, 91–92.

75 "Cat returned . . . Guy Village." *Prisoners of Hope*.

77 "At his 1960 . . . his actions." Michael Sullivan, *"Francis Gary Powers: One Man, Two Countries, and the Cold War," Military.com*, http://www.military.com/Content/MoreContent1/?file=cw_fgpowers (accessed July 20, 2012). Powers, Francis Gary. *Francis Gary Powers Makes Final Plea Before Moscow Court*, May 1, 1960, http://www.history.com/speeches (accessed July 21, 2012).

77 "Isn't it too . . . if he didn't." Hubbell 1976, 176.

78 "I don't know . . . as I live." National Archives, Records of the Central Intelligence Agency (263.2589), *CDR Jeremiah A. Denton, Jr.—Report from Inside a Hanoi Prison, 1966*, Hanoi, May 2, 1966. Reuters, "Pilot Captured by Hanoi Supports U.S. Policy," *Washington Post*, May 1966.

78 "When U.S. Intelligence . . . Morse code." Ron Shaffer, "Admiral Denton Decorated: Ex-POW Used His Eyelids to Signal 'Torture,'" *Washington Post*, November 20, 1974, C1.

6. MY DEAREST SYB

79–80 "My dearest Syb . . . my love, Jim." Stockdale 1984, 122–28.

81 "Boroughs, in turn . . . men had survived." Ibid., 135.

81–82 "That sounds dangerous . . . so to speak." Ibid., 136.

82 "The next day . . . POW matters." Vernon E. Davis, *The Long Road Home* (Washington, DC: Historical Office of the Secretary of Defense, 2000), 57.

7. LORD, I JUST NEED YOUR HELP

84–85 "For more than . . . Southeast Asia." Karnow 1983, 462.

85 "Major, we've got . . . their good-byes." Sam Johnson and Jan Winebrenner, *Captive Warriors: A Vietnam POW's Story* (College Station: Texas A&M University Press, 1992), 11–12.

86 "Sam relished . . . the vicinity." Sam Johnson, *"A Conversation with an American Hero,"* interview by Air Force Association, September 25, 2007.

87–88 "Two, go right . . . Silence answered." Johnson and Winebrenner 1992, 28–30.

91 "You are not entitled . . . sentenced to die!" Ibid., 45.

91–92 "Sam's mother . . . empty chambers." Johnson 2007. *Prisoners of Hope*. Johnson and Winebrenner 1992, 45–46.

92 "Still, from that . . . leave his side." *Prisoners of Hope*.

95–96 "Rabbit opened . . . repent your crimes." James A. Mulligan Jr., *The Hanoi Commitment* (Virginia Beach, VA: James A. Mulligan, 1981), 32–34.

96–97 "Untie the ropes . . . help me." Ibid., 35–36.

8. I LOVE A PARADE

98–99 "As she sat . . . want you to do." Stockdale 1984, 138–40.

99–100 "You will be tried . . . under bed!" Johnson and Winebrenner 1992, 106–7.

100 "Air raids . . . proximate targets." McNamara 1995.

100 "In the courtyard . . . and pants." Gary Foster and Michael McGrath, *The Hanoi March, July 6, 1966.* (Colorado Springs, CO: NAM-POW).

100 "Numbering lifted . . . finally arrived." *Return with Honor*.

101 "You must remember . . . do with you." Coffee 1990, 161. Hubbell 1976, 186.

102 "Now I give . . . your crimes." Hubbell 1976, 186.

102 "The procession . . . single step." Phóng Viên, "American Air Power Under the Eyes of the Victorious People of Hanoi," *People's Army Newspaper,* July 7, 1966, 1, 4.

102 "Over the growing . . . heads up." James S. Hirsch, *Two Souls Indivisible: The Friendship That Saved Two POWs in Vietnam* (New York: Houghton Mifflin, 2004), 136. Denton 1998, 111. Hubbell 1976, 187.

103 "Alvarez, Alvarez . . . they'd yell." *Return with Honor.* Hubbell, 187.

103 "Down with . . . get out." Viên 1966.

104 "A militiawoman . . . air power." Ibid.

105 "An elderly . . . in her eyes." Coffee 1990, 164.

105–8 "Newly arrived . . . Boyd deadpanned." July 6, 1966, fell on a Wednesday, but sources seemed certain the response was "Only on Saturdays."

107 "You fools . . . the people." Denton 1998, 114. Kiley and Rochester 1998, 199.

109 On July 20 . . . in view." Davis 2000, 83–84.

9. SUPERMAN!

110–11 "It is time . . . depends on you." Mulligan 1981, 73.

112 "The prisoner death . . . the exact number." The reported death rate in North Vietnamese and NLF prisons can vary based on a number of categories and considerations, including quality of data and category of personnel. This figure assumes all military personnel reported deceased out of 725 verified prisoners taken during the war (113 POW deaths, as noted by Kiley and Rochester, p. 597). Several American airmen, like Wilmer "Newk" Grubb, were documented to have survived their ejections but never appeared in the North Vietnamese detention system alive.

113 "Roaches terrorized . . . hard-liners alike." Kiley and Rochester 1999, 128, 211.

115–16 "Back in his cell . . . shameful exile." Hubbell 1976, 211.

116 "When an interrogator . . . Sleep, Storz." Joint Task Force—Full Accounting. "Debrief Extract, J2 1771, Ser: 185," Camp H. M. Smith, Hawaii, 1992, http://www.pownetwork.org/bios/s/s121.htm, (accessed May 25, 2013).

118 "At an early . . . beaten it." Jamie Howren and Taylor Baldwin

Kiland, *Open Doors: Vietnam POWs Thirty Years Later* (Washington, DC: Potomac Books, 2005).

121 "Tennessean Charles . . . at Yankee Station." Located in the South China Sea off Đà Nẵng and officially designated "Point Yankee," Yankee Station was the area where American carriers conducted air operations in support of the American mission in North and South Vietnam. An average of three carriers were on station at any one time.

125 "In Nels's . . . most dishonorably." Charles N. Tanner, Letter written by Charles N. Tanner, Hanoi, October 1966.

126 "It mentioned . . . Clark Kent." "Hanoi's Pavlovicms," *Time*, April 14, 1967, 43.

126 "On April 16 . . . waiting truck." Department of the Air Force, *Places and Dates of Confinement: Air Force, Navy and Marine Corps PWs, North Vietnam, 1964–1973*, SEAsia PW Analysis Program Report (Washington, DC: Department of the Air Force, 1975).

126–7 "He soon found . . . your *deceit*!" Hubbell 1976, 266.

10. YOUR ADORING HUSBAND

130 "With careful forethought . . . pass his letter." Mulligan 1981, 116–20. Hubbell 1976, 228–30.

131 "Dusk had . . . darkness." Mulligan 1981, 116–21.

131 "He prayed . . . Amen." Ibid., 121.

131–2 "You are too poor . . . in Bethlehem." Ibid., 128–29.

133 By the end . . . of writing home." Davis 2000, 373.

133–4 "Aircraft had . . . in Saigon." Chester L. Cooper, *The Lost Crusade: America in Vietnam* (Greenwich, CT: Fawcett Publications, 1972). Herring 2002, 203–04. McNamara 1995, 248–50. Karnow 1983, 506–9.

134 "The former air . . . bugs bite." Stockdale 1984, 185.

135–6 "On the occasion . . . she was here." Ibid., 188–90, 214.

137 "The instructions . . . Hang on." Ibid., 193–94.

138 "Jim had not . . . forgotten him." In his writings and interviews reviewed by the author, Jim Stockdale made no references to receiving letters during 1966, nor did Sybil, and the letters received by him at Christmas were written in the fall, making it likely that he received no mail during the preceding months of 1966.

138 "Jim's spirits . . . and left." Stockdale 1984, 197.

140 "Go, Muste . . . target list." Ibid., 201.

140 "In now-visible . . . government would act." Ibid., 207.

11. BACK US

142 "Đán! Đán . . . leave bucket." Stockdale 1984, 233.

142–43 "Jim heard . . . Saint." Ibid., 235–36.

145 "Some days . . . at home." Howes 1993, 96.

146 "At the week's . . . Go." Stockdale 1984, 244.

147–48 "Bow . . . let that happen." Stockdale 1984, 251–52. Johnson
        and Winebrenner 1992, 126–27. Howes 1993, 30–32.

149 "The guards thrust . . . 3 feet by 7 feet." Every inmate confined to
        the Mint interviewed by the author described the cells as measur-
        ing roughly 3 by 7 feet. Current layout and original French architec-
        tural drawings differ from each other and from the POW accounts,
        however. The book assumes the accounts of POWs to be accurate.

149 "The guards thrust . . . into the Mint." Rutledge 1973, 62.

149 "Twice each week . . . of the pigs." Coffee 1990, 193.

150 "Apology . . . nicer compliment." Ibid., 195.

150–51 "You are criminals . . . home together." Stockdale 1984, 253–
        54, 277.

151–52 "He pictured . . . individually." Ibid., 255–56.

152 "Harry Jenkins . . . depsondent of prisoners." Richard G. Capen,
        Finish Strong (San Francisco: HarperCollins/Zondervan, 2002),
        123–26.

153 "He announced . . . this cell." Mulligan 1981, 159.

153–54 "Efforts to win . . . the insurgency." Karnow 1983, 450.

154 "Jerry! . . . flew open." Mulligan 1981, 160.

155 "Jim didn't hesitate . . . to be correct." Ibid., 162.

156 "On August 6 . . . the next cell." Hubbell 1976, 298.

156 "Oh, God . . . been stronger." Coffee 1990, 201.

157 "In a different . . . same propaganda film." The film was almost
        certainly *Pilots in Pajamas*, produced in 1967 by an East German film
        crew based at the Plantation. Portions of the film run on continu-
        ous loop in Room Eighteen of the Hỏa Lò Prison Museum today.

157 "Shu's resistance . . . different explanation." Walter Heynowski and
        Gerhard Scheumann, *Piloten im Pyjama (Pilots in Pajamas)*, 1967,
        http://www.pownetwork.org/nvp/pilots_in_pajamas.pdf (accessed
        January 24, 2013).

157 "After being tortured . . . Jim Stockdale." Kiley and Rochester 1999, 305.

158–59 "George began yelling . . . Torture!" Hubbell 1976, 302.

159 "The staff soon . . . left arm." Ibid., 305.

12. A SNAKE YOU CAN'T KILL

161 "Eighty-two . . . actually seen." Michael McGrath, *U.S. POWs in North Vietnam* (Colorado Springs, CO: NAMPOW).

162 "You attack . . . be punished." Johnson and Winebrenner 1992, 135.

162 "Jim bid good . . . communication infraction." The Camp Authority had moved Nels Tanner out of the Mint shortly before transferring in Stockdale and Johnson.

163 "The stint together . . . talking so much." Hubbell 1976, 274.

163 "Prior to his . . . solitary confinement." Rutledge 1973, 59.

163 "Whereas George . . . children he had." Ibid., 60. Rochester 2010, 38.

164 "Suspecting the nature . . . international law." Hubbell 1976, 280.

165 "If Howie, Sam . . . summer of 1967." *Prisoners of Hope.*

165 "One fair-skinned . . . counted 243." Leo K. Thorsness, *Surviving Hell: A POW's Journey* (New York: Encounter Books, 2008), Kindle edition, 886.

168 "In a hushed voice . . . two years." Stockdale 1984, 267. Hubbell 1976, 324. Author John Hubbell attributes a similar line to Mao at the trial of Jim Stockdale. In his book *In Love and War,* Stockdale recalled it coming from Vy before the interview with the Russians.

168–69 "He leaned over . . . conference is finished." Ibid., 268–69.

169 "Why fool around . . . no repay." Ibid., 270.

170 "I have not been . . . Camp Authority." Ibid., 271.

170 "I am a war criminal . . . authority for mercy." Hubbell 1976, 324.

170–71 "Pigeye had untied . . . its own lot." Kiley and Rochester 1999, 309.

171 "In a happier . . . Job and Epictetus." James B. Stockdale, *Thoughts of a Philosophical Fighter Pilot* (Palo Alto, CA: Hoover Institution, 1995), 177–78.

171 "The Old Testament . . . southern Israel." Job lived in "the land of Uz," often thought to be territory in modern southwestern Jordan and southern Israel.

172 "While in Hỏa Lò . . . trust in God." James B. Stockdale, *A Vietnam*

Experience: Ten Years of Reflection (Palo Alto, CA: Hoover Institution, 1984), 35.

172 "When Jim and Rhinelander . . . the real danger." Stockdale 1995, 187–88.

172 "He listened intently . . . Jim Stockdale." Kiley and Rochester 1999, 308.

173–74 "Jim protested . . . matter seemed finished." Stockdale 1984, 273. Hubbell 1976, 326–27.

173 "The extensive list . . . more than 270." POW leaders had designated several gifted POWs as official memory banks, responsible for memorizing POW names and other information. Jim Mulligan was one such designated POW, and he repeated his list three times each day. Still today, Mulligan has a particularly sharp memory.

173–74 "Jim did his . . . matter seemed finished." Hubbell 1976, 124–27. Stockdale 1984, 272–74.

174–75 "He humbly accepted . . . ultimately triumph." Jim Collins, *Good to Great* (New York: HarperBusiness, 2001), 83–87.

175 "Two spiders . . . only companions." Johnson and Winebrenner 1992, 138.

175–76 "In August . . . of your imprisonment." Ibid., 140.

176 "It would be okay . . . woke up again." Ibid.

177–78 "Get up . . . shower and shave." Ibid., 142–43.

13. A HELLUVA STORY

179 "One location satisfied . . . human shields." Kiley and Rochester 1999, 317.

179 "One inmate . . . black dandruff." Ibid., 317.

182 "From the day in 1864 . . . from South Carolinians." Melvin Grigsby, *The Smoked Yank* (N.P.: Sam T. Clover, 1888).

184 "You know, George . . . your grandkids." Howren and Kiland, 11.

185 "On the road . . .'crost the bay." Rudyard Kipling, "*Mandalay*," *Poem Hunter*, December 31, 2002, www.poemhunter.com/poem /mandalay (accessed January 27, 2012).

14. THE BAD CAMP

187 "One afternoon . . . kept laughing." Mulligan 1981, 163.

187 "Three other American . . . know each other" Ibid., 164.

189 "Harry heard . . . guard barked." Johnson and Winebrenner 1992, 156.

190–91 "The French constructed . . . his leadership team." Robert Destatte, interview with Alvin Townley, March 5, 2012.

192 "Suddenly, his ears . . . Get up." Mulligan 1981, 167.

196 "After the guard . . . in camp with us." Ibid., 168.

199 "In Thy gentle . . . smiling our thanks." Rutledge 1973, 69.

199 "When he sensed . . . very long message." Denton 1998, 160.

200 "The guards made sure . . . CAG for weeks." Richard G. Capen, eulogy for Harry Tarleton Jenkins Jr, delivered in Coronado, CA, August 11, 1995.

203 "Eventually, Coker had . . . you were born." Hubbell 1976, 379–80.

206–7 "When Jerry told CAG . . . their entire lives." Denton 1998, 163.

207 "Once, he counted . . . before he stopped." Ibid., 164.

208 "During one walk . . . recurrent problem." Sam Johnson remembered Harry disconnecting wires behind the latrine to black out the camp. Harry's notes recall using the wires inside his cell, the scenario the manuscript relates since it comes from the most direct source.

208 "On some afternoons . . . myself all day." James B. Stockdale, interview by Dr. Albert C. Pierce, in *Moral Courage: An Evening in Honor of VADM James B. Stockdale*, recorded at the U.S. Naval Academy (November 30, 1999).

15. TO TELL THE WORLD

209 "Why do you want . . . from your home." Johnson and Winebrenner 1992, 169.

209–10 "Ultimately, U.S . . . . refuse to bear." James Willbanks, "Shock and Awe of Tet Offensive Shattered U.S. Illusions," *U.S. News & World Report*, January 29, 2009.

210–11 "What do you think . . . leaders were correct." Johnson and Winebrenner 1992, 169–72.

211 "By March 1968 . . . widespread." Herring 2002, 243.

211–12 "To say that we . . . best they could." Walter Cronkite, *Walter Cronkite's "We Are Mired in Stalemate" Broadcast, February 27, 1968,* https://facultystaff.richmond.edu/~ebolt/history398/Cronkite _1968.html (accessed July 28, 2012).

213 "Speaking from the Oval . . . duty may require." Lyndon John-
    son, *"President Lyndon B. Johnson's Address to the Nation—March 31,
    1968," Lyndon B. Johnson Presidential Library*, http://www.lbjlib.
    utexas.edu/johnson/archives.hom/speeches.hom/680331.asp
    (accessed January 29, 2013).

213 "Consequently, the final year . . . died in Vietnam." Comptroller,
    Secretary of Defense, *Casualty Statistics on Southeast Asia, by Month*,
    http://www.americanwarlibrary.com/vietnam/vwc24.htm (ac-
    cessed August 21, 2012). National Archives, *Statistical Information
    About Fatal Casualties of the Vietnam War*, http://www.archives.gov
    /research/military/vietnam-war/casualty-statistics.html#year (ac-
    cessed August 17, 2012).

214 "On May 26 . . . Thank you, Lord." Mulligan 1981, 183.

215 "Rat was seated . . . We will study." Denton 1998, 170–71.

215–16 "The appearance of Cat . . . your meal today." Mulligan 1981,
    184–85.

218 "Lieutenant Commander John . . . of early release." John McCain
    with Mark Salter, *Faith of My Fathers* (New York: Perennial, 1999),
    140–43.

218–19 "In response, Harriman . . . servicemen to uphold." Stockdale
    1984, 298–99.

219–20 "Heavens no . . . they should know." Ibid., 300.

221 "At Alcatraz, the summer . . . efficient administrator." Kiley and
    Rochester 1999, 344.

221 "Most important . . . summer heat." Ibid., 335.

221 "Here's to CAG . . . to the end." Stockdale 1984, 285.

223–24 "The League organized . . . secretary of defense." Evelyn Grubb
    and Carol Jose, *You Are Not Forgotten* (St. Petersburg, FL: Vanda-
    mere Press, 2008), 102.

224 "The new president . . . missing servicemen." Davis 2000, 408.

16. WE WILL BREAK YOU NOW

226 "A guard sprang . . . communicate." Denton 1998, 176.

227 "Purge, I say . . . comm." Ibid., 176.

227–28 "Jerry took it . . . break you now." Denton 1998, 177–79.

229 "Ah, Denton . . . back to Alcatraz." Ibid., 180.

230 "Mun, I take . . . of the Catholics." Mulligan 1981, 192.

230 "When the guards . . . so beautiful." Jim Mulligan identified

St. Joseph's as the cathedral he visited by using modern-day interior photographs; he was blindfolded while outside in 1968.

231–33 "The friendly gesture . . . you will be punished." Ibid., 193–94.

233 "Jerry responded that . . . summon a doctor." Hubbell 1976, 471.

234 "They want us to . . . long as you can." Johnson and Winebrenner 1992, 177.

234 "Bullshit . . . the same way." Mulligan 1981, 195.

234 "Quiet reigned . . . to shoot him." Stockdale 1999.

234 "They're beating . . . beating him." Johnson and Winebrenner 1992, 176.

235 "Sad sack rushed . . . No *bào cào*." Mulligan 1981, 196.

235 "Enraged and defiant . . . lazy son of a." Hubbell 1976, 472.

235 "Everybody goes . . . for three days." Stockdale 1984, 292.

235 "Their defiance reminded . . . to the last." Ibid., 292. Joseph Conrad, *Lord Jim* (New York: Doubleday, 1899), 64.

236 "Coughs or snorts . . . God bless you)." Mulligan 1981, 197.

236–37 "You must write . . . with my guards." Ibid., 197–98.

238 "When Sad Sack . . . I'll write." Ibid., 199.

239 "One confession . . . Gonzales." Kiley and Rochester 1999, 337.

239 "The United States is . . . will be punished." Johnson and Winebrenner 1992, 178–79.

240 "Oh, God, let . . . to the others." Ibid., 178–81.

240–42 "Some of his fellow . . . You will die here." Denton, Johnson, and Mulligan give different dates and accounts of Ron Storz's collapse; the narrative incorporates the most plausible information from all accounts to portray the most likely date and scenario.

241 "If something doesn't happen . . . the summer." Mulligan 1981, 205.

242 "What happened . . . gave Storz blood." Johnson and Winebrenner 1992, 183.

244 "When Sam Johnson . . . uncharacteristically pessimistic." Johnson and Winebrenner, 186.

244 "When Mickey Mouse woke . . . will go on." Denton 1998, 186.

17. BLACKMAIL

245–46 "It is you . . . say, or tape." Stockdale 1984, 326.

246–47 "Rabbit assigned Jim . . . bring you water." Ibid., 328–29.

247–48 "The next day . . . more comfortable." Ibid., 330–32.

250 "Pigeye screamed . . . to the ropes." Ibid., 332–33.

250 "Standing over his . . . my best regards, Jim." Ibid., 334–39.

251 "He now understood . . . it may lead." Fyodor Dostoyevsky. *Notes from Underground* (New York: Barnes & Noble, 2003), 254.

252 "I'm not going . . . Fast." H. R. Haldeman, *The Ends of Power* (New York: Dell, 1978), p. 120.

252 "We will not . . . our own." Herring 2002, 271.

252 "In his first . . . 157,000." Ibid., 182.

252 "Yet Vietnam . . . first term." National Archives. *Statistical Information About Fatal Casualties of the Vietnam War,* http://www.archives.gov/research/military/vietnam-war/casualty-statistics.html#year (accessed August 17, 2012).

253 "The wives believed . . . give them one." Richard G. Capen, e-mail, July 21, 2012.

254 "In the press . . . of their struggle." Richard G. Capen, interview by Alvin Townley, June 26, 2012.

255 "Before you leave . . . you to know." Ibid. Stockdale 1984, 307.

255 "The North . . . refused to do." Melvin R. Laird, "Statement by Secretary of Defense Melvin R. Laird." Washington, DC: Office of Assistant Secretary of Defense (Public Affairs), May 19, 1969.

255 "He and Laird saw . . . support would also." Davis 2000, 201, 419. Dale Van Atta, *With Honor: Melvin Laird in War, Peace, and Politics* (Madison: University of Wisconsin Press, 2008).

256 "I'm crazy to try . . . have an organization." Stockdale 1984, 309.

18. THE CAPTAIN OF MY SOUL

258 "As he walked . . . Jim's assessment." Hubbell 1976, 480.

259 "One POW who . . . locked in Alcatraz." Kiley and Rochester 1999, 309.

260–61 "The actual Nolan . . . their POWs." "Defectors: By Mutual Consent," *Time,* July 15, 1966.

261 "Dear McKinley . . . your arm move." Stockdale 1984, 351.

262 "The prisoners at Alcatraz . . . dead man." Johnson and Winebrenner 1992, 189.

263–64 "George refused to break . . . to do with you." Joanne Kimberlin, "Our POWs," *Virginian-Pilot,* November 11, 2008.

265 "Good-bye . . . old bastard." Stockdale 1984, 354.

265 "I only have one . . . like we do." Ibid., 355.

265–66 "Đán! Đán . . . brought down." Ibid., 356.

266–67 "Tomorrow is the day . . . nagged to death." Ibid., 356–58.

267–68 "That fall, the Politburo . . . families via postcards." Central Committee of the Vietnamese Communist Party, "Politburo Resolution 194: The Policy Regarding American Enemy Pilots Captured in Northern Vietnam," Hanoi, November 20, 1969.

268 "When a guard caught . . . punishment for communicating." Denton 1998, 195.

269 "One morning a guard . . . leg irons." Johnson and Winebrenner 1992, 193.

269–70 "Jerry and Softsoap . . . understand that." Denton 1998, 197.

270 "The POWs speculated . . . away with it now." Johnson and Winebrenner 1998.

270–71 "I'm freezing . . . get your clothes." Mulligan 1981, 208.

19. GBU

272 "Yes, Mrs. Stockdale . . . man with you." Stockdale 1984, 319.

273 "Before his visitors . . . own government." Ibid., 321.

274 "The more divided . . . negotiate at Paris." Richard Nixon, "Address to the Nation on the War in Vietnam," November 3, 1969, *University of California, Santa Barbara.* http://www.presidency .ucsb.edu/ws/index.php?pid=2303 (accessed March 21, 2013).

274 "In 1952 . . . same manner." *"Cold War: Feb. 21, 1972: Nixon Arrives in China for Talks." This Day in History.* http://www.history.com/this -day-in-history/nixon-arrives-in-china-for-talks (accessed August 25, 2012).

275 "When she heard . . . to your husband." Stockdale 1984, 362.

275 "Indeed, the volume . . . in 1970." Davis 2000, 376. Michael J. Allen, *Until the Last Man Comes Home* (Chapel Hill: University of North Carolina, 2009).

276 "For crying out . . . what I said." Stockdale 1984, 364.

276 "Many of us are . . . forces from Vietnam." Davis 2000, 416.

277 "Ladies and gentlemen . . . in my life." Richard Nixon, *"Remarks Following a Meeting with Wives and Mothers of Prisoners of War and Servicemen Missing in Action in Vietnam,"* December 12, 1969, *University*

of California, Santa Barbara. http://www.presidency.ucsb.edu/ws /index.php?pid=2368 (accessed September 28, 2012).

277 "Merry Christmas." Stockdale 1984, 368.

278–79 "You're all moving . . . do as he likes." Johnson and Winebrenner 1992, 200.

279 "Like so many . . . GBU." Mulligan 1981, 209.

280 "Softsoap had returned . . . tea basket." Denton 1998, 198.

280 "You bastards . . . going home!" Mulligan 1981, 211.

280–81 "When Howie . . . be together." Kiley and Rochester 1999, 508.

281 "He reported in . . . No talk!" Johnson and Winebrenner 1992, 200–201.

281 "Ron . . . no answer." Jim Mulligan reported hearing Ron Storz being interrogated in or near Stardust in December 1969, but nobody else could corroborate this. Mulligan recognized Storz's voice. Ron seemed to be refusing to cooperate, and to Jim it seemed as if he were irrational. The North Vietnamese threatened to return him to Alcatraz. Nobody recalled riding with Ron from Alcatraz to the Hilton, however. Nobody saw Ron after the group's December 9 transfer to the Hilton.

281 "When Jerry Denton . . . near Hanoi." Kiley and Rochester 1999, 509.

282 "Whatever the . . . to take over." Guarino 1990, 260.

282–83 "Ah, Denton . . . don't insult guards." Denton 1998, 202–3.

284 "The phantom . . . propaganda system." Johnson and Winebrenner 1992, 242.

286 "Feast yourselves . . . truly optimistic." Mulligan 1981, 214–15.

20. MAYDAY!

288–89 "Ah, Denton . . . think of something." Johnson and Winebrenner 1992, 220.

289 "They hate me . . . break me." Ibid., 222.

290 "Jerry issued . . . fast ceased." Denton 1998, 208.

290 "He began singing . . . up in Wing." MilitarySong, *"There Are No Fighter Pilots Down in Hell" Air Force Drinking Song,* http://www.you tube.com/watch?v=HtQQz8QcSiI (accessed March 6, 2012).

290 "On May 15 . . . another way out." Johnson and Winebrenner 1992, 227.

291 "In June . . . reporting, sir." *Return with Honor.*

292 "They remained . . . please, no more." Johnson and Winebrenner 1992, 233.

292–93 "Shirley refused . . . shaky and uneven." Ibid., 226.

294 "The Air National . . . among the audience." Allen 2009, 38–40.

295 "Dornan wore . . . wrist in America." Judy Davis, interview by Alvin Townley, August 20, 2012.

296 "Under the leadership . . . POW/MIA issue." Mike Anton, "Vietnam War Bracelets Come Full Circle," *Los Angeles Times*, November 4, 2010.

296–97 "Mary Helen . . . black-and-white flag." Mark Woods, "A Symbol Made for Memories," *Florida Times-Union*, August 9, 2009.

297 "Designing the flag . . . then forgotten." Andrea Brown, "Springs Man, Famous for POW Flag Design, Dies," *Gazette* (Colorado Springs), May 17, 2009. Valerie J. Nelson, "Newt Heisley Dies at Age 88; Veteran Designed POW/MIA Flag," *Los Angeles Times*, May 20, 2009.

298 "As Sam sized up . . . a while yet." Johnson and Winebrenner 1992, 233.

298 "He'll get better . . . without being punished." Ibid., 234.

299 "Ah, Sông . . . speak for Stockdale." Ibid., 234.

299 "I assure you . . . a while longer." Hubbell 1976, 527–28.

301 "At a press conference . . . Geneva Convention." David K. Bruce, "Violations of 1949 Geneva Convention by Democratic Republic of North Vietnam," *Commander's Digest*, January 16, 1971.

301 "Several weeks later . . . bring the men home." Richard Nixon, "A Pledge from the President," White House, press release, December 26, 1970.

301 "That last month . . . for Christmas." Davis 2000, 227.

301–2 "I am living . . . is alive." Rutledge 1973, 134.

21. O SAY CAN YOU SEE?

303 "Roughly 250 . . . in North Vietnam." Benjamin F. Schemmer, *The Raid* (New York: Avon, 1976), 307–10.

303–4 "The flight roared . . . captured servicemen." John Gargus, *The Son Tay Raid* (College Station: Texas A&M University Press, 2007).

303–4 "Over the bark . . . without any POWs." National Museum of the U.S. Air Force, *Rescue Attempt: The Son Tay Raid*, March 24,

2011, http://www.nationalmuseum.af.mil/factsheets/factsheet. asp?id=14410 (accessed August 22, 2012).

304 "The Sơn Tây . . . nearby facilities." Kiley and Rochester 1999, 522.

304–5 "It must be some . . . Heartbreak Hotel." Mulligan 1981, 233.

305 "Howie Rutledge had spent . . . through the wilderness." Rutledge 1973, 88.

305 "Bombardier-navigator . . . and they had." Hubbell 1976, 540.

306 "Hey, it's still . . . not allowed." Johnson and Winebrenner 1992, 245–46.

308 "How would you like . . . 1967 treatment?" Risner 1973, 216.

309 "In Jim . . . down a gauntlet." Kiley and Rochester 1999, 530.

309 "As they passed . . . are not tied." Risner 1973, 219.

310 "The POWs had begun . . . Eyes of Texas." Hubbell 1976, 545.

310 "In collegiate tradition . . . the hell is Six." Kiley and Rochester 1999, 531. Denton 1998, 223–24.

310 "For a time . . . Riot of 1971." Accounts of the Church Riot of 1971 vary in their details. The narrative draws on multiple sources, including writings and interviews from participants Jim Stockdale, Robbie Risner, Howie Rutledge, George Coker, Jeremiah Denton, Sam Johnson, and Bob Shumaker. Secondary sources such as Kiley, Rochester, and Hubbell were also consulted in developing the final narrative.

311 "Sure enough . . . Big deal." Johnson and Winebrenner 1992, 248.

311 "Well, I guess . . . Stockdale remarked." Byron Fuller with Mike McGrath and Paul Galanti, *Incredible Room Seven,* November 17, 2001, http://www.nampows.org/room_7.html (accessed March 1, 2012).

311 "The men's primary . . . having fun." Hubbell 1976, 545.

312 "In all of American . . . prisoners of war." For much of their time after 1970, Jim Thompson was imprisoned at the Plantation and Ev Alvarez was at the Zoo.

312 "Camp authorize . . . Thank you, Lord." Johnson and Winebrenner 1992, 248. *Prisoners of Hope.*

312 "Fellow naval . . . with a hangover." Hubbell 1976, 547.

312 "Orson Swindle . . . in that crowd." Fuller et al. 2001.

313 "Indignant, Sybil . . . thought to herself." Stockdale 1984, 386.

313–14 "Upon entering Zero . . . on their backs." Mulligan et al. n.d.

318 "From Rawhide . . . responded to Jim." Hubbell 1976, 558.

318 "Many prisoners still resented . . . the Damned Two." Howes 1993, 111.

318 "Many prisoners still resented . . . to the grave." Following Stockdale's wishes not to nag repentant sinners, the book does not include names of the Repentant Five. Upon return, senior POW officers did bring misconduct charges against the Damned Two, a Marine Corps lieutenant colonel and a navy captain. Charges were ultimately dropped by the government.

320–21 "It unfolded . . . in downtown Hanoi." Johnson and Winebrenner 1992, 252.

22. PEACE IS AT HAND

323 "U.S. Intelligence . . . made an attempt." Kevin Dockery, *Operation Thunderhead* (New York: Berkley Caliber, 2008), 213–33, 276–77.

323–24 "That spring, she . . . would not support." Karnow 1983, 657.

324 "Then he unleashed . . . bombed this time." Herring 2002, 307.

325 "Now he had . . . the proposed treaty." Andre Sauvageot, interview by Alvin Townley, December 10, 2011.

325 "In Camp Unity . . . spirits immediately fell." Johnson and Winebrenner 1992, 265.

326 "It's a B-52 raid . . . going home." Mulligan 1981, 267.

326 "Jim said . . . know we are here." Ibid., 272–73.

327 "The Christmas Bombing . . . harm's way." Tín 2002, 34–36.

327 "The air force lost . . . operational failures." McGrath, Michael. *Mac's Facts 46—B52 Combat Losses/Operational Losses in Vietnam*, Colorado Springs, CO: NAMPOW.

327 "As for the Americans . . . in modern dollars." Stephen Daggett, *Cost of Major U.S. Wars* (Washington, DC: Congressional Research Service, July 4, 2008). Department of the Navy, *American War and Military Operations Casualties*, http://www.history.navy.mil/library/online /american%20war%20casualty.htm (accessed March 16, 2013).

327 "As the United States prepared . . . U.S. interests alone." Karnow 1983, 668.

327–28 "From their courtyard . . . at long last, ended." Eugene B. McDaniel, *Scars and Stripes: The True Story of One Man's Courage in Facing Death as a Vietnam POW* (Alexandria, VA: American Defense Institute, 1981), 162.

328 "To all of you . . . prisoners of war." Richard Nixon, *Nixon's 'Peace with Honor' broadcast on Vietnam,"* *Watergate.info,* January 23, 1973. http://watergate.info/1973/01/23/nixon-peace-with-honor-broad cast.html (accessed August 17, 2012).

329 "Standing stiffly . . . in return." Kiley and Rochester 1999, 572.

329 "Each of the nine . . . dis . . . missed." Ibid., 572. Coffee 1990, 269–70.

329 "Later that afternoon . . . cautious optimism." Coffee 1990, 271.

330 "After some wrangling . . . khaki windbreaker." Kiley and Rochester 1999, 574. Keyes Beech, "POWs' Welcome Simple, Heartfelt," *Chicago Daily News Service,* February 1973.

330 "The former general staff . . . the Vietnamese government." Stockdale 1984, 436.

330–31 "I haven't answered . . . you're a good man." Denton 1998, 237–38.

331 "The optimists . . . February 1973." Mulligan 1981, 255.

23. GOD BLESS AMERICA

332 "The Camp Authority provided . . . the following weeks." Kiley and Rochester 1999, 581. Coffee 1990, 285.

333 "Behind Shu . . . July 1966." Defense Prisoner of War/Missing Personnel Office (DPMO), *Personnel Missing, Southeast Asia (PMSEA)* (Washington, DC: Department of Defense, 2005).

333 "He called to Ev . . .'er off, Ev." Everett Alvarez Jr. and Anthony S. Pitch, *Chained Eagle: The Heroic Story of the First American Shot Down over North Vietnam* (Washington, DC: Potomac Books, 2005), Kindle edition, 3790.

333 "For a man . . . suddenly upon them." Stockdale 1984, 436.

333–34 "The men boarded . . . two warring countries." *Return with Honor.*

334 "An American airman . . . will never know." *Prisoners of Hope.*

334–35 "The busses stopped . . . he said matter-of-factly." Denton 1998, 239.

335 "To his left . . . white linen." Davis 2000, 499.

335 "To his left . . . a blue uniform." Milton S. Baker, LCDR, USN, "Operation Homecoming: The Role of the Navy Public Affairs Officers: I: Hanoi," *Direction,* July 1973, 12.

336 "Within ten . . . B-52 crewmen." Hubbell 1976, 599. Davis 2000, 501.

336 "Thirty-eight-year-old . . . four turbofans." Department of the Air Force, *Hanoi Taxi—445th Airlift Wing*, January 13, 2006, http://www.445aw.afrc.af.mil/library/factsheets/factsheet.asp?id=3396 (accessed April 15, 2012).

336 "Marrott steered . . . on the ground." Associated Press, "POW Return Near," *Victoria Advocate*, February 5, 1973, 1.

336 "As the 340,000 . . . into the sky." Thomas Pepper, "1st POWs leave Hanoi on US Plane," *Baltimore Sun*, February 12, 1973, A1.

336 "What's the Super Bowl . . . POW responded." Kiley and Rochester 1999, 580.

336 "When the third . . . one surely is." Coffee 1990, 286.

336–37 "Mulligan turned back . . . except for this one." Mulligan 1981, 280.

337 "Once inside . . . 3-20-66." Ibid., 282.

338 "Do you show Ron . . . Eleven had made it." Johnson and Winebrenner 1992, 280.

338 "At 3:20 A.M. . . . in the Philippines." Beech 1973.

339 "People waved . . . WE LOVE YOU." "POWs Come Home," *Time*, February 26, 1973, 13–20. Rutledge 1973, 109.

339 "We are honored . . . God bless America." Denton 1998, 240. *Return with Honor*.

340 "After Sam Johnson's . . . rich American food." Baker 1973, 19.

340 "After Sam Johnson's . . . to order both." Johnson and Winebrenner 1992, 282–83.

341 "Originally limited to ten . . . averaged forty." "POWs Come Home," *Time*, February 26, 1973, 13–20.

341 "When his wife . . . who strengthens us." Rutledge 1973, 141.

341 "In his first . . . a little style.'" Stockdale 1984, 444.

342 "Jim Mulligan felt . . . get home." Mulligan 1981, 288.

342 "Not long thereafter . . . like many others." *Return with Honor*.

342 "By April 1 . . . of 566 military personnel." Davis 2000, 511. Kiley and Rochester 1999, 587. Michael McGrath, *U.S. POWs in North Vietnam* (Colorado Springs, CO: NAMPOW). Many Operation Homecoming figures differ slightly given various assumptions and data sets.

343 "When Jim completed . . . first plane with me." Mulligan 1981, 289.

345–46 "As the plane neared . . . enough of this for now." Johnson and Winebrenner 1992, 299.

346 "As he started . . . days straight." *Prisoners of Hope.*

346–47 "Lorraine turned . . . there's your daddy." *Return with Honor.*

349 "For the past seven . . . His grace on thee." Stockdale 1984, 440.

350 *"The New York Times* . . . neither until now." Davis 2000, 527.

SELECTED BIBLIOGRAPHY

Allen, Michael J. *Until the Last Man Comes Home*. Chapel Hill: University of North Carolina Press, 2009.

Alvarez Everett, Jr., and Anthony S. Pitch. *Chained Eagle: The Heroic Story of the First American Shot Down over North Vietnam*. Washington, DC: Potomac Books, 2005. Kindle edition.

Alvey, Carla. "Facing Torture." *Washington Times*, July 7, 2005. http://www.washingtontimes.com/news/2005/jul/07/20050707-090816-1280r/ (accessed August 8, 2012).

Annin Flagmakers. *About Annin—History*. http://www.annin.com/about.asp (accessed June 28, 2012).

Anton, Mike. "Vietnam War Bracelets Come Full Circle." *Los Angeles Times*, November 4, 2010.

Associated Press. "Hanoi Claims Photo Shows Downed Fliers," July 23, 1965.

———. "U.S. Planes Raid North Vietnam. . . ." *New York Times*, November 21, 1970, 1, 11.

———. "POW Return Near." *Victoria Advocate*, February 5, 1973, 1.

Atta, Dale Van. *With Honor: Melvin Laird in War, Peace, and Politics*. Madison: University of Wisconsin Press, 2008.

Austin, Anthony. *The President's War*. New York: J. B. Lippincott, 1971.

Baker, Milton S., LCDR, USN. "Operation Homecoming: The Role of the Navy Public Affairs Officers: I: Hanoi." *Direction*, July 1973, 11–28.

Beech, Keyes. "POWs' Welcome Simple, Heartfelt." *Chicago Daily News*, February 1973.

Bell, Garnett, and George J. Veith. *POWs and Politics: How Much Does Hanoi Really Know*. Center for the Study of the Vietnam Conflict Symposium, Lubbock, TX, Texas Tech University, April 19, 1996.

Booth, Peter. Interview by Alvin Townley. August 22, 2012.

Brown, Andrea. "Springs Man, Famous for POW Flag Design, Dies." *Gazette* (Colorado Springs), May 17, 2009.

Bruce, David K. "Violations of 1949 Geneva Convention by Democratic Republic of North Vietnam." *Commander's Digest*, January 16, 1971.

Capen, Richard G. *Finish Strong*. San Francisco: HarperCollins/Zondervan, 2002.

———. Interview by Alvin Townley. June 26, 2012.

Central Committee of the Vietnamese Communist Party. "Politburo Resolution 194: The Policy Regarding American Enemy Pilots Captured in Northern Vietnam." Hanoi, November 20, 1969.

Central Intelligence Agency. *Vietcong Policy Toward and Exploitation of U.S. Prisoners of War*. Declassified, Saigon, 1967.

Chance Vought/LTV History. http://www.utdallas.edu/library/special collections/hac/vought/history.pdf (accessed May 17, 2012).

Chesley, Larry. *Seven Years in Hanoi: A POW Tells His Story*. Salt Lake City, UT: Bookcraft, 1973.

Coffee, Gerald. *Beyond Survival*. New York: Berkley, 1990.

Collins, Jim. *Good to Great*. New York: HarperBusiness, 2001.

Comptroller, Secretary of Defense. *Casualty Statistics on Southeast Asia, by Month*. http://www.americanwarlibrary.com/vietnam/vwc24.htm (accessed August 21, 2012).

Conrad, Joseph. *Lord Jim*. New York: Doubleday, 1899.

Cooper, Chester L. *The Lost Crusade: America in Vietnam*. Greenwich, CT: Fawcett, 1972.

Cronkite, Walter. *Walter Cronkite's "We Are Mired in Stalemate" Broadcast, February 27, 1968*. https://facultystaff.richmond.edu/~ebolt/history398/Cronkite_1968.html (accessed July 28, 2012).

Daggett, Stephen. *Cost of Major U.S. Wars*. Washington, DC: Congressional Research Service, July 4, 2008.

Dalton, Anne Chancey. *Jeremiah A. Denton, Jr.: Vietnam War Hero.* Birmingham, AL: Seacoast, 2012.

Davis, Judy. Interview by Alvin Townley. August 20, 2012.

Davis, Vernon E. *The Long Road Home.* Washington, DC: Historical Office of the Secretary of Defense, 2000.

"Defectors: By Mutual Consent." *Time,* July 15, 1966.

Defense Prisoner of War/Missing Personnel Office (DPMO). *History of the National League of POW/MIA Families' POW/MIA Flag,* 1998. http://www.dtic.mil/dpmo/pow_day/history (accessed April 29, 2012).

———. *Personnel Missing, Southeast Asia (PMSEA).* Washington, DC: Department of Defense, 2005.

Denton, Jeremiah A., Jr. *When Hell Was in Session.* Los Angeles: WND Books, 1998.

Department of the Air Force. *Hanoi Taxi—445th Airlift Wing.* January 13, 2006. http://www.445aw.afrc.af.mil/library/factsheets/factsheet.asp?id=3396 (accessed April 15, 2012).

Department of the Air Force. *Places and Dates of Confinement: Air Force, Navy and Marine Corps PWs, North Vietnam, 1964–1973.* SEAsia PW Analysis Program Report. Washington, DC: Department of the Air Force, 1975.

Department of Defense. Letter from DoD to Mrs. Ronald E. Storz, November 27, 1973.

Department of the Navy. *American War and Military Operations Casualties.* http://www.history.navy.mil/library/online/american%20war%20casualty.htm (accessed March 16, 2013).

Destatte, Robert. Interview with Alvin Townley. March 5, 2012.

Dockery, Kevin. *Operation Thunderhead.* New York: Berkley Caliber, 2008.

Federation of American Scientists. *C-141B Starlifter.* http://www.fas.org/programs/ssp/man/uswpns/air/cargo/c141b.html (accessed April 18, 2012).

Foster, Gary. Interview by Alvin Townley. June 28, 2012.

Foster, Gary, and Michael McGrath. *The Hanoi March, July 6, 1966.* Colorado Springs, CO: NAMPOW.

Fuller, Byron, with Mike McGrath and Paul Galanti. *Incredible Room Seven.* November 17, 2001. http://www.nampows.org/room_7.html (accessed March 1, 2012).

Galanti, Paul. Interview by Michael Denton. September 7, 2012.

Galloway, John. *The Gulf of Tonkin Resolution.* Cranbury, NJ: Associated University Presses, 1970.

Gallup. *Public Opinion and the Vietnam War.* http://www.digitalhistory .uh.edu/learning_history/vietnam/vietnam_pubopinion.cfm (accessed June 26, 2012).

Gargus, John. *The Son Tay Raid.* College Station, TX: Texas A&M University Press, 2007.

Greer, W. L. *The 1972 Mining of Haiphong Harbor.* Washington, DC: Institute for Defense Analysis, 1997. http://www.dtic.mil/cgi-bin /GetTRDoc?Location=U2&doc=GetTRDoc.pdf&AD=ADA355037 (accessed January 23, 2012).

Grigsby, Melvin. *The Smoked Yank.* N.P.: Sam T. Clover, 1888.

Grubb, Evelyn, and Carol Jose. *You Are Not Forgotten.* St. Petersburg, FL: Vandamere Press, 2008.

Guarino, Larry. *A P.O.W.'s Story: 2801 Days in Hanoi.* New York: Ivy Books, 1990.

Haldeman, H. R. *The Ends of Power.* New York: Dell, 1978.

"Hanoi's Pavlovicms." *Time,* April 14, 1967, 43.

Herring, George C. *America's Longest War.* Boston: McGraw-Hill, 2002.

Heynowski, Walter, and Gerhard Scheumann. *Piloten im Pyjama (Pilots in Pajamas).* 1967. http://www.pownetwork.org/nvp/pilots_in _pajamas.pdf (accessed January 24, 2013).

Hiên, Nguyễn Thi. *Hỏa Lò Prison Historic Vestige.* Hanoi: Sun Advertising & Trading Co., 2010.

Hirsch, James S. *Two Souls Indivisible: The Friendship That Saved Two POWs in Vietnam.* New York: Houghton Mifflin, 2004.

"Home at Last!" *Newsweek,* February 26, 1973, 16–24.

Howes, Craig. *Voices of the Vietnam POWs.* New York: Oxford University Press, 1993.

Howren, Jamie, and Taylor Baldwin Kiland. *Open Doors: Vietnam POWs Thirty Years Later.* Washington, DC: Potomac Books, 2005.

Hubbell, John G. *P.O.W.: A Definitive History of the American Prisoner-of-War Experience in Vietnam, 1964–1973.* New York: Reader's Digest Press, 1976.

International Committe of the Red Cross. *International Humanitarian Law—State Parties/Signatories.* http://www.icrc.org/ihl.nsf/WebSign ?ReadForm&id=375&ps=P (accessed March 12, 2013).

Johnson, Lyndon. "President Johnson's Television Report Following Renewed Aggression in the Gulf of Tonkin," August 4, 1964. *University of Texas, School of Information.* http://solstice.ischool.utexas.edu/projects/index.php/LBJ_Gulf_of_Tonkin_Speech (accessed June 5, 2012).

————. *"President Lyndon B. Johnson's Address to the Nation . . . March 31, 1968."* Lyndon B. Johnson Presidential Library. http://www.lbjlib.utexas.edu/johnson/archives.hom/speeches.hom/680331.asp (accessed January 29, 2013).

————. "Report on the Gulf of Tonkin Incident (August 4, 1964)." *University of Virginia, Miller Center.* http://millercenter.org/president/speeches/detail/3998 (accessed July 6, 2012).

————. "Speech at Johns Hopkins University: Peace Without Conquest (April 7, 1965)." *Lyndon B. Johnson Presidential Library.* http://lbjlib.utexas.edu/johnson/archives.hom/speeches.hom/650407.asp (accessed May 25, 2013).

Johnson, Sam. "A Conversation with an American Hero." Interview by Air Force Association. September 25, 2007.

Johnson, Sam, and Jan Winebrenner. *Captive Warriors: A Vietnam POW's Story.* College Station: Texas A&M University Press, 1992.

Joint Task Force—Full Accounting. "Debrief Extract, J2 1771, Ser: 185," Camp H. M. Smith, Hawaii, 1992. http://www.pownetwork.org/bios/s/s121.htm (accessed May 25, 2013).

Karnow, Stanley. *Vietnam: A History.* New York: Penguin, 1983.

Kiley, Frederick, and Stuart I. Rochester. *Honor Bound: American Prisoners of War in Southeast Asia.* Annapolis, MD: Naval Institute Press, 1999.

Kimberlin, Joanne. "Our POWs." *Virginian-Pilot,* November 11, 2008.

Kraemer, Sven, and Marshall Wright. *Presidential Decisions: The Gulf of Tonkin Attacks of August 1964.* Washington, DC: Vietnam Information Group/Department of Defense, 1968. http://www.nsa.gov/public_info/_files/gulf_of_tonkin/chrono/rel2_wright_kraemer.pdf (accessed July 28, 2012).

Laird, Melvin R. "Statement by Secretary of Defense Melvin R. Laird." Washington, DC: Office of Assistant Secretary of Defense (Public Affairs), May 19, 1969.

Mather, Paul. Interview by Alvin Townley. June 22, 2012.

McCain, John, with Mark Salter. *Faith of My Fathers.* New York: Perennial, 1999.

McDaniel, Eugene B. *Scars and Stripes: The True Story of One Man's Courage in Facing Death as a Vietnam POW*. Alexandria, VA: American Defense Institute, 1981.

McGrath, Michael. *Mac's Facts 01—The Big Rooms—Camp Unity*. Colorado Springs, CO: NAMPOW, 2012.

———. *Mac's Facts 46—B52 Combat Losses/Operational Losses in Vietnam*. Colorado Springs, CO: NAMPOW.

———. *U.S. POWs in North Vietnam*. Colorado Springs, CO: NAMPOW.

McKnight, George. Letter to Monica and Mark Storz, January 18, 1985.

McNamara, Robert S. *In Retrospect*. New York: Random House, 1995.

MilitarySong. *"There Are No Fighter Pilots Down in Hell" Air Force Drinking Song*. http://www.youtube.com/watch?v=HtQQz8QcSiI (accessed March 6, 2012).

Moise, Edwin E. *Tonkin Gulf and the Escalation of the Vietnam War*. Chapel Hill: University of North Carolina Press, 1996.

Mulligan, James A., Jr. *The Hanoi Commitment*. Virginia Beach, VA: James A. Mulligan, 1981.

Mulligan, James A., et al. "Harry T. Jenkins." *The Brown Shoes*. http://thebrownshoes.org/AcrobatPDF/JENKINS,%20HARRY%20T.%20JR.%20%20%201-47.pdf (accessed June 3, 2012).

National Archives. Records of the Central Intelligence Agency (263.2589). *CDR Jeremiah A. Denton, Jr.—Report from Inside a Hanoi Prison, 1966*. Hanoi, May 2, 1966.

National Archives. *Statistical Information About Fatal Casualties of the Vietnam War*. http://www.archives.gov/research/military/vietnam-war/casualty-statistics.html#year (accessed August 17, 2012).

National Museum of the U.S. Air Force. *Rescue Attempt: The Son Tay Raid*. March 24, 2011. http://www.nationalmuseum.af.mil/factsheets/factsheet.asp?id=14410 (accessed August 22, 2012).

Naval Historical Center. *A-6E Intruder*. http://www.history.navy.mil/planes/a6.htm (accessed July 17, 2012).

Nelson, Valerie J. "Newt Heisley Dies at Age 88; Veteran Designed POW/MIA Flag." *Los Angeles Times*, May 20, 2009.

Nixon, Richard. *"Address to the Nation on the War in Vietnam,"* November 3, 1969. *University of California, Santa Barbara*. http://www.presidency.ucsb.edu/ws/index.php?pid=2303 (accessed March 21, 2013).

———. "Nixon's 'Peace with Honor' broadcast on Vietnam." January 23, 1973. *Watergate.info.* http://watergate.info/1973/01/23/nixon-peace-with-honor-broadcast.html (accessed August 17, 2012).

———. "*A Pledge from the President.*" White House press release, December 26, 1970.

———. "*Remarks Following a Meeting with Wives and Mothers of Prisoners of War and Servicemen Missing in Action in Vietnam.*" December 12, 1969. *University of California, Santa Barbara.* http://www.presidency.ucsb.edu/ws/index.php?pid=2368 (accessed September 28, 2012).

Nguyen, Lien-Hang T. *Hanoi's War: An International History of the War for Peace in Vietnam.* Chapel Hill: University of North Carolina Press, 2012. Kindle Edition.

PBS. "History of the USS Enterprise." *Frontline.* http://www.pbs.org/wgbh/pages/frontline/shows/navy/enterprise/enterprise2.html (accessed June 4, 2012).

Pepper, Thomas. "1st POWs leave Hanoi on US plane." *Baltimore Sun*, February 12, 1973, A1.

Powers, Francis Gary. *Francis Gary Powers Makes Final Plea Before Moscow Court.* May 1, 1960. http://www.history.com/speeches (accessed July 21, 2012).

"POWs Come Home," *Time*, February 26, 1973: 13–20.

Prisoners of Hope. Directed by Bernie Hargis. 2001.

Return with Honor. Directed by Freida Lee Mock and Terry Sanders. 2004.

Reuters. "Pilot Captured by Hanoi Supports U.S. Policy." *Washington Post*, May 8, 1966, A18.

Risner, Robinson. *The Passing of the Night: My Seven Years as a Prisoner of the North Vietnamese.* Old Saybrook, CT: Konecky & Konecky, 1973.

Rizor, Randy F., MD. Interview by Alvin Townley. September 15, 2012.

Robbins, Mark. *History of VA-95 Green Lizards.* http://95thallweatherattack.com/va95-history/va95-history-1952-1970.html (accessed July 6, 2012).

Rochester, Stuart I. *The Battle Behind Bars: Navy and Marine POWs in the Vietnam War.* Washington, DC: Department of the Navy, 2010.

Rubel, Robert. "The U.S. Navy's Transition to Jets." *Naval War College Review*, Spring 2010, 49–59.

Rutledge, Howard, and Phyllis Rutledge. *In the Presence of Mine Enemies.* Old Tappan, NJ: Spire Books, 1973.

Sauvageot, Andre. Interview by Alvin Townley. December 10, 2011.

Schemmer, Benjamin F. *The Raid.* New York: Avon, 1976.

Shaffer, Ron. "Admiral Denton Decorated: Ex-POW Used His Eyelids to Signal 'Torture.'" *Washington Post,* November 20, 1974, C1.

Solitary Confinement. http://www.alcatraz101.com/Page10.html (accessed April 16, 2012).

Sterner, Douglas. *The POW/MIA Flag.* http://www.homeofheroes.com /hallofheroes/1st_floor/flag/1bfb_disp9c.html (accessed June 26, 20112).

Stockdale, James B. "Captain Harry Tarleton Jenkins Jr. USN (ret.) Dies in Plane Crash in Arizona." *Coronado Eagle,* August 15, 1995, 1.

———. Interview by Dr. Albert C. Pierce. In *Moral Courage: An Evening in Honor of VADM James B. Stockdale,* recorded at the U.S. Naval Academy (November 30, 1999).

———. *Thoughts of a Philosophical Fighter Pilot.* Palo Alto: Hoover Institution, 1995.

———. *A Vietnam Experience: Ten Years of Reflection.* Palo Alto, CA: Hoover Institution, 1984.

Stockdale, Jim, and Sybil Stockdale. *In Love and War.* New York: Bantam Books, 1984.

Sullivan, Michael. "Francis Gary Powers: One Man, Two Countries, and the Cold War." *Military.com,* date unknown. http://www. military.com/Content/MoreContent1/?file=cw_fgpowers (accessed July 20, 2012).

Tanner, Charles N. Letter written by Charles N. Tanner. Hanoi, October 1967.

"Cold War: Feb. 21, 1972: Nixon Arrives in China for Talks. This Day in History. http://www.history.com/this-day-in-history/nixon-arrives-in -china-for-talks (accessed August 25, 2012).

Thorsness, Leo K. *Surviving Hell: A POW's Journey.* New York: Encounter Books, 2008. Kindle edition.

Tín, Bùi. *From Enemy to Friend: A North Vietnamese Perspective on the War.* Annapolis, MD: U.S. Naval Institute, 2002.

U.S. Department of State. *Foreign Relations of the United States, 1964–68, Volume XXVII, Document 53.* https://www.mtholyoke.edu/acad /intrel/vietnam/lbjbundy.htm.

U.S. House of Representatives. "Hearing on Servicemen Captured and Missing in Southeast Asia." Washington, DC, April 29, 1970.

USS *Lexington* Museum on the Bay. "*USS Lexington, CV-16.*" http://www.usslexington.com/index.php?option=com_content&task=view&id=38&Itemid=49 (accessed July 5, 2012).

Veith, George J. *Code-Name Bright Light.* New York, NY: Dell, 1998.

"Vernon Ligon, 73, Officer and POW in WWII and Vietnam." *Orlando Sentinel,* March 8, 1995. http://articles.orlandosentinel.com/1995-03-08/news/9503080083_1_kissimmee-vietnam-war-survivors (accessed March 1, 2012).

Vietnam Veterans Memorial Fund. *Search the Vietnam Veterans Memorial.* http://www.vvmf.org/thewall (accessed February 11, 2013).

Veteran Tributes—Ronald E. Storz. http://www.veterantributes.org/TributeDetail.asp?ID=29 (accessed February 28, 2012).

Viên, Phóng. "American Air Power Under the Eyes of the Victorious People of Hanoi." *People's Army Newspaper,* July 7, 1966, 1, 4.

———. "The Streets of the Capital Overflow with Victorious Zeal, Resound with Shouts of Hatred for the American Aggressors." *Hanoi Capital,* July 7, 1966, 1,3.

Watt, Barbara Powers, ed. *We Came Home.* Toluca Lake, CA: POW Publications, 1977.

Willbanks, James. "Shock and Awe of Tet Offensive Shattered U.S. Illusions." *U.S. News & World Report,* January 29, 2009.

Winchy, Eugene G. *Tonkin Gulf.* Garden City, NY: Doubleday, 1971.

Wolfe, Tom. *The Right Stuff.* New York, NY: Farrar, Straus, and Giroux, 1979.

Woods, Mark. "A Symbol Made for Memories." *Florida Times-Union,* August 9, 2009.

Young, Stephen. "How Hanoi Won the War." *Wall Street Journal,* August 3, 1995.

PHOTO CREDITS

Jerry and Jane Denton, courtesy of the Denton family.
Shumaker homecoming, *U-T San Diego*.
Stockdale homecoming, *U-T San Diego*.

INDEX